IT BEGAN WITH BABBAGE

It Began with Babbage

THE GENESIS OF COMPUTER SCIENCE

Subrata Dasgupta

OXFORD
UNIVERSITY PRESS

OXFORD
UNIVERSITY PRESS

Oxford University Press is a department of the University of Oxford.
It furthers the University's objective of excellence in research, scholarship,
and education by publishing worldwide.

Oxford   New York
Auckland   Cape Town   Dar es Salaam   Hong Kong   Karachi
Kuala Lumpur   Madrid   Melbourne   Mexico City   Nairobi
New Delhi   Shanghai   Taipei   Toronto

With offices in
Argentina   Austria   Brazil   Chile   Czech Republic   France   Greece
Guatemala   Hungary   Italy   Japan   Poland   Portugal   Singapore
South Korea   Switzerland   Thailand   Turkey   Ukraine   Vietnam

Oxford is a registered trademark of Oxford University Press
in the UK and certain other countries.

Published in the United States of America by
Oxford University Press
198 Madison Avenue, New York, NY 10016

Library of Congress Cataloging-in-Publication Data
Dasgupta, Subrata.
It began with Babbage : the genesis of computer science / Subrata Dasgupta.
    pages cm
Includes bibliographical references.
ISBN 978–0–19–930941–2 (alk. paper)
1.   Computer science—History—19th century.   2.   Computer science—History—20th century.
I. Title.   II. Title: Genesis of computer science, 1819–1969.
QA76.17.D36 2014
004.09—dc23
2013023202

9 8 7 6 5 4 3 2 1
Printed in the United States of America
on acid-free paper

To Amiya Kumar Bagchi

Contents

Acknowledgments

IN RETROSPECT, I now realize that this book on the genesis of computer science had its own genesis somewhere in my subconscious in summer 1977, when I was a visiting scientist in the Cambridge University Computer Laboratory. There, I had my first of many meetings with Maurice Wilkes, and it is also where I met David Wheeler. Twenty-eight years earlier, Wilkes, Wheeler, and their colleagues had designed and built the EDSAC, the world's first fully operational stored-program computer. As a graduate student, I had become seriously interested in the history and cognitive nature of scientific creativity, but computer science seemed different. For one thing, unlike physics, chemistry, or biology, the history of which stretched back centuries, the originators of computer science were, mostly, still living and active. When talking to Wilkes and Wheeler that summer, two pioneers, I was privy to a kind of oral history of our discipline.

Throughout the succeeding decades, my interest in the history and cognitive nature of science meandered in different directions, but I continued to think about computer science. Under the influence of Herbert Simon's *The Sciences of the Artificial*, I came to glimpse something about the nature of the discipline. I remember a conversation with B. Chandrasekaran of Ohio State University sometime during the early 1980s when we were, briefly, colleagues. Chandra said that computer science still had no intellectual tradition in the manner of physics or mathematics or chemistry. This obscurely disturbed me, but other preoccupations both within and outside computer science prevented me from pursuing this issue which, it seemed, required serious inquiry.

In November 2010, Wilkes passed away, and his death prompted me to give a lecture about him titled "The Mind of a Computer Pioneer" in the Center for Advanced Computer Studies at my university. After the talk, some graduate students approached me to offer a seminar course on the birth of computer science. An early draft of this book formed the basis for the course, which I taught in Fall 2011.

So I am indebted to Duane Huval, Charles LeDoux, Craig Miles, and the late Michael Sharkey for stimulating me in writing this book. They were the "first responders" to its contents. Their feedback was most valuable.

I have had the good fortune of many conversations with Maurice Wilkes, and conversations and lengthy e-mail discussions with the Herbert Simon, a polymath for our times on the origins of artificial intelligence. I was also privileged to know Donald Cardwell, historian of science and technology, when I was teaching at the University of Manchester Institute of Science and Technology during the early 1990s. These encounters have shaped my thinking, in different ways, on the historical, cognitive, and creative aspects of science, especially computer science. I have no doubt that their influence on me has found its way into this book.

I thank Simon Lavington, who made available to me a scarce, historical account of the Manchester University computers and for allowing me to read an unpublished paper by him on the Manchester machines. I thank D. F. Hartley for information on the academic status of computing during its earlier days in Cambridge.

Three anonymous reviewers, who read first drafts of the first few chapters on behalf of the publisher, offered very thoughtful comments. I thank them, as well.

Thank you, Jeremy Lewis, my editor at Oxford University Press who has been with this project from the day he received my first communication. It has been a pleasure working with him.

Thanks to Erik Hane, also of the editorial staff at Oxford University Press for all his help.

Thank you Terry Grow, a young artist who produced the images that appear in this book.

Bharathy Surya Prakash supervised all stages of the physical production of the book. Her professionalism was noteworthy. I thank her and her production team.

My thanks to Oxford University Press for giving me permission to adapt two diagrams (Figure 8.5, p. 135; Figure 8.7, p. 147) from *Technology and Creativity* (1996) authored by me.

Finally, as always, thank you Mithu, Deep, and Shome.

IT BEGAN WITH BABBAGE

Prologue

I

In 1819, a young English mathematician named Charles Babbage (1791–1871) began to design a machine, the purpose of which was to compute and produce, fully of its own steam, certain kinds of mathematical tables. Thus came into being the idea of *automatic computation*—performing computations without human intervention—and an intellectual tradition that eventually gave birth to a brand new and very curious scientific discipline that, during the late 1960s, came to be called *computer science*. This book tells the story of its genesis, a long birth process spanning some 150 years, beginning with Babbage and his dream of automatic computation.

The focus of every science (in fact, every intellectual discipline) is a certain kind of reality, a certain class of phenomena. The focus of computer science is the phenomenon called *computation*, which refers both to a concept and an activity that is associated historically with human thinking of a certain kind. The Latin root of the English word *compute* is *computare*—meaning, reckoning, calculating, figuring out. Thus, according to etymology, computation refers to the idea and the act of reckoning or calculating.

Etymologically, then, computation's domain would seem to be the realm of numbers. However, as we will see, we have come a long way from this association. We will see that the domain of computation actually comprises *symbols*—by which I mean *things that represent other things* (for example, a string of alphabetic characters—a word—that represent some object in the world, or a graphical road sign that represents a warning to motorists). The act of computation is, then, *symbol processing*: the manipulation and transformation of symbols. Numbers are just one kind of symbol; calculating is just one kind of symbol processing. And so, the focus of automatic computation, Babbage's original dream, is whether or how this human mental activity of symbol processing can be performed by (outsourced to) machines with minimal human intervention. Computer science as the science of automatic computation is also the science of automatic symbol processing.

II

However, computer science is not a *natural* science. It is not of the same kind as, say, physics, chemistry, biology, or astronomy. The gazes of these sciences are directed toward the natural world. In contrast, the domain of computer science is the artificial world, the world of made objects, *artifacts*—in particular, ones that perform computations. Let us call these *computational artifacts*.

Now, the natural scientist, when practicing her science, is concerned with the world *as it is*. As a scientist she is not in the business of deliberately changing the world. The astronomer looking through a telescope at the galaxies does not desire to change the universe but to understand it, explain it; the paleontologist examining rock layers in search of fossils is doing so to know more about the history of life on earth, not to change the earth (or life) itself. For the natural scientist, to understand the natural world is an end in itself. The desire is to make nature *intelligible*.[1] The computer scientist also wishes to understand, although not through nature but through computational artifacts; however, that wish is a means to an end, for she wants to *alter* the world in some aspects by creating new computational artifacts as improvements on existing ones, or by creating ones that have never existed before. If the natural scientist is concerned with the world *as it is*, the computer scientist obsesses with the world as she thinks *it ought to be*.

This, of course, highlights the venerable philosophical distinction between *is* and *ought*. We might say that computer science is a science of the *ought* in contrast to a natural science such as evolutionary biology, which is a science of the *is*.

III

Computer science is not unique because of this "oughtness," nor does its curious nature lie in this. In 1969, the polymath scientist and economics Nobel laureate Herbert Simon (1916–2001) pointed out that the main characteristic of artifacts is that they come into existence with a *purpose* and, consequently, the sciences that deal with artifacts—in his term, the "sciences of the artificial[2]"—are concerned with purpose (or goals), and in this sense they stand apart from the natural sciences. The objects of nature have no purpose. They just *are*. We don't ask about the purpose of the moon or the stars, of rocks or fossils, of oxygen or nitrogen. They just exist. It is true that anatomists and physiologists ask questions about the *function* of a particular organ or process in a living organism, but such functions are attributes that belong to some organ or life process as an outcome of natural evolution. They do not signify some *prior* purpose originating in the mind of a creative being. Artifacts, in contrast, have prior reasons for existence, reasons that were lodged in human minds prior to the beginning of artifact making. Thus, the sciences of the artificial must concern themselves with the characteristics of artifacts as they are related to the purposes *as intended for them by their (earthly) creators.* The structure and behavior of an artifact is meaningful only in respect to its purpose. Artifacts are *imbued* with purpose, reflecting the purposes or goals imagined for them by their human creators.

This is why a material artifact can never be explained solely in terms of natural laws even though the artifact must obey such laws. To explain or understand an artifact, even something as apparently simple as a piece of pottery, one must ask: What is it for? What does it do? What was the potter's intention?

This is why a computational artifact such as one's laptop can never be explained only by the laws of physics, even though the laptop's circuits and hard drive obey such laws. A computational artifact is intended to serve some purpose, and physics has nothing to say about purpose. *Computer science is a science of the artificial.* It must, therefore, embody principles, laws, theories, models, and so forth, that allow an explanation of how its structure and behavior relate to intended goals.

Computer science, then, involves the human mind in two ways. First, as we have noted, it is concerned with how artifacts can perform the mental activity of symbol processing. Second, as a science of the artificial, it must have a place in it for the minds of the human creators of computational artifacts—and how their imagined goals and purposes are transformed into artifactual forms.

IV

Of course, computer science is not the only science of the artificial. There are many disciplines that deal with the world of artifacts, that are concerned with changing the world to a preferred state, with pursuing the ought rather than the is. Some of them are of much earlier vintage than computer science. They include, for example, the traditional engineering disciplines—civil, mechanical, electrical, chemical, and metallurgical; they include architecture and industrial design. Others of more recent vintage include genetic engineering, biotechnology, and digital electronics design. Their concerns are, almost without exception, *material* artifacts: structures, machine tools, internal combustion engines, manufacturing and processing equipment, metals, alloys and plastics, aircraft, electronic systems, drugs, genetically modified organisms, and so forth.

Computer science stands apart because of the *peculiarity* of its artifacts. In fact, they are of three kinds.

They can be *material* objects—the physical computer system. These artifacts clearly resemble the material artifacts just mentioned because, like them, they obey the laws of physics and chemistry. They consume power, they generate heat, there is some physical motion involved, they decay physically and chemically over time, they have material extension, they occupy physical space, and their activities consume physical time.

Computational artifacts, however, can also be completely *abstract*, existing only as symbol structures (made visible on physical media such as paper or the computer screen). They are intrinsically devoid of any physical meaning. The laws of physical nature do not apply to them. As we will see, things called algorithms and purely mathematical machines called Turing machines exemplify such artifacts. Because they are abstract, once created they exist for ever. "They neither spin nor toil" in the physical world. They occupy no physical space nor do their activities consume physical time; rather, they live in their own *abstract* space–time frame.

Abstract computational artifacts such as algorithms resemble mathematical symbol structures (for example, algebraic equations, geometric objects) except that mathematical artifacts have no space–time characteristics at all, neither physical nor abstract.

The third kind of computational artifact is arguably the most interesting and unique of all. These artifacts are *in between* the material and the abstract. They themselves are abstract, yet their existence and usefulness depend on an underlying material substrate. We will call these *liminal* artifacts.[3] Computer programs and the entities called computer architectures are prime instances of this category; they themselves are abstract, yet they must have underlying material computational artifacts as substrates to make them useful or usable (just as the mind needs the brain for its existence).

Computer science, thus, must deal with computational artifacts that straddle the material, the abstract, and the liminal. Each of these types of artifacts can be studied, analyzed, understood, explained, and created autonomously, just as the mind and the brain can be studied autonomously, but—as in the case of the mind and the brain—only up to a point, because these classes of artifacts form *symbiotic relationships*: the abstract with the liminal, the liminal with the material. In fact, as we will see, automatic computation involves the constant interplay between the abstract, the liminal, and the material.

All of this separates computer science from most other sciences of the artificial—what makes computer science so peculiar, so curious, so distinctive. Because of the abstract and liminal artifacts, the laws governing computational artifacts are, in part only, physical laws. In fact, in a certain sense, the laws of nature are almost marginal in computer science. It is the abstract and the liminal artifacts that have come to dominate computer science, and *their* laws are necessarily of an entirely different nature. This raises the issue: What *is* the nature of the *science* in computer science?

V

The answer, in detail, is the story this book will tell. But, we must pause here on the concept of science itself. The sciences of the artificial differ from the natural sciences because the latter is concerned with natural phenomena and the former with the world of artifacts; they differ because the former *must* factor in purpose into the discourse whereas the latter *must not*. Yet, we call them both science. And, after all, this book is an account of the birth of computer *science*.

Throughout the centuries, especially since the 17th century—the age of Galileo and Newton, Descartes and Bacon, Kepler and Huygens—much ink has been spilled on the questions: What *is* science? What constitutes scientific knowledge? How does science differs from nonscience? How does scientific knowledge differ from other kinds of knowledge? Despite the vast, animated conversations on these issues, the debate continues. As one modern historian of physics has remarked, every attempt to "fix" the criterion of "scientificity" has failed.[4]

Etymologically, *science* is rooted in the Latin adjective *scientificus*, used by medieval scholars to mean "referring to knowledge that is demonstrable" as opposed to intuitive knowledge. During the 17th century, we find that it appears in the name of the Académie des Sciences in Paris (1666). However, in ordinary speech, even into the early 19th century, "science" was often used to mean knowledge acquired by systematic study or a skill. In Jane Austin's novel *Pride and Prejudice* (1813), we find a character that refers to dancing as a science.

In fact, until well into the 19th century, "science" and "philosophy" (especially as "natural philosophy") were more or less synonymous. In 1833, however, the word *scientist* was first deployed by the Englishman William Whewell (1794–1866), marking the beginning of the separation of science from philosophy.

During the 20th century, disciplines called *philosophy of science, sociology of science*, and *history of science*, and, most recently, the generic *science studies* have come into being with objects of inquiry that are the nature of the scientific enterprise. As one might expect, there has been (and continues to be) much debate, discussion, and (of course) disagreement on this matter.

Practicing scientists, however, harbor less anxiety about their trade. They broadly agree that "scientificity" has to do with the *method of inquiry*. They broadly subscribe to the idea that, in science, one gives primacy to observation and reasoning; that one seeks rational explanations of events in the world; that a highly critical mentality is exercised on a continuous basis by viewing a scientific explanation at all times as tentative—a hypothesis that must always be under public scrutiny, tested either by way of observation or experiment, and rejected if the evidence contradicts the hypothesis; and that scientific knowledge, being about the empirical world, is always incomplete. They also agree that a new piece of scientific knowledge is never an island of its own. It must cohere with other pieces of knowledge scientists have already obtained; it must fit into a network of other ideas, concepts, evidence, hypotheses, and so on.

All of this pertain to the natural sciences. What about the sciences of the artificial?

V I

There is, of course, common ground. The sciences of the artificial, like the natural sciences, give primacy to rational explanation, they demand a critical mentality, they acknowledge the tentativeness and impermanence of explanations, and they involve constructing hypotheses and testing them against reality by way of observation and experiment.

The crucial distinction lies in the nature of the things to be explained. For the natural sciences, these are natural objects. For the artificial sciences, these are artificial objects. Thus, the artificial sciences involve activities entirely missing in the natural sciences: the *creation of the things to be explained*—a process that (in general) involves the creation of a symbolic representation of the artifact (in some language), and then making (or *putting into effect*) that artifact in accordance with the representation.[5] The former is called *design*; the latter, *implementation*.

Design and implementation are thus the twins at the heart of the sciences of the artificial—activities entirely missing in the natural sciences. And the consequences are profound.

First, explanations in a science of the artificial will be of two kinds: (a) hypotheses about whether the design of an artifact satisfies the intended purpose of the artifact and (b) hypotheses about whether the implementation satisfies the design.

Second, a design is something specific. One designs a *particular* artifact (a bridge, the transmission system for a car model, a museum, a computer's operating system, and so on). So, really, the design of the artifact is a hypothesis (a theory) that says: If an artifact is built according to this design, it will satisfy the purpose intended for that artifact. A design, then, is *a theory of the individual artifact* (or a particular class of artifacts), and an implementation is *an experiment that tests the theory*.

Third, there is a consequence of this view of designs-as-theories. We noted that, within a natural science, an explanation (in the form of a law or a theory or a hypothesis or a model) does not stand on its own. It is like a piece of a jigsaw puzzle that must fit in to the jigsaw as a whole. If it does not, it is either ignored or it may lead to a radical rehaul of the overall network of knowledge, even the construction of a new jigsaw puzzle.

A science of the artificial has no such constraints. Because it deals with the design and implementation of artifacts, if the design and then the implementation result in an artifact that meets the intended purpose, *success has been achieved*. The particular artifact is what matters. The success of the artifact produces new knowledge that then enriches the network of knowledge in that science of the artificial. But, there is no obligation that this new knowledge *must* cohere with the existing network of knowledge. Thus, although a natural science seeks unified, consistent knowledge about its subject matter, an artificial science may be quite content with fragmented knowledge concerning individual artifacts or individual classes of artifacts.

One of the great glories of (natural) science is its aspiration for what scientists call *universal laws and principles*, which cover a sweeping range of phenomena that are true for all times and all places. Newton's law of gravitation, Kepler's laws of planetary motion, Harvey's explanation of the circulation of blood, the laws of chemical combination, the theory of plate tectonics in geology, Darwinian natural selection, and Planck's law are all examples of universal laws or principles.

The search for universals is also not unknown in the sciences of the artificial. For example, explanations of metallurgical techniques such as tempering and annealing, or the behavior of structural beams under load, or the characteristics of transistor circuits all have this universal quality. There is always an aspiration for universal principles in the artificial sciences.

However, the attainment of universal knowledge is not the *sine qua non* of progress in the sciences of the artificial. Design and implementation of the individual artifact always have primacy. A particular machine, a particular building, a particular system—these are what ultimately matter. If an architect designs a museum that, when built (implemented), serves the purpose for which it was intended, the project is deemed successful. Its relationship to other museums and their architectures may be of great interest to that architect and her colleagues, and to architectural historians, but that relationship is of no consequence as far as that museum project itself is concerned. So also for the design and implementation of a particular computer or a particular kitchen appliance or a particular medical device. *Ultimately, a science of the artificial is a science of the individual.*

In the chapters that follow, we will witness the unfolding of these ideas in the case of one particular science of the artificial: computer science.

VII

We will be traversing the historical landscape from a particular vantage point: the second decade of the 21st century. We will be looking to the past—admittedly, not a very remote past, because computational artifacts are a relatively recent phenomena.

One of the dilemmas faced by historians is the following: To what extent do we allow our current circumstances to influence our judgment, assessment, and understanding of the past? This question was first raised famously in 1931 by the (then-very young) British historian Herbert Butterfield (1900–1979).[6] Discussing the so-called English Whig historians of the 19th century (*Whigs* were the liberals or progressives, in contrast to the *Tories*, the conservatives), Butterfield offered a scathing critique of these historians who, he said, valorized or demonized historical figures according to their own 19th-century values. This viewing of the past through the lens of the present thus came to be called, derisively, *whiggism* or, more descriptively, *present-centeredness*.

Ever since Butterfield, conventional wisdom has advocated that present-centeredness should be avoided at all cost. The past must be judged according to the context and values of that past, not of the historian's own time. Yet, the fact is, historians *select* events and people of the past as objects of historical interest in the light of their current concerns and values. The cautionary point is that the historian must negotiate a narrow and tricky path, eschewing *judging* the past according to current values or concerns, yet *selecting* from the past according to his current concerns. We will also see, in this book, that *as 21st-century readers* (historians or nonhistorians, scientists or nonscientists, academics or general readers), we often understand aspects of the history of computer science better by appealing to concepts, words, terms, and phrases that are used *now*. And so, often, I allow the intrusion of present-centered language as a means to understanding things of the past. In other words, I strive to achieve a judicious blend of whiggism and antiwhiggism in this narrative.[7]

VIII

So, even before we embark on this story of the genesis of computer science, the reader is forewarned about the nature of this science. It is a science of many hues. To summarize:

1. Its domain comprises computational artifacts that can be material, abstract, or in between (liminal), and that can function automatically (that is, with minimal human intervention) to manipulate, process, and transform symbols (or information).
2. It is, thus, a science of symbol processing.
3. Its objective is to understand the nature of computational artifacts and, more fundamentally, their purposes (*why* they come into the world), and their making (*how* they come into the world).
4. It is, thus, a science of the artificial.
5. The *how* of their making comprises collectively the twin processes of design and implementation.
6. In general, design is both the *process* by which a symbolic representation of an artifact is created as well as the *symbolic representation* itself. Implementation is both the *process* by which a representation is put into effect, as well as the *artifact* that is the outcome of that process.
7. It is a science of the *ought* rather than of the *is*.
8. It is (primarily) a science of the individual. With these caveats in mind, let us proceed with the story.

NOTES

1. P. Dear., (2006). *The intelligibility of nature.* Chicago, IL: University of Chicago Press.

2. H. A. Simon., (1996). *The sciences of the artificial* (3rd ed.). Cambridge, MA: MIT Press.

3. *Liminality* refers to a state of ambiguity, of betwixt and between, a twilight state.

4. P. Galison., (2010). Trading with the enemy. In M. Gorman (Ed.), *Trading zones and interactive expertise* (pp. 26–51). Cambridge, MA: MIT Press (see especially p. 30).

5. I have borrowed the phrase *putting into effect* to signify implementation from P. S. Rosenbloom. (2010). *On computing: The fourth great scientific domain* (p. 41). Cambridge, MA: MIT Press.

6. H. Butterfield (1973). *The Whig interpretation of history.* Harmondsworth, UK: Penguin Books (original work published 1931).

7. E. Harrison. (1987). Whigs, prigs and historians of science. *Nature, 329,* 233–234.

I

Leibniz's Theme, Babbage's Dream

I

THE GERMAN MATHEMATICIAN Gottfried Wilhelm Leibniz (1646–1716) is perhaps best remembered in science as the co-inventor (with Newton) of the differential calculus. In our story, however, he has a presence not so much because, like his great French contemporary the philosopher Blaise Pascal (1623–1662), he built a calculating machine—in Pascal's case, the machine could add and subtract, whereas Leibniz's machine also performed multiplication and division[1]—but for something he wrote vis-à-vis calculating machines. He wished that astronomers could devote their time strictly to astronomical matters and leave the drudgery of computation to machines, if such machines were available.[2]

Let us call this *Leibniz's theme*, and the story I will tell here is a history of human creativity built around this theme. The goal of computer science, long before it came to be called by this name, was to delegate the mental labor of computation to the machine.

Leibniz died well before the beginning of the Industrial Revolution, circa 1760s, when the cult and cultivation of the machine would transform societies, economies, and mentalities.[3] The pivot of this remarkable historical event was steam power. Although the use of steam to move machines *automatically* began with the English ironmonger and artisan Thomas Newcomen (1663–1727) and his invention of the atmospheric steam engine in 1712,[4] just 4 years before Leibniz's passing, the steam engine as an efficient source of mechanical power, as an efficient means of automating machinery, as a substitute for human, animal, and water power properly came into being with the invention of the separate condenser in 1765 by Scottish instrument maker, engineer, and entrepreneur James Watt (1738–1819)—a mechanism that greatly improved the efficiency of Newcomen's engine.[5]

The steam engine became, so to speak, the alpha and omega of machine power. It was the prime mover of ancient Greek thought materialized. And Leibniz's theme conjoined with the steam engine gave rise, in the minds of some 19th-century thinkers, to a desire to automate calculation or computation and to free humans of this mentally tedious labor. One such person was English mathematician, "gentlemen scientist," and denizen of the Romantic Age, Charles Babbage.[6]

II

Charles Babbage (1791–1871), born into the English upperclass, did not need to earn a living. Son of a wealthy banker, he studied at Trinity College, Cambridge, and cofounded with fellow students John Herschel (1792–1871) and George Peacock (1791–1858) the Analytical Society, the purpose of which was to advance the state of mathematics in Cambridge.[7] Babbage left Cambridge in 1814, married the same year, and, with the support of an allowance from his father and his wife's independent income, settled in London to the life of a gentleman scientist, focusing for the next few years on mathematical research.[8] In 1816, he was elected a Fellow of the Royal Society (FRS), the most venerable of the European scientific societies, founded in 1662.[9]

In 1828, the year after he inherited his late father's estate and became a man of independent means in his own right, and a widower as well,[10] Babbage was elected to the Lucasian chair of mathematics in Cambridge—the chair held by Isaac Newton from 1669 to 1702,[11] (and, in our own time, by Stephen Hawking from 1979–2009), and still regarded as England's most prestigious chair in mathematics. Babbage occupied this chair until 1839, although—treating this appointment as a sinecure—he never actually took up residence in Cambridge nor did he deliver a single lecture while he held this chair.

In his memoirs, *Passages from the Life of a Philosopher* (1864), Babbage claimed that his first thoughts along the lines of Leibniz's theme came to him while he was still a student in Cambridge, around 1812 to 1813. He was sitting half-asleep in the rooms of the Analytical Society, a table of logarithms open before him. A fellow member of the Society, seeing him in this state, asked what he was dreaming about, to which he replied that he was thinking how these logarithms could be calculated by a machine.[12]

We do not know the truthfulness of this account. Anecdotes of scientists and poets ideating in a state of semisleep or in a dream are not uncommon. Celebrated examples include the German scientist Friedrich August von Kekulé (1829–1896), who dreamed the structure of the benzene molecule,[13] and the English poet Samuel Taylor Coleridge (1772–1834), who imagined the unfinished poem "Kubla Khan" while sleeping under the influence of opium.[14]

If this is true, the dream must have lain buried in Babbage's subconscious for a very long time—until about 1819—when, occupied with ways of calibrating astronomical instruments accurately, he began thinking about machines to compute mathematical tables.[15] Writing elsewhere in 1822, Babbage mentions working on a set of astronomical tables with his friend, the multidisciplinary scientist Herschel, and discussing with Herschel the possibility of a machine powered by a steam engine for performing the necessary calculations.[16]

Thus it was that, beginning in 1819, Babbage conceived the idea and began designing the first of his two computational artifacts, the *Difference Engine*. Its aim was the expression of Leibniz's theme in a specific kind of way—the fast, automatic, and reliable production of mathematical tables of a certain kind. The name of the machine was derived from the computational procedure it would use to compute the tables, called the method of differences, a method already well known for the manual preparation of tables.[17]

Babbage tells us what he wanted of his machine. First, it must be "really automatic"—that is, when numbers were supplied to it, it would be able to perform mathematical operations on them without any human intervention.[18] From an engineering point of view, this meant that after the numbers were placed in the machine, it would produce results by mechanisms alone—"the mere motion of a spring, a descending weight" or some other "constant force."[19] Second, the machine must be accurate, not only in the generation of numbers, but also in the printed tables, for this was an arena where inaccuracy and unreliability were known to creep in. This meant that the computing machine must be coupled directly with the printing device and, in fact, must drive the latter automatically so that no error-prone human intervention would be admitted.[20]

Mechanizing the preparation of mathematical tables would not only free human mental labor for other less tedious tasks, but also would speed up the process and eliminate human fallibility and replace it with machine infallibility. We are seeing here an elaboration of Leibniz's theme and of what Babbage had apparently dreamed of some half-dozen years before.

The Difference Engine was to be a "special-purpose" machine, because it could produce mathematical tables only. However, by deploying the method of differences, it was general within the confines of this special purposeness; the method of differences offered a general principle by which *all* tables might be computed by a single, uniform process.[21]

III

To understand the principle underlying the Difference Engine, consider the following example.[22] Suppose we compute the values of the expression $N^2 + N + 10$ for the consecutive integers $N = 0, 1, 2, \ldots, 5$. We can display the numbers thus produced by the two leftmost columns of Table 1.1.

In column D1, we display the differences between successive adjacent values of the column $N^2 + N + 10$. In column D2, we display the differences between the adjacent consecutive values of column D1. Notice that all the values of D2 are the same. This means

TABLE I.I

N	$N^2 + N + 10$	D1	D2
0	10		
1	12	2	
2	16	4	2
3	22	6	2
4	30	8	2
5	40	10	2

that we can compute further values of $N^2 + N + 10$ for $N = 6, 7, 8, \ldots$, and as long as we want by simply doing addition:

For $N = 6$, since the value of D2 = 2, the new value of D1 equals the previous value of D1 + 2—that is, $10 + 2 = 12$. Hence, the new value of $(N^2 + N + 10)$ = the previous value of $(N^2 + N + 10) + 12 = 52$.

In mathematical jargon, the expression $N^2 + N + 10$ is a polynomial of degree 2. We see that its second difference, D2, is a constant. The most general form of a polynomial is $a + bx + cx^2 + \cdots + dx^n$ (of degree n). There was a theorem discovered during the 19th century that states that any continuous function over an interval can be approximated as closely as desired by a polynomial. This means that most mathematical functions can be expressed approximately—but as accurately as one wishes—by such polynomials. And because all polynomials can be built up by difference tables, any mathematical function expressible by a polynomial can be computed by the method of differences.

In the case of our example, a second-degree polynomial required computing differences up to D2. A third-degree polynomial would require computing differences up to D3, and so on. Babbage's Difference Engine was planned to handle polynomials of up to degree 6. Thus, his machine would compute columns D1, D2, ..., D6.

IV

The subsequent history of the Difference Engine takes us into the trichotomy of *invention, design*, and *implementation*. In his book *The Nature and Aesthetics of Design* (1978), David Pye, a British industrial designer and design teacher characterized invention as the discovery of the "general principle of arrangement" that defines a class of artifacts,[23] and design as the application of such principles in some actual context leading to a particular embodiment of those principles. Implementation, we take to mean the actual realization of a working artifact conforming to the design—to put into effect the design (see Prologue, Section VI).

In fact, the distinction between these concepts is never always as neat as this. Invention is a term that can easily apply to *any* sort of ideation, not just in the realm of artifacts. We speak of Charles Darwin and Alfred Russel Wallace as the co-inventors of the theory of natural selection, of Newton and Leibniz as the co-inventors of the calculus. Design does not enter the discourse in these contexts. On the other hand, invention, design, and implementation may be so entwined that we cannot unravel them into distinct activities or phases. We speak of Thomas Newcomen as having invented the Newcomen engine because he conceived the basic principles, but his invention is linked inextricably with his design of a particular form of the atmospheric steam engine, and the construction (that is, implementation) of the first working engine in 1712 along the lines of its design, which was used to operate a mine drainage pump in Staffordshire in England.[24] Here, invention, design, and implementation form a unified activity.

Ultimately, the litmus test of inventionhood is the *originality* of the conceived product—whether it is the principle governing an artifact or a technique or a theory. Inventionhood entails creativity.[25] Designs may or may not be original. Implementations may or may not be original. Throughout the course of this story, we will come across instances of these diverse situations.

V

In 1822, Babbage built a prototype Difference Engine that he used to demonstrate the viability of its principle—a preliminary experiment to test his design-as-theory (see Prologue, Section VI). With the support of the Royal Society, he obtained a grant from the British government of £1500 to begin work on a full-scale engine, a comprehensive experiment in effect.

He employed a leading machine builder and "mechanician" of the time, Joseph Clement (1779–1844), who had been trained under two of Britain's most eminent mechanical engineers: Joseph Bramah (1748–1814; most well known for his invention of the hydraulic press) and Henry Maudslay (1771–1831). Clement was especially known as a machine tool builder and for his improvements of lathes and precision tools (for which he was awarded the Isis gold medal of the Society for the Encouragement of the Arts in 1827 and the silver medal of the Society of Arts in 1828).

Thus, Clement's pedigree as an engineer was impeccable, but he came from a humble background, far removed from Babbage in formal education and social class. In class-ridden Victorian England, Babbage treated Clement as an inferior, a minion, and Clement was apparently extravagant in the charges he demanded for his services.[26] Eventually, they fell out, with Clement—according to the laws of the time—retaining possession of the engineering drawings he had prepared and the machine tools he had made for the project.

Nevertheless, by 1833, Babbage had managed to assemble a part of the Difference Engine—without the printing unit that, of course, he had considered a *sine qua non* for his machine. This version of the engine is now on display at the Science Museum in London.

VI

Figure 1.1 shows a simplified and schematic diagram of the Difference Engine for computing polynomials of degree 2. The machine consisted of three columns, each with six "cages," with each cage holding one "figure wheel." The rightmost column was called the "table column"; the middle one, the " first difference column"; and the leftmost, the "second difference column".

Ignoring the lowest figure wheel on the table column (which served no purpose), the five figure wheels above it could each be set manually to any one of 10 digits: 0, 1,..., 9. The setting on the lowest figure wheel represented the unit's digit of a number, the one above it the 10s digit, and so on. So the highest figure wheel represented the 10,000s digit, and the entire table column could be set to any number from 00000 through 99999. As its name suggests, the figure wheels on the table column would hold the table with the values to be calculated.

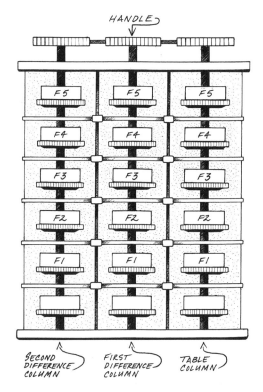

FIGURE 1.1 The Difference Engine.

The five figure wheels (again, ignoring the redundant bottom one) on the first difference (middle) column were exactly identical to those in the table column, except they represented the values of the first difference. Likewise, the figure wheels on the leftmost column stored the values of the second difference.

When initial numbers were placed on the figure wheels of each of the columns and the handle was cranked, the number held in the second difference column would be added to that held in the first difference column, thereby changing the latter; and the number in the first difference column would be added to the number in the table column, thus altering the latter. By this simple movement of the machine, tables would be computed using the method of difference.[27]

A fully operational Difference Engine was never built in England, and although Babbage would return to its design and construction later in his life, he could not interest the government in continuing their financial support. The failure of this project was, apparently, something of a trauma in Babbage's scientific life and, according to one historian, he never recovered fully from this blow.[28] Yet, he must have taken comfort that the Difference Engine would eventually get built—by Swedish printer Georg Scheutz (1795–1873) and his son Edvard—based on a description of the machine in a 1834 article by Dionysius Lardner (1793–1859), a science writer.[29] The Scheutz Difference Engine took nearly 20 years to complete, in 1852. It was exhibited at the Paris Exhibition in 1855. In 1856, the Scheutz engine was purchased by the Dudley Observatory in the United States, and in Britain a copy of this machine was built under the supervision of William Farr (1807–1883), statistical superintendent of the General Register Office, where it was set to work churning out new English life expectancy tables.[30] So, in fact, Babbage lived to see his design carried to full implementation. His theory for an automatic calculating machine was validated experimentally.

The Difference Engine, as we have seen, was a special-purpose computing machine. It speaks to Babbage's inventiveness and creativity, certainly; but, it might have been assigned to the prehistory of computer science had it not led its inventor to a much more ambitious project—the idea of a general-purpose or "universal" computer, capable of any mathematical computation. This was Babbage's grand conception of the Analytical Engine. And here we have an invention of a technological idea, along with a design, but no implementation.

NOTES

1. H. H. Goldstine. (1972). *The computer from Pascal to von Neumann* (Chapter 1). Princeton, NJ: Princeton University Press.

2. Ibid., p. 8n.

3. T. S. Ashton. (1969). *The Industrial Revolution*. London: Oxford University Press.

4. L. T. C. Rolt. (1963). *Thomas Newcomen*. London: David & Charles/Dawlish MacDonald.

5. R. L. Hills. (1989). *Power from steam: A history of the stationary steam engine*. Cambridge, UK: Cambridge University Press.

6. R. Holmes. (2008). *The age of wonder*. New York: Vintage Books.

7. C. Babbage. (1994). *Passages from the life of a philosopher* (p. 21). Piscataway, NJ: IEEE Press (original work published 1864).

8. M. Campbell-Kelly. (1994). Introduction (pp. 7–35). In Babbage, op cit., p. 12.

9. By the 20th century, to be elected an FRS was the Holy Grail of most British and Commonwealth scientists. In Babbage's time, however, the society was still very much a community of upper-class Oxbridge-educated gentlemen, not all of whom were interested in scientific research. E. N. da C. Andrade. (1960). *A brief history of the Royal Society* (p. 11). London: The Royal Society.

10. Campbell-Kelly, op cit., p. 17.

11. Babbage, op cit., p. 22.

12. Ibid., pp. 30–31.

13. A. Findlay. (1948). *A hundred years of chemistry* (pp. 36–38). London: Gerald Duckworth.

14. J. L. Lowes. (1930). *The road to Xanadu*. Boston, MA: Houghton-Mifflin.

15. Babbage, op cit., p. 31.

16. C. Babbage. (1822). *The science of numbers reduced to mechanisms*. Quoted in Campbell-Kelly, op cit., p. 14.

17. This method had been used, for example, in the French manual table-making project for the French ordinance survey during the 1790s. Campbell-Kelly, op cit., p. 13.

18. Babbage, op cit., 1994, p. 30.

19. Ibid.

20. Ibid., p. 31.

21. Ibid.

22. See also Goldstine, op cit., pp. 17–19.

23. D. Pye. (1978). *The nature and aesthetics of design* (p. 21). London: Herbert Press.

24. G. Basalla. (1988). *The evolution of technology* (pp. 35–40). Cambridge, UK: Cambridge University Press.

25. S. Dasgupta. (1996). *Technology and creativity* (p. 55). New York: Oxford University Press.

26. Campbell-Kelly, op cit., pp. 217–222.

27. Babbage, op cit., 1994, pp. 47–49.

28. Campbell-Kelly, op cit., p. 29.

29. D. Swade. (2001). *The Difference Engine: Charles Babbage and his quest to build the first computer*. New York: Viking.

30. Campbell-Kelly, op cit., p. 31.

2

Weaving Algebraic Patterns

᠍᠊᠍

I

THE ANALYTICAL ENGINE has a startling place in the history of computing. To the best of our knowledge, no machine had ever before been conceived along its lines. More remarkably, some of its key principles of design would actually be reinvented a century later by people who were, apparently, ignorant of it. If imitation is the sincerest form of flattery, then so is *re*invention or *re*discovery, at least when born from ignorance. It tells us much about how ahead of one's time the original creator was. This reinvention of Babbage's idea was particularly poignant because it would become the fount of fruitful and rich phylogenetic pathways in the later evolution of the digital computer and the emergence of computer science.[1]

II

Dissatisfaction is a prime generator of the creative urge, dissatisfaction with the status quo and the desire to change it to something better.[2] Charles Babbage was unhappy with the waste of human mental labor in computing mathematical tables, which led to his desire to free human beings from this tedium—hence, the Difference Engine.

However, the Difference Engine produced its own discontent. As Luigi Frederico Menabrea (1809–1896), an Italian military mathematician (and, later, prime minister of Italy) would explain *apropos* the Difference Engine, its use was limited to one particular kind of computation. It could not be applied to the solution of "an infinity of other questions" of interest to mathematicians. It was this limitation and the attendant discontent that led Babbage to conceive the machine he called the *Analytical Engine*, the operation of which he believed would encompass the full range of algebraic problems.[3]

The Difference Engine was not general enough. Babbage desired a computing engine that could range over the whole of "mathematical analysis." As he explained in a letter to the Earl of Rosse, then president of the Royal Society, his Analytical Engine would have the power to perform the "most analytical complicated operations."[4] Here, then, is Babbage's promise: a mathematical machine with "nearly unlimited" powers.

Babbage's name for his new machine is significant. The Difference Engine could only compute functions according to the method of differences—hence its name. In mathematics, the study of infinite processes, also called *transcendental functions* (for example, the function $\sin x = z/1! - z^3/3! + z^5/5! - \cdots$), is called *analysis*[5]—hence, Analytical Engine, a mathematical machine of the most general sort.

We get a sense of how general the Analytical Engine's capabilities would have been if it had been implemented (which it was not) by reading both Menabrea's *Sketch of the Analytical Engine* (1842) as well as the notes on the machine appended to the "Sketch" (written originally in Italian) by its translator into English, Augustus Ada, Countess of Lovelace. (We read more about this remarkable woman later in this chapter.) Thus, Menabrea takes us, in great detail, through the sequence of operations the engine would execute to solve a pair of simultaneous linear equations.[6] And in one of her notes, Lovelace demonstrates, again in detail, the execution sequence by the engine for computing Bernoulli's numbers.[7]

There was another source of discontent regarding the Difference Engine. Babbage was disappointed with the slowness of its adding mechanism. To speed it up, he invented a complex scheme called "anticipated carriage" (a forerunner of the carry look-ahead adder in modern computers). However, in the Difference Engine, this mechanism would have to be replicated for the many different stages in which addition was performed—involving the difference columns and the table column—and this would be prohibitively expensive. So the problem was to implement this faster arithmetic mechanism at a reasonable cost.

III

In the language of modern computer science (we are indulging in present-centeredness [see Prologue, section VII]), the logical or functional organization of a computer is called its *architecture* (discussed much more later). One of Babbage's major acts of creation in conceiving the Analytical Engine was in response in part to this need to realize an economic implementation of the anticipatory carriage-based addition mechanism. This response was to separate the function of representing numbers in the machine from the task of performing operations upon those numbers—the creation of a single, *centralized* arithmetic unit (or, in present-centered language, *processing* unit) and to separate it from

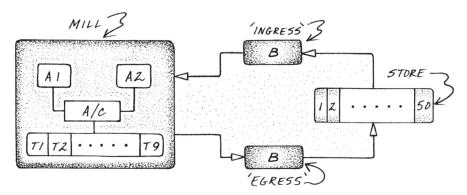

FIGURE 2.1 Architecture of the Analytical Engine A1/A2, accumulators; A/C, arithmetic/control mechanism; B, buffer; T1, T2,... T9, table of constants 1, 2,...9.

the means to hold these numbers. In the Difference Engine, the two mechanisms were conjoined.

This separation of processing from storage was an architectural innovation of the highest order. Babbage named the part of the machine that would perform the arithmetic operations the *mill*, and the part that would hold the numbers or values of algebraic variables the *store*. The contents of the store would pass to the mill and, after an operation is performed by the mill, the resulting value would be returned from the mill to the store.[8]

Schematically, the situation is as depicted in Figure 2.1. As for the terms *store* and *mill*, a noted Babbage scholar suggests that Babbage drew on these terms metaphorically by appealing to the milieu of textile making wherein yarns were brought from the store to the mill, therein woven into fabric, which was then returned to the store.[9]

IV

If the separation of storage from processing was a profoundly significant innovation (to an extent, as we will see later, that even Babbage may not have appreciated), the other was the manner in which Babbage achieved the "unlimited" power for his mathematical engine as he had promised in the letter mentioned earlier, and as extolled by Menabrea and Lovelace. Where did this generality come from? A generality that, Lovelace said, would even allow the engine to compute functions of any number of other functions, such as

$$F(x, y, z, \log x, \sin y, x^n, ...)[10]$$

Babbage envisioned his promised generality by way of an *analogy*. The use of analogy is one of the most common ways of creative thinking. The process is roughly along the following lines: First, search for a similarity between the problem with which a person is grappling and some other situation with a solution that is well understood. Second, establish a correspondence between features of the two situations. Third, extract from the familiar, understood situation relevant aspects and "map" them to the unfamiliar problem. Fourth, and last, use these mappings to solve the problem.[11]

There are no guarantees that analogical thinking will always work, but when it does, the outcome can be fruitful, rich, unexpected, and consequential. Sometimes, the analogy may become embedded in one's language and thus becomes a *metaphor*.[12]

We must remember that there is nothing mechanical about this process of analogical thinking. Creativity may be demanded in all its stages, not the least of which in detecting similarity between the problem situation and something else, which might be completely unconnected, far removed from the problem at hand.

Babbage's great insight was to construct an analogy between his problem of establishing a general or "universal" computing capability for his Analytical Engine and a technique from the realm of textile manufacture, as textile was clearly much in his mind as he grappled with the idea of his new engine.

In the simplest terms, weaving involves the intercrossing of longitudinal threads called the *warp* with transverse threads called the *woof*. When cloth with an intricate design (and, perhaps, many colors, as in brocade) is woven, it becomes necessary to allow certain warp threads to cross the woof threads and to prevent other such crossings. This is how designs are woven, and the weaving process follows a *pattern*. The pattern, in other words, dictates the sequences of crossing and noncrossing of warp and woof.

In 1801, a Frenchman Joseph-Marie Jacquard (1752–1834) acquired a patent for automating pattern weaving. As so often happens in technology, Jacquard combined features developed by earlier textile machine inventors, made slight modifications, and produced a machine that came to be called the *Jacquard loom*—an invention that won him a gold medal, glory, and (presumably) wealth.[13]

The crux of Jacquard's invention was to encode the pattern in a batch of stiff, punched cards. Each card carried a part of the overall pattern according to the pattern of holes punched into the card; the whole stack represented the entire design. By an elaborate arrangement of mechanisms, the holes would be sensed (or not, in their absence) and the loom would accordingly weave patterns of threads by crossing each other (or not). The batch of cards formed a "closed loop," and so their repeated presence would ensure that the same design was repeated in the woven cloth.[14]

Again, taking a present-centered view of the past, we easily recognize the punched cards in the Jacquard loom for what they are—as a *memory* that holds the pattern the loom will "recall" and "obey," as a *blueprint* for how a piece of cloth is to be woven, and as a *program* that drives the loom. All these metaphors, of course, share the following: that the pattern to be woven by the loom into a cloth can be altered by simply changing the patterns of holes in the stack of punched cards. *This* was the source of Babbage's insight.

V

So here was the analogy. In the Jacquard loom, each distinct pattern to be woven is defined by a specific encoding of the pattern in a closed-loop series of punched cards. The loom reads this pattern and weaves the cloth accordingly. By changing the batch of punched cards, the loom weaves a different pattern. The same loom, a *finite* device, has the capability for, potentially, an *infinity* of weaving patterns.

In the Analytical Engine, computation of each distinct mathematical function is determined by an ordered sequence of (arithmetic) operations on the values of variables. These sequences of operations (in present-centered language, programs) can be encoded as patterns of holes on punched cards. The machine reads a particular set of punched cards and performs the sequence of operations they represent. By changing the set of punched cards, a different sequence of operations corresponding to a different mathematical computation is performed. In the evocative words of Lovelace, the Analytical Engine would weave "algebraic patterns" much as the Jacquard loom wove "flowers and leaves."[15]

It is, thus, in its architecture—the separation of store from mill certainly, but even more in its universal character, rendered possible by the use of punched cards—that the Analytical Engine stood apart from its historical precedents. But, we also recognize the *modernity* of these architectural principles—a recognition coming from the fact that this architecture was reinvented for the electronic digital computer a century later.

For Lovelace, the punched-card principle placed the Analytical Engine on a different plane from all that had gone before. The machine had stepped beyond "the bounds of arithmetic." It was no longer a "mere" calculating device. Lovelace recognized that the punched-card mechanism imbued the Analytical Engine with an ability to "combine together general symbols" of "unlimited variety." It was no mere number cruncher but a *symbol processor*. By this virtue, it established a link between the strictly material artifact (which the Analytical Engine was) and abstract mental processes characteristic of mathematics itself—a link, in other words, between the machinations of a material artifact and the kinds of symbol manipulations the mind carries out in mathematical reasoning.[16]

There was more to the Analytical Engine than this philosophical advance. There was technological promise. A new language was at hand to manage the "truths" of mathematical analysis in a far speedier, more accurate, yet practical manner than had ever existed before. The Analytical Engine promised not only to bridge the material and the mental, but also the theoretical and the practical.[17]

The use of punched cards to communicate the sequence and nature of the operations to the machine led to other possibilities that added to the machine's universality. For one, the initial values of the variables (numbers) on which to be operated could be set either manually in the store or by way of additional cards that Babbage called "variable cards". More interestingly, it was possible in Babbage's scheme to *iterate* through a sequence of operations. For this purpose, he proposed a combination of what he called "combinatorial cards" and "index cards", the roles of which were to direct, at specific intervals, the return of variable cards to particular "places" in the computation, and to direct the number and nature of the repetitions to be performed.[18] From a present-centered perspective, Babbage's index cards were the forerunners of what later came to be called index registers.[19]

VI

Babbage did not, of course, just conceive the architectural principles for his machine. In the long years he devoted to the project—from 1833 until 1849, and then again from about 1856 until his death in 1871[20]—he obsessed incessantly over its actual physical design and implementation. He kept extensive notes, now in the collections of the Science Museum in London. The massiveness of the documentation is impressive: 300 sheets of engineering drawings; 600 to 700 representations of the mechanisms in the form of (what we would now call) timing diagrams, flowcharts, logic diagrams, and walk-throughs; and 6000 to 7000 pages of notes.[21]

Of course, the Analytical Engine, like the Difference Engine, was a mechanical machine, a complex of gears, wheels, chains, levers, rack-and-pinions, weights, barrels, pulleys, and the like.[22] Babbage's was a mechanical world[23]; yet, despite this, his work illustrates vividly that there are logical, conceptual, organizational, and behavioral (in other words, what in present-centered language we would call architectural) principles that can be abstracted out of the purely physical, purely technological. To put this in another way, there was something that computer scientists of the late 20th century would recognize: what makes a digital computer a digital computer is not the material or the kind of physical technology out of which it is built, it is its conceptual, organizational, and architectural principles.

One person who studied Babbage's Analytical Engine documents in great detail was Australian computer scientist and Babbage scholar Allan Bromley. Through his eyes we get a detailed sense of Babbage's mechanical world. Bromley, however, belongs to what is called the age of electronic computers. To describe the machinations of the Analytical Engine, he *had* to translate Babbage's ideas into present-centered language. He could do this, fortunately, because the concepts Babbage invented had direct modern correspondences, which is why Bromley could say (using modern-day jargon), that the Analytical Engine was a "decimal machine" and that it used the "sign-and-magnitude" scheme to represent numbers.[24]

A particularly vivid instance of the modernity of Babbage's ideas was discussed by the British electronic computer pioneer (later, Sir) Maurice Wilkes (on whom much will be said in later chapters), who was probably the first to examine Babbage's notebooks on the Analytical Engine (in 1971, the centenary of Babbage's death).[25] One of Wilkes's discoveries was that Babbage's design of what we now call the computer's *control unit*—as the name suggests, that part of the computer that directs the very basic step-by-step actions to carry out the operations encoded in the punched cards (the program in present-centered language)—bears a remarkable resemblance to the very technique Wilkes invented in 1951. Babbage had anticipated, a good 100 years earlier, the principle of microprogramming.[26]

VII

A significant portion of the Difference Engine was built by Babbage, and there was the Scheutz implementation.[27] Alas, the Analytical Engine was never built, not even as a prototype, not even some substantial portion of it, although Babbage made a number of experimental components.[28]

We have seen that government funding of the Difference Engine (totaling about £17,000[29]) evaporated completely by 1833. Thereafter, Babbage could not interest the government in financing his work on the Analytical Engine. Without such support, there was never a possibility of the machine being built. As it was, he had spent some £20,000 of his own money on the Difference Engine.[30] Yet, during the first 16 years (1833–1849) that he devoted to the project and then again during the later period (1856 until his death), he was at it constantly, ideating, thinking, refining, elaborating, conceptualizing, obsessing. There is something quite poignant in our imagined vision of this man, working in complete isolation, obsessed with an idea, the archetypal lonely inventor, the solitary scientist of Romantic lore,[31] churning out drawing after drawing, in their hundreds, note after note, in the thousands, conceiving new ideas, designing new mechanisms, for a machine he must have realized would never get built in his lifetime. There lies, perhaps, the poignancy of his venture. Babbage was leaving something *for posterity*, a time capsule to be retrieved in the future—as, indeed, it was, by such Babbage scholars as Martin Campbell-Kelly, Bromley, and Wilkes.

Babbage's work on the Analytical Engine is an example *par excellence* of what it means to be a designer–inventor rather than a craftsman–inventor. His vast outpouring of documents on the project not only represents a design activity of almost epic proportions, but also demonstrates the separation of designing from making, of the role of designs as blueprints, of the separation between designer and builder.

This separation of designing from making marks the distinction between someone like Babbage and the traditional craftsman (for example, even in Babbage's time in Victorian England, the wheelwright[32]). For the craftsman, designing and making are inextricably intertwined: one designed while making and one made while designing, and, indeed, one made while using and one used while making.[33] In separating designing—and the creation of drawings and explanatory and descriptive notes *are* acts of design—from building, Babbage left a blueprint for posterity. In fact, more excitingly, he left behind a *theory* for, and of, the Analytical Engine. We find in Babbage's work an idea that I have already mentioned (see Prologue, section VI), to which I return to later, that has a vital place in the history of computer science: the idea of designs-as-theories.[34]

VIII

We cannot end Babbage's story without further mention of Lovelace, whom we have, so far, encountered only cursorily as the translator of Menabrea's 1842 memoir on the Analytical Engine, and one who added a lengthy gloss on the translated article. The exclusion of women from intellectual establishments such as universities and scientific organizations is a well-known feature of the Western intellectual tradition[35]—thus, their absence in most histories of science. It would not be until the 19th century that women began to have a presence—although still a devastatingly minor one—in science and mathematics, and their minority status continued to prevail into and through the 20th century. The history of science, including mathematics, is a long, sad history of misogyny.[36]

There were, of course, stellar exceptions, especially in the mathematical sciences, some of whom were noblewomen who were privileged with "a room of their own" (to borrow from Virginia Woolf). In 18th-century France, for example, there was the grandiosely named Gabrielle-Emilie Le Tonnier de Breteuil Marquise du Châtelet (1706–1749), mistress to philosopher and writer Voltaire (1694–1778), who discoursed on Newtonian physics for the French Enlightenment *philosophes*, espoused Leibnizian ideas, and even embroiled herself in intellectual disputes with the likes of the mighty Swiss mathematician Leonhard Euler (1707–1783).[37] Across the English Channel, born the year after du Châtelet died, the German–born observational astronomer Caroline Herschel (1750–1848)—aunt of Babbage's friend Herschel—when not assisting older brother, Sir William Herschel (1738–1822) in his discovery of the planet Uranus and unimagined cosmic universes, would go on to find many comets on her very own.[38] In 19th-century Britain there was the remarkable Scotswoman Mary Fairfax Somerville (1780–1872), mathematician and natural philosopher (as physicists were then called), who wrote the first paper (on magnetism) by a woman to be read before the Royal Society and published in its venerable *Philosophical Transactions*[39]; who wrote *The Mechanism of the Heavens* (1831), an exposition on the mechanical philosophy of the French *savant* Pierre Simon, Comte de Laplace (1748–1827); who wrote *On the Connection of the Physical Sciences* (1834), a scientific "bestseller" in her lifetime; who became associated with Babbage's friend Herschel; and yet who would be denied fellowship in the Royal Society because she was a woman.[40]

And then there was Augustus Ada, the Countess of Lovelace (1815–1852), born Ada Byron, a daughter of Lord Byron (1788–1824). The poet and his daughter had no relationship, although they apparently pined for each other, and Byron wrote her into his long narrative poem, "Childe Harold's Pilgrimage"(1812–1818). They were buried next to each other in a church in Nottinghamshire; both died at age 36.

Married at 20 to the First Earl of Lovelace (hence her title), she showed mathematical ability at an early age. While in her teens, she came to know Somerville,[41] and was tutored by the mathematician Augustus de Morgan (1806-1871)—a pleasing coincidence as de Morgan's celebrated theorems in Boolean algebra play a role in the later design of computer circuits (as we will see).

Babbage was a regular visitor at the Lovelace's country seat.[42] When he learned that Lovelace had translated Menabrea's French article on the Analytical Engine into English, he suggested that she add notes to the English memoir,[43] which she did. Her notes, appended to the Menabrea memoir, were three times as long as the original article. The most celebrated of these was Note G, the last one, for two very different reasons.

The first was because of her remark that the Analytical Engine could not initiate any task. It had no such "pretensions"; it could only do what it was ordered to do by humans.[44] Here, Lovelace anticipated an issue that was much debated more than a century after she wrote these words (as we will see): whether computers can exhibit "intelligence" or "original thought."

The second point worthy of mentioning in Note G is that it laid out in great detail the sequence of operations (an *algorithm*) for the computation of a mathematical entity called Bernoulli's numbers; this computation would be performed on the Analytical Engine.

Whether this algorithm was constructed by Lovelace or whether she was communicating Babbage's work remains unresolved. Babbage himself remembered that he and Lovelace discussed possible problems to use as illustrative examples. He suggested several, but ultimately the ones selected were chosen by Lovelace. As for the algorithm to compute Bernoulli's numbers, this was originally written by Babbage but there was a "grave mistake" in it that Lovelace detected and returned to him for amendment.[45]

If we accept this account, the algorithm for computing Bernoulli's numbers was really Babbage's work, not Lovelace's. Claims made about her of being "the world's first programmer" in this light are thus exaggerated. Lovelace's place in the history of computing lay in her translation of the Menabrea article, and in her lengthy gloss on how mathematical functions could be reduced to operations on Babbage's engine. And even had she been the originator of this particular algorithm, she could scarcely be called its programmer. At the very least, she would have had to write a program that *executes correctly* on an actual Analytical Engine, but such a machine did not exist physically.

Still, if not the world's first programmer, Lovelace must be regarded, along with Menabrea, as the one who demonstrated how an analytical problem in mathematics could be executed by a machine.[46] We must also appreciate her sharp insight into the very nature of a computing machine, its scope and limits, as her comment cited earlier illustrates, and which is amplified further by her remark that a machine such as the Analytical Engine would have *consequences* for the course of science itself, for many problems in science would become resolvable and "more profoundly" tractable with the help of the Analytical Engine.[47]

She was anticipating the role of this machine as an instrument of science itself. We must also not forget that she was a poet's daughter with a flair for an elegant turn of phrase—that she could speak of the engine as a machine for "weaving algebraic patterns."

NOTES

1. I have appropriated the word *phylogeny* from evolutionary biology. In the words of biologist, paleontologist, and scientific essayist Stephen Jay Gould (1941–2002), phylogeny is "the evolutionary history of a lineage conventionally depicted as a sequence of adult stages" (S. J. Gould. (1977). *Ontogeny and phylogeny* (p. 483). Cambridge, MA: Belknap Press of Harvard University Press). In other words, phylogeny refers to the evolutionary history of a type of organism, a species, or a genus, seen through their adult forms.

2. S. Dasgupta. (1996). *Technology and creativity* (p. 22). New York: Oxford University Press.

3. L. F. Menabrea. (1842). "Sketch of the Analytical Engine", *Bibliothéque Universelle de Genève* [On-line], October, no. 42. Available: http://www.fourmilab.ch/babbage/sketch.html

4. Letter from Charles Babbage to the Earl of Rosse, President, Royal Society, June 8, 1852 (pp. 77–81). In C. Babbage. (1994). *Passages from the life of a philosopher* (p. 79). Piscataway, NJ: IEEE Press (original work published 1864).

5. C. Boyer. (1991). *A history of mathematics* (2nd ed., Rev., pp. 443–445). New York: Wiley.

6. Menabrea, op cit.

7. A.. A. Lovelace. (1842). Notes. In Menabrea, op cit.

8. Menabrea, op cit.

9. M.. Campbell-Kelly. (1994). Introduction (pp. 7–36). In Babbage, op cit., p. 23.

10. Lovelace, op cit.

11. M. B. Hesse. (1966). *Models and analogies in science*. London: Sheed & Ward; J. Holland, K. J. Holyoak, R. E. Nisbett, & P. R. Thagard. (1986). *Induction* (Chapter 10). Cambridge, MA: MIT Press.

12. S. Dasgupta. (1994). *Creativity in invention and design* (pp. 27–33). New York: Cambridge University Press.

13. R. L. Hills. (1990). Textiles and clothing. In I. McNeil (Ed.), *An encyclopaedia of the history of technology* (pp. 803–854). London: Routledge (see especially pp. 822–823); J. Essinger. (2004). *Jacquard's web*. Oxford: Oxford University Press.

14. Essinger, op cit. D. S. L. Cardwell. (1994). *The Fontana history of technology*. London: Fontana Press.

15. Lovelace, op cit.

16. Ibid.

17. Ibid.

18. C.. Babbage. (1837). *On the mathematical power of the calculating engine*. Unpublished manuscript, December 26, Oxford University, Buxton MS7, Museum of the History of Science; printed in B. Randell. (1975). *The origins of the digital computer* (2nd ed., pp. 17–52). New York: Springer-Verlag (see especially p. 21).

19. R. Moreau. (1984). *The computer comes of age* (p. 15). Cambridge, MA: MIT Press.

20. A. G. Bromley. (1982). Charles Babbage's Analytical Engine, 1838. *Annals of the History of Computing*, 4, 196–217 (see especially p. 196).

21. Ibid., p. 197.

22. Bromley (op cit.) has several drawings that show some of the mechanisms designed by Babbage.

23. M. V. Wilkes. (1981). The design of a control unit: Reflections on reading Babbage's notebooks. *Annals of the History of Computing*, 3, 116–120.

24. Bromley, op cit., pp. 197–198.

25. M. V. Wilkes. (1971). Babbage as a computer pioneer. *Historia Mathematica, 4*, 415–440.

26. Wilkes, 1981, op cit.

27. See chapter 1.

28. Campbell-Kelly, op cit., p. 24.

29. Babbage, 1994, op cit., p. 79.

30. Ibid.

31. The Age of Romanticism, circa 1770 to 1835, was a time when not only poetry, fiction, and art were imbued with the spirit of wonder about nature and ourselves, but also science was touched by the same spirit. See R. Holmes. (2008). *The age of wonder.* New York: Viking Books.

32. G. Sturt. (1923). *The wheelwright's craft.* Cambridge, UK: Cambridge University Press.

33. J. C. Jones. (1980). *Design methods: Seeds of human future* (2nd ed.). New York: Wiley; C. Alexander. (1964). *Notes on the synthesis of form.* Cambridge, MA: Harvard University Press.

34. S. Dasgupta. (1999). *Design theory and computer science* (pp. 368–379). Cambridge, UK: Cambridge University Press (original work published 1991).

35. L. Pyenson & S. Sheets-Pyenson (1999). *Servants of nature* (p. 336). New York: W. W. Norton.

36. Nor is the history of art any better. See W. Chadwick. (2007). *Women, art and society* (4th ed.). London: Thames & Hudson.

37. Pyenson & Sheets-Pyenson, op cit., pp. 342–344.

38. Holmes, op cit.

39. S. Wood (2010). *Mary Fairfax Somerville* [On-line] (original work published 1995). Available: http://www.agnesscott.edu/lriddle/women/somer.htm

40. Pyenson & Sheets-Pyenson, op cit., pp. 347–348.

41. B. Toole (2011). *Ada Byron, Lady Lovelace* [On-line]. Available: http://www.agnesscott.edu/lriddle/women/love.htm

42. Campbell-Kelly, op cit., p. 27.

43. Babbage, 1994, op cit., p. 102.

44. Lovelace, op cit., Note G.

45. Babbage, 1994, op cit., p. 102.

46. Ibid.

47. Lovelace, op cit., Note G.

3

Missing Links

IN CHAPTER 2, I suggested that Babbage's place in the history of computing was twofold: first, because his Analytical Engine represented, for the first time, the *idea* of automatic universal computing and how this idea might be implemented, and second, because some of his design ideas—the store, mill, control, user interface via punched cards—anticipated some fundamental principles of the electronic universal computer that would be created some 75 years after his death. There is a modernity to his idea that makes us pause. Indeed, it led Babbage scholar Allan Bromley to admit that he was "bothered" by the architectural similarity of the Analytical Engine to the modern computer, and he wondered whether there is an inevitability to this architecture: Is this the only way a computer could be organized internally?[1]

Thus, Babbage's creativity lay not only in conceiving a machine that had no antecedent, but also it lay in his envisioning an idea of universal computing that disappeared and then reappeared many decades later, and came to be the dominant architectural principle in computing. This observation is, of course, present-centered; we might be perilously close to what Herbert Butterfield had called the "Whig interpretation of history" (see Prologue, section VII), for we seem to be extolling Babbage's achievement because of its resonance with the achievements of our own time. But were there any direct consequences of his idea? What happened after Babbage? Did he have any influence on those who came after? And, if not, what took place in the development of what we have come to call *computer science*?

II

In fact, there is a view that between Babbage's mechanical world of computing and the electronic age, nothing really happened—that the time in between represented the Dark

Ages in the history of computing. This is, of course, as misguided a view as another held by historians at one time that Europe, between the end of the Roman Empire (circa fifth century) and the Renaissance (the 15th–16th centuries)—the Middle Ages—was in a state of intellectual and creative backwardness. Which is why the Middle Ages was also once called the Dark Ages.

Just as modern historical scholarship revealed that the Middle Ages was anything but Dark,[2] so also must we discount vigorously the idea that the period between Babbage and the age of the electronic computer was a Dark Age in the history of computing. In fact, when we examine what transpired after Babbage, we find that it was a period when two very different and lively views of computing took shape. I will call these the *abstract* and the *concrete* views, corresponding—broadly—to the conception of computational artifacts that are abstract and physical, respectively.

Let us dwell, for the moment, on the concrete view. What we find is that this was a period (roughly between 1880 and 1939) during which several species of material computational artifacts were created. These species were linked in that they were invented with a common *purpose*: to automate computing as much as possible. Yet, the linkages differed in that, although some machines aspired to universal computing, others had more modest aspirations.

I use the word *species* metaphorically, of course. Biology offers us yet another metaphor. Ever since the 18th century (well before Darwin, Wallace, and the advent of their particular theory of evolution), physical anthropologists and natural historians[3] interested in the connection between man and ape have quested for the "missing link" between the two.[4] After Darwin, the very credibility of Darwinian natural selection rested, at least in part, on the discovery of missing links in the fossil record.[5] I am tempted to term collectively the period between Babbage's design of the Analytical Engine (circa 1840s) and the advent of the electronic computer (circa 1940s) the Age of Missing Links, for they constituted designs and inventions that paved pathways of ideas from Babbage's vision of a universal automatic computing engine to the practical realization of that vision.

III

The punched card, used by Jacquard for his loom and then Babbage's key to the universality of the Analytical Engine, developed an identity and a universality of its own. It became a repository of information or symbol structures—a memory device, in fact. And a whole new genus of machines, now powered by electricity, came into existence just to manipulate and process the contents of these punched cards. "Computing" not only signified esoteric mathematical computation, but also came to mean an activity called *data processing*—a genre of computing involving data pertaining to human beings; to human society, commerce, health, welfare, economy, and institutions. "Tables" meant not only tables of logarithms or trigonometric functions, but also printed tables of such data on the nitty-gritty of individual life—name, place and date of birth, age, gender, religion, occupation, ethnicity, educational level, date of death, and so on.

And the United States entered the history of computing.

IV

In 1890, Herman Hollerith (1860–1929), American-born son of German immigrants, inventor and statistician, submitted a dissertation bearing the title *In Connection with the Electric Tabulation System which Has Been Adopted by U.S. Government for the Work of the Census Bureau* to the Columbia University School of Mines, for which he received a PhD. This must surely be the first doctoral degree awarded in the field of computing, the first recognition of computing as an academically respectable discipline.

Hollerith obtained an engineering degree from the Columbia School of Mines in 1879; his academic record was such that, after graduating, one of his professors, William P. Trowbridge (1828–1892), appointed him his assistant. It was a fateful appointment. When Trowbridge became chief special agent in the U.S. Bureau of Census, Hollerith moved with him as a statistician. At the Bureau, Hollerith met John Shaw Billings (1839–1913), a surgeon in the U.S. Army who had been assigned to the Bureau earlier to help with statistical work related to census data. At the time Hollerith joined the agency, Billings was in charge of collecting and tabulating data for the 1880 U.S. census.[6]

The history of computing repeatedly tells a story of dissatisfaction with the use of human mental labor for tasks of a mechanical nature. Thus it was with Babbage (as we saw); thus it was with Hollerith. Although accounts differ,[7] the essence of the story is the same: Billings, remarking in Hollerith's presence, that there ought to be a mechanical way of tabulating census statistics. Thus was planted a seed in Hollerith's mind. In 1882, he spent some time teaching in the mechanical engineering department at the Massachusetts Institute of Technology (MIT)—between Babbage and Hollerith we find the first of many appearances of the two Cambridges in the history of computing—and during his brief tenure there (he left in 1884 to take a post in the U.S. Patent Office), he worked on the problem of converting information punched as configurations of holes in cards into electrical impulses that, in turn, would drive mechanical equipment. This was the beginning of *electromechanical computing*.

V

Analyzing the way census and other similar kinds of demographic data had been gathered before, Hollerith identified some basic data processing operations involved in the process: *sorting* data in some order, *counting*, and *tallying* such data.[8] The operations seem simple enough, involving mental activity that any literate, numerically competent person can carry out—clerical operations, in other words. The problem is that of volume.

The amount of data that may have to be sorted and tallied may be unmanageably vast. In the case of Census data—and this was the original *need* posed to Hollerith—it may entail records on the population of a city, a state, a whole country. Rather than process such massive volumes of data manually, perhaps this work could be done mechanically, as far as possible.[9] We are, once more, reminded of Leibniz's remark: "excellent men" should not have to waste time in the drudgery of calculation that could be "delegated" to machines.[10]

Leibniz's theme, as I called it, may have been meant for mathematical computation; his "excellent men" referred to astronomers and mathematicians. His theme, however, echoed by Babbage, also became Hollerith's theme: to automate computation—not the kind of computation Leibniz and Babbage had in mind, involving transmutations of complex mathematical functions into sequences of machine operations, but computation nonetheless: sorting, counting, tallying, and organizing large volumes of data. To Hollerith, automatic computation meant automatic data processing. We might say that if Babbage initiated the realm of automatic scientific computing, Hollerith commenced the realm of automatic commercial or business computing, and the latter responded to a particular need. Hollerith's major intellectual achievement was to invent "an electric tabulating system," which also gave him a doctoral degree from Columbia University.

Tabulation entails printing a summary obtained by counting. Electromechanical machines that did this came to be called tabulators or, sometimes, accounting machines.[11] A well-known example was the IBM 407 Accounting Machine. In fact, Hollerith invented not just a single machine but a *system* comprising machines and a *process* that would be carried out by the system. His electric tabulating system involved a device called a keyboard punch, a tabulator, and a device that he called a sorting box (a distant forerunner to the later automatic sorter). Curiously, the printing of tabulated data was done by hand in Hollerith's system—a situation that would be improved in later developments by others—to include an automatic printer as part of the system.[12] What was processed was data transcribed onto punched cards.

In Hollerith's hands, the original Jacquard card (or its Babbageian version) became something entirely different. His cards were 3 inches by 5.5 inches,[13] and each card held relevant information about an individual. Hollerith described, as an example, the format of the card used by the U.S. Surgeon-General for compiling U.S. Army health statistics.[14]

Each card represented an individual soldier. The card's surface was partitioned into several sections (or "fields", to use a later term), each devoted to particular, relevant aspects. Each field, in turn, consisted of an array of subfields, with numbers or abbreviated codes assigned to the subfields. One field was given, for instance, to the division to which the soldier was assigned, and the subfields corresponded to the various divisions. A hole punched in one of the subfields would indicate the soldier's division.

Thus, a single Hollerith card became a memory device that held data that, in a manner of speaking, defined the "identity" of that individual (from the Army's perspective, that is). It held a record about a person, such as rank, the branch of the armed services, age,

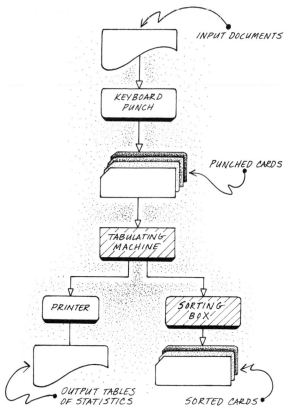

FIGURE 3.1 A Hollerith Data Processing System.

race, nationality, and length of service.[15] To paraphrase a comment by a character in Don DeLillo's novel *White Noise* (put in an altogether different context), one is the sum total of one's data.[16]

The system was completely general—universal in the same sense that the Jacquard card (in the realm of weaving) and the Babbage card (in the realm of mathematical computing) were universal. By changing the format design a different card would obtain, as was used by New York City's Board of Health to compile mortality statistics[17] and, of course, a different format design would be used to compile statistics in the 11th U.S. Census of 1890, in which Hollerith's system played a central role.

His system can be depicted by a system diagram, as shown in Figure 3.1. From the census returns documents, a keyboard punch transcribes the information for each individual onto a card. The cards are then placed, one by one, on a part of the tabulating machine Hollerith called "the press", which has sensors that read the data by sensing the holes, and send electrical signals to the other main component of the tabulator comprising mechanical counters in the form of dials. Specific counters are wired through circuits to the sensors that read specific fields in the card. For example, one counter could be connected to the sensors in the press so that it counted the number of males in a district, whereas another, the number of females. This is done manually by establishing the electrical connections between sensors and counters. If some combination of fields are to be compiled, for instance the number of white males and females, respectively, additional circuits are established manually that connect sensors for the fields "male" and "white" to a separate counter.

The cards may need to be sorted in some order or separated into stacks according to some particular field or combination of fields. In the case of census processing, for example, they may have to be separated and/or ordered by district so that statistics for each district can be compiled. The sorting box is used for this purpose. It consists of a box divided into compartments, each of which is closed by a lid that springs open when an electromagnetic circuit is closed. The lids of the sorting box are connected to the press component of the tabulator in the same way as the counters. When a particular district number is read by the appropriate sensor in the press, the lid wired to that sensor springs open. The card is then deposited manually in the opened compartment, the lid is closed manually, and the next card is read. If a different district number is now read, a different lid opens, and so on.

In present-centered language, Hollerith's tabulating system was a human–machine system. Human intervention was necessary to transcribe the data onto punched cards; to feed the cards one by one into the press part of the tabulator; to set up the connections between sensors and counters, and between sensors and the compartment lids in the sorting box; to transfer cards from the tabulator to the sorting box; and to print out the values held in the counters. However, the time-consuming, tedious, and error-prone task of actually tallying and compiling information was automated.

VI

Hollerith was not content in being "just" an inventor. Like his great contemporary and compatriot Thomas Alva Edison (1847–1931), he was also an entrepreneur, and in this capacity he enters into the corporate history of the computer.

In 1896, Hollerith left government service to found his own company, the Tabulating Machine Company. In 1911, this firm merged with two others to form the Computing Tabulating Recording Company (CTR), of which a certain Thomas J. Watson (1874–1956) became head in 1914. Watson changed the name of the company's Canadian subsidiary to International Business Machines (IBM) in 1917; the parent company, CTR itself, became IBM in 1924, with more than 300,000 employees.[18] In 1920, CTR formed a British subsidiary named British Tabulating Machine (BTM), which parted ways from IBM in 1947 and, after merging with another company, became International Computers and Tabulators (ICT). In 1968, ICT merged with English Electric Computers and became International Computers Limited (ICL), a firm that no longer exists, having been acquired by Fujitsu in 2002.

VII

Punched-card electromechanical data processing is part of the fossil record that unveils a part of what I am calling *missing links* in the evolutionary history, the phylogeny, of computing—links that connect Babbage's mechanical world to the age of digital electronics. Throughout the course of the first four decades of the 20th century, led by IBM—the undisputed leader in this technology—a whole range of electromechanical machines were designed that refined, improved, enlarged, and automated further the process of data processing. The objective, always, was to improve automation in terms of extent of automation (and thus minimizing human intervention) and speed of processing.

The punched card itself—at the heart of data processing systems—would change quite radically from Hollerith's original card. It would be standardized in size (7 1/8 inches by 3 1/4 inches), thickness, and format: 12 rows spaced one-quarter inch apart with 80 columns. Alphabetic, numeric, and special characters were represented by specific combinations of holes down a column, according to what is known as "extended binary-coded decimal interchange code".

The basic data processing functions would evolve, and machines to perform these functions came into being, including a typewriterlike device, the *keypunch* to punch cards; a similar device called the *verifier* to verify the correctness and accuracy of the transcribed punched cards; the *automatic punch* to reproduce or copy a deck of punched cards; the *sorter* to arrange a deck of cards automatically according to some hierarchy (such as in alphabetic sequence of names or in numeric sequence of dates of birth); the *collator*, which merged two previously sorted decks of cards into one larger sorted deck; the *tabulator*, with varying degrees of functional sophistication; the *calculator*, which read data from input cards (such as the number of hours one employee worked in a pay period and his hourly rate) and performed numeric calculations (such as gross pay, tax, benefit deduction, net pay), then punched the results onto cards; and the *printer*.

Machines such as tabulators, calculators, and collators were *programmable* in that, by changing the wiring connections on the control panel or "plugboard," they could be made to read different fields on a card and to perform variations on their central functions. After a plugboard was wired a certain way, it constituted a "program" that could be used repeatedly, or that plugboard could be exchanged for a differently wired plugboard.

VIII

In the world of punched-card data processing, each type of machine performed a specialized function, but no one machine type really had an "identity" of its own. One would not purchase a sorter by itself, nor a keypunch, nor a tabulator, not even a calculator. Each was in symbiotic relation with the others; they "fed" off one another. They formed a system. A *data processing center* (such as IBM had) would have an army of keypunches and verifiers, some automatic punches, some printers, a few sorters, one or two tabulators, and one or two calculating machines—a factory, in other words, in which some of the machines worked in parallel, some in sequence, and some in "pipeline" mode. But what was being processed, what flowed from one machine to another, were not the punched cards—they were only the medium—but data or information or *symbol structures* carried in the punched cards. Data processing factories or centers were *symbol* processing systems.

These systems unveiled a fundamental character of symbol processing: numbers are only one kind of symbol. Insofar as machines such as Babbage's Difference Engine and Analytical Engine were concerned with numbers and arithmetic operations, they were calculating machines, as Babbage readily admitted, but the punched-card data processing system that Hollerith pioneered entailed much more than calculation. It performed operations such as comparing, matching, sorting, merging, and copying. These operations did not alter the symbol structures they were processing. Indeed, these operations were indifferent to the symbols themselves as signifying anything out there in the world. Their only concern was the *relationship* among the symbols, such as whether 3 was higher than A (in some sense). In other words, the punched-card data processing paradigm revealed that *computing and calculating are not synonymous.* In concrete terms, the calculating machine and the tabulator were not the only machines that mattered.

IX

On the other side of the Atlantic, Babbage had not been forgotten. At least one person, an Irishman named Percy Ludgate (1883–1922), was much aware of him.[19] Writing in 1909 on the design of an analytical machine capable of performing calculations without human intervention, he recalled, in admiration, Babbage's work.[20]

What little we know about Ludgate is largely a result of British computer scientist and computer historian Brian Randell, who composed a brief biography of this man.[21] Born in County Cork, Ireland, Ludgate studied accountancy at Rathmere College of Commerce in Dublin, passed his final examination with distinction, and was awarded a gold medal by the Corporation of Accountancy. His deplorably short working life was spent as an auditor with a Dublin firm, and so his work on the analytical machine was almost certainly done in his spare time in the privacy of his home. He appeared to be an unassuming person; he was described by some who knew him as modest, gentle, courteous, and humble,[22] although his intellectual abilities were evident to colleagues and he was even regarded as possessing a touch of genius.[23]

During World War I, Ludgate played a major role as a member of a government committee responsible for overseeing the production and supply of oats for a large area of the country to maintain a regular supply to the cavalry division of the army. His work in planning and organizing this large-scale enterprise drew praise from his bosses.[24] Unmarried, he died of pneumonia in 1922, just short of his 40th birthday.

Although Ludgate was aware of Babbage, this did not inspire his own efforts, at least during the earlier stages. It was only after the initial design of his machine that he came to know of Babbage's work. However, he freely acknowledged that, thereafter, he benefited greatly from the latter's writings.[25] If there was, as he conceded, a certain similarity between his own design and that of the Analytical Engine, this was not a matter of happenstance, but rather a reflection of the fact that his tenor of thinking about automatic computing followed a path Babbage had walked.[26] Bromley's comment, made some 70 years, later comes to mind (refer back to Section I).

This resemblance, however, is at the most general functional or architectural level. As to the detailed structure—the design of the actual mechanism—the differences between his machine and Babbage's were considerable.[27]

Ludgate appealed to both Babbage's autobiography and the Menabrea–Lovelace memoir as evidence of the viability of mechanical, automatic computation of analytical (in the mathematical sense of this word) problems.[28] We may imagine how, working in virtual isolation, in the tradition of the mythic lone inventor, probably with not a single person to discuss his work, his later discovery of Babbage *confirmed* his own conviction regarding the viability of his own thinking. He must have surely taken solace from his discovery of Babbage's work. It must have given him greater confidence in articulating the functional requirements demanded of *any* analytical machine.

In one long, breathless paragraph, Ludgate stipulated what an analytical machine must achieve. It must have the means to hold or store the numeric data required as input to the problem of interest, as well as the results produced by the computation. It must have the means to send pairs of numbers to the unit that performs arithmetical operations, the means to select from the stored numbers the correct ones on which to operate, and the ability to select the proper operations to perform on such selected numbers. It must have the means of recalling numbers previously computed should they be needed for a later part of the computation. And, of course, there must be a means of sequencing the operations and numbers according to the "laws" of evaluations of algebraic equations. And, he asked, how could a machine follow such algebraic laws?[29]

All roads keep leading back to Jacquard and his loom.[30] However, rather than cards, Ludgate resorted to a sheet or roll of perforated tapes[31]—thus the appearance, in the domain of computing, of perforated *paper tape* as the functional equivalent of punched cards. Ludgate called this "formula-paper".[32] In contrast to Babbage, who used two sets of cards—one to specify the operations to be performed and the other to select the numbers on which to be operated—each row of the formula-paper specified both the operation to be performed as well as the selection of the numbers on which to be operated.[33]

Even more distinctive were Ludgate's schemes for storing numbers and for performing arithmetic. His store comprised "shuttles." Each variable was stored in a separate shuttle. Each shuttle carried protruding metal rods—one rod for the sign and one rod for each digit of a 20-digit number. The actual digit stored on a rod would be represented by the protrusion of the rod out of the shuttle by a distance from 1 to 10 units. The shuttles would be held in "two co-axial cylindrical shuttle-boxes."[34] A particular variable would be accessed during an arithmetic operation by rotating the carrying shuttle box through an appropriate angle. As for his scheme for performing arithmetic, the basic operation was to be multiplication.[35]

The idea of a multiplication machine was not new in Ludgate's time. The French inventor Léon Bollée (1870–1913) had built such a machine, which won him a gold medal at the Paris Exposition in 1889; and there had been other patents awarded to inventors even earlier. Ludgate's scheme used a version of the logarithmic method of multiplication. In the latter method, the product $a * b$ would be computed as $c = \log a + \log b$, and then it would take the antilog of c. Ludgate did not use logarithms; rather, each digit was translated into a unique "index number." The index numbers of the two original digits to be multiplied were added, then a reverse translation (anti-index number, so to speak) was performed to obtain the two-digit product.

For example, Ludgate showed a table of digits and corresponding simple index numbers. For the digit 4, the index number is 2; for the digit 6, it is 8. So to calculate $4 * 6$, the corresponding index numbers are added ($2 + 8 = 10$). A second table showed the compound index numbers corresponding to each double-digit product. For the compound index number 10, the corresponding product is 24. Hence, the result, 24, could be read off from the table.

Ludgate admitted the difficulty of describing the mechanism of the index system without drawings.[36] Basically, the actual addition of the index numbers and the reading off of index numbers and products were to be effected by a system of movable blades and slides, and their relative displacements from each other, rather like the operation of a slide rule, which—before the advent of pocket calculators—was the primary handheld calculation aid for engineers and scientists.

The multiplication of two multidigit variables—say, $a = 9247$ and $b = 8132$—would be performed by a cycle of operations, each operation involving a set of movements of the blades. The operation first computed the partial product $8132 * 9$ (using the index numbers), then $8132 * 2$, followed by $8132 * 4$, and finally $8132 * 7$. Each of these partial products was stored in the shuttle system, and then the final product was computed as the sum of the partial products, the addition effected by the relative displacements of the slides and blades.

As for division, here, too, Ludgate deviated markedly from the convention of dividing by repeated subtraction of the divisor from the dividend. This method was inadequate for the purpose of his machine. He noted that Babbage used this method, but it gave rise to many mechanical difficulties.[37] Instead, Ludgate adopted a method of division that began with the assumption that the machine could add, subtract, and multiply.[38] His method drew on the fact that an expression p/q, where p and q are the variables, can be expanded, using the Binomial Theorem to a series expression so that

$$p/q = Ap\left(1 - x + x^2 - x^3 + x^4 - x^5 + \cdots\right)$$

where A and x are both computed from the original variables p and q. Finding the sum of the expression as far as x to the power 10 would produce a result correct to at least 20 digits.[39]

Another distinctive feature of Ludgate's design was (using present-centered language) its user interface. The machine would be controlled by two keyboards—one allowed numbers to be communicated to the machine and would thus substitute for feeding in numbers through paper tape; the other would control the working of the machine and would thus serve as a substitute for the formula-paper.

As in Babbage's case, Ludgate's was a mechanical world—perhaps surprising for his time, when electric power had taken over many of the tasks energized by steam power in Babbage's time. Like Babbage, whom Ludgate quoted frequently and approvingly, Ludgate never built his machine. Unlike Babbage, Ludgate did not seem even to have attempted to build his machine. In fact, in a paper written in 1914, he mentioned that he had discarded his machine in favor of a new design that combined the best of both of Babbage's Analytical and Difference Engines.[40] Nothing, however, seems to be known about this later design.

Ludgate's optimism about the place of a machine such as his—of the place of computing machines in general—is clear in the concluding paragraph of his 1909 paper. Reflecting, as it were, the collective thoughts of his illustrious predecessors, Leibniz, Babbage, and Lovelace, Ludgate wrote that he could not imagine a single branch of science—pure or applied—that depended on mathematics for its development that would not benefit from automatic computation. By transforming abstract algebraic expressions into numeric computations, the scientist would be relieved of the tedium of complex calculations that could then be performed in a fast, precise, and automatic manner.[41]

For Ludgate, computing machines of the analytical kind were an instrument of science—in contrast to the data processing systems built by Hollerith and his successors, which were instruments of commerce. These two broad faces of computing were thus visible before World War I.

Ludgate's work on the analytical machine did not go unnoticed. In the July 1, 1909, issue of the preeminent British science journal *Nature*, a notice was published titled "A New Analytical Machine," authored by Sir Charles Vernon Boys (1855–1944), a distinguished English experimental physicist and inventor, and a fellow of the Royal Society.[42] Ludgate, an accountant by profession and an inventor by avocation, must have been pleased with the recognition of his work by such a distinguished professional scientist.

X

To reiterate: The central aim of this book is to trace the historical pathways to the emergence of the new science we now call computer science, and to understand the peculiar and unique character of this science. And so, at this point in the story, it seems appropriate to ask: What evidence do we find that a science surrounding computing was emerging? Or was it at all?

I think it is fair to say that at least one characteristic that makes a field of study or a human endeavor begin to seem scientific, whether it deals with the natural or artificial world, is when someone surveys what has been achieved to date and then abstracts from the evidence certain unifying principles. Such principles may take the form of a theory or a critical analysis of the domain of interest, or they may touch on the very nature of that field (what philosophers would call its ontology) or the character of its constituent knowledge (its epistemology), or they may address its methods of investigation (its methodology).

Such a general, possibly abstract, meditation on the nature of computing machines, and the first peek at a fetal form of a science of computing, is found in the writings of a Spaniard, Leonardo Torres y Quevedo (1852–1936). Son of a railway engineer, Torres y Quevedo studied civil engineering at what is now the Universidad Politécnica de Madrid, graduating in 1876. After working for a time in the railways, he came into an inheritance, resigned from the railways, and set himself up as an independent inventor and engineer with his own laboratory. Later, he was appointed director of the Laboratory of Applied Mechanics in the Athenaeum in Madrid (an institution dedicated to making scientific instruments). In later life, he received many honors for his inventions and engineering work both in Spain and abroad, including election to the Royal Spanish Academy of Sciences, the award by King Alfonso XIII of Spain of a prestigious gold medal of the Academy, presidentship of the Academy, an honorary doctorate from the Sorbonne, and, in 2007, the American Institute of Electrical and Electronics Engineers (IEEE) recognized one of his electrical inventions as an IEEE Milestone in Electrical Engineering and Computing—the first Spaniard to be so honored. He was also commemorated by his country by the issue of two stamps in his honor.[43]

But let us return to 1915 and to a long article written by Torres y Quevedo in Spanish and published in the journal of the Royal Spanish Academy of Sciences. The English translation bears the title "Essays on Automatics."[44] The word *automaton*, Torres y Quevedo wrote, is often used to refer to a machine that mimics the behavior of a human or an animal; an automaton is driven by its own power source and can go about its actions, usually repetitive ones, without outside intervention.[45]

He offered as an example the self-propelled torpedo. Its behavior involves establishing certain fixed mechanical relationships between its main moving parts. This is a problem in kinematics, the science of bodies or systems of bodies in motion, a branch of engineering mechanics that enters into the design of mechanical machinery.

The word *automaton* derives from the Latinized Greek word *automatos*, and the invention of mechanical automata reaches back to antiquity, to such Hellenistic engineers/inventors as Ctesibius (fl. 285–222 BCE), Philo of Byzantium (circa 270–200 BCE), and Hero of Alexandria (fl. first century CE)—all scholars who, along with so many others, found their way to the great Museum at Alexandria, where they taught, studied, and did research. They imagined into existence automata more as amusement for the wealthy than for practical use.[46] Still, Hero was credited for the invention of that most useful of artifacts, the water clock.[47]

Truly spectacular water clocks were made during the early Middle Ages by Chinese, Arabs, and Europeans.[48] But, undoubtedly, the most visible, successful, and consequential automaton was the mechanical weight-driven clock—the successor to the water clock. The most reliable evidence to date places the invention of the mechanical clock to some time between 1335 and 1344 in Milan and Padua, Italy.[49] The Padua clock of 1344 has been associated fairly firmly with Jacopo di Dondi (1290–1359), a scholar and physician who supervised the construction of this clock and may have contributed to its design.

XI

So mechanical automata have a venerable pedigree. In "Essays," however, they are not what interested Torres y Quevedo, but rather automata that imitated not human movement but human thought—to the extent that such a machine could, conceivably, replace humans.[50]

This, of course, is a very different notion of automata from its original roots. Torres y Quevedo was contemplating "thinking" machines. People such as Babbage and Ludgate had designed machines that embodied their respective theories of automatic computation. Torres y Quevedo, however, abstracted still further—machines that imitated the "thoughtful action" of humans. And thought included, certainly, calculation, but went beyond to making judgment, making choices. These are thoughtful actions, and machines that do this are his second type of automata. He called the study of such machines *automatics*.[51]

Such automata must have "sense organs"—"thermometers, magnetic compasses,…, etc"; they must have "limbs"—mechanisms that execute the operations demanded of them. However, the essential feature of such automata is that they be "capable of discernment"[52]—that they have the capacity to use information received immediately from the environment or even information obtained at some prior time to dictate their operations. Such automata must, then, imitate organisms in controlling their behavior according to information received from outside their own physical boundaries. Remarkably, Torres y Quevedo wrote, they must *adapt* their behavior according to "changing circumstances."[53]

Torres y Quevedo's theory of automata is that such a machine is an *adaptive system* that can alter its "conduct" according to "changing circumstances." He does not stop with this general definition. His science of automatics goes deeper. His aim in "Essays" was to try and show, at least theoretically, that such an adaptive automaton can be created according to principles ("rules") that can be built into the machine itself.[54] To illustrate this theoretical possibility, he resorted to real devices (he was, after all, an engineer), using electrical switches, each of which could be in one of a number of positions ("states," in present-centered language), representing input information to the automaton, and electromagnets that could be "excited," thus attracting their respective armatures as instances of operations.

He probed further. He referred to the French philosopher René Descartes (1596–1650), who in his most famous work, *Discourse on Method* (1637), discounted the possibility of automata being rational in the way humans are. In response, Torres y Quevedo imagined a machine in which there are "thousands or millions" of switches, each of which can be in one of as many different positions (states) as there are distinct written characters (such as letters, numbers, punctuation marks).[55] He wrote that it is quite possible that these switches could be set to represent any phrase or sentence, short or long. A speech, then, would be represented by the setting of switches. In fact, he was anticipating the possibility of storing symbol structures (a phrase or a speech) electrically, made up of letters, numbers, punctuation marks, and so on—that is, he was imagining the possibility of an automaton that processes symbols of *any* kind, not just numbers *à la* Babbage (to whom, incidentally, he refers extensively in his essay). But, Torres y Quevedo stopped short of actually positing machines that *reason on their own*. Like Lovelace, who cautioned that the Analytical Engine could not originate computational action, so, too, did Torres y Quevedo respond to Descartes somewhat cautiously. Descartes, he wrote, had been mistaken in assuming that for an automaton to provide reasoned responses it must do the reasoning itself. Rather, it is the creator of the automaton who does the reasoning.[56]

Still, in Torres y Quevedo's "Essays," we find the first inkling of a general theory of what a computing device might be. It is an automaton capable of symbol processing and adapting itself to variations in its input.

NOTES

1. A. B. Bromley. (1982). Charles Babbage's Analytical Engine, 1838. *Annals of the History of Computing, 4*, 196–217.

2. See, for example, F. B. Artz. (1980). *The mind of the Middle Ages* (3rd ed., Rev.) Chicago, IL: University of Chicago Press.

3. *Natural history* was the term commonly used until the end of the 19th century to designate the study of life at the level of the individual organism, especially organisms in their natural habitat. See M. Bates. (1990). *The nature of natural history* (p. 7). Princeton, NJ: Princeton University Press (original work published 1950). The term still prevails in some contexts such as, for example, in the term *natural history museum*.

4. A. E. Lovejoy. (1936). *The great chain of being* (pp. 233–236). Cambridge, MA: Harvard University Press.

5. E. Mayr. (1982). *The growth of biological thought* (p. 430). Cambridge, MA: Belknap Press of Harvard University Press.

6. H. H. Goldstine. (1972). *The computer from Pascal to von Neumann* (p. 67). Princeton, NJ: Princeton University Press.

7. Ibid., pp. 67–68.

8. H. Hollerith. (n.d.). "An electric tabulating system". Reprinted in B. Randell. (Ed.), (1975). *The origins of the digital computer* (2nd ed., pp. 129–139). New York : Springer-Verlag (see especially p. 129). The original source of this article is not specified by Randell. However, the following article was published with the same title: H. Hollerith. (1889). An electric tabulating system. *The Quarterly, Columbia University School of Mines, X*, 238–255.

9. Ibid.

10. Goldstine, op cit., p. 8*n*.

11. F. P. Brooks, Jr. & K. E. Iverson (1969). *Automatic data processing: System/360 edition* (p. 120). New York: Wiley.

12. Goldstine, op cit., pp. 70–71.

13. Hollerith, op cit., p. 131.

14. Ibid.

15. Ibid., pp. 132–133.

16. D. DeLillo (1994). *White noise* (p. 203). New York: Penguin (original work published 1985).

17. Hollerith, op cit., p. 133.

18. R. Moreau (1984). *The computer comes of age* (p. 24). Cambridge, MA: MIT Press.

19. P. E. Ludgate. (1909). On a proposed analytical machine. *Proceedings of the Royal Dublin Society, 12*, 77–91. Reprinted in Randell (pp. 71–87), op cit., p. 71.

20. Randell, op cit., p. 71.

21. B. Randell. (1971). Ludgate's Analytical Machine of 1909. *The Computer Journal, 14*, 317–326.

22. Ibid., p. 319.

23. Ibid.

24. Ibid., 318.

25. Ludgate, op cit., p. 72.

26. Ibid.

27. Ibid.

28. Ibid.

29. Ibid., pp. 72–73.

30. Ibid.

31. Ibid., p. 73.

32. Ibid., p. 74. Perforated paper tape also had a place in looms, reaching back to the 18th century. More prominently, paper tapes were used in electrical telegraphy in the mid 19th century.

33. Ibid.

34. Ibid.

35. Ludgate, op cit., p. 75.

36. Ibid., p. 74.

37. Ibid., p. 80.

38. Ibid., p. 81.

39. Ibid.

40. Quoted in Randell, 1971, op cit., p. 320.

41. Ludgate, op cit., p. 85.

42. C. V. Boys. (1909). A new analytical machine. *Nature, 81*, 14–15.

43. This biographical information was extracted from several websites on the Internet, most notably, http://www.wvegter.hivemind. Last accessed July 19, 2013.

44. L.. Torres y Quevedo. (1975). Essays on automatics (R. Basu, trans.). Randell, 1975, op cit., pp 87–106. (Original work published in Spanish as "Essais sur l'automatique. Sa definition. Étendue théoritique de ses applications," *Revue Générale des Sciences Pures et Appliquées*, 601–611 (15 Nov. 1915).

45. Torres y Quevedo, op cit., p. 87.

46. A. P. Usher. (1985). *A history of mechanical inventions* (Rev., pp. 162–163). New York: Dover Publications (original work published 1954).

47. H. Hodges. (1971). *Technology in the ancient world* (pp. 180–181). Harmondsworth, UK: Penguin Books.

48. D. L. Landes. (1983). *Revolution in time* (pp. 18–20). Cambridge, MA: Harvard University Press.

49. Usher, op cit., p. 196.

50. Torres y Quevedo, op cit., p. 87.

51. Ibid., p. 88.

52. Ibid.

53. Ibid.

54. Ibid., p. 89.

55. Ibid., p. 90.

56. Ibid., p. 91.

4

Entscheidungsproblem: What's in a Word?

I

IN 1900, THE celebrated German mathematician David Hilbert (1862–1943), professor of mathematics in the University of Göttingen, delivered a lecture at the International Mathematics Congress in Paris in which he listed 23 significant "open" (mathematicians' jargon for "unsolved") problems in mathematics.[1]

Hilbert's second problem was: Can it be proved that the axioms of arithmetic are consistent? That is, that theorems in arithmetic, derived from these axioms, can never lead to contradictory results?

To appreciate what Hilbert was asking, we must understand that in the *fin de siècle* world of mathematics, the "axiomatic approach" held sway over mathematical thinking. This is the idea that any branch of mathematics must begin with a small set of assumptions, propositions, or *axioms* that are accepted as true without proof. Armed with these axioms and using certain *rules of deduction*, all the propositions concerning that branch of mathematics can be derived as theorems. The sequence of logically derived steps leading from axioms to theorems is, of course, a *proof* of that theorem. The axioms form the foundation of that mathematical system.

The axiomatic development of plane geometry, going back to Euclid of Alexandria (fl. 300 BCE) is the oldest and most impressive instance of the axiomatic method, and it became a model of not only how mathematics should be done, but also of science itself.[2]

Hilbert himself, in 1898 to 1899, wrote a small volume titled *Grundlagen der Geometrie (Foundations of Geometry)* that would exert a major influence on 20th-century mathematics. Euclid's great work on plane geometry, *Elements*, was axiomatic no doubt, but was not axiomatic enough. There were hidden assumptions, logical problems, meaningless definitions, and so on. Hilbert's treatment of geometry began with three undefined objects—point, line, and plane—and six undefined relations, such as being parallel and being between. In place of Euclid's five axioms, Hilbert postulated a set of 21 axioms.[3]

In fact, by Hilbert's time, mathematicians were applying the axiomatic approach to entire branches of mathematics. For example, the axiomatization of the arithmetic of cardinal (whole) numbers formulated by the Italian Giuseppe Peano (1858–1932), professor of mathematics in the University of Turin, begins with three terms—"number", "zero", and "immediate successor"—and are assumed to be understood. The axioms themselves are just five in number:

1. Zero is a number.
2. The immediate successor to a number is a number.
3. Zero is not the immediate successor of a number.
4. No two numbers have the same immediate successor.
5. The principle of mathematical induction: Any property belonging to zero, and also to the immediate successor of every number that has the property, belongs to all numbers.

Exactly a decade after Hilbert's Paris lecture, British logician and philosopher Bertrand Russell (1872–1970), in collaboration with his Cambridge teacher Alfred North Whitehead (1861–1947), published the first of the three-volume *Principia Mathematica* (1910–1913)—not to be confused with Newton's *Principia*—which attempted to develop the notions of arithmetic from a precise set of logical axioms, and which was intended to demonstrate that mathematical knowledge can be reduced to (or, equivalently, derived from) a small set of logical principles. However, Russell and Whitehead did not address Hilbert's second problem.

Hilbert returned to the foundations of mathematics repeatedly throughout the course of the first three decades of the 20th century, establishing what came to be known as "Hilbert's program".[4] In 1928, in an address delivered at the International Congress of Mathematicians in Bologna, Italy (the home, incidentally, of the world's first university), and in a monograph titled "Die Grundlagen der Mathematik" ("The Foundations of Mathematics), he asked: (a) Is mathematics *complete*, in the sense that every mathematical statement could be either proved or disproved? (b) Is mathematics *consistent*, in the sense that a statement such as $2 + 2 = 5$ could never be arrived at by a valid proof, or in the sense that two contradictory propositions $a = b$ and $a \neq b$ could both be derived? (c) Is mathematics *decidable*, in the sense that there exists a definite method that can be followed to demonstrate that a mathematical statement is true or not?

Hilbert, of course, believed that the answer to all three questions was yes. For his program to work, certain matters needed to be clarified. In particular, certain key concepts had to understood. These included, in particular, the concepts of absolute proof, formal system, and meta-mathematics.

Intimidating words, especially the last.

By *absolute proof* is meant that the consistency of a mathematical system must be established without assuming the consistency of some other system.[5] In other words, a mathematical system must be self-contained, a solipsistic world of its own.

A system that allows for absolute proofs, not admitting anything outside of itself, is what mathematicians and logicians call a *formal system*, and no term, expression, or proposition in the system has any meaning. And because terms or expressions in a formal system have no meaning, they are not even symbols, for a symbol represents something else, it is *about* something else, whereas the terms or propositions in a formal system are just squiggles. For example, the entities 2, +, 4, and = carry no meaning in a formal system of arithmetic; they are squiggles. Likewise, the expression 2 + 2 = 4 is a string of squiggles that is also meaningless, but is derived by putting together the "primitive" squiggles according to certain rules (often called a *calculus*).

Which leads us to meta-mathematics. It is one thing to write

$$2 + 2 = 4$$

This is a meaningless squiggle composed out of primitive squiggles. It is another thing to write

"2 + 2 = 4" is a valid proposition in arithmetic.

The former is an expression *within* arithmetic, whereas the latter is a statement *about* that expression and, thus, a statement *about* arithmetic. The one is a mathematical proposition; the other, a meta-mathematical statement.

This distinction was important for Hilbert's program and, as we will see, it plays a significant role in the development of the science of computing. In Hilbert's context, it means that statements such as

"mathematics" is consistent
"mathematics" is complete
mathematical propositions are decidable

are meta-mathematical. They are meaningful assertions about mathematics.

To return to Hilbert's three questions. The answers were provided in 1931 by an Austrian mathematician Kurt Gödel (1906–1978), then at the University of Vienna, who later emigrated to America and became a member of the extraordinary constellation of scientific thinkers that included Albert Einstein (1879–1955) at the Institute of Advanced Study, Princeton, New Jersey,[6] (This institution plays a role of its own in *our* story, as we will see.)

Gödel's response to Hilbert, published in a German journal, bears the title, when translated into English, "On Formally Undecidable Propositions of Principia Mathematica and Related Systems," and it would have devastating implications for how mathematicians would see the nature of their craft. Gödel showed that axiomatic systems have certain inherent limitations, that the complete axiomatization of even the arithmetic of whole numbers is not possible. He demonstrated that it is impossible to establish the internal consistency of a large range of mathematical systems, including arithmetic—that is, there was no guarantee that a system of mathematics was free from internal contradictions. He showed that there are true propositions in arithmetic (the truth of which could be established by appealing to concepts *outside* arithmetic) that could not be proved *within* the axiom system of arithmetic itself. He established what came to be called the *undecidability problem* in mathematics: that there are certain propositions in a mathematical system that can be neither proved nor disproved.[7]

All of this meant that a mathematical system (such as arithmetic) is both incomplete and inconsistent. These results came to be called *Gödel's Incompleteness Theorem*. In proclaiming the limits of mathematical reasoning, it has the same status as Heisenberg's celebrated Uncertainty Principle in physics.

II

We seem to be far removed from the story of computing. The world shared by Hilbert, Russell and Whitehead, and Gödel belongs to the furthest reaches of abstraction, a veritable platonic universe seemingly having nothing to do with computing machines, even those that address the solution of algebraic problems. But let us consider another of Hilbert's famous *fin de siècle* problems: his 10th problem concerning a family of equations of the form

$$P(x_1, x_2, \ldots, x_n) = 0$$

where P is a polynomial with integer coefficients, known as "Diophantine equations."

Hilbert asked whether one could devise a procedure by which it can be decided in a finite number of steps whether a given Diophantine equation is solvable in rational integers (that is, zero, and positive and negative integers, ± 1, ± 2, and so forth). This is called a *decision problem* or, to use its impressive German term, *Entscheidungsproblem*. As for a "procedure" that can be performed in a "finite number of steps," what Hilbert was asking was whether there is (using present-centered language) an *algorithm* to decide whether a given Diophantine equation has a solution.

Now, the *Entscheidungsproblem* bears a connection with Gödel, for, although Gödel had shown that certain mathematical propositions are undecidable, the *Entscheidungsproblem* asks whether there is an algorithm that can decide whether any proposition is or is not decidable.

This is where Alan Turing enters this story.

III

As Lord Byron's estranged daughter and Babbage's interpreter, as a woman uncommonly gifted in mathematics, and as one who more than anyone else (save for Babbage) can claim to have understood something of what it is to program a computer a century before her time, it is not surprising that Augustus Ada, Countess of Lovelace, has drawn a measure of popular attention. However, among all the characters who people the history of computer science, no one has excited more attention of the nonmathematical, nonscientific world than Alan Mathison Turing (1912–1954).

Apart from biographies, two plays about him were written, produced, and performed in London and New York (one even garnering three Tony Award nominations). A television film about his life was shown by the BBC. A novel has been written with Turing as its main character. A musical has been made. In Manchester, England, where he lived and taught in the university's mathematics department in the final years of a short life, and where he died, a bridge and a road were named after him. Statues of the man have been installed in several places in England. Computer laboratories and auditoria and entire buildings have been named after him in universities in Europe, South America, and the United Kingdom. The world's premier prize in computer science is called the Turing Award. And, in 2012, the centenary of his birth, commemorative events, both scientific and cultural, were held in many parts of the world. One wonders what he would have made of this posthumous adulation.

No doubt, a significant part of the popular fascination with Turing stems from the tragic aspect of his later life. A homosexual in England in a time when homosexuality was illegal, under the same law as in Oscar Wilde's time a half-century before, Turing was prosecuted for "gross indecency" in England.[8] His death in June 1954 by cyanide poisoning was officially attributed to suicide. His personal eccentricities, as recollected by people who knew him, added to the legend surrounding him. But, all of this would not have meant a thing if he had been an "ordinary" man. This, he most certainly was not. His place in the history of computer science lies in his remarkable contributions to at least three different aspects of this story. Here, we consider the first and, arguably, his most profound contribution.

At the time Gödel published his massively consequential results, Turing was an undergraduate in King's College, Cambridge, reading for a mathematics degree or "tripos" (in Cambridge jargon).[9] As an undergraduate, Turing read Bertrand Russell's *Introduction to Mathematical Philosophy* (1919) and was introduced to the problems of the foundations of mathematics.[10] He read a paper on mathematical philosophy to the Moral Science Club ("moral science" being the term Cambridge used to denote philosophy). At King's College, he came to know, among the college fellows, philosopher of science Richard Braithwaite (1900–1990), and attended a course of lectures on the methodology of science by astrophysicist Arthur Stanley Eddington (1882–1944).[11] Working on his own and responding to Eddington's lectures, some of which touched on probability and statistics,

Turing "discovered" a key result in probability theory called the Central Limit Theorem, only to learn that this theorem had actually been published in 1922.[12]

He graduated in 1934 and his results in the tripos were good enough for King's College to offer him a research studentship. He began writing a dissertation that, if accepted, would give him a fellowship in King's. Dissertation completed and submitted to the college for their consideration, Turing attended a course of lectures offered by Max Newman (1897–1984), a fellow of St. John's College in Cambridge and distinguished for his contribution to topology, a major branch of mathematics that deals with the properties of spatial objects like curves and surfaces that remain unchanged under such transformations as deformation, twisting, and stretching. Newman will have a later influence on Turing, but in 1935, this particular encounter proved to be fateful. Newman lectured on the foundations of mathematics and the problems Hilbert had laid out in 1928. And he discussed Gödel's incompleteness theorem.

Still, Gödel had not dealt with the third of Hilbert's problems: *Entscheidungsproblem.* Is there a procedure for determining whether a mathematical proposition was provable or unprovable?

That same year, at age 22, on the strength of his dissertation and backed by such senior and illustrious King's College fellows as economists John Maynard Keynes (1883–1946) and Arthur Pigou (1877–1959), Turing was elected a fellow of King's College.

IV

Entscheidungsproblem: a mechanical process to "do" mathematics. What does it mean to call a process mechanical? Does it entail a machine? A mathematical machine?

Babbage's Analytical Engine was a mathematical machine. Was this the kind of thing Hilbert had in mind when he formulated his *Entscheidungsproblem*? Did he at all know of Babbage's engine? When Turing became interested in Hilbert's third question, did *he* know about Babbage? According to his biographer, he did indeed know of Babbage's work, but probably not until the 1940s.[13] At any rate, so his biographer tells us, sometime during the early summer of 1935, in the village of Grantchester, just outside Cambridge—a place immortalized by the poet Rupert Brooke (1887–1915), once a fellow himself of King's College, in his poem "The Old Vicarage, Grantchester" (1912)—lying in the meadow watching the Cambridge sky, as in Brooke's poem, Turing began to think of a machine to deal with the *Entscheidungsproblem.*[14]

However, the mathematical machine about which Turing began thinking that summer in 1935 was a far cry from the world of gears, levers, and Jacquard cards. Babbage's engine was a mathematical machine in that it solved mathematical problems of a certain kind. Turing's idea of a mathematical machine was, to begin with, far larger in scope regarding what such a machine could do. But also, *it was itself a mathematical object.* Turing's vision of a machine belonged not to the world of physical artifacts that obeyed the laws of physics, it belonged to the world of squiggles or, as we will see, squiggles that represented things—hence, it was a world of symbols and symbol processing. It could process symbols but was itself also a symbolic object; it belonged to the abstract world. Turing envisioned a purely abstract artifact.

In May 1936, he submitted a long paper bearing the forbidding title "On Computable Numbers with an Application to the *Entscheidungsproblem*" to the London Mathematical Society. The paper was accepted and published in the society's *Proceedings* later that year.[15] Notice the title of the paper. It is as if "computable numbers" was the main issue "with an application to" the *Entscheidungsproblem* as a secondary concern.

As Nobel laureate biologist and scientific essayist Sir Peter Medawar (1915–1987) memorably wrote, a scientific paper never tells the story of how science *actually* takes shape in a person's mind. A scientific paper rarely represents the actual creative thought process that produced the results described in the paper. All the messiness that enters into thinking, all the false trails, blind alleys, muddle-headedness, short-sightedness, and limited rationality that scientists (or any problem solver) experience during actual thinking are cleaned up or shoved under the carpet. What is communicated is a sanitized "portrait of the scientist as a rational being." It is for this reason that Medawar claimed that the scientific paper is "a fraud."[16]

So, also, we should not take the title of Turing's paper and the organization of its contents as a reflection of his actual thought process. Rather, we should accept it as an image of how he probably rationalized his thinking after the fact, an image of how he wanted to present his thoughts to readers.

He began with the concept of *computable numbers*. What are these? They are "real numbers whose expressions as a decimal are calculable by finite means."[17] More simply, "a number is computable if its decimal can be written down by a machine."[18] A real number is a quantity that has a decimal expansion, such as 0.25 and 3.14159. Notice, in Turing's definition, the clause "by finite means." The calculation of a computable number must eventually come to a stop; it cannot go on forever. In the case of a number such as $\pi = 3.141592653\ldots$, although it is an infinite decimal, it is a computable number in that one can compute the first n decimal digits in a finite number of steps. At the heart of the matter, for Turing, was to determine how a machine could perform the task that we—intuitively and naturally—call *computing*.

In 1936, the year his paper "On Computable Numbers" was published, the word *computer* still meant a human being who computes. And Turing began by sketching out how a (human) "computer" goes about the task of computing.

It entails reading and writing symbols on paper. But, rather than a two-dimensional paper, imagine a long tape, a "one-dimensional" affair divided into squares (much as a child's arithmetic book in Turing's time was divided into squares). Each square can hold a single symbol.

The computer, being human, has certain obvious perceptual and cognitive traits that affect her behavior. How she behaves at any particular time is dependent on the symbols she is observing and her "state of mind." Let us suppose that there is a limit to the number of symbols the computer can observe at any moment—there is a bound, in other words, to her perceptual range. If she wants to observe more symbols, she must take successive observations. We also suppose that, although the number of "states of mind" can be large, there is a finite limit to that number.

We also imagine (Turing wrote) that the computer can only perform very simple or "atomic" operations, and that a computational task is decomposable into a sequence of these atomic operations.

So what are these atomic operations? They must include operations that (a) change a symbol on an observed square on the tape; (b) move the computer's "eye" from an observed square to another, within a certain window of squares bounding the observed square; and (c) change the computer's state of mind. The change of state of mind can accompany either change of symbol on the observed square or change of the observed square.

Turing then drew an analogy between his human computer and a machine that does the work of the person. To each state of the human's mind there is a machine state (so the number of machine states is finite). The machine can scan the tape and "read" its squares. In any one move, the machine can change a symbol on the square being read, or move from one square to another on its left or right, and undergo a change of state.[19]

Turing then claimed that the atomic operations—scanning a symbol in a square, moving to the right or left of the scanned square, writing a symbol or erasing it, changing the state—are all those that are involved in performing a computation.[20] He also stipulated that, at any point in time, the motion of this machine is determined *completely* by the machine state along with the symbol then being scanned.

This is what Turing named a *computing machine.* Suppose, now, that such a machine is given a tape with some "input" set of symbols (or no symbols at all, a blank tape) and, placed in an "initial" configuration, is set into motion. Then, any sequence of symbols printed by the machine onto the tape is said to be *computed by the machine.*

It might be convenient to translate Turing's description into present-centered language:

A computing machine consists of a *tape* that is unbounded in length. Each *square* of the tape can hold one of a vocabulary of *symbols*, Si, Sj, …. At any point in time, a *read/write head* is positioned on one square of the tape; call it the *current square*. The corresponding symbol is the *current input symbol*. The machine can be in one of a finite number of *states*, Qk, Ql, …. The state of the machine at any given time is its *present state*. Depending on the current input symbol and the present state, the read/write head can *print* a symbol on the current square (possibly overwriting the prior symbol) or *erase* the current symbol, move one square to the right or to the left, and place the machine into the *next state*. This next state then becomes the present state of the machine.

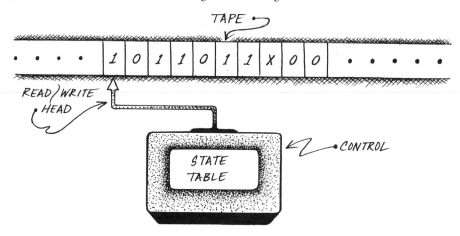

FIGURE 4.1 A "Parity-Detecting" Turing Machine in the Initial State.

Turing called his machine, simply, a computing machine. In present-centered language, it is called, in his honor, a *Turing machine*.

Consider, as an example, a very simple Turing machine (Figure 4.1). Its task is to "read" an input string of 0s and 1s written on the tape, and print a 1 on the tape if the number of 1s in the string is odd—0, otherwise—and come to a *halt* (in mathematical jargon, this machine is a parity detector). A special symbol X on the tape indicates the end of the input string. The machine replaces the input string with 0s and replaces the X with a 1 or 0, depending on the parity.

This machine needs three states. Qo corresponds to an odd number of 1s detected in the input string at any point of the machine's operation. Qe corresponds to an even number of 1s detected up to any point of the machine's operation. The third state is H, the halting state. The machine begins its operation with the read/write head positioned on the square holding the first binary digit of the input string.

Consider, for instance, that the tape has the following input string. The initial position of the read/write head is indicated by the digit in bold type.

...00...10**1**1011X00...0...

The behavior of this Turing machine is defined by what, in present-centered language, is called a *state table*, which looks like Table 4.1.

The first row of this table can be read as follows: Given current state Qe and input symbol 0, the next state will be Qe, an output symbol 0 is written onto that square, and the read/write head moves one square to the right. The last row tells us that given the current state Qo and input symbol X, the next state will be the halt state H, output 1 will be written on the tape, and there will be no further motion of the read/write head. The other rows of the state table can be interpreted similarly.

Tracing the machine's operation on the example input string, we see that it goes through the following sequence of states and tape configurations. Again, the position of

TABLE 4.1 State Table for the "Parity-Detecting" Machine

Current state	Input symbol	Next state	Output symbol	Read/write head motion
Qe	o	Qe	o	R
Qe	I	Qo	o	R
Qe	X	H	o	—
Qo	o	Qo	o	R
Qo	I	Qe	o	R
Qo	X	H	I	—

the read/write head at the start of each step in the sequence of operations is indicated by the digit in bold type.

$Qe:$ **1**011011X
$Qo:$ 0**0**11011X
$Qo:$ 00**1**1011X
$Qe:$ 000**1**011X
$Qo:$ 0000**0**11X
$Qo:$ 00000**1**1X
$Qe:$ 000000**1**X
$Qo:$ 0000000**X**
$H:$ 00000001

Figure 4.2 shows the state of the tape and the position of the read/write head after the leftmost symbol on the tape has been read. The 1 is overwritten by a 0, and the read/write head moves one square to the right.

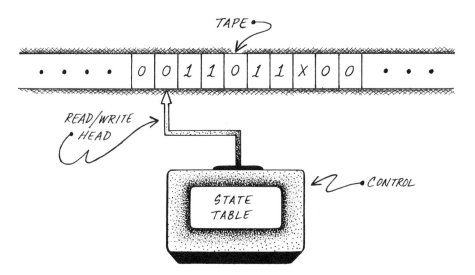

FIGURE 4.2 The "Parity-Detecting" Turing Machine after First Move.

There is, then, a distinct Turing machine for each distinct computational task. Each Turing machine so constructed is a special-purpose machine. Each such special-purpose machine specifies the initial contents of the tape, the desired content of the tape, the initial position of the read/write head, and a state table that defines the possible behavior of the machine. A Turing machine can be constructed to add two integers *n, m* represented by *n* 1s followed by a blank followed by *m* 1s, leaving the result of *n + m* 1s on the tape. Another machine can be constructed to perform the multiplication of two numbers *n, m* leaving the result on the tape. Yet another machine could be built that, say, given an input string of *a*'s *b*'s, *c*'s would produce its mirror image (a palindrome). For example, from input string *aaabbaacc* the output would be *ccaabbaaa*, and so on.

The parity detection machine described here is not a device for performing arithmetic. It is, rather, a pattern recognition machine. Indeed, the parity detector is a *decision* machine, for it can decide whether the number of 1s in an input string has odd or even parity. Turing's computing machine, then, is not just a calculating engine *à la* Babbage or Ludgate. It is a *symbol processing* machine. More precisely, it is a "squiggle" processing machine in that, for an input string of squiggles on the tape, it will generate an output string of squiggles. That the squiggles represent something else—that they are actually symbols—is determined by the designer of the machine. Sometimes, the strings of squiggles do not represent anything, as in the palindrome producer.

In more mathematical terms, a Turing machine's output will be a *function* of its input. It's value is, say, $F(X)$, *where X* is the input or "argument" to the function F. The state table determines how F is to be computed. Indeed, we might say that a Turing machine's state table *is* that function.[21] If a Turing machine can be constructed to compute $F(X)$, then that function is said to be *Turing computable*.[22]

V

A particular Turing machine is (to use another present-centered term) *programmed* to do what it does. The state table describes this program. As already noted, each Turing machine is a special-purpose computing device in the sense that the Difference Engine was a special-purpose device; it computes a *particular* function $F(X)$. It does not have the universality dreamed of by Babbage when he was designing the Analytical Engine, but Turing quickly rectified the situation. As he tells us, one can invent a single machine **U** that can compute *any* computable function. If **U** is provided with a tape that begins with a symbolic description of some *other* computing machine **M**, then **U** will perform the same computation as **M**.[23] He called this machine **U** a "universal computing machine." Later, it came to be known as a *universal Turing machine*.[24] From a present-centered point of view, it can be described in the following way.

A universal Turing machine **U** can compute any Turing-computable *function* $F(X)$ by specifying the description of the Turing machine **M** that computes $F(X)$ on the same tape of **U** as the input argument *X*. When **U** halts, the *value* **F**(*X*) will be printed on the tape.

In a universal Turing machine, the tape will contain not only the argument of the function to be computed, but also the program (state table) that would compute that function on a "regular" Turing machine. The state table of the universal Turing machine will "read" the program from the tape and *interpret* this program. The universal Turing machine will *simulate* each Turing machine that is described on its tape. It is programmed to be programmable, so to speak—in the fashion of the Analytical Engine—although it is far more universal than the Analytical Engine, for it is capable of simulating *any* other Turing machine.

VI

Turing's 1936 paper had the clause "with an application to the *Entscheidungsproblem*" in its title. Recall Hilbert's third question: is there a definite method that can decide the provability (or otherwise) of a mathematical problem? This was what had excited Turing in the first place, what had started him on this particular intellectual journey leading to his universal Turing machine. And, in his paper, addressing this question, he would reply that Hilbert's *Entscheidungsproblem*, in fact, had no solution. There can be no computing machine that, provided with a mathematical expression, can determine whether the expression is provable.

His argument was complex and ingenious and dense, and because it drew on the construction and operation of a Turing machine, completely original in style. Heretofore, mathematical (or meta-mathematical) proofs had never relied on the operation of a machine that scanned symbols on a tape. And, of course, it sounded the death knell of Hilbert's third problem, just as Gödel had sounded the death knell of Hilbert's first two problems. Turing's argument also demonstrated the limits of his computing machine. There were problems that were not Turing computable; they were *unsolvable* so far as Turing computability was concerned.

VII

So what had Turing wrought in his paper of 1936? He had created, as we have seen, a symbol processing machine in the sense that its behavior is determined by precise rules. A description of a set of rules of behavior is also called, in the mathematical world, an *effective procedure*, and in the computational world, an *algorithm*. There is a sense in which we speak intuitively or naturally of effective procedures performed by human beings. For example, we talk of a procedure for multiplying two multidigit numbers. That procedure is "effective" because its rules guarantee us a correct solution. What Turing did was to declare that any process that "naturally" or "intuitively" seems to be an effective procedure can be realized by a Turing machine.[25]

This claim would come to be known as *Turing's thesis*. Using a very different formalism, American mathematician and logician Alonzo Church (1903–1995) arrived, that same year although earlier, at a similar conclusion, deploying a notion he called "effective calculability" and using a very different formalism called "recursive function theory".[26] Turing acknowledged this in his paper and demonstrated that Church's concept of effective calculability and his notion of computability were equivalent. Thus, Turing's thesis is also called *Church's thesis* in the context of Church's result, and it was Church who, in a review of Turing's paper, called the latter's result *Turing's thesis*. In 1936, Turing would go to Princeton, where Church was on the mathematics faculty, and write a doctoral dissertation. His dissertation committee included Church.[27]

The use of the word "thesis" is noteworthy. Turing's claim was not a theorem. It could not be proved, because the notion of effective procedure or algorithm is intuitive, informal. In fact, the Turing machine is a formalization of this intuitive notion.

The Turing machine is an abstract artifact. No one would think seriously of building a physical model of the Turing machine. Its significance in the history of computing lay in the future: It was *consequential* in a number of ways.

First, per Turing's thesis, the fact that anything "naturally" deemed computable can be realized by a Turing machine meant that for every physical entity that one might call a computer (artificial or human) there exists a Turing machine equivalent. The Turing machine is the great unifier: Babbage's Difference Engine, his Analytical Engine, Ludgate's analytical machine, and all other computing engines that could be conceived and built or are yet to be built have their functional commonality in the Turing machine. Despite its breathtakingly simple architecture, the Turing machine is (to use a mathematical term) a canonical form for digital computers.

Second, Turing's invention of his machine initiated its own intellectual adventure; the mathematical foundations of computing began with Turing's work (along with the work of a handful of other contemporaries such as Church). The term *automaton* (which, as we have seen, has a long pedigree; see Chapter 3, Section X) was appropriated to establish a discipline and a field of study called *automata theory*—the systematic study of the structure, behavior, capabilities, and limitations of abstract computing machines—the Turing machine and its variants certainly, but other abstract kinds also (some of which we will encounter later). What Turing launched with his 1936 paper was the founding of *theoretical computer science*, even though it was a time when a "computer" was still a human being! It is because of this that the year 1936 may well be called an *annus mirabilis*, a miracle year in the annals of computing.

VIII

The spirit of Alan Turing, like that of Charles Babbage but much more, permeates the history of computer science, as we will see—"now you see him; now you don't," rather like the Orson Welles character Harry Lime in Carol Reed's classic film *The Third Man* (1949). And, like Harry Lime, even when not actually visible, Turing's presence is forever palpable, although not menacingly or threateningly, but challengingly.

The conventional wisdom is that Turing's 1936 paper had no influence on the practical development of the digital computer that would take place in the decade or so thereafter. This conventional wisdom seems plausible. After all, both Turing and Church were "pure" mathematicians and logicians. Their respective papers were published in mathematical journals. And even among mathematicians, Turing's approach—creating a machine (albeit an abstract one) that generates a process involving space (the squares on the tape), time (the succession of steps required to perform a computation), and motion (of the read/write head)—must have seemed quite alien. Indeed, according to Turing's biographer, there was no one in England who could referee the paper prior to its acceptability for publication.[28] He had created a new kind of mathematics that would eventually migrate out of mathematics into the new science of computing under the banner of automata theory.

The main protagonists in the next chapters of our story were not at all concerned with such issues as computability, unsolvability, decidability, and so on. They were not interested in what could *not* be computed, but rather with what *could* be computed and *how*—in the "real" world. Some of these people had a formal mathematical background, but in "mainstream" mathematics, not where mathematics met logic. Others were trained in physics or engineering. They would have been blissfully unaware of Turing's 1936 paper.

There were, however, two factors that might challenge the conventional wisdom. One was the interaction among scientists, not just within the close-knit community in Cambridge, London, or Oxford in England, or the "other" Cambridge in America, but across the Atlantic. The other was World War II, which made teams out of individuals in a way the scientific world had never experienced before.

The making of "laboratory societies" was not unknown. In Cambridge, not far from King's College, was the Cavendish Laboratory (founded in 1874), arguably the world's most distinguished center for experimental physics between the two World Wars, when first Sir Joseph Thomson (1856–1940) and then Sir (later Lord) Ernest Rutherford (1871–1937) presided over a glittering galaxy of physicists, British and otherwise.[29] But science—even experimental physics—was still done on a relatively small scale. World War II changed all that, as much in Britain as in the United States and in Germany. The "purest" of scientists became "applied scientists"; engineers, mathematicians, physicists, and chemists hobnobbed with one another in pursuit of common goals in a manner never witnessed before. They were forced to mingle with bureaucrats, civil servants, politicians, and the military. The era of *Big Science* had begun.

Turing, with all his eccentricities (sometimes recorded by those who knew him) would also become a participant in Big Science as it emerged in England, especially in Bletchley Park, where scientists and engineers were in the business of building code-breaking machines. Here, he would encounter Max Newman, whose lectures in Cambridge on

Hilbert's program had started him on the path to the Turing machine. Indeed, Newman had been instrumental in ensuring that Turing's paper could be published—despite Church's priority by a few months—arguing that the two approaches were very different and that Turing's was a more direct approach to solving the *Entscheidungsproblem.* He also helped Turing to go to Princeton to work with Church.[30] So at least one person who was heavily involved in the development of real computers during World War II was intimately familiar with Turing's machine.

In Princeton, beside the university where Church taught, there was the fabled Institute of Advanced Study, the "one true Platonic heaven,"[31] whose denizens included Albert Einstein (1879–1955) and the prodigious John von Neumann (1903–1957), whose place in this history is among the most profound (as will be seen). Einstein may well have been a distant, ephemeral figure for Turing, but not von Neumann. They had met in 1935 when von Neumann spent a term as a visiting professor in Cambridge[32]; their acquaintance was renewed in Princeton, and von Neumann even wrote a letter of support on Turing's behalf to obtain a fellowship that would allow him to extend his stay in Princeton for a second year (which he did),[33] this enabling him to complete a doctoral dissertation under Church. Strangely enough, von Neumann's letter had no mention of Turing's work on computable numbers. It would seem plausible that, at some point during their encounter in Princeton, von Neumann would come to know of this work, but there is no evidence of this.[34]

At any rate, let us put aside Turing for the moment. Let us venture into an astonishing chapter in the history of computing that began during the late 1930s but received its most intense stimulus during, and because of, World War II. Its outcome was the emergence, during the course of the 1940s, of the fully operational, general-purpose, programmable, electronic computer.

NOTES

1. More precisely, in the spoken version of the lecture, for want of time, he presented only 10 of these problems. C. B. Boyer. (1991). *A history of mathematics* (2nd ed., Rev., p. 610). New York: Wiley.

2. Thus, Sir Isaac Netwon's *Philosophae Naturalis Principia Mathematica* (1687) [Mathematical Principles of Natural Philosophy]—called, simply, *Principia*—although a work about physical nature, was couched in a mathematical–axiomatic framework.

3. Boyer, op cit., p. 609.

4. R. Zach. (2003). Hilbert's program. *Stanford encyclopedia of philosophy* [On-line]. Available: http://www.plato.stanford.edu/entries/hilbert-program/

5. E. Nagel & J. R. Newman. (1959). *Gödel's proof* (p. 26). London: Routledge & Kegan Paul.

6. For a delightful "postmodern" fictional portrait of some of these actual thinkers at this institute circa 1940s and 1950s, see J. L. Casti. (2003). *The one true platonic heaven.* Washington, DC: Joseph Henry Press.

7. For a beautiful and highly understandable (from a nonmathematician's point of view) of Gödel's work, see Nagel & Newman, op cit.

8. In September 2009, the then-British Prime Minster Gordon Brown issued a formal apology to Turing on behalf of the government.

9. A. Hodges. (1983). *Alan Turing: The enigma* (p. 59 *ff*). New York: Simon and Schuster.

10. Ibid., p. 85.

11. Ibid., p. 87.

12. Ibid., p. 88.

13. Ibid., p. 297.

14. Ibid.

15. A. M. Turing. (1936). On computable numbers with an application to the *Entscheidungsproblem*. *Proceedings of the London Mathematical Society*, *2*, 230–236. This paper has since been reprinted in M. Davis. (Ed.). (1965). *The undecidable*. New York: Raven Press. It is also available on the Internet at http://www.abelard.org/turpap2.htm. The pagination I refer to later in this chapter is based on this retrieved paper.

16. P. B. Medawar. (1990). Is the scientific paper a fraud? In P. B. Medawar, 1990. *The threat and the glory: Reflections on science and scientists* (pp. 228–233). Oxford, UK: Oxford University Press.

17. Turing, op cit., p. 2.

18. Ibid.

19. Ibid., pp. 16–18.

20. Ibid., p. 3.

21. M. Minsky. (1967). *Computation: Finite and infinite machines* (p. 132). Englewood-Cliffs, NJ: Prentice-Hall.

22. Ibid., p. 135.

23. Turing, op cit., p. 11.

24. Minsky, op cit., p. 132 *ff*.

25. Ibid., p. 108.

26. A. Church. (1936). An unsolvable problem of elementary number theory. *American Journal of Mathematics*, *58*, 345–363.

27. Hodges, op cit., p. 145.

28. Ibid., p. 113.

29. J. G. Crowther. (1974). *The Cavendish Laboratory, 1874–1974*. New York: Science History Publications.

30. Hodges, op cit., p. 112–113.

31. Casti, op cit.

32. Hodges, op cit., p. 131.

33. Ibid.

34. Ibid.

5

Toward a Holy Grail

∽ ───

I

SOMETIME BETWEEN 1936 and 1946, there was a change in etymology, at least in the English language. The word *computer* came to mean the machine not the man. Old habits, of course, die hard. And so, such terms as *automatic calculating machines* and *comput ing machines* remained in common use, along with the cautious adoption of computer, until the end of the 1940s.

But at the beginning of that war-ravaged, bomb-splattered decade, George Stibitz (1904–1995), a mathematical physicist working for Bell Telephone Laboratories in New Jersey, wrote a memorandum on a machine he and his colleague Samuel B. Williams had built in which *computer* unequivocally meant a machine. Indeed, they named their creation the Complex Computer because it was designed to perform arithmetic operations on complex numbers—computations necessary in the design of telephone networks, which was Bell's forte.[1]

There was, of course, much more happening in the realm of computing than a change in the meaning of a word. Computers were actually being built, increasingly more complex, more ambitious in scope, more powerful, faster, and physically larger than the punched-card machines that largely dominated automatic calculation. They were being built in at least three countries: America, Germany, and England.[2]

These machines, developed in different centers of research, formed evolutionary families, in the sense that machine X built at a particular center gave rise to machine $X + 1$ as its successor. The word "evolution" carries with it much baggage. Here, I am speaking not of biological evolution by natural selection *à la* Darwin, but *cultural* evolution. The latter differs from the former in a fundamental way: biological evolution is not driven by goal or purpose; cultural evolution is *always* goal driven. In the realm of computers—artifacts, therefore part of culture—for example, a goal is established by the designers/engineers or potential client, and a machine is built that (one hopes) satisfies the goal. If it does satisfy the goal, then well and good (at least for a time); otherwise, a new effort will be initiated that strives to correct the flaws and errors of the earlier machine. Thus, a new artifact emerges "out of the ashes" of the old.

Over time, there may emerge new goals, new priorities that the existing machine does not meet. These new goals initiate a new design problem, a new project that usually draws on earlier experience, earlier knowledge, earlier designs. What cultural evolution shares with biological evolution is, first, that they both are (usually) gradual. Second, they both constantly entail "testing" the organism or artifact against the environment, discarding those that do not meet the environmental conditions and ensuring the "survival" of those that do. The fundamental difference between the two lies in the *mechanism* by which organisms and artifacts respond to the environment. In the case of organisms, it is natural selection, which is purposeless; in the case of artifacts, it is purposeful adaptation to new environments. In fact, the difference lies in the dichotomy of chance and purpose.[3]

Let us see what some of these first evolutionary families of computers were.

II

Stibitz's memorandum of 1940 began with the somewhat obvious observation that an essential mission of Bell Telephone Laboratories was the design of electrical (telephone) networks.[4] The implications of this statement for this story were, however, anything but mundane. The design of telephone networks entailed computations involving complex numbers—numbers of the form $a + ib$ or $a - ib$, where a, b are real numbers (in the mathematical sense) and $i = \sqrt{-1}$ is an imaginary number (in the mathematical sense). The scientists at Bell Laboratories had long felt the need for machines that could take over the burdensome performance of these complex calculations.[5]

The machine named Complex Computer, designed by Stibitz and Williams between 1938 and 1940, was a response to this need. Its primary purpose was to perform arithmetic on complex numbers, but it was also useful in another task common in network design, finding roots of polynomials—that is, finding values of x that would satisfy a polynomial equation such as, for example, $2x^3 - 5x^2 + 3x - 1 = 0$.

Thus, the Complex Computer was a relatively special-purpose electromechanical device that used electrical *relays* (basic switching circuit elements used in telephone networks and, so, a familiar technology in the Bell Laboratories culture). This machine became the first and the progenitor of the Bell Laboratories series of "relay computers" referred to as Model I through Model VI, but some also given specific names. Thus, Model I was also called the Complex Computer.

After America entered World War II, military needs, of course, had priority over all else. Weapon systems had to be designed, built, and tested for accuracy and reliability before they could be deployed in battle. Civilian scientists, mathematicians, and engineers were assigned to military establishments or projects under military command. Stibitz was seconded to the National Defense Research Council. One of the projects in which he became involved was the development of precise test equipment for checking the accuracy of a certain kind of "gun director" called the *M-9*.[6] Stibitz suggested that an all-digital computer made from relays as the basic circuit element might do the job.[7] Thus came about the second of the Bell Laboratories machines—the Model II, or Relay Interpolator—so named because its principal computational task was the mathematical process called interpolation, although it was also used for other kinds of tasks, such as calculating roots of polynomials and solving differential equations.[8] Like the Complex Computer/Model I, the Relay Interpolator/Model II was controlled by "orders" punched on paper tape and communicated through teletype readers.

In 1942, Stibitz conceived the concept of floating-point arithmetic, which is vital for scientific computation because it allows numbers ranging from the very small to the very large to be represented in a common fashion.[9] As we will see later, he was not the first to conceive this idea; however, it seems likely that he invented it in ignorance of other prior work done elsewhere in Germany.

The war dominated all. Ideally, the proof positive of the accuracy and reliability of antiaircraft guns could only be established in the battlefield. To test the gun director's accuracy or correctness before deployment, the field conditions would have to be simulated. A plane would be flown, as if on a bombing run. The shells, of course, would not be fired at it; instead, the indicators on the gun director would record data on the plane's movement on a moment-by-moment basis, along with data recording the succession of "gun orders," and one would have to calculate the relative positions of plane and shell at the moment the shell would burst. Such calculations would take "a team of five computers" a week to perform.[10] Old habits die hard! Here, *computer* referred to a person.

And so began a project to build a relay computing machine to carry out these calculations automatically. The outcome was named the Ballistic Computer. This machine—Bell's Model III relay machine—was still a relatively special-purpose, electromechanical, perforated paper tape-controlled machine. The Model II had an adder circuit that would do multiplication by repeated addition, and subtraction by complementing the number to be subtracted (the "subtrahend") and adding this complement to the number to be subtracted from (the "minuend").[11] The Model III had specialized circuits for multiplication and division.[12] The Model II had five registers to store numbers during a computation.[13] In the Model III, there were four registers dedicated to the arithmetic circuits themselves, but in addition there were a set of 10 "storage registers" used to hold both intermediate results of the arithmetic calculations and the final results.[14] Perhaps the most compelling difference between the two models was that although the Model II contained about 500 relays,[15] the Model III was composed of more than 1300 relays.[16]

The most significant computer in the Bell Laboratories lineage was the Model V. (The Model IV was only slightly different from the Model III, whereas the Model VI was a simplified version of the Model V.[17]) In the Model V, the Bell Laboratories family reached its fullest efflorescence; it was seen as a genuine general-purpose programmable computer.[18] The project, begun in 1944, was a quantum jump over its predecessors in physical size and complexity. It contained 9000 relays, 50 different pieces of "teletype apparatus," weighed about 10 tons, and occupied a floor space of some 1000 square feet. It also exhibited a marked improvement in its flexibility, generality of purpose, reliability, and capacity to operate autonomously without human intervention. Two "copies" of the Model V were built—one completed in 1946 that went to a federal agency in Langley, Virginia, that was the forerunner to the National Aeronautics and Space Administration, and the other, completed in 1947, was sent to the U.S. Army's Ballistic Research Laboratory (BRL) in Aberdeen, Maryland.[19]

Here, then, comparing the Model V with its Bell predecessors, is an exemplar of evolution in technological complexity[20]—a complexity manifested even in its complete documentation, estimated at the time of its development to fill "hundreds of pages."[21] We get a sense of the "general-purposeness" of the Model V from the range of problems it was capable of solving, which included systems of linear equations, ordinary differential equations, interpolation, evaluation of functions of different kinds, and partial differential equations.[22]

A remarkable aspect of the Model V was that each copy of the machine was comprised of two "computers."[23] Each computer was self-sufficient in that it had all the components necessary for solving a problem except for the "tape-reading devices"—the input system, in present-centered language.[24] Each computer had a set of 15 storage registers, several special registers, and an arithmetic unit that performed all four arithmetics as well as square root extraction; control units that accepted "orders" from tape and directed the execution of these orders; registers that received and stored tables of numbers from an input tape; printer control; and teletype printers (the output unit).

However, the two computers in each computing system shared "permanent tables" that held values of trigonometric and logarithmic functions.[25] They also shared the "input organs"—several paper tape transmitters through which orders and data were communicated to the individual computers. A problem could be assigned to a single computer or, for large problems, distributed to the two computers.[26] In present-centered language, the Model V provided an early form of *multiprocessing*—that is, the ability to execute a single computational job by distributing its component tasks to more than one machine, which could then operate simultaneously.

Another significant feature of the Model V was the "problem tape," one of the input tapes to the system. One of its functions was to identify the start and end of a problem or a subproblem; another function was to provide a check that the routines and data tapes required for a given problem were the correct ones. A third function was to control the printing of headings on the output "answer sheets." When the machine began operation, the problem tape was the first to be activated. Indeed, it was responsible for "supreme control" of the progress of a computation.[27]

It would be misleading to call the problem tape a rudimentary "operating system" (in present-centered language). Yet, by exerting supreme control over the execution of a problem, it has features of what later would be called a *system program*.

III

Let us return to 1938, the year in which Stibitz and Williams began their work on the Complex Computer and the decision to use relays as the basic circuit element. A relay is just a switch. When it is closed, or ON, the current flows from its input terminal to its output terminal; when open, or OFF, current flow is blocked. If two relays are connected in series, a current will flow through the circuit only if both relays are ON; if either is OFF, current will not flow. If two relays are connected in parallel, then current flows if either one or the other or both relays are ON.

So a relay has two "states": ON and OFF (in present-centered language, a *bistable device*). Suppose the two states, instead of being termed ON and OFF are called TRUE and FALSE. Let us call these two states TRUE and FALSE *logical* or *truth values*. In that case, we may also say that if a current flows through a circuit, its value is TRUE; if no current can flow through, its value is FALSE.

So now, a series connection of two relay switches, X and Y, behaves according to the following statements:

If X = TRUE and Y = TRUE, **then** X **and** Y = TRUE; **otherwise,** X **and** Y = FALSE.

If X = FALSE and Y = FALSE, **then** X **or** Y = FALSE; **otherwise,** X **or** Y = TRUE.

Now, if a relay switch is ON, its *complementary* state is OFF and vice versa. Let us call the complement of a state by the symbol **not**. In which case, we also have a behavior pattern for a relay X:

If X = TRUE, **then not** (X) = FALSE; **otherwise, not** (X) = TRUE.

All this is no mere esoteric conceit. During the mid 19th century, at about the time Babbage was still fretting over his Analytical Engine, another Englishman quite unlike him in social origin named George Boole (1819–1864), born into an impecunious working-class family in Lincoln, England—possessed of the most modest of ordinary school education, almost entirely self-taught in Greek, Latin, German, Italian, French, mathematics, logic, and philosophy—would contribute many papers to mathematical journals and write several books on mathematics and logic. Among them was *The Mathematical Analysis of Logic* (1847) that, according to one historian of mathematics, probably earned him a professorship of mathematics in Queen's College in Cork, Ireland, in 1849.[28] However, it was a later book, the loftily titled *An Investigation of the Laws of Thought* (1854), that granted Boole a lasting place in the annals of modern thought.

What Boole did was to establish the basis of a new algebra of logic. The variables of this algebra could only have the two truth values—TRUE and FALSE—and were thus called *logical variables* or *symbolic variables*. The rules of this algebra—its "calculus"—allowed one to deduce the truth or falsehood of logical expressions or propositions built up by combining logical variables with the logical operations **and**, **or**, and **not**.

Boole died at age 49 in Cork of an illness brought on by getting a drenching in the rain, but not before receiving much recognition, including an honorary LLD degree from the University of Dublin and a medal from the Royal Society. More than a century later, a crater on the moon was named after him.

Boole's *Laws of Thought* had consequences; the laws would later be systematized by other eminent mathematicians, including Augustus de Morgan, Lovelace's one-time tutor; American mathematician–philosopher Charles Sanders Peirce (1839–1914); and British economist and logician William Stanley Jevons (1835–1882). The result came to be called *Boolean algebra* and the development in mathematical logic of the *propositional calculus* for making formal inferences about logical propositions.

In 1937, Boolean algebra formed the logical foundation of the design of circuits composed of switches, such as relays, later called the discipline of *switching circuit design*. Thus, a Victorian professor of mathematics laid one of the cornerstones in the making of a science of computing. If Babbage's ghost hovers continually over this story, Boole's spirit does as well, making his appearance 75 years after his death—and, unlike Babbage, Boole contributed directly to the logical basis of computer design.

IV

In 1937, Claude Shannon (1916–2001), a 21-year-old graduate student, submitted a thesis for a master's degree in electrical engineering at MIT. The thesis was titled *A Symbolic Analysis of Relay and Switching Circuits*.[29] In this work, Shannon drew an analogy between the basic idea in propositional calculus (or, equivalently, in Boolean algebra) and the basic behavior of relay circuits along the lines shown in Table 5.1 (where + does *not* mean the arithmetic operation of add).

In 1938, Shannon published a paper, based on his thesis, in the *Transactions of the American Institute of Electrical Engineers*. The timing of this publication turned out to be important for Shannon's reputation. In the Soviet Union, a Russian logician and engineering theorist named Victor Shestakov (1907–1987) had proposed a theory of switching circuits based on Boolean algebra in 1935. However, he did not publish his work (in Russian) until 1941.

Shannon would later co-invent (with Warren Weaver [1894–1978]) a branch of applied mathematics called *information theory* that laid the theoretical foundation for

TABLE 5.1 Correspondence Between Relay Circuit and Propositional Calculus Concepts

Symbol	Interpretation in relay circuits	Interpretation in propositional calculus
X	The circuit X	The proposition X
o	The circuit X is open	Proposition X is false
I	The circuit X is closed	Proposition X is true
$X + Y$	The parallel connection of X and Y	The proposition that is true if X or Y is true
XY	The series connection of X and Y	The proposition that is true if X and Y is true
X'	The circuit that is open when X is closed, and closed when X is open	The contradiction of proposition X

communication. As a scientific eclectic, his work crossed several scientific boundaries. When he died in 2001, Shannon was a much-honored scientist, but his place in this story rests primarily (but not solely, as we will later see) in that 1937 master's thesis.

It was not only Boolean algebra that he introduced into switching circuit design, but also the fact that the binary states ON and OFF (or open and closed, in Shannon's terminology) could be represented by the truth values TRUE and FALSE from propositional logic, and the binary digits 1 and 0, respectively. Boolean algebra or propositional logic, switching circuit design, and binary arithmetic came together by way of Shannon.

Thus we find George Stibitz, in his 1940 memorandum, explicating the advantages of the binary system in the context of computers—notably, the simplicity of binary addition: $0 + 0 = 0, 0 + 1 = 1, 1 + 0 = 1, 1 + 1 = 10$. This "extraordinary" simplicity, Stibitz wrote, made it so much easier to design computing machines composed of relays, for a relay has only two positions: open and closed. The former represents the binary digit 0; the latter, the digit 1.[30]

One of the earliest textbooks on the design of arithmetic units for digital computers, published in 1955, described the role Boolean algebra could play in computer design. It is enough for any basic circuit element having just two states (that is, is a bistable device) to be represented by a Boolean variable—not just relays, but other circuit elements that came to be used in later computers, such as vacuum tubes and diodes. Associated with Boolean variables are three fundamental Boolean operations AND (logical product), OR (logical sum), and NOT (complement). Using these operations, Boolean expressions can represent *any* circuit composed of bistable or binary circuit elements.[31]

For example, a switching network with four inputs A, B, C, D and a single output E such that 1 is produced on E only when both A and B are 1s or when both C and D are 1s (Figure 5.1) can be expressed by the Boolean expression $E = AB + CD$, where AB and CD represent A AND B, C AND D, respectively, and the + represents OR.[32] A very different

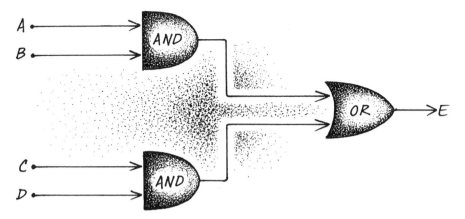

FIGURE 5.1 A Logic Circuit for $E = AB + CD$.

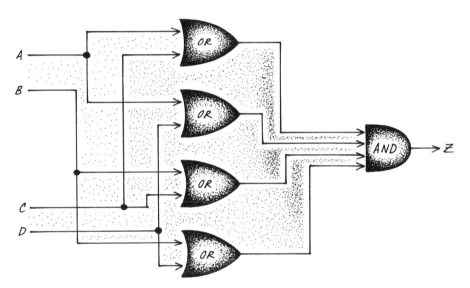

FIGURE 5.2 A Logic Circuit for $Z = (A + C)(A + D)(B + C)(B + D)$.

switching network is shown in Figure 5.2, represented by the Boolean expression $Z = (A + C)(A + D)(B + C)(B + D)$. However, using the *laws* of Boolean algebra, one can transform this last expression to the expression $E = AB + CD$, corresponding to the much simpler and economic circuit of Figure 5.1.[33] So the power of Boolean algebra lay not only in its concise notation, but also as a *calculus*.

V

We have seen that, ever since Babbage, the desire for automatic computation was stimulated by the felt need for the speedy, accurate, and reliable production of tables of all sorts. In Babbage's time, these tables were mathematical in nature. Later, after Hollerith, punched-card tabulators were used busily through the first decades of the 20th century in compiling statistical tables and mortality data, and in accounting and other business-related statements.

Beginning in about 1928, Hollerith-style data processing machines began to be used extensively to produce astronomical tables. In particular, a Cambridge-educated New Zealander, Leslie John Comrie (1893–1950), superintendent of the Nautical Almanac Office in England, used the Hollerith machine to compile tables of the moon's position.[34] In the United States, Wallace J. Eckert (1902–1971), an astronomer, teaching in Columbia University, and seriously interested in automating astronomical calculations, established in 1926 a computer laboratory in the university.[35] This invoked the interest of Thomas J. Watson (1874–1956), president of IBM, the undisputed industrial leader in punched-card data processing machines. Watson was persuaded to establish a computational bureau at Columbia. In 1933, financed by IBM, this computer laboratory— for that is what it was—was expanded and named the Thomas J. Watson Astronomical Computing Bureau, a joint enterprise of IBM, the department of astronomy in Columbia, and the American Astronomical Society.[36] Eckert was one of those in the electromechanical era who understood the need for automatic digital computing machines to support the mathematical work of scientists. So did Stibitz at Bell Laboratories, as we have seen. And so did a graduate student in physics in Harvard University named Howard H. Aiken (1900–1973).

These seemed to be times when memoranda were being written on computing and computers, not with a view to publication, but as exploratory documents to be circulated and read by a select group of people to stimulate discussion and instigate practical action. Stibitz's 1940 paper was an example. Three years earlier, Aiken wrote a memorandum titled "Proposed Automatic Calculating Machine," which would be published in 1964 as a historical document.[37] Aiken acknowledged Babbage's pioneering work and that of his successors, including Hollerith. Like all those who preceded him, Aiken was driven by a dissatisfaction and a resulting need.

He observed that recent developments in the exact sciences (such as physics, chemistry, and astronomy) entailed the definition and use of many new mathematical relationships, most of which were described in terms of infinite series or processes. The methods of tabulating these functions were inadequate, and so their application to scientific problems was severely hindered.[38] Indeed, it was not just that the methods of tabulation were insufficient, because of their slowness and propensity for errors, but also there were problems in physics that could not be solved because of the lack of means for their computation.[39]

There were, then, problems in physics that were unsolvable—not in the Turing theoretical sense that no machine could *ever* solve them (see Chapter 4, Section VI), but in the technological sense that computing machines of the time did not have the power or the capacity to perform the necessary computations. Aiken laid the basic requirements that had to be met for the purpose of automatic scientific computation.

He pointed out that accounting machines were concerned only with problems involving positive numbers, whereas machines meant for *mathematical* purposes must be able to handle both positive and negative numbers. Furthermore, such machines must be able to cope with a wide variety of transcendental functions, such as trigonometric, elliptic, Bessel, and probabilistic functions. Third, because most mathematical computations involve iterative processes that compute repetitively over entire ranges of values of some variables, machines dedicated to the mathematical sciences must be fully automatic after a process is initiated without any (or at least minimal) human intervention.[40] Aiken concluded that such features could be realized by converting existing punched-card, data processing machines of the kind made by IBM into scientific computing machines.[41]

If attracting IBM's attention was Aiken's immediate purpose in making this point— a means to a larger scientific end—he succeeded spectacularly. Through appropriate connections in Harvard, Aiken linked with Eckert, and through Eckert with the right people at IBM. Thus, in 1939, a project was initiated involving Aiken and a team of IBM engineers led by Clair D. Lake (1888–1958), one of IBM's major engineer–inventors, to build a machine according to Aiken's design.[42] The result was the Automatic Sequence Controlled Calculator (ASCC), more widely known as the *Harvard Mark I*—the first of an evolutionary family of machines built by Aiken and others in Harvard, and also the machine with which IBM began its spectacular reign in the realm of automatic programmable computers.

The Mark I was built at the IBM Laboratory in Endicott, New York, and was shipped to Harvard, where it became operational in 1944. Aiken would later formally acknowledge Lake and two other IBM engineers, Frank. E. Hamilton and Benjamin M. Durfee, as his co-inventors of this machine.[43] The Mark I was described in some detail in a series of three articles published in 1946, coauthored by Aiken and Grace Murray Hopper (1906–1992).[44]

VI

If Lovelace was the first female computer scientist (using a present-centered term), then, so far as is currently known, Hopper was the second. Because Hopper was situated in a more opportune time and place, her place in this history is somewhat more prominent.

Aiken obtained his PhD in physics from Harvard in 1939, leaving him unencumbered to pursue his computer project. Hopper, 6 years younger, graduated in mathematics and physics from Vassar College in 1928, then went to Yale, where she earned a PhD in mathematics in 1931. At the time Aiken and Hopper began collaboration on the Mark I, Hopper was on the mathematics faculty in Vassar and had begun service in the U.S. Naval Reserves, and it was in this capacity that she was assigned to the Mark I computer project.

Hopper reappears later in this story. For the present, it suffices to note that, although she was employed by private computer manufacturing corporations later in her life, she remained in the U.S. Navy for her entire working life, always (it seems) in uniform, retir-ing with the rank of Rear Admiral. She would become a legendary figure in the world of computing and beyond, and was referred to as "Amazing Grace". Such was her presence in the development of computer science, a major professional award in computer program-ming, given annually by the Association for Computing Machinery, America's foremost computing organization, was named in her honor, and a series of conferences titled The Grace Hopper Celebration of Women in Computing has been established.

Hopper shared something else with Lovelace. If the latter was the first explorer (with Babbage) of the *idea* of programming a computer, then Hopper was, even more surely, among the very first in the modern era to be concerned with the science and *practice* of programming.

VII

The Harvard Mark I, like the Bell Laboratories Models I and II (its contemporaries) was an electromechanical machine, although the mechanical dominated. On the one hand, it was powered by electric motors; used relays, contacts, and electromagnets; and printed its results on electric typewriters. On the other hand it, was a conglomerate of gears, shafts, chains and sprockets, clutches, cams, counterwheels, and so on,[45] perhaps reflect-ing the tradition of the punched card data processing machines with which its IBM engi-neers were supremely familiar.

The machine normally operated on numbers of 23 digits of significance, although for particular greater accuracy problems, the number of significant digits could be extended to 46.[46]

The machine's storage capacity was composed of 60 memory registers to hold constant numbers and 72 registers to hold variable numbers that could serve as inputs to compu-tations. There were processing units for addition, multiplication, and division, and tables to hold values of transcendental functions (for example, trigonometric functions such as sine, cosine and tan, and logarithmic values). The output of calculations could be recorded on punched cards (which, in turn, were usable as inputs to other computations or shared between computational laboratories) or printed out on paper by way of electric typewriters.[47]

An important architectural difference between the Mark I and the contemporary Bell Laboratories computers was that the former was a decimal machine whereas the latter used binary numbers and arithmetic. The overall control of computation was directed by perforated paper tapes read into and decoded by the "sequence control unit," with each perforated line specifying the operation to be performed, the data source of the opera-tion, and the destination of the result (in present-centered language, the *operands*).

The Mark I was, physically, a massive machine, more than 50 feet long, containing 800,000 components, many of which were adapted from IBM punched-card machines.[48] Functionally and architecturally, it must count as an important contribution to the pursuit of what we might call a Holy Grail—the development of *the* automatic, programmable, general-purpose digital computer.

Clearly, such a machine was in Aiken's mind when he wrote his 1937 memorandum.[49] The problem lay in the elusive nature of this Holy Grail—a moving ghost, in fact. How general purpose was general purpose? How automatic was automatic? What did it mean to be programmable?

In Aiken's eyes, in the eyes of Stibitz and his codesigners of the Bell Laboratories machines, and in the eyes Eckert of the Watson Astronomical Computing Bureau in Columbia, *general purpose* meant the ability to perform mathematical calculations characteristic of scientific and engineering problems. A general-purpose computing machine was a *numeric analysis machine* (an expansion of Babbage's idea of an Analytical Engine). The Mark I was designed with this kind of generality in mind, in which the various processes of mathematical analysis were reduced to sequences or combinations of five basic arithmetic operations—addition, subtraction, multiplication, division, and referencing tables of previously computed results. The Mark I could carry out any sequential combination of these operations fully automatically.[50]

We note Aiken's and Hopper's identification of *five* arithmetic operations—elsewhere, they also call them "the five fundamental operations of numerical analysis."[51] The fifth operation is what, in present-centered language, we would call *table lookup* or *table search*—the capacity to draw on (previously computed) tables of mathematical functions such as trigonometric functions as a means of avoiding unnecessary calculations. Here we have a very early reference to searching as a computational operation. As we will see later, searching (and its near kin, sorting) will form fundamental topics as computer science gradually matures.

VIII

To repeat, the Holy Grail of computing was itself an evolving entity. After all, the whole point of automatic computation was to overcome certain frailties of the human mind—its slowness in performing computations, its tendency to make mistakes, its proneness to fatigue and, thus, reliability. *Speed, accuracy, reliability.* These were, of course, the desiderata of all scientific instruments reaching back to antiquity. They assumed still more imperative roles in the design of computers. It was not enough for a computer to be automatic and general purpose. It was not enough for it to be programmable. It must also be fast, it must be accurate, and its mode of computing must be reliable.

Even programmability raised questions and debates. This was not just a matter of infusing generality to a computing machine, it also had an effect on the extent of automaticity as well as on the effective speed of performing computational tasks.

The point is that there are no absolute or optimal criteria for recognizing that one has found this particular Holy Grail. There is also the deplorable limit to human cognitive capacity; humans are limited in their ability to make the best possible decisions in their ability to optimize. Aiken was trained as a physicist, Stibitz as an engineer, and Comrie and Eckert as astronomers. Their training, their professional upbringing, shaped their mentalities as computer pioneers; and it limited their computational worldviews.

IX

How is this important? During the 1940s, as Aiken and colleagues and Stibitz and associates were going about their projects; as World War II raged; as a huge galaxy of scientists assembled in Los Alamos, New Mexico, to build the most unimaginably destructive weapon of all time; at the University of Chicago, not too far from where the Italian-American physicist Enrico Fermi (1901–1954) and his team were producing the first controlled nuclear chain reaction in the world's first nuclear reactor, a precocious social scientist named Herbert Alexander Simon (1916–2001)—who, like Fermi, would one day receive a Nobel Prize—was writing a PhD dissertation in political science. His topic was how human decisions are made in organizations. This dissertation, duly completed and accepted by the University of Chicago, was fine-tuned and published in 1947 as a book titled *Administrative Behavior*.[52]

One of Simon's major insights—indeed, a Nobel Prize-winning insight, as it turned out to be—was that humans, being limited in their cognitive capacity, are severely limited in their ability to make rational decisions. Such limits originate in the fact that, to make fully rational decisions, a person must have access to all possible information relevant to that situation; moreover, the information must be complete and correct, and the decision maker must be able to process the information speedily, reliably, and accurately to arrive at the best possible course of action to follow.

In actuality, in most situations, the available information is neither complete nor correct, or a person may not have all the relevant information even if it is somewhere "out there" in the cultural environment. Even if the person is fortunate enough to have all the relevant and correct information, his capacity to process it and produce the most rational decision in a speedy, accurate manner may be severely limited. In his later writings, Simon would call this cognitive limitation on rational decision making *bounded rationality*.[53]

So, under the condition of bounded rationality, how *do* humans make decisions? Simon suggested that, rather than seek the best, good human decision makers strive for what is *good enough*; they establish certain goals as aspirations that seem within their cognitive capacity and strive to reach those aspirations. If they succeed, they may not have made the best possible decision, but one that is satisfactory. Instead of trying to optimize, decision makers *satisfice*.[54] Satisficing, not optimizing, is the name of the decision maker's game.

What Simon theorized about administrative decision making applies equally well to the realm of much of human problem solving, as Simon has himself explored[55]—and that includes design processes.[56] The designer of any reasonably complex artifact suffers from bounded rationality, and she has very little choice other than to satisfice her design.

An artifact, then, is the product of satisficing choices. When the artifact is then tested "in the field," its limitations, flaws, and weaknesses will be revealed. There will inevitably be such limitations because satisficing is a matter of compromise. A new cycle of design may then begin with the current design as the starting point. A new aspiration level may be identified and new goals established that correspond to it, and the designer proceeds to a new, hopefully improved, design. And so it goes. Artifacts lead to new artifacts as their "descendants." Over time, a phylogenetic family of artifacts will appear. Or, over time, one phylogenetic pathway may spawn the beginning of an entirely new one.

Of course, even satisficing is constrained by bounded rationality. The satisficing goals may not be attainable after all; all kinds of cultural factors (the "environment") may intrude, including unforeseen, unanticipated changes in the cultural environment. In the case of computing machines, new technologies may appear, for example.

X

Thus it was with the Bell Laboratories series of machines. Thus it was with the computers that followed the Harvard Mark I.

Physical technology, an aspect of computing's cultural environment, played a vital role in this evolution. Electronic components as digital devices—the "offspring" of analog electronic devices, such as vacuum tubes long used in radio engineering—became a rival to relays. The speed at which the vacuum tube could switch states (ON to OFF or vice versa) was much faster than in the relay. However, digital electronic components were still regarded as unreliable by some, and so Aiken, having parted ways with IBM after the Mark I project, embarked, in 1945, on the development of the Mark II using electromagnetic relays.[57] The storage capacity of this paper tape-controlled machine was larger than that of the Mark I. The latter had 72 storage registers[58]; the former could hold 100 decimal floating-point numbers (see Section II, this chapter).[59] Computational power was also greater; there were two adders and four multipliers that could operate simultaneously, and several more input and output devices.

This machine became operational in 1947. Because of its use of relays, it was also faster than the Mark I. Like its predecessor, the Mark II was a decimal machine; however, it used the binary coded decimal notation (described in an early form first by Stibitz in 1940) for representing decimal numbers.

As for IBM, with two of the ASCC/Mark I engineers, Lake and Burfee as members of the design team, the company built the Pluggable Sequence Relay Calculator that, in the proper IBM tradition of its electromechanical tabulating machines, used plugboards to input "programs." On the other hand, like the Mark II, it used relays. This machine became operational at the end of 1944[60]—in fact, the same year the Mark I, although completed in 1942, also became operational. In 1945, a design team led by Eckert (now director of pure science in IBM as well as director of the Watson Astronomical Computing Laboratory in Columbia University), and Hamilton from the Mark I project, began work on the IBM Selectric Sequence Electronic Calculator. Electronics had arrived at IBM. However, well before the dedication of this machine in 1948, electronic computing had turned up in Philadelphia 2 years earlier. The Holy Grail seemed to be within reach.

XI

World War II played two different roles in the annals of computing. On the one hand, it stimulated the development of automatic computing; on the other, the normal channels of scientific communication so deeply cherished by scientists working in different countries and so profoundly necessary to maintain the openness of the scientific enterprise were, "for reason of state," blocked—especially between scientists of the Allies and those of Germany.

We have seen the first of these effects in the case of the Bell Laboratories' Ballistic Computer. The Harvard Mark I was also used, initially, by the U.S. Navy.[61] The Mark II was also intended for the U.S. Navy, although by the time it was completed in 1947, the war was over.[62] The first "copy" of IBM's Pluggable Relay Sequence Calculator was sent, in 1944, to the Aberdeen Proving Ground in Maryland, the place where the U.S. Army conducted its testing of weapons systems. By the end of World War II, the military–scientific complex was firmly established, and the computer was undoubtedly in the thick of this complex.

The other effect of the war meant that work going on in Germany on computing (as in atomic physics) during the war years was unknown in the Allied countries until well after the war ended. Maurice Wilkes (1913–2010), whom we will encounter at length later in this story, tells us in his autobiography that it was not until well after the war that he first heard the name of Konrad Zuse (1910–1995).[63]

During the early 1930s, as a civil engineering student at the Technische Hochschule Berlin, Zuse, like so many others we have encountered in this story, was frustrated by the tedium of manual calculation. Like others, he, too, began to think about automatic computation. In 1936, he filed a patent for the design of a paper tape-controlled mechanical binary computer.[64] In his patent application, he described a memory device comprised of "cells" that could hold both input numbers entering into a computation and the results of computations. He wrote of a "computational plan," punched onto a paper tape, that would specify the arithmetic operations to be performed, the locations of the memory cells that contained the input data, and the locations of cells where the computational results would be placed. The computational plan would initiate the necessary operations automatically.[65]

Zuse's design included the possibility of multiple arithmetic units, memories, tape readers, and punches so that several operations could be performed simultaneously (in present-centered language, the possibility of parallel processing).[66] He recognized that certain computational situations might demand data that would be constant across parts of a process, in which case, rather than be input to the machine every time they were needed, they could be specified as part of the computational plan[67] (in present-centered terms, these constants are called "literals").

Zuse recognized that a distinction could be made between a human performing computations and a computing machine. Typical "human habits" could be cast off, and simpler mechanisms, conducive to automatic computation could be used instead. An example was the use of binary arithmetic. Zuse also recognized that scientific and technical computations (in contrast to accounting calculations) may need to deal with numbers ranging from the very small (for example, the coefficient of thermal expansion, $e = 0.000012$) to the very large (for example, the modulus of elasticity, $E = 2,100,000$ kg/cm^2), with both kinds perhaps appearing in the same computation.[68]

To accommodate such variation, he proposed the use of "semilogarithmic notation"[69]—in present-centered language, floating-point representation. Thus, Stibitz was not the *original* inventor of floating-point notation for numbers (see Section II, this chapter), although it is quite likely that the American did not know of Zuse's patent application, which meant that he independently (re)invented the concept.

Zuse's proposal was the basis for his first computer called the Z1, completed in 1938. It was a purely mechanical machine, with a 16-word binary memory, and was the progenitor of his next machine, which combined a mechanical memory with an arithmetic unit made of some 200 electromagnetic relays, and was called the Z2.[70] The Z2 was a perforated paper tape-controlled machine that could calculate "certain simple formulae" and demonstrate the "principle of program control," but it was not a practical computer.[71]

Zuse's further work was interrupted temporarily when he was called up for military service. During that time an associate, Helmut Shreyer (1912–1984), an engineer–inventor, began building an electronic version of the Z1 that, using vacuum tubes ("valves" as Shreyer called them), was able to compute at much higher speeds than relays.[72]

The electronic components in this design were a combination of valves and neon tube diodes. Shreyer built a small binary arithmetic unit with about 100 valves. Unfortunately, the unit was destroyed by war damage.[73]

A positive outcome of Shreyer's memorandum was that Zuse was released from military duty and given government backing to pursue his computer research.[74] The first fruit of this was the Z3—an electromechanical machine built in Berlin between 1939 and 1941, and financed mainly by the German Aeronautical Research Institute. Unfortunately, it was destroyed in an air raid in 1944.[75] Zuse does not tell us the extent to which it was actually in productive operation, save to comment laconically: "A series of interesting programs was tested and calculated on the machine."[76] This machine was controlled by commands punched on paper tapes; its two "parallel" arithmetic units used floating-point binary, 22-bit representation of numbers (a sign bit, a 7-bit exponent, and a 14-bit mantissa).[77] The machine not only performed standard arithmetic operations, but also square root extraction and multiplication by common factors such as 2, 1/2, 10, 0.1, and −1. Data were input in decimal form through a keyboard and converted internally to binary, and the reverse was done to produce output results in the form of a "lamp display with four decimal places and a point."[78] A total of 2600 relays were used.

In present-centered language, the Z3 was a single-address machine, with each instruction on the program tape specifying the storage address of a single operand and an operation. Presumably, the second operand was "implied," an internal register in the arithmetic unit.

The immediate successor to the Z3 was the Z4. Its design, planning, and construction began "immediately" after the completion of the Z3.[79] In general architecture, it was "fundamentally" identical to Z3, but with some changes. The word length (in present-centered terminology) was increased to 32 bits; the store was mechanical, and there were "special units for program processing," although Zuse did not specify what these were. However, he mentioned the addition of conditional branch commands so that, one may presume, these special units included the capacity to execute conditional branches. There were also "various technical improvements."[80] The Z4 was completed in 1945, to the extent that "it could run simple programs." It was the only one of the wartime Z computers that survived.[81] It was also the last of Zuse's wartime computers. In 1950, after German recovery and reconstruction, the Z4 was transferred to the Eidgenössiche Technische Hochschule (ETH) Zurich,[82] but the Z series phylogeny continued on with the Z5, built in the 1950s and still a relay machine, and the later development of electronic successors.[83]

We will encounter the highly original Zuse later in this chronicle in another context: the development of notation for communicating with the computer—in present-centered language, the development of programming languages.

XII

World War II harbored innumerable secrets. One was the development of an evolutionary series of computers in Bletchley Park, a manor house and estate in what is now the town of Milton Keynes not far from London. Bletchley Park now houses Britain's National Museum of Computing. During the war, it was the site of that country's cryptanalytical center, responsible for decrypting codes and ciphers used by the Axis countries. Computing machines played a critical role in Bletchley's wartime mission. Naturally, the work carried out there was highly classified and remained so long after the war was over.

Like other major technoscientific centers created specifically for the war effort, Bletchley Park was populated by mathematicians, scientists, and engineers, many of whom had either already achieved distinction or would do so in later life. Mathematician Max Newman, whose lectures in Cambridge on Hilbert's problems had been the catalyst for Turing's work on computability (see Chapter 4), was one of the team leaders. There was William T. Tutte (1912–2002), who would achieve great distinction for his contribution to combinatorial mathematics. There was Thomas H. Flowers (1905–1998), an electronics engineer who had conducted research on the use of electronic valves (vacuum tubes, in American parlance) in telephone switching networks almost a decade before he entered Bletchley Park.[84] There was the eclectic Donald Michie (1923–2007), a classics scholar who, after the war, would turn into a mammalian geneticist before self-transforming into one of Britain's leading figures in a branch of computer science called *artificial intelligence*. There was the mathematician and statistician Irving J. Good (1916–200), a student of the renowned Cambridge mathematician Godfrey H. Hardy (1877–1947). There was Allan Coombs (1911–1993), an electronics engineer; and the Welshman Charles Wynn-Williams (1903–1979), a physicist whose doctoral research in the Cavendish Laboratory, Cambridge, was supervised by Lord Ernest Rutherford (1871–1937), and who became especially known before the war for his work on electronic instrumentation for use in nuclear physics and radioactivity research. Among his prewar contributions was the invention of the binary counter, which became a standard component in digital systems, including the digital computer. And there was Alan Turing.

As it turned out, Turing was involved in some of the early computer developments at Bletchley, but not the later work that produced the most significant products.[85] Turing's contributions lay, rather, in actual cryptanalysis—the analysis and deciphering of codes—and with the Enigma—the generic name for a type of electromechanical encryption machine (invented by a German engineer after World War I) and used by such civilian organizations as banks in peacetime, and by both Allied and Axis intelligence during the war. Turing was concerned with deciphering intercepted code produced by the German Enigma.[86]

The Colossus, a prototype machine, and its production grade, the Mark II Colossus, belong to this story because they were certainly among the very first binary electronic digital computers to be built. They were, in fact, the descendents of a series of earlier machines built at Bletchley Park—the Robinson family, with Heath Robinson as the first, followed by Peter Robinson, and then Robinson & Clearn. The Colossi were followed, as the war came to an end, by other more specialized machines all with quirky names.[87]

The prototype Colossus, completed in the remarkably short period of about 11 months, became operational in December 1943.[88] The Mark II Colossus was completed in June 1944, just 5 days before D-Day.[89] These machines also interest us because, in Babbage's country—and Turing's—they represent England's first serious engagement with the design and construction of digital computers in the 20th century. As we will see later, they more than compensated for this tardiness by the end of the 1940s.

XIII

At the physical level, as a material artifact, the Colossus had several novel features. It was a binary machine. It used a clock pulse to time operations throughout the machine; it was a "synchronous" machine. It used some 1500 electronic valves (the Mark II had some 2400 valves).[90] It had a "shift register"—a register in which the binary digits could be shifted one position to the left or right in each clock step, a common feature in later digital computers. It had bistable circuits to perform counting, binary arithmetic, and, strikingly, Boolean logical operations. This latter mirrored its most original architectural feature: a capacity to perform complicated Boolean functions. Indeed, the Colossus was designed as a "Boolean calculating machine" rather than as an "ordinary number cruncher."[91] It could also execute conditional branch operations.

Data were input through punched paper tape read by a photoelectric tape reader, whereas output was printed out on an electric typewriter.[92] The only memory comprised "[e]lectronic storage registers changeable by automatically controlled sequence of operations."[93] Such automatically controlled sequence of operations—its program (although the term did not yet exist in this context)—was fed to the machine by setting switches and plugs manually.

The Colossi machines were designed as special-purpose computers, with a function to facilitate and expedite code breaking—hence, a "Boolean calculating engine." Yet, it was sufficiently flexible "[w]ithin its own subject area" that it could be used to perform jobs that were not considered at the design stage[94]—although this was, apparently, a forced flexibility, for it necessitated cumbersome manual intervention.[95]

XIV

What was the legacy of the Colossus for the history of computing? Because of the classified nature of its mission, the work at Bletchley Park would not be known to the public for some three decades following the end of the war.[96] Thus, the design details of the Colossi machines could not be transmitted to other later computer projects in Britain or abroad. In this sense, this series of machines came to an evolutionary dead end.

On the other hand, the people involved left Bletchley Park after the war, carrying with them a great deal of valuable and original *knowledge*, both theoretical and experiential, into their peacetime lives. Among them, at least four would be involved with computers and computing.

Newman became a professor of pure mathematics at the University of Manchester, and Good went with him.[97] Manchester University (as we will see) became a hugely important site for original research in computing—and remained so into the 1950s, and through the 1960s and 1970s—and Newman had no small role in establishing this tradition. Indeed, not long after taking his position in Manchester, he applied to the Royal Society for a grant to establish a "calculating machine laboratory" in the university, which was duly awarded in July 1946. Thus was initiated the Manchester tradition. Good was involved in its early years.

Turing joined, as a "scientific officer," the newly established mathematics division in the National Physical Laboratory (NPL) in Teddington, a London suburb.[98] The mission of this division included "[i]nvestigation of the possible adaptation of automatic telephone equipment to scientific computers" and the "[d]evelopment of an electronic counting device suitable for rapid computing."[99] This appointment marked Turing's first systematic foray into building a practical version of his "universal computing machine"—the Turing machine. He conceived and developed the detailed proposal for what came to be called the NPL's ACE computers, with ACE being an acronym for *Automatic Computing Engine*.[100]

Michie, the classics scholar-turned-cryptanalyst, although he became a geneticist after the war, never quite forgot his interest, nurtured at Bletchley Park and shared by Turing, in chess-playing machines. In 1965, Michie was appointed professor of machine intelligence in Edinburgh University and was instrumental in making Edinburgh a leading world center in artificial intelligence.

The consequence of the Colossi projects for the future history of computer science was its people and the knowledge they held, rather than its actual machines.

NOTES

1. G. R. Stibitz. (1940). *Computer*. Unpublished memorandum. Later printed in B. Randell. (Ed.). (1975). *The origins of digital computers* (2nd ed., pp. 241–246). New York: Springer-Verlag.

2. It is no coincidence that these were the main countries battling it out during World War II—nothing like the imperative of war to facilitate machines that expedited the mathematics of warfare.

3. The literature on the evolutionary nature of creativity in technological, scientific, artistic, and literary cultures is vast—and controversial. See especially D. T. Campbell. (1960). Blind variation and selective retention in creative thought as in other knowledge processes. *Psychological Reviews, 60*, 380–400; P. Steadman (1979). *The evolution of designs*. Cambridge, UK: Cambridge University Press; G. Radnitzky & W.W. Bartley, III. (Eds.). (1987). *Evolutionary epistemology*. La Salle, IL: Open Court; G. Basalla. (1988). *The evolution of technology*. Cambridge, UK: Cambridge University Press; A. K. Sen. (1992). On the Darwinian view of progress. *London Review of Books, 14*; S. Dasgupta. (1996). *Technology and creativity*. New York: Oxford University Press; D. K. Simonton. (1999). *Origins of genius: Darwinian perspectives on creativity*. New York: Oxford University Press; S. Dasgupta. (2004). Is creativity a Darwinian process? *Creativity Research Journal, 16*, 403–413; D. K. Simonton. (2010). Creative thought as blind-variation and selective-retention: Combinational models of exceptional creativity. *Physics of Life Reviews, 7*, 190–194; S. Dasgupta. (2011). Contesting (Simonton's) blind variation, selective retention theory of creativity. *Creativity Research Journal, 23*, 166–182.

4. Stibitz, op cit., p. 242.

5. Ibid.

6. O. Cesareo. (1946). The Relay Interpolator. *Bell Laboratories Records, 23*, 457–460. Reprinted in Randell (pp. 247–250), op cit., p. 247. (All citations to this and other articles reprinted in Randell will reference the reprint.)

7. Ibid.

8. Ibid., p. 239.

9. R. Moreau. (1984). *The computer comes of age* (p. 29). Cambridge, MA: MIT Press.

10. J. Juley. (1947). The Ballistic Computer. *Bell Laboratories Records, 24*, 5–9. Reprinted in Randell (pp. 251–255), op cit., p. 251.

11. Cesareo, op cit., p. 249.

12. Juley, op cit., p. 253.

13. Cesareo, op cit., p. 249.

14. Juley, op cit., p. 254.

15. Cesareo, op cit., p. 250.

16. Juley, op cit., p. 254.

17. Randell, op cit., p. 239.

18. Ibid.

19. F. L. Alt. (1948a). A Bell Telephone Laboratories computing machine: I. *Mathematical Tables for Automatic Computation, 3*, 1–13. Reprinted in Randell (pp. 257–270), op cit., p. 257.

20. For more on technological complexity see G. Basalla, op cit. S. Dasgupta. (1997). Technology and complexity. *Philosophica, 59*, 113–139.

21. Alt, op cit., p. 257.

22. F. L. Alt. (1948b). A Bell Telephone Laboratories computing machine: II. *Mathematical Tables for Automatic Computation, 3*, 69–84. Reprinted in Randell (pp. 271–286), op cit., pp. 283–284.

23. Alt, 1948b, op cit., p. 277.

24. Ibid.

25. Ibid., p. 276.

26. Ibid.

27. Alt, 1948a, op cit., p. 270.

28. C. S. Boyer. (1991). *A history of mathematics* (2nd ed., Rev., p. 579). New York: Wiley.

29. C. E. Shannon. (1940). *A symbolic analysis of relay and switching circuits.* Unpublished thesis, Department of Electrical Engineering, MIT, Cambridge, MA. For some reason, although Shannon submitted the thesis in 1937, it was approved formally in 1940.

30. Stibitz, op cit., pp. 243–244.

31. R. K. Richards. (1955). *Arithmetic operations in digital computers* (p. 33). Princeton, NJ: Princeton University Press.

32. Ibid.

33. Ibid.

34. L. J. Comrie. (1928). On the construction of tables by interpolation. *Monthly Notices of the Royal Astronomical Society, 88*, 506–523. L. J. Comrie. (1932). The application of the Hollerith tabulating machine to Brown's tables of the moon. *Monthly Notices of the Royal Astronomical Society, 92*, 694–707.

35. H. H. Goldstine. (1972). *The computer from Pascal to von Neumann* (p. 109). Princeton, NJ: Princeton University Press.

36. Ibid.

37. H.. H. Aiken. (1975). Proposed automatic calculating machine. Reprinted in Randell (pp. 191–197), op cit. (original work published 1937). Page citation to this chapter refers to the Randell reprint.

38. Ibid., p. 192.

39. Ibid.

40. Ibid., pp. 192–193. Aiken also listed a fourth, more technical, mathematical requirement that we can ignore here.

41. Ibid., p. 193.

42. Randell, op cit., p. 187; Goldstine, op cit., p. 111.

43. H. H. Aiken & G. M. Hopper. (1975). The Automatic Sequence Controlled Calculator [in three parts]. *Electrical Engineering, 65,* 384–391, 449–454, 522–528 (original work published 1946). Reprinted in Randell (pp. 199–218), op cit., See footnote, p. 199. All page citations to these articles refer to the Randell reprint.

44. Ibid.

45. Ibid., p. 201 *ff.*

46. The number of significant digits indicate the range and precision of the real numbers that can be represented. For example, the value of π as a real number, 3.14285..., can be represented to more decimal digits with an increase in the number of significant digits.

47. Aiken & Hopper, op cit., p. 201.

48. Moreau, op cit., p. 30.

49. Aiken, op cit.

50. Ibid., p. 201.

51. Aiken & Hopper, op cit., p. 203.

52. H. A. Simon. (1976). *Administrative behavior* (3rd ed.). New York: Free Press (original work published 1947).

53. See, for example, H. A. Simon. (1983). *Reason in human affairs.* Oxford: Basil Blackwell; H. A. Simon. (1996). *The sciences of the artificial* (3rd ed.). Cambridge, MA: MIT Press.

54. Ibid., 1996, op cit., pp. 27–30.

55. A. Newell & H. A. Simon. (1972). *Human problem solving* (pp. 681, 703). Englewood-Cliffs, NJ: Prentice-Hall.

56. Simon, 1996, op cit., pp. 111–138; S. Dasgupta. (2009). *Design theory and computer science* (pp. 32–35, 62–65). Cambridge, UK: Cambridge University Press (original work published 1991).

57. Randell, op cit., p. 188.

58. Aiken & Hopper, op cit., p. 203.

59. Recall that floating-point arithmetic had been conceived by Stibitz at least as far back as 1942.

60. Randell, op cit., p. 188.

61. Ibid., p. 187.

62. Ibid., p. 188.

63. M. V. Wilkes. (1985). *Memoirs of a computer pioneer* (p. 157). Cambridge, MA: MIT Press.

64. K. Zuse. (1975a). *Method for automatic execution of calculations with the aid of computers.* Patent application. Extract reprinted in Randell (pp. 159–166), op cit., Trans. R. Basu (original work published 1936).

65. Ibid., p. 159.

66. Ibid., p. 162.

67. Ibid.

68. Ibid.

69. Ibid.

70. K. Zuse. (1975b). *The outline of a computer development from mechanics to electronics.* Reprinted in Randell (pp. 171–186), op cit., p. 179 (original work published 1962 in German).

71. Ibid.

72. H. Shreyer. (1939). *Technical computing machines.* Unpublished memorandum. Published in Randell (pp. 167–169), op cit., p. 168.

73. Zuse, op cit., p. 178.

74. Randell, op cit., p. 156.

75. Zuse, op cit., p. 179.

76. Ibid.

77. Ibid. This article was written in 1962 in German. My reference is to the excerpted English translation in which such terms as *program*, *word*, *exponent*, *mantissa*, and *single address code*— very much established during the 1960s—were used.

78. Ibid.

79. Ibid.

80. Ibid.

81. Ibid.

82. Ibid., p. 180.

83. Ibid., pp. 183–184.

84. B. Randell. (1980). The Colossus. In N. Metropolis, J. S. Howlett & G. C. Rota. (Eds.), *A history of computing in the twentieth century* (pp. 47–92). New York: Academic Press (see especially p. 55).

85. Ibid., op cit., p. 78.

86. A. Hodges. (1987). *Alan Turing: The Enigma* (pp. 166–170). New York: Simon & Schuster.

87. Randell, 1980, op cit., p. 71.

88. Ibid., pp. 47, 65.

89. I.. J. Good. (1980). Pioneering work on computers at Bletchley. In Metropolis, Howlett, & Rota, op cit., pp. 31–45 (original work published 1976).

90. Randell, 1980, op cit., p. 71.

91. Ibid., p. 74.

92. Good, op cit., p. 42; Randell, 1980, op cit., p. 66.

93. Randell, 1980, op cit., p. 72.

94. Ibid., p. 73.

95. Ibid., p. 74.

96. Ibid., p. 47.

97. Ibid., p. 80.

98. Hodges, op cit., p. 305.

99. Quoted in Hodges, op cit., p. 306.

100. J. H. Wilkinson. (1980). Turing's work at the National Physical Laboratory and the construction of pilot ACE, DEUCE and ACE. In Metroplois, Howlett, & Rota, op cit., pp. 101–114.

6

Intermezzo

BY THE END OF World War II, independent of one another (and sometimes in mutual ignorance), a small assortment of highly creative minds—mathematicians, engineers, physicists, astronomers, and even an actuary, some working in solitary mode, some in twos or threes, others in small teams, some backed by corporations, others by governments, many driven by the imperative of war—had developed a shadowy shape of what the elusive Holy Grail of automatic computing might look like. They may not have been able to define *a priori* the nature of this entity, but they were beginning to grasp how they might recognize it when they saw it. Which brings us to the nature of a *computational paradigm*.

Ever since the historian and philosopher of science Thomas Kuhn (1922–1996) published *The Structure of Scientific Revolutions* (1962), we have all become ultraconscious of the concept and significance of the *paradigm*, not just in the scientific context (with which Kuhn was concerned), but in all intellectual and cultural discourse.[1]

A paradigm is a complex network of theories, models, procedures and practices, exemplars, and philosophical assumptions and values that establishes a framework within which scientists in a given field identify and solve problems. A paradigm, in effect, defines a *community* of scientists; it determines their shared working culture as scientists in a branch of science and a shared mentality. A hallmark of a mature science, according to Kuhn, is the emergence of a *dominant* paradigm to which a majority of scientists in that field of science adhere and broadly, although not necessarily in detail, agree on. In particular, they agree on the fundamental philosophical assumptions and values that oversee the science in question; its methods of experimental and analytical inquiry; and its major theories, laws, and principles. A scientist "grows up" inside a paradigm, beginning from his earliest formal training in a science in high school, through undergraduate and graduate schools, through doctoral work into postdoctoral days. Scientists nurtured within and by a paradigm more or less speak the same language, understand the same terms, and read the same texts (which codify the paradigm).

However, rather like a nation's constitution, a paradigm is never complete or entirely unambiguous. There are gaps of ignorance within it that need to be filled—clarifications, interpretations, and unknowns that must be known, and open problems that must be solved. These are the bread-and-butter activities of most practitioners of that science. Kuhn called the sum of these activities *normal science*. In doing normal science, the paradigm as a whole is never called into question; rather, its details are articulated.

We will see, as our story unfolds, that there is much more to Kuhn's theory of paradigms and how it can explain scientific change. We also note that Kuhn's theory has been explored widely and criticized severely.[2] But here, rather as he had postulated paradigms as frameworks for doing science, we can use his theory of paradigms as a framework for interpreting history, to lend some shape to this unfolding history of computer science.

Let us consider, for our immediate purpose, one of his key historical insights. This is the situation in which a paradigm has yet to emerge within a discipline. The absence of a paradigm—the *preparadigmatic* stage—marks a science that is still immature and perhaps even marks uncertainty that it *is* a science. In this condition, there might exist several "competing schools and subschools of thought."[3] They vie with one another, with each school having its own fierce adherents. They may agree on certain aspects of their burgeoning discipline, but they disagree on other vital aspects. In fact, according to Kuhn, leaving aside such fields as mathematics and astronomy, in which the first paradigms reach back to antiquity, this situation is fairly typical in the sciences.[4]

And, in the absence of a shared framework, in the absence of a paradigm, anything goes. Every fact or observation gleaned by the practitioners of an immature science seem relevant, perhaps even equally significant.

III

This was the situation in computing circa 1945. No one had yet ventured to speak of a science of computing, let alone something as precise as a disciplinary name such as computer science. As we have seen, even the word *computer* was not yet widely in place to signify the machine rather than the person. For a science of computing to be spoken of, there had to be some semblance of a paradigm to which the current, few dozen practitioners of the field could pay allegiance. There was no solid evidence of a paradigm—yet.

On the other hand, certain elements had emerged as common ground—in fact, some reaching back to Babbage himself.

First, the central focus of all the protagonists in this story so far, beginning with Babbage, was a machine to perform automatic computation: a computational artifact (see Prologue). This artifact was basically a material one, and so the physical technology was always at the forefront in the minds of the people involved. Yet (again, beginning with Babbage and his sometime collaborator Lovelace), the material artifact was not an island of its own. Unlike almost all material artifacts that had ever been invented and built before, there was an intellectual activity involved in preparing a problem to be solved by automatic computing machines. As yet, there was no agreed-on name for this activity or its product. The term *program* was still some way off.

Second, a fundamental organization of an automatic computing machine—its *internal architecture*—had been clarified: there must be a means of providing the machine with information, and a means by which the results of computation could be communicated to the user—input and output devices. There must be a store or memory to hold the information to be used in a computation or the results of computation. There must be an arithmetic unit that can actually carry out the computations. Even the possibility of parallel processing—using two more arithmetic units, even multiple input and output devices—was "in the air." There was also the possibility of specialized units for specific kinds of mathematical operations such as multiplication and the extraction of square roots, or for operations to "look up" mathematical tables. There must be a means for controlling the execution of a computational task and a means for specifying what the computational task is to be.

Third, the distinction between special-purpose and general-purpose computers was rather vague. The machines that had been conceived or actually built and used thus far were designed to perform specific kinds of computational tasks (some very specific, some spanning a range of problems within a problem class). The dominant class of problems for which computing machines were developed, up to this point, were mathematical or, at least, numeric. The Colossus, in contrast, was specialized toward the class of logical (or, equivalently, Boolean) problems. A general-purpose machine must provide capabilities to process tasks spanning different classes of problems. This means that the physical machine itself must provide the means for the efficient execution of these different tasks. Such capability was yet lacking.

Fourth, as noted earlier, the words *programmable* and *computer program* had yet to emerge. The terms still in common use circa 1945 were "paper tape controlled" or "plugboard controlled". Zuse, as we have seen, used the term "computational plan", which is perhaps closest to *program*. Aiken and Hopper spoke of "sequence tape". But, the *idea* of programmability, reaching back to Babbage and Lovelace, was, circa 1945, a shared concept.

Fifth, and last, certain other terms had emerged to form the nucleus of a computing vocabulary: "floating-point representation", "binary", and "binary coded decimal" in the

context of numbers. Another was "register" to signify the individual units of information storage, linked either directly with arithmetic units or as collections to serve as the
machine's memory.

This much seemed to be agreed on. However, there were different opinions and views
on other fundamental matters. How should numbers be represented? Some had come to
appreciate the advantages of binary notation whereas others clung to the familiar decimal
system. How large should the unit of information storage (in present-centered language,
the *word size*) be? What should be the form of the computational plan?

Then there was the matter of the physical technology of computers. Purely mechanical technology—gears, levers, cams, sprocket and chain, the stuff of kinematics, the
domain of mechanical engineering—still prevailed, but had also given way to the guile
of electrical technology. Electrical relays and electromagnets had become the preferred
and trusted physical basis for building computing machines. There was even an elegant
mathematics—Boolean algebra—that could be applied to the design of binary switching
circuits out of which electrical components would be made.

However, World War II raged on, and the imperatives of faster means of computation became more urgent, the lure of *electronic* circuit elements became increasingly more
attractive. On August 14, 1945, 5 days after America exploded its second atomic bomb
upon Nagasaki, the Japanese surrendered. The Germans had already surrendered in May.
World War II was finally over. The state of computing was scarcely in the minds of anyone
in the world, save for a few dozen of those who were involved in its development before
and during the war years—in America, Britain, and Germany. But for these few people,
the state of computing and computing machines *mattered*. In the light of a Kuhnian
framework, the situation, however, was very much in a preparadigmatic state.

IV

An aspect of this preparadigmatic state included the larger theoretical questions: What
kind of discipline was computing? Was it a discipline at all?

We noted at the beginning of this book that scientists, as a community, agree implicitly and broadly that what makes a discipline scientific is, above all, its methodology (see
Prologue, Section V)—the use of observation, experimentation, and reasoning; a critical
stance; and an ever-preparedness to treat explanations (in the form of hypotheses, theories,
laws, or models) as tentative and to discard or revise them if the evidence demands this.

In the artificial sciences, explanations are about artifacts, not nature. Here, scientists
address the question whether such and such an artifact satisfies its intended purpose (see
Prologue, Section III). We also noted that, in the case of artifacts of any reasonable complexity, design and implementation are activities that lie at the heart of the relevant artificial sciences, activities missing in the natural sciences. Designs serve as theories about a

particular artifact (or class of artifacts), and implementations serve as experiments to test the validity of the theories (see Prologue, Section VI).

We have observed thus far in this story the emergence of several of these features. From as far back as Charles Babbage, we see, for example, the separation of design from implementation. In fact, in Babbage's case, it was all design, never implementation. It was left to others to implement the Difference Engine and to test Babbage's theory. The Analytical Engine was detailed in theory, but the theory was never tested.

With the advent of electromechanical machines, we observe the strongly empirical/experimental flavor of computing research. The families of machines, whether at Bell Laboratories, IBM, Bletchley Park, or Zuse's workplace in Germany, reveal the emphasis on building individual, specific machines; ascertaining their appropriateness for their intended purposes; revising or modifying the design in the light of their performance; or even creating a new design because of changes in purposes and new environmental factors (such as the availability of new technologies).

Although computing research had enjoyed a very short life thus far, evolution was in evidence. Phylogenies were created. However, this evolutionary process was not Darwinian, for the latter demands lack of purpose, randomness, chance. Rather, it was evolution driven by purpose. Each member of an evolutionary family was the product of an intended goal or purpose, a design that constituted a theory of the proposed artifact— and a hypothesis that if the artifact was built according to the design, it would satisfy the intended purpose; and an implementation that tested the theory followed by modification or revision of the design as a result of the experiment or modified purposes; and a new design. Each design became a theory of (or for) a particular computing machine. Each implementation became an extended experiment that tested the associated theory.

Almost as an aside stood Alan Turing's work. His abstract machine was a purely logico-mathematical device, albeit a device quite alien to most mathematicians and logicians of the time. At this stage of our story, Turing's machine stands in splendid isolation from the empirical, experimental design-as-theory, implementation-as-experiment work that was going on in Britain, the United States, and Germany before and during the war years. The Turing machine had had no impact on the design of computing machines thus far. Even in Bletchley Park, despite the fact that Turing had worked there, despite the fact that many of his colleagues there knew of his 1936 paper, the architecture of the Colossus was quite uninfluenced by Turing's machine.[5]

On the other hand, the inventors and designers of computing machines during the 1930s and throughout the war years, be they mathematicians, physicists, astronomers, or engineers, clearly envisioned their machines as mathematical and scientific (and, in the case of the Colossus, logical) instruments. In *this* sense, they were mathematical machines.

The data processing, punched-card machines pioneered by Hollerith and evolved by such companies as IBM during the first third of the 20th century were, if not mathematical, certainly *number processors*. So mathematics in some form or another was the central preoccupation of these designers. Unlike the Turing machine, though, they were *real* artifacts. They had to be built. And machine building was the stuff of engineering.

This is where matters stood circa 1945. If people recognized that a discipline of computing was emerging, they had no name for it, nor was there a firmly established shared framework, a paradigm, in place. At best, these early pioneers may have thought their unnamed craft lay in a kind of no-man's land between a new kind of mathematics and a new kind of engineering.

NOTES

1. T. S. Kuhn. (1970). *The structure of scientific revolutions* (2nd ed.) Chicago, IL: University of Chicago Press (original work published 1962).

2. The literature on Kuhn's theory of paradigms is vast. An early set of responses is the collection of essays in I. Lakatos & A. Musgrave. (Eds.). (1970). *Criticism and the growth of knowledge*. Cambridge, UK: Cambridge University Press. An important later critique is L. Laudan. (1977). *Progress and its problems*. Los Angeles, CA: University of California Press. See also G. Gutting. (1980). *Paradigms and revolutions*. Notre Dame, IN: University of Notre Dame Press. For a more recent critical study of Kuhn, see S. Fuller. (2000). *Thomas Kuhn: A philosophical history for our times*. Chicago, IL: University of Chicago Press. This book also has an extensive bibliography on Kuhn and his theory. Kuhn's own thoughts following the publication of the second edition of *Structure*, in response to his critics, are published in J. Conant & J. Haugeland. (Eds.). (2000). *The road since* Structure. Chicago, IL: University of Chicago Press.

3. Kuhn, op cit., p. 12.

4. Ibid., p. 15.

5. There was an idea that Max Newman, the principle architect of the Colossus, was influenced by Turing's work, but this claim was never substantiated. See B. Randell (1980), "The Colossus". In N. Metropolis, J.S. Howlett, & G.-C. Rota (Eds.). *A history of computing in the twentieth century*. (pp. 47–92). New York: Academic Press.

7

A Tangled Web of Inventions

⌒ ———————————————————————————————————————

I

ON FEBRUARY 15, 1946, a giant of a machine called the *ENIAC*, an acronym for Electronic Numerical Integrator And Computer, was commissioned at a ceremony at the Moore School of Electrical Engineering at the University of Pennsylvania, Philadelphia.

The name is noteworthy. We see that the word *computer*—to mean the machine and not the person—had cautiously entered the emerging vocabulary of computer culture. Bell Laboratories named one of its machines Complex Computer; another, Ballistic Computer (see Chapter 5, Section I). Still, the embryonic world of computing was hesitant; the terms "calculator", "calculating machine", "computing machine", and "computing engine" still prevailed. The ENIAC's full name (which, of course, would never be used after the acronym was established) seemed, at last, to flaunt the fact that this machine had a definite identity, that it was a computer.

The tale of the ENIAC is a fascinating tale in its own right, but it is also a very important tale. Computer scientists and engineers of later times may be ignorant about the Bell Laboratories machines, they may be hazy about the Harvard Mark series, they may have only an inkling about Babbage's dream machines, but they will more than likely have heard about the ENIAC. Why was this so? What was it about the ENIAC that admits its story into the larger story?

It was not the first *electronic* computer; the Colossus preceded the ENIAC by 2 years. True, no one outside the Bletchley Park community knew about the Colossus, but from a historical perspective, for historians writing about the state of computing in the 1940s, the Colossus clearly took precedence over the ENIAC. In fact (as we will soon see), there was another electronic computer built in America that preceded the ENIAC. Nor was the ENIAC the first *programmable* computer. Zuse's Z3 and Aiken's Harvard Mark I, as well as the Colossus, well preceded the ENIAC in this realm.

As for that other Holy Grail, *general purposeness*, this was, as we have noted, an elusive target (see Chapter 6, Section III). No one would claim that the Colossus was general purpose; it had been described as a "Boolean calculating machine" (see Chapter 6, Section XIII).[1] But, the ENIAC provoked more uncertainty. For one person who was intimately involved in its design and construction, the ENIAC was "a general-purpose scientific computer"[2]—that is, a computer capable of solving, very fast, a wide variety of scientific, mathematical, and engineering problems.[3] For another major participant in the ENIAC project, it was "a mathematical instrument."[4] A later writer somewhat extravagantly called it a "universal electronic calculator."[5] A more tempered assessment by a computer scientist and historian of computing spoke of the ENIAC as comparable with the Colossus; both were special-purpose machines—the former specialized for numeric computation; the latter, for Boolean calculations.[6]

Perhaps, then, it seems reasonable to claim that the ENIAC was a general-purpose *numeric* computer, specialized for solving mathematical and scientific problems using methods of numeric analysis. It was an analytical engine as Babbage had dreamed of.

However, the ENIAC's historical significance, its *originality*, lay in other directions. There was, first, its sheer scale physically, technologically, and computationally. Physically, the machine was a mammoth, occupying three walls of a 30-foot-by-50-foot room and much of the central space. Technologically, it used 18,000 vacuum tubes of 16 different types.[7] Added to that, it used 70,000 resistors, 10,000 capacitors, 1500 relays, and 6000 manual switches.[8] This was an order of technological complexity far in excess of anything achieved in computing before. And, computationally, because of its electronic technology, it was vastly faster than any other previous computing machines— about 1000 times faster than its nearest competitor, the electromechanical Harvard Mark I.[9]

The significance of using 18,000 vacuum tubes from the perspective of reliability is worth noting. The ENIAC was a synchronous machine, pulsed by a clock signal every 10 microseconds. If any one of these vacuum tubes malfunctioned, an error would occur every 10 microseconds. With this many tubes, the reliability of the components was of the essence. Even the failure of a single vacuum tube could cause a digit to be erroneous.[10] By carefully selecting rigidly tested components that were then operated well below their "normal ratings,"[11] the reliability of the computer was maintained at an acceptable level. Writing several months after its commission, Arthur Burks (1915–2008)—a mathematician who would later become known as much as a computer theorist and philosopher of science, as one of the ENIAC's lead engineers—commented that, after the initial phase of testing, the failure rate was about two or three per week. These failures, however, could be identified and corrected quickly by operators thoroughly conversant with the ENIAC design so that, in effect, only a few hours were lost per week as a result of failures.[12]

This, then, was one of the ENIAC's major achievements: it demonstrated the *viability* of large-scale use of electronic components in digital computers. It heralded the viability and the advent of large-scale electronic digital computers.

The other historically significant factor was that the ENIAC had *consequences*. Experience with its design, especially its organizational principles, and the resulting dissatisfaction showed the way for a new, crucial concept: the stored-program computer (discussed much more later). This concept was like the crucial missing piece of a jigsaw puzzle. It was instrumental in the formation of a style for the logical and functional organization of computers—for computer architecture (in present-centered language). So compelling was this style, so quickly was it accepted by the fledgling computer culture of its time, that it became the foundation of the first genuine paradigm in computing (in Thomas Kuhn's sense; see Chapter 6). As we will see, discontent with the ENIAC was a catalyst that led to the birth of computer science.

For these various reasons—its general-purposeness in the domain of numeric computation; its scale of physical size, technological complexity, and speed of operation; its consequence for the making of the paradigm for a science of computing—the ENIAC has a compelling place in our story. But there is more. The story of the ENIAC, both in terms of the genesis of its principles—that is, the past that fed into it—and the future it helped to shape form a tangled web of ideas, concepts, insights, and personalities. We learn much about the *ontogeny* of artifacts (to use a biological term)—its developmental history—from the story of the ENIAC.[13]

II

The ENIAC was, of course, a child of World War II, although it never saw wartime action. The ENIAC project began in June 1943 and the machine was commissioned in February 1946, exactly 6 months after the Japanese surrender and the end of the war. The project began in the Ballistics Research Laboratory (BRL) of the Aberdeen Proving Ground in Maryland. With the American entry into the war in December 1941, this laboratory established a scientific advisory committee of some of the country's leading scientists.[14] One of them was Hungarian-born John von Neumann (1903–1957), mathematician extraordinaire, a professor at the Institute of Advanced Study, Princeton (along with the likes of Einstein and Gödel), and an influential figure in the corridors of power in Washington, DC.

Among the scientists—mathematicians, physicists, chemists, astronomers, and astrophysicists—assembled as BRL's scientific staff for the war effort was the young Herman Goldstine (1913–2004), an assistant professor of mathematics at the University of Michigan until 1942, when he was called into wartime service. His charge at the BRL was ballistic computation.[15]

Ballistic computation, solving differential equations to compute ballistic trajectories, demanded computing machines. The aim of these computations was to prepare firing tables that, for a particular shell, meant that up to some 3000 trajectories had to be computed for a particular range of initial firing conditions, such as muzzle velocity and firing angle.[16]

As it happened, the Aberdeen Proving Ground had acquired, in 1935 (well before the BRL was founded) a "copy" of a machine called the *differential analyzer* that was quite unlike the kind of computers developed in places like Bell Laboratories or Harvard. The differential analyzer was an *analog* computer and, as the war came to America, was considered the most powerful device for the solution of differential equations, which was what it was designed expressly to do.

In 1931, an engineer named Vannevar Bush (1890–1974), a professor in the department of electrical engineering at MIT in Cambridge, Massachusetts, had invented the differential analyzer, a machine powered by an electric motor, but otherwise a purely mechanical device. It was an analog machine because, rather than transform an analytical expression (such as a differential equation) into a digital computational problem (as was the tradition ever since Babbage), the mathematical behavior of the "system" of interest (a ballistic trajectory, for example) would be modeled by another physical system with behavior that corresponded exactly (or as approximately as close as possible) to the system of interest. The model served as an *analog* to the problem system. By manipulating the model, the desired computation would be performed.

Just as the numeric "digital style" of computing reached back to Victorian Britain so also did the "analog style." The *doyen* of late Victorian British science, Scottish mathematical physicist William Thomson, Lord Kelvin (1824–1907), conceived, in 1876, the "harmonic analyzer" for solving equations that described tidal behavior.[17] Kelvin's harmonic analyzer was never actually built. In any case, Bush, apparently unaware of Kelvin's ideas until much later, went his own way to build his differential analyzer.[18]

The principal computing unit in the differential analyzer was comprised of a set of six "integrators" for performing integration, the means by which differential equations would be solved. In addition, systems of gears performed the four arithmetic operations.[19] A differential equation to be solved for y as a function of x, say, would be prepared in the form of one or more integrals. An integrator would be supplied with values of x, the variable of integration, and y, the integrand, and would produce the value of $\int y dx$. The input values would be translated into amounts of physical movements (linear displacements, angular rotations) of disks, wheels, gears, shafts, and styluses, although the output could also be printed out on a printer. The whole system was driven electrically by the main shaft rotated by an electric motor, with this shaft representing the independent variable x.[20] Other than this, the machine's components and their interconnections were entirely mechanical.

In the words of Bush's biographer, the differential analyzer was an "imposing contraption" yet "brutish."[21] Its operation would cause metal to "clank" with metal.[22] Setting up a problem for solution entailed disassembling the machine and reassembling it to set the linear and angular displacements of its mechanical components to represent the input values; various adjustments would be made to the components. More specifically, solving a particular set of differential equations involved the following steps:

> *Problem preparation*: The equation would be transformed into an integral form. *Determination of the interconnections of the units*: This was undertaken to solve the equation. *Manual connection of the physical units*: This entailed placing gear wheels, addition units, and shafts into positions and tightening them manually. *Problem running*: This necessitated the setup of the initial conditions corresponding to the initial values of the variables.

Typically, a problem setup would take 2 or 3 days.[23] To obviate some of these problems, in a second version of the MIT differential analyzer built by Bush and his student (and, later, colleague) Samuel Caldwell (1904–1960), and completed in 1942, transmission of the values of variables through shafts and gears was replaced by electrical methods. Very soon thereafter, circumstances would overtake the differential analyzer completely.

III

During the 1930s, Bush's differential analyzer attracted a great deal of attention. It was a "smashing success" according to Bush's biographer.[24] As we have noted, the Aberdeen Proving Ground acquired its own copy of the machine in 1935. Early during the 1940s, the Moore School of Electrical Engineering of the University of Pennsylvania in Philadelphia took charge of this machine on behalf of the BRL and started a program to train people in ballistic computation—especially women who had science degrees.[25] In September 1942, Goldstine was put in charge of this operation at the Moore School,[26] and thus was established the nexus between the Moore School of Electrical Engineering and the BRL—more fatefully, between the Moore School and computers. Through the exigencies and happenstance of wartime decisions, the Moore School planted for itself a secure place in the history of computing.

After America entered World War II, the school became a center for computing firing tables.[27] The differential analyzer was fully occupied. But then, as Burks recalled, a certain John Mauchly (1903–1980) suggested to Goldstine that these firing tables could be compiled must faster with electronic devices. On Goldstine's request, Mauchly and two colleagues, Presper Eckert (1919–1995) and John Brainerd (1904–1988), wrote a proposal for an "electronic differential analyzer" in April 1943, for which it was calculated that this machine would compute ballistic trajectories 10 times faster than the electromechanical differential analyzer. The proposal was submitted on behalf of the Moore School to the BRL.[28]

Thus, two new protagonists enter this story, Mauchly and Eckert, whose names are for-ever twinned, as are other scientific "couples" in the annals of science, such as Cockcroft and Walton in atomic physics, Watson and Crick in molecular biology, Yang and Lee in theoretical physics, and Hardy and Littlewood in pure mathematics.

Mauchly was a physicist who, at the time the war broke out, was on the physics faculty at Ursinus College, a liberal arts college just outside Philadelphia, and a person with a long-standing interest in automatic computing. Eckert (no relation to Wallace Eckert [see Chapter 5, Section V]) was a graduate student in electrical engineering, "undoubt-edly the best electronic engineer in the Moore School."[29] The third author of the pro-posal, Brainerd, was a professor of electrical engineering at the Moore School, with a deep interest in using the differential analyzer. Goldstine persuaded the powers that be in the BRL to finance the project, which they did. The electronic differential analyzer later became the ENIAC.[30]

So began a new chapter of this story, but a chapter embedded in a tangled web of means and ends, of people and personalities, of insights and ideas, of controversies.

IV

This part of the story must begin, in 1939/1940, in Ames, Iowa, with another pair of collaborators: John Vincent Atanasoff (1903–1995) and Clifford Berry (1918–1963). The former was on the faculty of the physics department at Iowa State College (later Iowa State University); the latter, a just-graduated electrical engineer and Atanasoff's graduate student in physics. An unpublished memorandum authored by Atanasoff in 1940 spoke of the occurrence of systems of linear simultaneous algebraic equations in many fields of physics, technology, and statistics, and the necessity of solving such equations speedily and accurately.[31]

The time to solve such equations of even moderate complexity manually—by a (human) computer[32]—was prohibitively large; equations containing a very large num-ber of "unknowns" (that is, variables) were well nigh unapproachable. Like almost all his predecessors who have appeared in this story, Atanasoff was dissatisfied with the status quo. He sought help from automata. Some 7 years earlier, Atanasoff wrote in a 1940 memorandum that he had begun to investigate the possibility of automating the solution to such problems,[33] although it was only in 1939 that he began an actual project to build a computer for solving linear simultaneous equations with Berry as assistant. This machine was completed in 1942. Later, it would be called the *Atanasoff–Berry Computer* (ABC).[34]

However, Atanasoff's approach differed in some respects from his contemporaries. He considered, then discarded, punched-card tabulators because of their insufficient com-putational power. He dwelled on binary computation and concluded that it was supe-rior to other number systems. He then considered the design of the actual mechanisms to use and decided, first, that he would use small electrical condensers (capacitors, in present-centered language) to represent the binary digits o and 1—a positive charge representing 1 and a negative charge, o.[35] As for the computing unit, it would be made of vacuum tubes.[36]

The ABC became an operational electronic digital computer in 1942, capable of performing the task (up to some limit) it was designed to do. Later, it would be acknowledged as the world's *first* operational electronic digital computer, preceding the Colossus. More important, for this story, it embodied a number of noteworthy innovations.

First, as noted, vacuum tube circuits were used for the computational (arithmetic) units. By the mid 1930s, the use of vacuum tubes, resisters, and capacitors in radios was well established. However, these circuits operated in analog or continuous mode. Digital circuit elements such as flip-flops, counters, and simple switching circuits had also been implemented, but the digital use of vacuum tubes for building such circuits was quite rare.[37]

Second, memory was implemented in the form of electrical condensers (capacitors) mounted on two rotating Bakelite drums 8 inches in diameter and 11 inches long. A positive charge on a condenser represented 1; a negative charge, o. Each drum could store 30 50-bit numbers. As the drum rotated, these numbers could be read, processed, and replaced serially. The two drums were mounted on the same axle so that they could operate synchronously.

Third, the ABC was designed to solve simultaneous linear equations by the widely used method of Gaussian elimination. For this purpose, the coefficients in the equations were read from punched cards onto the drums. By a succession of binary additions, subtractions, and shifting binary numbers right or left, the computation would be performed.

Fourth, the computation units consisted of 30 add–subtract units that took numbers from the storage drums and performed the adds or subtracts in parallel. Circuits were also available for shifting binary numbers. There were no separate circuits for multiplication or division.

Fifth, internally, the ABC was a binary machine. However, input data fed to the computer through punched cards were in decimal form, and so decimal-to-binary conversions were done before numbers were stored on the drums; conversely, binary-to-decimal conversions were performed before outputting results in decimal form. These outputs were displayed on dials.[38]

Sixth, and last, intermediate results were stored in binary form on cards. For this purpose, Atanasoff recorded binary digits on the card with electric sparks that carbonized the card at those locations. These binary digits could then be read by applying a voltage to the card because a carbonized spot provided less resistance to the reading voltage than a spot that had not been carbonized.[39]

When the ABC was completed, all components worked well except the electric spark mechanism, which would fail occasionally. Because of this, the ABC could solve small sets of equations correctly, but not large ones because the latter demanded very large numbers of binary digits to be both recorded as intermediate results and then read. It was because of this weakness that the ABC was almost (but only almost) fully operational. Atanasoff and Berry never resolved this problem. In fall 1942, they were both called into war research. Neither returned to Iowa State College after the war, and the ABC was eventually dismantled.[40] Yet, as would be acknowledged later, in designing and building the ABC, Atanasoff and Berry demonstrated the viability of electronic switching circuits across a range of units desirable in a computer—to perform arithmetic operations, base conversions, and control functions.

Here was a science of the artificial in action (see Prologue, Section VI): a design for a particular computer representing a theory of the machine, the purpose of which was the solution of linear algebraic equations; a theory that embedded the logical organization of the computer (its architecture) and the physical characteristics of its parts; and an implementation that afforded the crucial experiment to test whether a computer built according to the design would serve its intended purpose. The design constituted a theory of an *individual* machine (see Prologue, Section VI). The implementation constituted an experiment about such a singular theory, and the implementation revealed not only the broad validity of the design-as-theory, but also where the theory–experiment ensemble failed—in the fact that the machine was limited to small systems of equations. The next logical step would be either to modify the design or the implementation to eliminate the error. But, as noted, this never happened because of the exigencies of war.

Atanasoff also realized that the ABC could do more than solve systems of linear equations. Becoming aware, in spring 1941, of the improved differential analyzer being built by Bush and Caldwell, he realized that his machine could also be used to solve differential equations by way of numeric integration.[41]

V

In June 1941, Mauchly, then a physics faculty member at Ursinus College, visited Atanasoff in Ames, Iowa, to learn about the ABC, which was still a work in progress at that time. The two had met at a scientific conference in December 1940, at which time Mauchly had come to know of Atanasoff's computer project. In fact, even before his visit to Ames, Mauchly was told by Atanasoff, in a letter written in May 1941, of the idea of using the ABC to solve differential equations.[42]

During the 4 days Mauchly stayed in Ames, he had extensive opportunity to examine the ABC and hold discussions with his host about electronic computers.[43] Mauchly also read, and made notes from, Atanasoff's memorandum of August 1940.[44]

In September 1941, Mauchly wrote to Atanasoff of his "hope" to "outdo the analyzer electronically." He mentioned some "different ideas" that had occurred to him, some of which combined Atanasoff's ideas with others, some quite different.[45] More pointedly, he asked Atanasoff whether the latter would object to his (Mauchly's) incorporating some of the ABC's features into his own design.[46]

Clearly, then, when Mauchly proposed to Goldstine his idea of an electronic version of the differential analyzer and when, in August 1942, he wrote his short memorandum *The Use of High Speed Vacuum Tube Devices for Calculating*,[47] he not only had considerable knowledge of both the differential analyzer (he had enrolled in a defense training course at the Moore School soon after his visit to Iowa in June 1941) and the ABC, he was also imagining how to use features of the ABC in his own concept of an electronic computer. His memorandum of 1942 contained a detailed discussion of the advantages of using electronic circuitry but contained no reference to Atanasoff's work. We thus see that the ENIAC had its genesis in Mauchly's *dissatisfaction* with the Bush differential analyzer. However, this dissatisfaction may itself have been triggered by his encounter with Atanasoff and the ABC.

If Mauchly was the originator of the *idea* of a digital electronic version of the differential analyzer and was the overall architect of the ENIAC, the mind behind its physical *realization* was Presper Eckert. As chief engineer of the ENIAC project, he was its "mainspring," according to Goldstine who, as the representative of the BRL, oversaw the entire enterprise.[48] Eckert, Goldstine wrote, was omnipresent, and it was his energy that imbued the project with its "integrity" and guaranteed its success.[49]

Thus, in conceiving the artifact, Mauchly was the principal designer and Eckert was the principal implementer. Eckert, in turn, assembled a group of talented engineering minds including, most notably, Arthur Burks and Adele Goldstine (1920–1964), a mathematician and Herman Goldstine's wife, respectively.[50]

Thus far, we have seen that Mauchly's idea of an electronic differential analyzer was prompted by his encounter with both Bush's invention and Atanasoff's ideas. However, the ENIAC is a remarkable case study in how the past infiltrates the present in creative work. To understand this, let us consider the nature of this computer.

VI

Architecturally, the ENIAC consisted of four distinct classes of units. In present-centered language, they were the input/output units, a read/write memory, a computational unit, and a control unit (Figure 7.1).

Data were fed to the machine from a punched-card reader, and from there to a set of relays called, collectively, the *constant transmitter*, which in modern terms served as an input buffer. Conversely, the result of a computation was sent through the "printer" (a misnomer for the ENIAC's output control device) to a card punch.

The ENIAC's memory comprised a set of 20 "accumulators," each of which could hold a signed, 10-digit decimal number. It was, thus, a decimal computer with a memory capacity of 20 decimal numbers. Additional storage capacity of up to 300 numbers was provided by way of three "function tables," which could hold read-only tabulated data. The function values were set to values by means of manual switches.

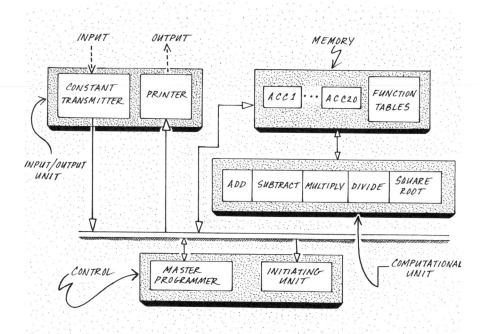

FIGURE 7.1 Architecture of the ENIAC. ACC, accumulator. Adapted by permission of the publisher from S. Dasgupta, *Technology and Creativity*, © 1996 Oxford University Press, Fig. 8.5.

The word *accumulator* enters the language of computer culture. It once meant a capacitor—a device for storing electric power. This use of the word is now largely obsolete, although in Britain it is still sometimes used to mean a battery. It seems plausible that the word was appropriated into the language of computer design from this electrical context. In the realm of digital computers, accumulator came to refer to a unit that combined a storage register with arithmetic circuits; it could store a number in the register and, when another number was received from elsewhere in the computer (usually, its main memory), it would add (or subtract) the two and store the result back in the accumulator register.[51] In the ENIAC, each accumulator could store a 10-digit, signed number.[52]

Other computing capabilities were provided by means of a multiplication unit and a divider/square root extractor. Both these units performed their operations on the values held in the accumulators and placed their results back into the accumulators.

The different units were controlled individually by switches that could be set manually. To perform a computation, the switches associated with the relevant unit would be set to specify which operations were to be performed. The various units would also be connected by means of cables to enable transmission of signals between the units. The "initiating unit" was responsible for clearing the computer, turning on power, and initiating a task. Last, the sequencing of these operations would be established by setting switches on the "master programming unit."

The ENIAC designers seem to be the earliest users of some variant of the word *program* (or programme, in British English spelling) in the context of computers. The *Oxford English Dictionary* finds the earliest appearance of the word in computing in a 1945 report on the ENIAC by Eckert, Mauchly, Goldstine, and Brainerd in which they expressed a desire to "program" the accumulator in a certain way.[53] And, in summer 1946, the Moore School offered a course on Theory and Design of Electronic Computers, probably the first formal course on electronic computers.[54] The *Oxford English Dictionary* tells us that, in his lectures, Presper Eckert spoke of "automatic checking" that "may be programmed" into the computer as an integral component as part of the problem being solved.[55]

To understand the general nature of this "programming" of the ENIAC, let us consider a trivial example.[56]

Suppose it is required to produce a table of squares for $n = 0, 1, \ldots, 99$. Assume first that accumulator 1 already contains some value n and accumulator 2 contains n^2. The machine is next to compute $(n + 1)$ and $(n + 1)^2$. It does so as follows:

Set a switch so that the initiation unit transmits a signal that causes accumulator 1 to transmit its contents twice and accumulator 2 to receive these contents twice. The result is that accumulator 2 will contain $(n^2 + 2n)$. If now a switch is set that causes the constant transmitter to send a 1 to both accumulators, then accumulator 1 will contain $(n + 1)$ and accumulator 2 will have $(n^2 + 2n + 1) = (n + 1)^2$.

This "program" can be used *iteratively* to build a table of squares by setting switches in the master programmer. Initially the accumulators have been set to 0. The initiation unit enables the master programmer to start counting the number of outputs, initiate the first output (that is, record $n = 0, n^2 = 0$), and activate the first computation. This causes the accumulators to send and receive values as described. The first cycle of the iteration produces $n = 1, n^2 = 1$. The iterative process continues until 100 pulses have been emitted by the master programmer. The output, a table of squares for numbers 0, 1, ..., 99 is punched out on cards.

VII

At this point in the ENIAC story, a small diversion is necessary. In the history of biological thought, there is a celebrated (if controversial) theory that actually goes back to Aristotle (384–322 BCE) but was given modern shape by some 19th-century German biologists, most notably Ernst Haeckel (1834–1919). This is the so-called law of recapitulation (also called the biogenetic law), and it is pithily expressed as *ontogeny recapitulates phylogeny*—meaning that, in the development from embryo to adult stage (ontogeny), an organism passes through stages resembling the successive stages in the evolution (phylogeny) of its remote ancestors.[57]

In the realm of artifacts (and here I am speaking of technological artifacts, "useful things"), we also speak of their evolutionary history.[58] Artifacts, of course, neither evolve "naturally" nor do they develop from embryonic to mature state "organically." They are created things, reflecting their creators' mental states—dissatisfaction, curiosity, purposiveness. Yet, a kind of analogy with the law of recapitulation applies to artifacts; in the realm of artifacts, *phylogeny conditions ontogeny.*[59]

This does not mean that the process by which an artifact comes into existence passes through stages that reflect the phylogeny of ancestor artifacts. Rather, it means that the thinking an inventor, designer, or engineer puts into the creative act will embody *knowledge of past artifacts.* This knowledge shapes the invention process.

The ENIAC is a vivid example of this phylogeny law of artifacts.

VIII

Figure 7.2 shows the landmarks in the phylogeny of the ENIAC.[60] Perhaps the most notable of the evolutionary pathways shown here involves the use of vacuum tubes. These, used widely during the 1930s as analog circuit elements in radio, were used (as we have seen) in the ABC as digital circuit elements, in its arithmetic and control circuits. We recall that Mauchly was much familiar with Atanasoff's project. In the ENIAC, the use of vacuum tubes was extended beyond the computational unit to the read/write memory, the accumulators.

Another notable pathway was the one depicted on the rightmost side of Figure 7.2: the influence of the overall architecture of the differential analyzer on the ENIAC architecture. Mauchly's original intention was to outperform the differential analyzer by electronic means. He stated this in a letter to Atanasoff in September 1941.[61] His memorandum of 1942 reiterated this goal.[62] The ENIAC project was driven by this goal. And the report submitted by Mauchly, Eckert, and Brainerd to the BRL in April 1943, the eve of the beginning of the ENIAC project, emphasized this connection. But, the relationship between the differential analyzer and the ENIAC went beyond this sense of dissatisfaction with the one leading to the other; it was more than "competitiveness" between the analyzer and the proposed machine. The ENIAC designers drew on the differential analyzer's organization as an analogical source for the ENIAC's design[63]; just as the differential analyzer could be envisioned as a set of interconnected "submachines," along the same lines the proposed ENIAC would comprise a collection of interconnected units. And, indeed, when the ENIAC was completed, the analogy between the internal organization of one with the other held.[64]

There are mappings between units of one and the other. Corresponding to input tables in the analyzer are the function tables and constant transmitter in the ENIAC. The latter's printer corresponds to the former's output table and printer; the differential analyzer's integrators mapped to the ENIAC's accumulator–arithmetic unit complex. There was even a correspondence between the interconnections of the shafts in the analyzer and those connecting the ENIAC units.[65]

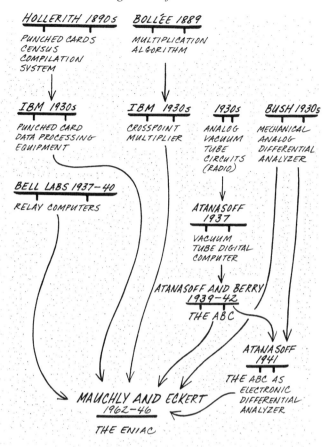

FIGURE 7.2 Phylogeny of the ENIAC. Adapted by permission of the publisher from S. Dasgupta, *Technology and Creativity*, © 1996. Oxford University Press, Fig. 8.7.

One other phylogenetic feature is noteworthy: the genesis of the ENIAC's multiplier. In terms of the amount of circuitry, this was the single most complicated unit in the machine. In fact, this multiplier was an electronic implementation of a fast multiplication algorithm invented in 1889 by the French inventor–manufacturer Léon Bollée (1830–1913). This algorithm, which Bollée implemented in his own mechanical multiplication machine of 1899, was used in later machines, including electromechanical calculators[66]—including the IBM 601 multiplier, one of that company's family of data processing machines and considered the most powerful commercially available data processing device in the 1930s.[67] There were strong similarities between the multiplication procedure implemented in the ENIAC and that used in the IBM 601.[68]

Last, the IBM plugboard concept was used by the ENIAC designers to implement their problem setup procedure—their method of programming. When a problem had been transformed into a form suitable for the ENIAC, the units would be interconnected and their switches set to enable the execution of the desired task. The ENIAC problem setup procedure was derived from, and an extension of, the IBM plugboard procedure.[69]

IX

The ENIAC, then, was spun out of a web of past inventions. This itself is not especially unusual; phylogeny conditions ontogeny—and this, incidentally, is true as much in the realms of science, art, poetry, and fiction as in technological invention and design.

But the web in which the ENIAC was spun was tangled for other reasons, which had to do with the following kinds of questions about *inventionhood*. Who invented the first electronic computer? And who invented the ENIAC? These kinds of questions are of great interest to historians of science and technology, and to those who study creativity. In the case of the ENIAC, they were also of legal interest—hence the tangled web.

The legal aspect stemmed from a long-drawn-out and celebrated court trial over the ENIAC patent. The issue before the court was the validity of a patent, applied for in 1947 and granted in 1964, to Presper Eckert and John Mauchly for their "invention" of the ENIAC. In 1967, a lawsuit was filed by Honeywell Corporation against Sperry Rand concerning the ENIAC patent. Sperry Rand entered the picture in the often-tortuous ways of corporate mergers and acquisitions. In 1948, Mauchly and Eckert formed the Eckert Mauchly Computer Corporation.[70] This company was acquired by Remington Rand in 1950, which itself merged with Sperry Gyroscope to form Sperry Rand in 1955.[71] Many of the patent rights on the ENIAC awarded to Eckert and Mauchly were acquired by Sperry Rand. Honeywell's suit challenged the very validity of the ENIAC patent. To add to the complications over inventionhood, as part of the same lawsuit, some other leading participants in the ENIAC project, including Arthur Burks, also filed claims as co-inventors of the ENIAC, along with Eckert and Mauchly.[72]

The ruling by Judge Earl Larson had many components to it, but the ones of immediate interest to our story were the following points. First, the judge stated that Eckert and Mauchly were the sole co-inventors of the ENIAC and that Burks and others had no claims as co-inventors.[73] Second, the judge also found that Eckert and Mauchly did not *themselves* invent "automatic electronic computing," but rather derived their ideas from "one Dr. John Vincent Atanasoff."[74] This ruling rendered the ENIAC patent invalid.

Third, Larson also ruled that the ENIAC patent was invalid because of the amount of time that had lapsed between the publication of its main features and the filing of the patent. The latter was done on June 26, 1946. However, in 1945, a document titled "First Draft of a Report on the EDVAC" was written by John von Neumann (whom we have encountered briefly [see Chapter 4, Section III, and this chapter, Section II], but will soon meet at length). This report, as we will see, will initiate another chapter of our story, and make the whole matter of inventionhood in the realm of computing even murkier. What mattered to Larson, however, is that on June 30, 1945, Herman Goldstine disseminated this report on a machine that was intended to be the ENIAC's successor. The report was legally deemed a publication and an "enabling disclosure" of the ENIAC almost a year before the ENIAC patent application was filed, which also rendered the patent invalid.

So, legally, the ENIAC patent (and Eckerd and Mauchly's claim to that patent) was rendered invalid. Legally, Eckert and Mauchly had "derived" its principles from Atanasoff's work. Yet, outside the law court, the question of who *really* invented the automatic electronic computer poses much difficulty. We now know, for instance, that the ABC and the ENIAC became operational after the Colossus. So if we allow that becoming operational is a reasonable criterion of inventionhood, the first automatic electronic computer was neither the ABC nor the ENIAC.

Then there is the fact that (like the Colossus), the ABC was designed as a special-purpose computer, to solve linear algebraic equations. Atanasoff recognized that it could also be applied to the solution of differential equations using numerical integration, but this possibility was never tested; it remained in the realm of possibility. The ENIAC was also special purpose, but much less so than the ABC. Even though it was envisioned as an electronic differential analyzer, thus intended to do the kinds of computations required to produce ballistic firing tables, its computational capabilities were such that its first use was computations needed for the hydrogen bomb project, which began in Los Alamos during the early 1940s.

Arthur Burks, one of its lead engineers and, later, one of its historians, had no doubts about the generality of the ENIAC. To him it was "the first electronic, digital, general-purpose scientific computer."[75] Writing in 1981, Burks defined a general-purpose computer as a digital computer that manifests two features. First, it affords arithmetic and memory capabilities that enable numbers to be entered automatically through an input unit and stored in an alterable memory, arithmetic operations to be performed on numbers, and the outcome transmitted to the outside world through an output device. Second, it provides a two-level programming facility. At the lower level are facilities for the execution of common sequences of arithmetic, input and output operations; at the higher level there is a capacity to combine these sequences into larger units—entire programs. Given these two features, according to Burks, one has a general-purpose computer that can solve a variety of problems—differential equations and number theoretical as well as data processing—commonly encountered in science, engineering, and accounting.[76] The ENIAC, meeting these criteria, according to Arthur and Alice Burks, was a general-purpose device.

Computer scientist and historian of computing Brian Randell would have none of it. He charged that the Burks's definition was "rather vague." For instance, a machine that did not have a multiplier unit (which the ENIAC did) but could perform multiplication by repeated addition, met their definition. But, *should* such a computer count as general purpose?[77] At the programming level, Randell suggested that any computer claiming to be general purpose must have the "crucial" facility to select among items held in its read/write memory based on previously computed results—in present-entered language, a branching capability. The ENIAC did not meet this condition.[78]

The problem is that both Burks and Randell used somewhat arbitrary criteria to define a general-purpose computer. Furthermore, both, writing in 1981, suffered from the pitfalls of present-centered (whiggish) history (see Prologue, Section VII). Their judgment of what was a general-purpose computer was colored by their perspectives circa 1981; they both imposed their latter-day perceptions on earlier situations.

It is interesting to compare these opinions voiced a quarter century after the near completion of the ENIAC with a contemporary account by Herman and Adele Goldstine. Writing in 1946, they described the ENIAC as a general-purpose electronic computer that, although developed primarily for the purpose of calculating firing tables, could, in fact, produce solutions to a variety of numeric problems.[79]

A slightly later commentator, also (as we will see) a major participant in this story, would write about the ENIAC that its tiny memory along with its manual programming feature severely limited its use for many problems.[80]

Clearly, even among the protagonists of this early part of our story, the notion of a general-purpose computer had no well-defined or well-accepted features. As I have noted before, the ENIAC can best be described as a computer that had sufficient generality across a range of mathematical (or numeric) problems (see Chapter 6, Section III, and this chapter, Section I).

Last, we pause on the judgment rendered by Larson in the court case that the ENIAC was "derived" from the ABC and so cannot count as the "first automatic electronic computer." We must not forget that the ABC was never a fully, correctly operating machine. On the contrary, it died a quiet death when Atanasoff and Berry both joined war projects. A machine's claim to priority (not the ideas underpinning the machine) must lie not just in the design, but also in its implementation. It is the operational machine that becomes a functioning artifact, not its underlying principles or its partial operationalism.

This never happened with the ABC. The ENIAC, on the other hand, was actually operational even before its formal dedication in February 1946. Its first computation was on a problem that pertained to the fledgling hydrogen bomb project in Los Alamos, and this computation was performed in December 1945.[81] The machine was running "satisfactorily" before its dedication.[82] In November 1946, it was transferred from the Moore School to the Aberdeen Proving Ground, although it was not started up until February 1947. Thereafter, it operated continuously "until 11.45 pm on 2 October 1955."[83] The contrast between the fate of the ABC and that of the ENIAC was stark. In speaking of the first *operational* electronic computer, there was what logicians might call a category mistake in comparing the one with the other.

NOTES

1. B. Randell. (1980). The Colossus. In N. Metropolis, J. Howlett, & G.- C. Rota. (Eds.), *A history of computing in the twentieth century* (pp. 47–92). New York: Academic Press (see especially p. 74).

2. A. W. Burks. (1980). From ENIAC to the stored program computer: Two revolutions in computers. In Metropolis, Howlett, & Rota (pp. 311–344).

3. A. W. Burks & A. R. Burks. (1981).The ENIAC: First general-purpose electronic computer. *Annals of the History of Computing, 3,* 310–399 (see especially p. 311).

4. H. H. Goldstine. (1972). *The computer from Pascal to von Neumann* (p. 156). Princeton, NJ: Princeton University Press.

5. R. Moreau. (1984). *The computer comes of age* (p. 33). Cambridge, MA: MIT Press.

6. Randell, op cit., pp. 74–75.

7. Goldstine, op cit., p. 153.

8. Burks & Burks, op cit., p. 337.

9. Ibid., p. 311.

10. A. W. Burks. (1947). Electronic Computing Circuits for the ENIAC. *Proceedings of the Institute of Radio Engineers, 35,* 756–767.

11. Ibid.

12. Ibid., p. 767.

13. *Ontogeny* is "the life history of an individual, both embryonic and postnatal." S. J. Gould. (1977). *Ontogeny and phylogeny* (p. 483). Cambridge, MA: Belknap Press of Harvard University Press.

14. Goldstine, op cit., p. 128.

15. Ibid., pp. 131–133.

16. Burks & Burks, op cit., p. 311.

17. W. Thomson. (1878). Harmonic analyzer. *Proceedings of the Royal Society of London, 27,* 371–373.

18. G. P. Zachary. (1977). *Endless frontier: Vannevar Bush, engineer of the American century* (p. 49). New York: Free Press.

19. V. Bush. (1931). The differential analyzer, a new machine for solving differential equations. *Journal of the Franklin Institute, 212,* 447–488.

20. Burks & Burks, op cit., p. 314.

21. Zachary, op cit., p. 51.

22. Ibid.

23. Burks & Burks, op cit., p. 314.

24. Zachary, op cit., p. 73.

25. Goldstine, op cit., p. 130.

26. Ibid., p. 133.

27. Burks, 1980, op cit., p. 314.

28. Ibid.

29. Goldstine, op cit., p. 149.

30. Burks, 1980, op cit., p. 314.

31. J. V. Atanasoff. (1940). *Computing machine for the solution of large systems of linear algebraic equations.* Unpublished memorandum. Printed in B. Randell. (Ed.). (1975). *The origins of digital computers* (2nd ed., pp. 305–325). New York: Springer-Verlag (see especially p. 305).

32. Ibid., p. 306.

33. Ibid.

34. J. V. Atanasoff. (1984). Advent of electronic digital computing. *Annals of the History of Computing, 6*, 229–282.

35. Atanasoff, 1940, op cit., pp. 307–308.

36. Ibid., p. 309.

37. Atanasoff, 1984, op cit., p. 242; Burks & Burks, op cit., p. 317.

38. Burks & Burks, op cit., p. 329.

39. Ibid.

40. Ibid., p. 330.

41. Atanasoff, 1984, op cit., p. 255.

42. C. R. Mollenhoff. (1988). *Atanasoff: Forgotten father of the computer* (p. 255). Ames, IA: Iowa State University Press.

43. Atanasoff, 1984, op cit., pp. 254–255; Mollenhoff, op cit., pp. 55–58.

44. Mollenhoff, op cit., p. 57.

45. Quoted by Burks & Burks, op cit., p. 332.

46. Ibid.

47. J. V. Mauchly. (1942). *The use of high speed vacuum tube devices for calculating.* Unpublished memorandum. Printed in Randell (pp. 329–332), 1975, op cit.

48. Goldstine, op cit., pp. 155–156.

49. Ibid., p. 154.

50. Ibid., p. 155.

51. R. K. Richards. (1955). *Arithmetic operations in digital computers* (p. 98). Princeton, NJ: Van Nostrand.

52. Burks, 1947, op cit., p. 760.

53. Quoted from J. P. Eckert, J. W. Mauchly, H. H. Goldstine, & J. G. Brainerd. (1945). Description of the ENIAC and comments on electronic digital computing machines. Contract W670 ORD 4926. Philadelphia, PA: Moore School of Electrical Engineering. *Oxford English Dictionary* [On-line]. Available: http://oed.com.

54. Goldstine, op cit., p. 241.

55. *Oxford English Dictionary,* op cit.

56. This example is taken from Goldstine, op cit., p. 160.

57. P. B. Medawar & J. S. Medawar. (1983). *Aristotle to zoo: A philosophical dictionary of biology* (pp. 225–226). Cambridge, MA: Harvard University Press. For an authoritative text on this law see Gould, op cit.

58. J. P. Steadman. (1979). *The evolution of designs.* Cambridge, UK: Cambridge University Press; G. Basalla. (1988). *The evolution of technology.* Cambridge, UK: Cambridge University Press; H. Petroski. (1988). *The evolution of useful things.* New York: Alfred A. Knopf; S. Dasgupta. (1996). *Technology and creativity* (Chapter 8). New York: Oxford University Press.

59. Dasgupta, op cit., p. 146.

60. This diagram is taken from Dasgupta, op cit., p. 147.

61. Mollenhoff, op cit., p. 59.

62. Mauchly, 1942, op cit., p. 329.

63. Burks & Burks, op cit., pp. 334–335.

64. Ibid.

65. Ibid., p. 341.

66. Ibid., p. 364.

67. Ibid., p. 363.

68. Ibid.

69. Ibid., pp. 371–372.

70. N. Stern. (1980). John William Mauchly: 1907–1980 (obituary). *Annals of the History of Computing*, 2, 100–103.

71. Goldstine, op cit., p. 326.

72. The records of the trial documented as *The ENIAC Trial Records,* U.S. District Court, District of Minnesota, Fourth Division: Honeywell, Inc. *v.* Sperry Rand Corp. et al, No. 4-67, Civ. 138. Decided October 19, 1973: Judge Earl Larson. Judge Larson's decision was published in the *U.S. Patent Quarterly*, *180*, 673–773. The court records are available at the Charles Babbage Institute of the History of Computing, Minneapolis, Minnesota, and also online. Available: www. cbi.umn.edu

73. Burks & Burks, op cit., p. 312.

74. Larson, as cited in the records of the ENIAC Trial, www.cbi.umn.edu, op cit.

75. Burks & Burks, op cit. (pp. 311–312).

76. Ibid., p. 385.

77. Randell, 1980, op cit., pp. 74–75; see Comment by B. Randell in Burks & Burks, op cit., p. 397.

78. Burks & Burks, Comment by B. Randell, op cit., pp. 396–397.

79. H. Goldstine & A. Goldstine. (1946). The Electronic Numerical Integrator and Computer (ENIAC). *Mathematical Tables and Other Aids to Computation*, 2, 97–110. Reprinted in Randell, 1975, op cit. (pp. 333–347). (See especially p. 333.)

80. D. J. Wheeler. (1951). *Automatic computing with the EDSAC* (p. 5). PhD dissertation, University of Cambridge.

81. Goldstine, op cit., p. 226.

82. Ibid., p. 231.

83. Ibid., p. 235.

8

A Paradigm Is Born

IN THE ENIAC story so far, John von Neumann has had a fleeting presence. We saw that the BRL formed a high-powered scientific advisory committee at the start of World War II, well before the United States entered the war. von Neumann was a member of this committee and it is unlikely that anyone in the committee was as influential in the American scientific world or, for that matter, in the corridors of power in Washington, DC, than him.

By the beginning of the 1940s, von Neumann had a massive reputation in the mathematical universe. His contributions spanned many regions of pure and applied mathematics, mathematical physics, even formal logic. He was one of the six mathematicians originally appointed as professors at the Institute of Advanced Study, Princeton, when it was founded in 1933[1]—another was Einstein. In 1944, von Neumann and economist Oskar Morgenstern (1902–1977) published a book titled *The Theory of Games and Economic Behavior*, thus founding and establishing for posterity the scientific discipline known as game theory.

Herman Goldstine, who came to know von Neumann very well—first through their involvement with the BRL and then, after the war, at the Institute of Advanced Study, where Goldstine went to work with von Neumann on what came to be called the IAS computer project[2]—wrote vividly about von Neumann's intellectual persona, of his ever-ready receptiveness to new ideas, his responsiveness to new intellectual challenges, his mental restlessness when between projects, and the single-mindedness with which he pursued an idea that captured his attention.[3]

Oddly enough, despite his involvement with the BRL, he was apparently unaware of the ENIAC project until a chance meeting with Goldstine in a railway station in

Aberdeen, Maryland. Goldstine recalls how the entire tone and tenor of their first conversation, initially casual and relaxed, changed when von Neumann realized that Goldstine was involved with the development of a high-speed electronic computer. Thereafter, Goldstine writes, he felt as he was being grilled in a doctoral oral examination.[4] Thus began their association, a relationship that only ended with von Neumann's death from cancer in 1957.[5] And thus began von Neumann's engagement with computers.

Soon after this meeting in August 1944, von Neumann accompanied Goldstine to Philadelphia to witness the ENIAC.[6] From that point on, von Neumann was a regular visitor to the Moore School, attending meetings with the ENIAC designers.[7]

However, von Neumann's interest in computers did not originate *only* out of intellectual curiosity. Like every one else, his engagement with automatic computing stemmed from dissatisfaction with the status quo. Working in the field of applied mathematics called hydrodynamics (or fluid dynamics), he had pondered on the use of computational approaches for solving analytical equations.[8] Beginning in 1943, von Neumann was also associated with the Los Alamos Scientific Laboratory (later renamed the Los Alamos National Laboratory), where the Manhattan Project was underway to develop the atom bomb and, in this context, concerned with solutions to nonlinear systems of equations, he was in search of methods for expediting solutions to such problems.[9]

II

Even as the ENIAC was being implemented, its designers were recognizing its weaknesses. Its memory, constructed of vacuum tubes, was far too small in capacity for handling many large problems, but larger memories using tubes were deemed unrealizable. A different electronic technology was needed for the memory. Besides, the use of plugboards, cables, and manual switches to program and set up the machine for each fresh task was too cumbersome, too slow. Goldstine would recall that, by August 1944, he was chafing at how clumsy the mechanism was for programming the ENIAC.[10] Clearly, despite what he and Adele Goldstine would write in their report on the ENIAC in 1946 (see Chapter 7, Section IX), well before that report was written, the ENIAC was *not* deemed general-purpose enough.

The very act of implementation revealed not only that the design-as-theory was inadequate in satisfying the ENIAC's intended purpose, but also that the purpose itself needed to be extended. Perhaps further thought during the design and planning process revealed these shortcomings. But, human beings—even the most intellectually brilliant and the most creative of them—are ultimately limited in their cognitive capacities. People suffer from what polymath scientist Herbert Simon, conceiver of the idea of the sciences of the artificial (see Prologue, Section III), famously termed *bounded rationality*.[11] This is why the empirical approach is so important in the sciences—natural or artificial. The act of experimentation (in the case of the artificial sciences, this entails implementation) is a way of circumventing bounded rationality. The ENIAC's implementation yielded information about the ENIAC that thinking alone about the design did not.

Changing the design of the ENIAC midstream was out of the question. The needs of ballistic calculation for a war still raging were urgent. Instead, the ENIAC team envisioned a new project that could be initiated after the ENIAC was completed. A new contract was signed between the BRL and the Moore School to build "a new ENIAC of improved design."[12]

Meetings ensued at which von Neumann was present. The outcome was that, by the end of August 1944, certain very specific requirements for the new ENIAC were identified. The machine would (a) contain many fewer tubes than the then-current machine and hence would be cheaper and easier to maintain, (b) be capable of handling many types of problems not easily adaptable to the current ENIAC, (c) be capable of storing cheaply and at high speed large quantities of numeric data, (d) be of such a character that the setup of a new problem would require very little time, and (e) be smaller in size than the current ENIAC.[13]

In fact, there was already a candidate for a memory device that would meet requirement (c). It was called a *mercury delay line* (or ultrasonic memory) with which Presper Eckert had worked in connection with the development of radar (one of the major technoscientific products of World War II). As for requirement (d), what was needed was a means of setting up a problem "automatically," providing a capability for "automatic programming of the facility and processes."[14]

More meetings ensued in which, along with Eckert, Mauchly, Goldstine, Burks, and other members of the ENIAC group, von Neumann participated. A name was given to the proposed computer: Electronic Discrete Variable Arithmetic Computer (EDVAC). By March 1945, a first report on this machine would state that "problems of logical control" had been discussed and analyzed, and that von Neumann would submit a summary analyzing the logical organization of the EDVAC.[15]

More discussions followed on the proposed EDVAC design.[16] More significantly, von Neumann had by then written up the promised "preliminary draft."[17]

This draft of 1945, comprising 100 mimeographed pages, was titled *First Draft of a Report on the EDVAC*. Its sole author was von Neumann. Thus was born a myth—that the ideas and principles articulated in this report were von Neumann's alone. In a sense, anyone reading this document cannot be blamed for thinking so. When a scientific or scholarly or technical paper of any sort shows the names of people in its byline, the reader infers that these are the names of the authors. If others also contribute, then at the very least a list of names is usually inserted in a footnote or at the end of the document. However, the EDVAC report of 1945 showed only von Neumann's name as the author. Nor were there any acknowledgments in the document to anyone else.

Perhaps von Neumann was not to blame. The report was intended as a preliminary document (as the title announced) for circulation within the ENIAC group. What it became, however, was an unpublished paper authored by von Neumann that entered into computer lore.

Needless to say, this myth created much controversy. It fostered resentment. Maurice Wilkes (soon to enter this story), writing in 1985, felt that a serious injustice had been done to Eckert and Mauchly, who had not been given their rightful credit for the ideas von Neumann described in the EDVAC report, some of which they had, apparently, arrived at even before von Neumann entered the project.[18]

III

Let us then admit that the contents of the EDVAC report represented the collective thoughts of several minds. Yet, the fact is that von Neumann synthesized it all into a masterly monograph. He was its sole writer, if not the only author of its contents. He created a scientific text of a depth and elegance that was *his* art and no one else's. In earlier centuries, certain texts (such as *Two New Sciences* [1638] by Galileo [1564–1642] or *Principles of Geology* [1830–1833] by Charles Lyell [1797–1875]) created paradigms in their respective domains. *First Draft of a Report on the EDVAC* falls in this same category (as we will see), and John von Neumann was its author.

Let us consider what made this report so important to our story.

The first major contribution made by the EDVAC report was its emphasis on the *logical* design and principles of a computer and their delineation from *physical* principles. We now refer to the logical design of a computer—which must not be confused with logic design, a term used to mean the design of circuits with behavior that can be described by Boolean algebra (see Chapter 5, Sections III and IV)—as *computer architecture*. Although this latter term would not enter the language of computer science for several more years, what the EDVAC report ushered in was the explicit recognition that there was a distinction to be made between a computer's architecture and its physical implementation. The architecture is an *abstraction* of the physical machine and concerns itself with a computer's logical and functional elements and their relationships, and how they relate to the tasks the computer is intended to perform. Conversely, by articulating a computer architecture, decisions concerning the physical implementation may be deferred.

In fact, computer architectures are important examples of liminal computational artifacts (see Prologue, Section IV). They lie at the borderline between the purely abstract and the purely material. Computer architectures have an abstract identity of their own; one can describe them, analyze them, design them without referring (to any large extent) to anything physical. Yet, the identity of a computer architecture is made complete only when there is an implementation in the form of a material artifact, a physical computer (again, a rough analogy of the mind and brain is useful here). This explicit distinction, emphasized in the EDVAC report, between logical design and physical design, between architecture and implementation of that architecture was entirely new.

The second major contribution of the EDVAC report is its most significant one. It concerned the nature and function of a computer's internal memory. For a machine to perform long sequences of operations without human intervention, it must have a large memory.[19] For example, the partial or intermediate results of a complex operation such as finding square or cubic roots of a number, or even multiplication or division must be "remembered."[20] Tables of values of commonly used mathematical functions (such as logarithmic or trigonometric functions) and values of certain analytical expressions, if stored in memory, can expedite computation.[21] In the case of differential equations, initial conditions and boundary conditions would also have to remembered for the duration of a computation.

Information such this was, of course, long recognized as essential to computation. What made the EDVAC report stand apart was the recognition that in a long and complicated calculation the *instructions* themselves may need to be remembered, for they may have to be executed repeatedly.[22] In present-centered language, a program (that is, the sequence of instructions or orders needed to carry out a computation) requires its own memory. And even though these various memory requirements are distinct functionally or conceptually, it seemed natural and, indeed, tempting to conceive such different types of memory, for storing input data and results, for holding tables of values, and for remembering instructions as a single "organ."[23]

In these thoughts lie history, for what they expressed were the first significant hints of a paradigm (see Chapter 6, Section II). Why it was a paradigm is discussed later. Eventually, these ideas will be conceptualized collectively by the term *stored-program computer*, wherein the instructions to be executed are not only stored in an alterable read/write memory but there is no distinction between instruction/program memory and the memory holding all the information that is input to the computation and is the result of the computation. There is just one memory organ.

These two principles—the concept of the stored-program computer in which the same memory organ holds both data and program, and the principle of separating architecture from implementation, logical design from physical design—constitute two of the fundamental elements of the newly emergent paradigm. With historical hindsight, the Holy Grail seemed within reach.

IV

Most of the American engineers, mathematicians, and physicists who were embroiled in the development of automatic computers in the decade 1936 to 1946, culminating in the production of the ENIAC, may not have heard of Alan Turing, let alone have read his 1936 paper on the *Entscheidungsproblem* (see Chapter 4). Babbage's name appears sporadically in papers, reports, and memoranda written during that period, but neither Turing's name nor his work have any presence (with the exception, of course, of the scientists and engineers in Bletchley Park [see Chapter 5, Sections XII–XIV]).

One person outside Bletchley Park and engaged with automatic computation who knew Turing well was von Neumann. As we have seen, von Neumann first met Turing in

1935 in Cambridge. They met again when Turing went to Princeton in fall 1936, where he stayed for 2 years and worked toward his PhD under Alonzo Church (see Chapter 4, Section VIII). There is no direct evidence that von Neumann had read Turing's paper on the *Entscheidungsproblem* and his mechanical concept of computability.[24] There is, however, sufficient indirect and circumstantial evidence. First, given that offprints of his paper arrived while Turing was in Princeton,[25] given von Neumann's legendary interest in all things mathematical including formal logic—indeed, his first field of interest was mathematical logic and the foundations of mathematics (in 1925 and 1927, he published two papers in this area)[26]—and given that von Neumann wrote a letter of support to Cambridge University on Turing's behalf for a fellowship that would allow him to stay a second year at Princeton to complete his thesis,[27] it seems inconceivable that von Neumann did not know of Turing's paper on computability. Certainly Goldstine was sanguine that von Neumann was aware of Turing's work.[28] More definite evidence was offered by Stanley Frankel (1919–1978), a physicist who participated in the Manhattan Project in Los Alamos that led to the production of the atom bomb. In Los Alamos, Frankel had known von Neumann. He would recall, in 1972, that sometime during 1943 or 1944, von Neumann referred Turing's 1936 paper to Frankel and urged him to study it (which he did).[29]

This inevitably raises the question: was the idea of the stored-program concept as enunciated by von Neumann in the EDVAC report—involving a single memory organ for both instructions and data—shaped by von Neumann's knowledge of Turing's universal computing machine of 1936? In that machine, we recall, the tape (the Turing machine memory) held symbols representing both the operations to be performed and the effect of those operations, the data on which operations are performed, and the results of such operations (see Chapter 4, Section IV). Was there *any* connection linking von Neumann's knowledge of the Turing paper and the architecture of the EDVAC computer?

According to Frankel's letter to Brian Randell, there was indeed such an influence. von Neumann apparently told Frankel that the basic idea of the stored-program computer was due to Turing. Frankel went on to write that he believed that von Neumann's "essential role" was to introduce Turing's fundamental concept to the larger world.[30]

If, in fact, there was such an influence then, of course, Turing's 1936 paper would have great *practical* significance in the story of the birth of this new paradigm. In any case, even assuming that the stored-program concept was not influenced by von Neumann's knowledge of Turing's work (if, for instance, it were Eckert and Mauchly who had originally conceived the idea), it is quite inconceivable that, after the concept had emerged, von Neumann did not think of the Turing machine, and that he did not immediately realize a rather beautiful relationship between the architecture of a purely abstract artifact such as the Turing machine and the architecture of a practically conceived material artifact such as EDVAC, that they were the theoretical and practical faces of the same computing coin.

V

Let us recall Thomas Kuhn's concept of a scientific paradigm (see Chapter 7).[31] The essence of "paradigmhood" is that a substantial majority of scientists (or certainly the most influential ones) working in a particular discipline should agree on certain core concepts governing their science—notably, its core philosophical, theoretical, and methodological components. If, in fact, the community was deeply divided on these issues, then, according to Kuhn, the science would be in a "preparadigmatic" state.

The second essence of paradigmhood is that a paradigm is neither complete nor unambiguous, for if a paradigm is complete, then, of course, there is no more to be done in that science! So there are significant clarifications to be made, interpretations to be given, unsolved problems to be solved, and so forth. All such activities Kuhn called "normal science." A paradigm, then, offers a broad map, a framework, within which scientists carry out their normal research.

We can relate the Kuhnian notion of a paradigm (which is a social concept, involving a community) with the cognitive concept of schemas. The term *schema* was first used most famously in 1932 by English psychologist Sir Frederick Bartlett (1886–1969) in his studies of the process of remembering.[32] Bartlett characterized a schema as an organization of past experiences held in a person's memory that participates in how the person responds to a new situation, and how and what he remembers of his past experiences.[33]

Since Bartlett, the original concept of the schema (schemas or schemata in plural) has been adapted, developed, and applied not only by psychologists, but also by anthropologists, philosophers, art historians, cultural and intellectual historians, creativity scholars, and researchers in artificial intelligence, and refined into a *schema theory*.[34]

According to this theory, an individual stores in her long-term memory an assemblage of schemas. A schema is a kind of pattern or template that serves to represent in that person's mind a certain stereotypical experience, concept, or situation. For example, we carry in our minds schemas for what it is like to attend a church wedding, go to a football game, or eat at a restaurant. When that person is confronted with a new situation, she attempts to make sense of it in terms of matching it against some existing schema that then guides the person in responding to the situation. And so, even if we have never eaten at a Japanese restaurant, we "cope" with it by referencing our restaurant schema. Schemas, then, enable expectations about a person's social, cultural, or physical milieu and how to respond to new kinds of encounters within that milieu. Beginning in early childhood and over time (as Swiss psychologist Jean Piaget [1896–1980] suggested[35]), humans constantly construct, use, instantiate, and reconstruct their mental stock of schemas.

Schemas, then, provide a kind of *cognitive map* whereby people negotiate new territories of knowledge, physical, social, and cultural situations and experiences. But, to be effective, schemas must be flexible, they must be both elastic and plastic; one must be able to stretch or reshape them, often in surprising ways. Austrian-British art historian Sir Ernst Gombrich (1909–2001) wrote famously of making art as a process of starting with an initial schema and gradually correcting or modifying it.[36] It is helpful if the initial schema selected by the artist is loose, flexible, even a bit vague, for then it can be extended or modified according to the artist's need. Indian filmmaker Satyajit Ray (1921–1992) once remarked that, when looking for stories to adapt to film, he preferred novellas to full-scale novels because the former allowed more possibilities for expanding or interpreting or changing into a script for a film than the latter. For Ray, novellas afforded schemas more readily than full-length novels, which were more tightly bound, leaving little scope for enlargement. These examples from art and filmmaking suggest that schemas are not only useful—indeed, essential—for everyday thinking, remembering, and making sense of our day-to-day experiences, but also they are at the root of creative thinking.

In the context of science, *a paradigm, when internalized by a scientist, becomes her dominant schema for that science.*

A paradigm is a social entity; inside an individual's mind it becomes a cognitive entity, a very elaborate schema that governs the scientist's entire approach to, and conception of, that science. What Kuhn called "normal science" means, for the individual scientist, the elaboration and refinement of the schema representing the paradigm. It entails adding new elements (subschemas) to a schema, or altering some elements, or sometimes deleting subschemas altogether.

When we say that "a paradigm is born," in cognitive terms this means that a common schema has been established in the minds of the scientists who work in that science. It also suggests that the schema is initially a mere skeleton, a backbone of related concepts, ideas, theories, and so forth, that need to be elaborated, refined, enlarged, even reshaped without destroying the overall skeleton.

A schema held in a person's mind is something personal; a paradigm belongs to a community. So when an individual scientist absorbs a paradigm and it becomes a schema in her mind, her interpretation of the paradigm may be quite different from a fellow-scientist's interpretation of the same paradigm.

VI

Which brings us back to our story. Around 1945/1946, such a paradigm was just born. Those few people in the world who were engaged in the development of computers and computing would acquire and hold in their minds schemas representing the new-born paradigm. For someone like von Neumann, his computational schema would have two connected but separate subschemas: one representing the ideas and concepts contained in the EDVAC report, the other representing his understanding of the universal Turing machine. For someone like Mauchly or Presper Eckert, a subschema corresponding to the Turing machine was probably absent.

But, people like Mauchly, Eckert, Goldstine, Burks, and others who developed the ENIAC, and also von Neumann, would also possess a schema representing the idea of the

ENIAC. There would be linkages between the ENIAC schema and the stored-program computer schema, for there were obvious common concepts. For example, central to the ENIAC schema was the presence of the idea of vacuum tubes to implement both memory and arithmetic units. The stored-program computer schema also had a place for vacuum tubes, according to the EDVAC report.[37]

However, the ENIAC schema was *not* a subschema of the stored-program computer schema. The differences were too fundamental. The ENIAC and the stored-program computer schemas, in the minds of the people involved in their development, stood apart. And the vital point is that the ENIAC schema *never became a paradigm*, whereas the stored-program computer schema did.

VII

Paradigms in the natural sciences differ in a fundamental way from paradigms of the kind that concerns us in this story. Consider, for example, the Darwinian paradigm in biology. Its vital element is the theory of natural selection, and this is a statement about the organic world as it is. Philosophers would call it a *descriptive* theory. The Darwinian paradigm is, accordingly, a descriptive paradigm, concerning the organic world as it is.

In contrast, what we are calling the *stored-program computer paradigm* is about an artificial world; the computer is an artifact, an invented thing. Any possible science that might be represented by this paradigm is a science of the artificial (see Prologue).[38] And any paradigm characterizing an artificial science, dealing with an artifact (or a family of artifacts) is necessarily *a prescriptive* paradigm. It speaks of a world as it ought to be (see Prologue, Section II).

Natural scientists may agree or disagree about how the world really is; artificial scientists may agree or disagree about how the world ought to be. This distinction between *is* and *ought* is, equivalently, the distinction between what is *true* and what is *right*. It is the distinction between empirical statements that are true or false, and value judgments that distinguish between right or wrong with respect to some purpose or goal. The paradigms that govern the artificial sciences, being prescriptive, express value judgments; the paradigms that govern the natural sciences, being descriptive, express statements about facts. Thus, one can argue whether the special theory of relativity is true—that is, whether it is a correct description of some aspect of the physical world. One cannot argue whether the ENIAC is true—only whether it is achieves its stated purpose, or how well it achieves its stated purpose, how good or bad it is with respect to its intended purpose.

Let us keep this in mind for the purpose of this unfolding story. Let us always keep in mind that any science we associate with computers (which are artifacts), is a science of the artificial. A paradigm for an artificial science is, then, unconcerned fundamentally with truth or falsehood. It is concerned fundamentally with goodness or badness, rightness or wrongness—not in an ethical or moral sense, but relative to goals and purposes.

The EDVAC report, although intended for a few eyes only, was circulated widely. Its status for paradigmhood was a matter of social acceptance by those who were either working on, or were seriously interested in, computers.

One of those who read the EDVAC report was Alan Turing, who, at the end of World War II, joined (in June 1945) the newly formed mathematics division of Britain's National Physical Laboratory (NPL) in Teddington, outside London.[39] Turing's boss at NPL, the man who had recruited him, mathematician John R. Womersley (1907–1958), head of the mathematics division, had shown Turing the EDVAC report.[40] On joining NPL, Turing began working immediately on the preliminary design of a stored-program electronic computer.

The critical element in the EDVAC report—the critical factor in the viability of a stored-program computer—was the means to achieve an economical yet fast, large internal memory. Turing's own "universal machine," the product of his 1936 *Entscheidungsproblem* paper postulated a linear tape that would move left and right across a read/write head. In a lecture delivered to the London Mathematical Society in 1947 on his new project, he alluded to this abstract machine, but he pointed out that, although in the kind of computing machine he had envisioned it was necessary for the memory to be infinite, an infinite tape would be impractical in a "real" stored-program machine because of the time that would be spent in searching the tape for information needed at any given point of time.[41]

In fact, there *was* a physical artifact corresponding to Turing's abstract idea. Prior to joining NPL, Turing had been sent to Germany as a member of an Anglo-American team to determine the status of German wartime communication technology.[42] One of the captured German army devices was the magnetophone, an early form of the tape recorder.[43] However, Turing rejected this mechanism for the reason mentioned earlier; it required too much back-and-forth movement.[44] Instead, he favored the acoustic delay line as a memory device.

Such a delay line had been built by Presper Eckert and others at the Moore School in summer 1943, and was studied for application to radar.[45] When plans for the EDVAC were being drawn up, Eckert and another member of the ENIAC team worked on a preliminary design of an acoustic delay memory using mercury.[46] The credit for the idea lay entirely with Eckert, according to Goldstine.[47]

In the EDVAC report, von Neumann made no reference to any specific acoustic memory, Eckert's or otherwise. Rather, he discussed at great length, in an abstract sort of way, a "delay memory" and its characteristics.[48] He also described an alternative (and for him, preferred) form of memory "along the lines of the *iconoscope*,"[49] an electrostatic storage tube that stored electrical charges and that, he believed, held distinct advantages over the delay line as memory.

The basic principle of the acoustic delay line memory is that because sound takes a certain amount of time to travel through a physical medium such as a liquid like mercury, for that duration of time, the medium may be said to be storing the sound wave. Consider a tube of mercury of some length. An electrical signal could be transformed into an acoustic disturbance, propagate through the mercury in the tube from one end, and be transformed back into an electrical signal at the other end. If this "output" electrical signal was fed back to the "input" to the tube, then one would have a memory device. Sound travels through mercury at the rate of 1450 meters/second. A tube of mercury 1.45 meters long will give a delay of 1 millisecond.

Translation of electrical pulses into an acoustic wave and the reverse could be done using a phenomenon called the piezoelectric effect, discovered in 1880 by French scientists Pierre Curie (1859–1906) and his brother Jacques (1856–1941). In this instance, an electrical disturbance imposed on a quartz crystal would cause the crystal to oscillate. When such a crystal was attached to the input side of a tube of mercury, the oscillation produced an acoustic pulse, which propagated through the mercury, taking a certain amount of time. After a delay, it caused another quartz crystal to vibrate, producing, in turn, an electrical pulse. The latter is returned, through appropriate circuits that reshape and amplify the pulse, to the input side of the tube.[50]

Suppose now a binary 1 is represented by a pulse 0.5 microsecond wide and a 0 is noted by the absence of a pulse. A pulse position (corresponding to a 1 or a 0 followed by a gap before the next pulse [1] or nonpulse [0]) would be 1 microsecond. Then, a single delay tube 1.45 meters long would hold a sequence of 1000 binary digits. To reshape and amplify the output pulse before recirculating it would need about 10 vacuum tubes. Thus, 1000 binary digits could be stored on a mercury tube at the cost of 10 vacuum tubes. If, on the other hand, vacuum tubes were used for memory (as in the ENIAC), then 1000 binary digits would need 1000 vacuum tubes. In terms of vacuum tube use, the cost of an acoustic memory reduces by a factor of 100 to 1.

Acknowledging that Eckert was the originator of the idea of using a delay line as memory, Turing chose this mechanism over alternatives because it was "already a going concern."[51]

IX

Turing named the machine he began to design the ACE (Automatic Computing Engine). In 1945, he wrote *Proposal for Development in the Mathematics Division of an Automatic Computing Engine (ACE)*, which was perhaps as extensive in scope and length as the EDVAC report.[52] Although believing his own paper to be a completely comprehensive account of the design of his proposed machine, he added that his paper should be read alongside the EDVAC report.[53] Thus, von Neumann's paper appeared to have played a part in shaping Turing's ideas about a practical stored-program computer—a curious and pleasing *quid pro quo* if, in fact, von Neumann's idea had been shaped by Turing's 1936 work.

It was an ambitious plan. The ACE would use a delay line memory of some 6400 words of 32 binary digits each, held in 200 long mercury delay lines.[54] Unfortunately, the ACE project had more than its share of problems, mainly in communications among its designers in NPL's mathematics division and the implementers who were in the electronics section. Eventually, the problems were resolved and, in 1949, detailed design began on a much-stripped down version of the ACE, called *Pilot ACE*. Its memory capacity was much smaller than what Turing had originally planned, comprising 300 words of 32 binary digits each.[55]

Public demonstrations of the Pilot ACE were given in May 1950,[56] but by then at least two other stored-program computers were operational (as we see later) both, as it happened, in England. The ACE project is significant to this story not because of priority-of-invention reasons; rather, it represents an almost instant recognition by Turing (and Womersley) at NPL of the significance of the stored-program concept. It was an important piece of evidence pointing to the acceptance of the stored-program computer as a computational paradigm.

Well before the public demonstrations of the Pilot ACE, however, Turing had left NPL. In September 1947, he took sabbatical leave from NPL and returned to Cambridge to resume his war-interrupted fellowship at King's College.[57] A year later, he resigned from NPL and moved to Manchester to take up a position created for him and funded by the Royal Society at the University of Manchester. His new position was deputy director of the Royal Society Computing Laboratory.[58] The University of Manchester harbored computational ambitions.

X

If a paradigm, when born, elicits prompt recognition and acceptance by members of the relevant scientific community, if it initiates research programs ("normal science" in Kuhn's language), if it is quickly assimilated and internalized as a mental schema by individuals, then, like Turing, but more *effectively*, the work by Englishman (later Sir) Maurice Wilkes (1913–2010) and his colleagues in Cambridge University between 1946 and 1949 epitomized these phenomena. Wilkes recognized the significance of the ideas put forth in the EDVAC report as soon as he first encountered them in May 1946. In his memoirs, written in 1985, he records how, on reading the report, he immediately recognized that this was "the real thing," that this was the way the development of the computer would follow.[59]

It would be a travesty to call the work that Wilkes and his collaborators did in those first 3 years of peacetime as "normal science." There was nothing remotely normal about it. Wilkes was on *terra incognita*, a terrain unknown not just to him, but also to everyone else. What Wilkes did was design and implement successfully and completely a computer called the Electronic Delay Storage Automatic Calculator (EDSAC) that not only adhered to the general principles of the stored-program computer, but also demonstrated *empirically* the viability of the concept. It was, in the realm of the artificial sciences, what in the natural sciences is called *experimentum crucis*, a crucial experiment that could make or break a theory or hypothesis. It was not the only experiment under way at that time to test the viability of the stored-program concept, but it was the first such *complete* experiment. In fact, it is fair to say that beginning with the EDSAC project, Wilkes's scientific life entailed one long series of experiments that revealed how an artificial science (in this case, computer science) can be an empirical science.

The EDSAC project was significant in another sense. It opened up an entirely new region of the stored-program computer paradigm, a new class of artifacts the likes of which had never been seen before: computer programs or software.

XI

Wilkes obtained his BA degree in mathematics from Cambridge University ("mathematics tripos" in Cambridge language) in 1934, the same year as Turing. While Turing was a student (and later, fellow) of King's College, Wilkes studied at (and would later become a fellow of) St. John's College a few hundred yards away, but apparently they did not meet until much later.[60]

Wilkes was very much a "Cambridge man" who, on entering the university in 1931 as an undergraduate, spent his entire academic life in Cambridge until his retirement in 1980. When he died in Cambridge, he was emeritus professor of computer technology and a much-honored man, including the award of a knighthood.[61]

Wilkes's forte during his early years was in applied mathematics, especially as applied to radio physics. He did his doctoral research at the Cavendish Laboratory (where the fabled Lord Rutherford was still the Cavendish professor and director), and obtained his PhD in 1938.[62]

By then, however, he had already encountered the lure of automatic computing. While working at the Cavendish, he came to know of the differential analyzer from a lecture in 1936 given by Douglas Hartree (1897–1958), a mathematician and numeric analyst and professor of applied mathematics at the University of Manchester. Hartree had built a differential analyzer for his department. The lecture was followed by a demonstration of a model version of the analyzer (built from components of what, in England, is called a meccano set and in America, an erector set), and was housed in the physical chemistry department of the university.

Working on the properties of long-wave radio waves, Wilkes was having to deal with the solution of differential equations. The machine beckoned, and soon he had obtained permission to use it.[63] Not long after, he was put in charge of the machine. By a happy coincidence, the University of Cambridge had ambitions of acquiring a full-scale differential analyzer. By 1937, plans to establish a computing laboratory in the university were underway. It was named the University Mathematical Laboratory and it came into exis-tence in 1937 as an independent academic department of the university.[64] The part-time director of the laboratory was (later, Sir) John Lennard-Jones (1894–1954), professor of theoretical chemistry at the university, who had initiated the building of the model ana-lyzer. In late 1937, Wilkes, still a doctoral research student, was appointed, a demonstra-tor at the university—effectively, a very junior academic position, in the Mathematical Laboratory.

After the end of World War II (during which Wilkes was engaged in radar develop-ment, application, and deployment), he returned to Cambridge, where he was promoted to the rank of university lecturer and appointed acting director of the Mathematical Laboratory. His main mandate was "to take part in the development of new machines and new methods of computing and to provide for the instruction of students."[65] The year after, in late 1946, he was formally appointed director of the laboratory, a posi-tion he would only relinquish on retirement 34 years later. In 1965, he was appointed to Cambridge's first chair in computer technology—almost a decade after his election as an FRS, Britain's most coveted scientific honor.

XII

At the time the war ended, Wilkes knew nothing about the developments in electronic digital computing, not in America and certainly not in Germany. Because of its highly classified nature he was not privy to the Colossus work in Bletchley Park, either.[66] This situation was soon remedied—first, through Hartree, an authority in Britain on the dif-ferential analyzer and automatic computing, and through Comrie (whom we encoun-tered much earlier in the story [see Chapter 5, Section V]), who had recently returned from a visit to America, bringing back with him a copy of the EDVAC report, which he gave to Wilkes. Therein lay, Wilkes recalled later, the fundamental principle of the stored-program computer.[67]

Soon after this, Wilkes received "suddenly" an invitation from Harold Pender (1879–1959), dean of the Moore School of Electrical Engineering, to attend a course offered by the school on electronic computers.[68] The outcome was a first visit to the United States, meeting some of the main players in the development of automatic computing in America, including Goldstine and Mauchly in Philadelphia, and Howard Aiken and Samuel Caldwell in the "other" Cambridge. He observed the ENIAC and learned about the use of mercury delay lines as the basis for improved memory.[69]

Wilkes, like von Neumann in the EDVAC report, recognized the main disadvantage of the acoustic delay line memory: its slow access speed, because of the time needed for the acoustic pulse to circulate (hence the word *delay*), and the complicated timing cir-cuits this entailed.[70] But Wilkes, although formally trained as an applied mathematician, had a profoundly engineering mind. His was a pragmatic disposition. Whatever doubts he may have harbored about acoustic delay line memory were put aside when, on return to England (on the *Queen Mary*) in September 1946, he met an Austrian-born research student in the Cavendish Laboratory, Thomas Gold (1920–2004), later a distinguished astrophysicist, who put before his "wondering eyes" a scale drawing of a mercury tank that would do the job.[71] Gold's wartime work was on radar, and in this context he had been involved in designing mercury tanks. Somewhat like Turing's choice of delay lines for ACE, Wilkes's choice of memory technology was dictated by pragmatics—in his case, not just the availability of technology, but also of human expertise to go with it.

XIII

The machine that Wilkes and his group built was called the Electronic Delay Storage Automatic Calculator—EDSAC, for short—and, like the ENIAC, the full name would be quickly forgotten or ignored (Figure 8.1).

Initially, apart from Gold (who helped him during the first experiments with mercury tanks),[72] a workshop assistant, and a laboratory assistant, Wilkes was by himself. Later, an instrument maker, an electronic technician, and several research students would join the project. The latter included, in particular, William Renwick (1924–1971) and David Wheeler (1927–2004), both of whom would author or coauthor with Wilkes

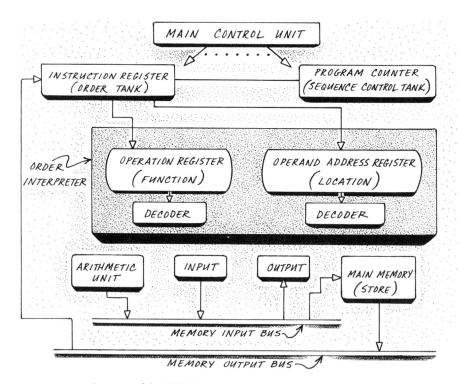

FIGURE 8.1 Architecture of the EDSAC.

publications on the early Cambridge computers. Wheeler (as we will see) has a particularly important place in the consolidation of the stored-program computer paradigm.

The full name of this machine suggests how much memory considerations were at the forefront of Wilkes's consciousness. The EDVAC report paid much attention to this issue, but the EDVAC report also paid much attention to all aspects of the stored-program computer principles, including what von Neumann called "orders."[73] This was the word frequently used at the time to mean *instructions*. The collection of orders comprised the "order code" (in present-centered language, *instruction set*).

In the EDVAC report, the orders were separated into four groups: orders to perform arithmetic operations, those to transfer numbers from one location to another, ones to go to particular locations in memory to access the orders as and when required, and input and output orders.[74]

The transfer orders were made uniform. If a number had to be moved from one memory location to another, it must first be transferred, using a single order, from the source location to the accumulator in the arithmetic unit and then, using a second order, from the accumulator to the destination memory location. Each order would, thus, specify a single memory location (the source or the destination).[75] In present-centered language, the stored-program computer prescribed in the EDVAC report would have a single-address architecture.

The EDSAC adhered to these principles. It was designed as a serial, binary machine with an acoustic delay line memory implemented by means of 32 mercury tanks (Figure 8.2), each about 5 feet long and each holding 32 17-binary digit numbers (including a sign digit). The machine's memory capacity, thus, comprised 1024 locations. Per the EDVAC proposal, a single-address architecture was used.[76]

Wilkes and Renwick introduced the EDSAC at a conference in June 1949. This was the first formal communication of the world's *first fully operational stored-program computer*. The emphasis here is important. In this new field—still without a name—priority of invention was as important as priority of discovery or invention in any other more established science.

In this matter of priority, the EDSAC had a rival—not the successors to the ENIAC group in America, as one might expect, not the ACE project at the NPL, but in Manchester, at the University of Manchester, already a site of automatic *analog* computing because of Hartree and his differential analyzer, a project to build an electronic digital computer also begun in 1946. The principals of this project were (later, Sir) Frederic C. Williams (1911–1977), an electrical engineer and an international authority on electronics ("the best-known electronics circuit engineer in the world"[77]), who had worked in the Telecommunications Research Establishment (TRE) in Malvern on radar during the war, and Tom Kilburn (1921–2001), who had worked with Williams at TRE on radar. After the war ended, Williams joined the University of Manchester as professor of electrotechnics; Kilburn, a Cambridge mathematics graduate-turned-circuit designer, went with Williams as a scientific assistant before becoming a research student. Kilburn would

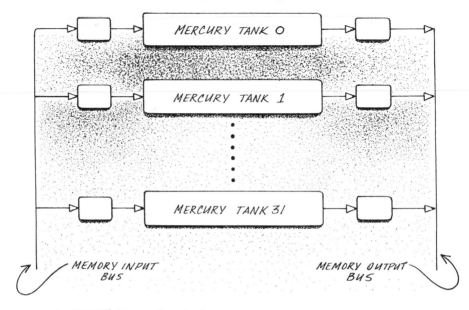

FIGURE 8.2 EDSAC's Memory Organization.

later be appointed professor of computer engineering (in 1960) and then head of the department of computer science (in 1964), elected a fellow of the Royal Society and, like Wilkes, much honored.

Williams, who had visited the Moore School in summer 1946 and was familiar with the ENIAC, chose the electrostatic storage tube as the basis of memory for his planned computer. He invented, in collaboration with Kilburn, a cathode ray tube (CRT) storage device (on which he had done some contributory research at the TRE[78]) that came to be called the *Williams tube*. A patent application for this device was filed in December 1946.[79] As Williams described it, binary digits were represented by a pattern of charges on the screen of a CRT. He distinguished between short-term memory, of a duration of about 0.2 second, and long-term memory, obtained by regenerating the charge pattern.[80]

Williams's use of "short-term memory" and "long-term memory" is interesting for an electronics engineer. The anthropocentric *memory* was used, for example, in the EDVAC report. Wilkes preferred the more artifactual word *store* (as Babbage had used). Williams further connected computing machines to psychology by his choice of the two terms. As we will see, the idea of the mind–brain as computer and the computer as mind–brain will soon enter into the making of computer science.

The Manchester computer was at first called the Manchester University Digital Computing Machine.[81] Later, and more permanently, mirroring the name of Aiken's machine at Harvard (see Chapter 5, Section V), it came to be called the Manchester Mark I. Like the EDSAC, and faithful to the EDVAC plan, the Mark I used single-address orders.[82]

The most obvious difference between the Mark I and the EDSAC was undoubtedly in the memory. The latter used acoustic delay lines; the former, a cathode ray storage tube.

Although the EDSAC's memory capacity was 1024 17-bit "words," the Mark I memory consisted of 256, 40-binary digit words.[83] However, the Mark I also incorporated an architectural principle that would long outlive the use of electrostatic or delay line memory, and which the EDSAC did not have—the concept of the "B-line."[84]

B-lines were (in present-centered language) index registers that allowed locations of numbers specified in the instruction to be changed without actually altering the contents of the instruction itself. Recall that Babbage had conceived this idea for his Analytical Engine (see Chapter 2, Section V). So a Mark I instruction would be of the form (in present-centered language)

Memory address (S), B-line, Function (f)

and so the execution of this instruction would be

Accumulator ← Accumulator f Memory[S + B-line]

and the contents of a B-line could be modified as

B-line ← B-line ± Memory [S]

Another original feature of the Mark I was (in present-centered language) a secondary (or backup) memory—a drum with up to a 16K-word capacity.[85] There were special commands to transfer from drum to machine and vice versa. Yet another noteworthy feature of the Mark I absent in the EDSAC was that the former's order code included orders to perform the Boolean (logical) operations AND and OR.[86]

A "baby" Mark I was built first. On June 21, 1948, Williams wrote a 17-instruction program to calculate the highest factor of a number, the program just small enough to be held in the 32-by-32-array CRT. He entered the program into the computer through a keyboard. The procedure took 10 minutes to execute. "Suddenly" the correct answer appeared on the screen, accompanied by much cheering by the observers.[87]

So, strictly speaking, the baby Mark I was the first stored-program computer to *become operational*.[88] However, when the baby first ran, it had no provision for automatic input and output. It was not a complete—that is, it was not a *fully* operational—automatic stored-program computer.

The Manchester designers acknowledged that the baby was only a first step—a pilot study. It was a small-scale experimental machine intended to test the viability of the storage principle and to gain some experience of working with this kind of a machine.[89] Yet, the baby was a universal machine in the sense that it could be used to solve any problem that could be reduced to a program of elementary instructions.[90]

In the case of the EDSAC, by February 1949, the input (paper tape reader) and output (teleprinter) mechanisms had been attached to the computer. On May 6, a program to compute a table of squares and print the results was read into the machine, and all of a sudden the results were printed out. Wheeler then wrote a program to compute a table of prime numbers that was soon after executed correctly.[91]

In the light of what happened in the future in the realm of computers and computing—and what in present-centered language is called *information technology*—this event of May 6, 1949, must count as a small step for a small group of people working obscurely in a Cambridge laboratory that would entail a giant leap for humankind.

Wilkes, no doubt, had a flair for the dramatic. A month and a half later, he hosted a conference on automatic computing in Cambridge, which began with a demonstration of the EDSAC in action.[92] The program, written by Wilkes for computing and printing the squares of numbers and their first difference, and Wheeler's program to compute and print a table of primes were run.

As for the Manchester group, a fully operational machine, the Mark I, with input and output facilities was completed in October 1949.[93] Hence, the place of EDSAC as the world's first fully operational automatic stored-program computer.

XIV

An architectural concept: the stored-program computer principle. For both Wilkes in Cambridge and Williams in Manchester, this shared paradigmatic core became the foundation of their respective mental schemas for an automatic digital computer (see Section V, this chapter). Thereafter, their respective schemas were refined and elaborated in two different ways. Each researcher instantiated his schema differently, with the outcome being two distinct schemas with a common core. Each postulated a particular design for a particular machine that conformed to the stored-program computer architectural concept. Each design became the theory for a particular computer such that each of them, Wilkes and Williams, believed that if a computer was built according to their respective designs it would "best" realize the stored-program computer architectural principle as laid out in the EDVAC report.

The implementations of the two machines were two distinct experiments, each a test of a distinct design-as-theory. However, the separation in time between design and implementation, theory and experiment, was not "clean." Rather, the process of implementation went hand in hand with the process of design; theory and experiment overlapped.

Of course, neither Wilkes nor Williams was on his own. Each built a small team; each communicated his respective schema (inner vision, as it were) of what a stored-program computer *should be like* to members of his team. Their schemas were externalized and shared with others. If there was an unfolding paradigm for which the stored-computer concept was the core architectural principle, then we find here the nucleation of two *subparadigms*, each expanding and refining the core principle in a different way.

Something else is noteworthy here. If we think of the EDSAC and the Manchester Mark I designs as representing subparadigms within the overall emerging paradigm, they did not become alternative, competing, mutually exclusive theories of how a stored-program computer should look. Rather, each project was a complementary experiment as a whole that tested the validity of the stored-program computer concept. At the same time, we must keep in mind that the latter concept was an abstract entity. The two projects, in Cambridge and Manchester, represent different pathways to how the abstract stored-program computer concept could give rise to a material computational artifact. Each project was in the business of producing an individual computer with its own design-as-theory. The emerging paradigm of this particular science of the artificial was to be populated, at this early stage in its life, with at least two distinct designs-as-theories, two distinct implementations—using a biological analogy, two distinct species of computational artifacts. Like biological species, these two cultural species (for artifacts are aspects of culture) might survive or might become extinct in the future, or they may give rise to evolutionary descendants. There was nothing to suggest that these two species (and others that might arise in the future either as their descendants or from other principles) embodied alternate, mutually exclusive scientific theories as, for example, Darwinian and Lamarckian evolutionary theories were in 19th-century biology, or deterministic and probabilistic theories were in 20th-century subatomic physics. The subparadigms representing the EDSAC and the Manchester Mark I designs could coexist peacefully, perhaps in friendly competition, as part of the larger computational paradigm.

XV

But what of the EDVAC itself, with a theory and design that had given birth to the stored-program computer paradigm?

As it happened, the ENIAC team dispersed soon after the ENIAC was commissioned. Eckert and Mauchly left to form their own company, and Goldstine and Burks joined von Neumann at the Institute of Advanced Study at Princeton to plan, design, and build a machine along the EDVAC principles using an electrostatic storage tube as the basis for memory.[94] This device was to be developed at the nearby RCA Laboratory by electrical engineer and inventor Jan A. Rajchman (1911–1989); the device was called the *Selectron*.

The detailed principles of the machine (the IAS computer, as it would be called)—its logical design—was delineated in a report issued in June 1946 titled *Preliminary Discussion of the Logical Design of an Electronic Computing Instrument*.[95] Like the EDSAC and the Manchester Mark I, the IAS computer was designed as a single-address computer. The main memory was to be 4096 40-binary digits words; physically, the memory was comprised of 40 Selectron tubes each of 4096 binary digit capacity. A single word of memory would comprise identical locations on all 40 Selectron tubes.

Like the EDVAC report, this report by Burks and colleagues was highly influential in consolidating the stored-program paradigm. However, the IAS computer was not finished until 1952.[96] The main contribution of the paper by Burks and colleagues was, thus, to refine further the logical, conceptual, and theoretical aspects of the paradigm along a separate pathway from those of the Cambridge and Manchester projects.

As for the EDVAC, even though the original conceivers of this machine had left, work on building this machine continued at the Moore School until 1949, when it was trans- ferred to the BRL in Aberdeen, Maryland, where it was completed and became opera- tional in 1951. The EDVAC was discontinued in 1962.[97] With the transfer of the EDVAC, the Moore School's place in the history of computing came to an end.

XVI

A paradigm in science is created by a process that is part social, part cultural, and part intellectual. That a paradigm entails acceptance by a community of practitioners of a sys- tem of ideas and beliefs is undoubtedly a social process. Sometimes, it is even a political process. And it is cultural insofar that it is consistent with the belief systems, the manners and mores of the practitioners. But, it is never an irrational or unintellectual process. There is reason and logic at the core of paradigm formation.

However, science also entails *communication*. Scientists need to let others *know* about their work—others outside their own laboratories. In a natural science such as physics, scientists (or natural philosophers, as they were once called) would correspond with one another. This also enabled scientists to examine, criticize, and test one another's ideas. When Sir Isaac Newton (1642–1727) wrote to fellow natural philosopher Robert Hooke (1635–1703) that "If I have seen further it is by standing on the shoulders of giants," he was surely referring as much to his living contemporaries (such as Hooke) as to his dead predecessors.

During the 17th century, the means of communicating scientific results was greatly enriched, indeed altered, by two related events: the formation of *scientific societies* such as the Royal Society of London, founded in 1660, and the Académie des Sciences, founded in Paris in 1666; and the establishment of *scientific periodicals*, of which the oldest (and still preeminent) was the *Philosophical Transactions of the Royal Society* (1665). Scientific societies formalized the social nature of the scientific enterprise by enabling its members to meet in a common space and for a common cause. Scientific periodicals facilitated com- munication of results in more permanent and public form than letters between scientists.

Implicit in the founding of both societies and periodicals is the presumption that there is a shared field of interest and common agreement about the broad principles underpin- ning the field. They contribute to the social fabric of paradigm formation.

The 1940s witnessed the emergence of this communicative element among the small but growing community of people interested in computers. On January 7–10, 1945, Aiken organized, at Harvard University, a Symposium on Large-Scale Digital Calculating Machines, sponsored jointly by the university and the U.S. Navy's Bureau of Ordinance. The meeting was synchronized with the formal opening of Harvard's new Computation

Laboratory (later renamed the Aiken Computation Laboratory). The program included a demonstration of the Harvard Mark I, and the formal sessions included papers on such topics as the Mark I, the Bell Telephone Laboratory relay computers, delay line memory, electrostatic storage tubes, computational methods for the solution of mathematical problems, and the preparation of problems for automatic computation. The official list of registrants for the symposium numbered more than 325 people from academia, industry, and government, mostly from within the United States (but including Turing).[98]

And (as we have noted) Wilkes organized, in 1949, the Conference on High-Speed Automatic Calculating-Machines in Cambridge, England, sponsored by the University Mathematical Laboratory and the Ministry of Supply of the U.K. government.[99] This was attended by more than 140 participants from Britain, France, Sweden, Holland, and Germany (but none from the United States). In addition to the EDSAC demonstration, there were sessions on relay computers, electrostatic storage tubes, methods of preparing problems for automatic computation, different kinds of storage technologies, the Manchester Mark I, the NPL's ACE, and circuit design.

As for societies, in 1947, some people in the United States began floating the idea of starting an association of those interested in computing machines.[100] Thus began a "mimeographed campaign" for founding the world's first computer society. Originally named Eastern Association for Computing Machinery and formed at a meeting on September 15, 1947 (attended by 78 people), the organization's name was changed to Association for Computing Machinery (ACM) in January 1948.[101] And so, even before the successful completion of the first stored-program computers, a society was in place. Mauchly was the vice-president in the first year and president in the second.

As for periodicals devoted exclusively to computing, the process was rather more tardy. The first such periodical was *Mathematical Tables and Other Aids to Computation* (*MTAC*), a quarterly founded in 1943 and published by the National Research Council (United States).[102] People like Wilkes and Renwick (on the EDSAC); Womersley, head of the NPL's mathematics division; Herman and Adele Goldstine (on the ENIAC); Wallace Eckert (on IBM's plugboard relay machines), Leslie Comrie (on scientific computing); and Franz Alt (on the Bell Laboratory computers) published papers in the *MTAC*. The ACM was surprisingly sluggish; its first journal, *Journal of the ACM,* a quarterly, first appeared in 1954.[103] Clearly, the social aspect of the new paradigm—in terms of the formation of societies and periodicals—was very sparse during the 1940s, perhaps evidence that a paradigm, although born, was still very much in its earliest infancy.

NOTES

1. J. L. Casti. (2003). *The one true platonic heaven* (p. xii). Washington, DC: Joseph Henry Press.
2. H. H. Goldstine. (1972). *The computer from Pascal to von Neumann* (p. 245). Princeton, NJ: Princeton University Press.
3. Ibid., p. 179.

4. Ibid., p. 182.

5. Ibid., p. 183.

6. Ibid., p. 182.

7. Ibid., p. 186.

8. S. M. Ulam. (1980). Von Neumann: The interaction of mathematics and computing. In N. Metropolis, J. Howlett & G.- C. Rota (Eds.), *A history of computing in the twentieth century* (pp. 93–99). New York: Academic Press (see especially p. 94).

9. N. Stern. (1980). John von Neumann's influence on electronic digital computing, 1944–1946. *Annals of the History of Computing, 2*, 349–362.

10. Goldstine, op cit., p. 185.

11. H. A. Simon. (1996). *The sciences of the artificial* (3rd ed.). Cambridge, MA: MIT Press; H. A. Simon (1988). *Reason in human affairs*. Oxford: Basil Blackwell.

12. Goldstine, op cit., p. 183.

13. H. Goldstine. (1944). Draft memorandum. August. Quoted in Goldstine, 1972, op cit., p. 186.

14. J. P. Eckert. (1944). *Disclosure of magnetic calculating machine*. Memorandum. January. Quoted by Stern, op cit., p. 354.

15. Goldstine, op cit., p. 187, citing a report coauthored by J. P. Eckert, J. W. Mauchly, and S. R. Warren, March 31, 1945.

16. Quoted by Goldstine, op cit., p. 187, from a second report by Eckert, Mauchly, and Warren, July 10, 1945.

17. Ibid.

18. M. V. Wilkes. (1985). *Memoirs of a computer pioneer* (p. 109). Cambridge, MA: MIT Press. In this context, I recall vividly a private conversation I had with Sir Maurice Wilkes at a conference in Palo Alto, California, in fall 1983 on this issue. Wilkes was uncompromising in his view: the "logician" von Neumann got all the credit, whereas the true begetters of the main ideas presented in the EDVAC report—the "engineers" Eckert and Mauchly—were denied their deserved plaudits.

19. J. von Neumann (1945). *First draft of a report on the EDVAC.* (Unpublished memorandum). Philadelphia: Moore School of Electrical Engineering. Printed in B. Randell (Ed.), 1975. *The origins of digital computers* (2nd edition). New York: Springer Verlag (pp. 349–354) (see especially, p. 2). All citations to this report will refer to the Randall publication, op cit., p. 2.

20. Ibid.

21. Ibid.

22. Ibid.

23. Ibid., op cit., p. 3.

24. A. Hodges. (1983) *Alan Turing: The Enigma* (pp. 131–132). New York: Simon & Schuster.

25. Ibid., p. 128.

26. F. Smithies. (1959). John von Neumann (obituary). *Journal London Mathematical Society, 34*, 373–384 (see especially p. 374).

27. Hodges, op cit., p. 131.

28. Goldstine, op cit., p. 174.

29. S.. Frankel to B. Randell, private communication, 1972. Quoted in B. Randell. (1972). On Alan Turing and the origins of digital computers. In B. Meltzer & D. Michie (Eds.), *Machine intelligence 7* (pp. 3–22). New York: Wiley (see especially p. 10).

30. Frankel, 1972, as quoted in Randell 1972op cit., p. 10.

31. T. S. Kuhn. (1970). *The structure of scientific revolutions* (2nd ed.). Chicago, IL: University of Chicago Press.

32. F. C. Bartlett. (1932). *Remembering*. Cambridge, UK: Cambridge University Press.

33. Ibid., p. 210.

34. For discussions of schema theory in these various contexts, see, for example, E. H. Gombrich. (1969). *Art and illusion*. Princeton, NL: Princeton University Press; J. Piaget. (1976). *The child and reality*. Harmondsworth, UK: Penguin Books; G. Mandler. (1985). *Cognitive psychology*. Hillsdale, NJ: Lawrence Erlbaum Associates; M. A. Arbib & M. B. Hesse. (1986). *The construction of reality*. Cambridge, UK: Cambridge University Press; R. D'Andrade. (1995). *The development of cognitive anthropology*. Cambridge, UK: Cambridge University Press; S. Dasgupta. (2007). *The Bengal Renaissance*. New Delhi: Permanent Black.

35. Piaget, op cit.

36. Gombrich, op cit., p. 89.

37. von Neumann, op cit., p. 5.

38. Simon, 1996, op cit.

39. Hodges, op cit., p. 307.

40. Ibid.

41. A. M. Turing. (1992). Lecture to the London Mathematical Society. Reprinted in D. C. Ince. (Ed.). *Collected works of A.M. Turing: Mechanical intelligence* (pp. 106–142). Amsterdam: North-Holland (see especially p. 106; original work published 1947).

42. Hodges, op cit., p. 311.

43. Ibid., pp. 314–315.

44. Ibid.

45. Goldstine, op cit., pp. 188–189.

46. A. W. Burks. (1980). From ENIAC to the stored program computer: Two revolutions in computers. In Metropolis, Howlett, & Rota (pp. 311–344), op cit., p. 336.

47. Goldstine, op cit., p. 180.

48. von Neumann, op cit., pp. 12–13, 25–32.

49. Ibid., p. 32. Italics in the original.

50. Burks, op cit., p. 336.

51. Turing, op cit., p. 108.

52. A. M. Turing. (1945). *Proposal for development in the Mathematics Division of an Automatic Computing Engine (ACE)*. Unpublished report, National Physical Laboratory, Teddington. Printed in Ince (pp. 20–105), op cit.

53. Ibid., p. 21.

54. J. H. Wilkinson. (1980). Turing's work at the National Physical Laboratory. In Metropolis, Howlett, & Rota (pp. 101–114), op cit., p. 102.

55. Ibid., p. 111.

56. Ibid., p. 110.

57. Hodges, op cit., p. 370.

58. Ibid., pp. 376, 390.

59. Wilkes, op cit., pp. 108–109.

60. Wilkes, op cit., p. 135.

61. After formal retirement from the university, Wilkes served on the staff of Digital Equipment Corporation, Maynard, Massachusetts, as an engineering consultant (1980–1986) and then with the Olivetti Company in Cambridge, England, as an advisor (1986–2002).

62. Wilkes, op cit., p. 34.

63. Ibid., p. 25.

64. Ibid., p. 28. In 1970, the laboratory was renamed University Computer Laboratory—its current name.

65. Ibid., p. 105.

66. Ibid., p. 135.

67. Ibid., pp. 108–109.

68. Ibid., p. 116.

69. Ibid., pp. 121–124.

70. Ibid., p. 121.

71. Ibid., p. 127.

72. Ibid., p. 129.

73. von Neumann, op cit., p. 37 et seq.

74. Ibid.

75. Ibid.

76. M. V. Wilkes & W. Renwick. (1949). The EDSAC. In Anon. (1950). *Report of a conference on high speed automatic calculating-machines, June 22–25 1949* (pp. 9–11). Cambridge, UK: University Mathematical Laboratory (see especially p. 9).

77. M. Hewett. (1998). Interview of Tom Kilburn. *Personal Computer World, May,* 186–188 (see especially p. 186).

78. Ibid., p. 186.

79. S. H. Lavington. (1980). Computer development at Manchester University. In Metropolis, Howlett, & Rota (pp. 433–443), op cit., p. 433.

80. F. C. Williams. (1949). Cathode ray tube storage. In Anon.>, 1950, op cit., pp. 26–27. The original paper in which this excerpt appeared is F. C. Williams & T. Kilburn. (1949). A storage system for use with binary digital computing machines. *Proceedings of the Institution of Electrical Engineers, 96,* Part 2, No. 30, 183 *ff.*

81. T. Kilburn. (1949). The Manchester University digital computing machine. In Anon, 1950, op cit. (pp. 119–122).

82. Kilburn, op cit., p. 119.

83. Lavington, op cit., p. 435.

84. Kilburn, op cit., p. 121.

85. Lavington, op cit., p. 435.

86. Kilburn, op cit., List of Instructions, (p. 122).

87. Kilburn, in Hewett, op cit., p. 188.

88. Lavington, op cit., pp. 433–434.

89. F. C. Williams & T. Kilburn. (1948). Electronic digital computers. *Nature, 162,* 487.

90. Ibid.

91. Wilkes, 1985, op cit., p. 142.

92. W. Renwick. (1949). The EDSAC demonstration. In Anon, 1950, op cit., pp. 12–16.

93. Lavington, op cit., p. 433.

94. Goldstine, op cit., pp. 240–241.

95. A. W. Burks, H. H. Goldstine, & J. von Neumann. (1946). *Preliminary discussion of the logical design of an electronic computing instrument.* Unpublished report. Princeton, NJ: Institute of Advanced Study. This report has been published widely. See, for example, C. G. Bell & A. Newell. (1971). *Computer structures: Readings and examples* (pp. 92–199). New York: McGraw-Hill. See also B. Randell. (Ed.). (1975a). *The origins of digital computers* (2nd ed., pp. 34–79). New York: Springer-Verlag.

96. B. Randell. (1975b). Stored program electronic computers. In Randell (pp. 349–352), 1975a, op cit., p. 352.

97. Ibid., p. 352.

98. Anon. (1985). *Proceedings of a Symposium on Large-Scale Calculating Machines: The Harvard Computation Laboratory.* (W. Aspray, Introduction). Cambridge, MA: MIT Press (original work published 1947).

99. Anon, 1950, op cit.

100. Notice on organization of an Eastern Association for Computing Machinery. June 25, 1947. Quoted in L. Revens. (1972). The first twenty five years: ACM 1947–1972. *Communications of the ACM, 15,* 485–490 (see especially p. 485).

101. Ibid., p. 485.

102. E. A. Weiss. (1972). Publications in computing: An informal review. *Communications of the ACM, 15,* 491–497.

103. Ibid., p. 494.

9

A Liminal Artifact of an Uncommon Nature

I

THE STORY SO far has been a narrative about the development of two very contrasting types of computational artifacts. On the one hand, Alan Turing conceived the idea of a purely abstract and formal artifact—the Turing machine—having no physical reality whatsoever, an artifact that belongs to the same realm of symbols and symbol manipulation, as do mathematical objects. On the other hand, the major part of this narrative has been concerned with a material artifact, the computer as a physical machine that, ultimately, must obey the laws of physics—in particular, the laws governing electromagnetism and mechanics. This was as true for Babbage's machines (which were purely mechanical) as for Hollerith's tabulator, as true for the electromechanical machines, as for the Harvard Mark I and the Bell Telephone computers, as true for the ABC and the ENIAC, as for the EDSAC and the Manchester Mark I.

Beginning with the EDVAC report, and especially manifest in the development of the first operational stored-program computers, was the dawning awareness of a totally new *kind* of artifact, the likes of which had never been encountered before.

Philosophers speak of the ontology of something to mean the essential nature of that thing, what it means to be that thing. The ontology of this new kind of artifact belonged neither to the familiar realm of the physical world nor the equally familiar realm of the abstract world. Rather, it had characteristics that looked toward both the physical and the abstract. Like Janus, the Roman god of gates, it looked in two opposite directions: a two-faced artifact—which, as we will see, served as the interface between the physical and the abstract, between the human and the automaton; a *liminal* artifact, hovering ontologically between and betwixt the material and the abstract (see Prologue, Section IV). So uncommon was this breed that even a name for it was slow to be coined.

During the Cambridge conference in England in 1949, we find a session devoted to programming and coding.[1] Some years earlier, the ENIAC designers had named the ENIAC's control unit the "master programming unit", and a 1945 report on the ENIAC had referred to a "wish to program the first accumulator to transfer its contents" (see Chapter 7, Section VI). Thus the words *program* and *programming* were in cautious use by 1949, although the more common term was still *coding*.

In 1947, Herman Goldstine and John von Neumann coauthored a three-part report titled *Planning and Coding Problems for an Electronic Computing Instrument*, a lengthy and detailed discussion of preparing programs (or codes) for their IAS computer (yet to be built).[2] At the Cambridge conference, David Wheeler, one of the main designers of the EDSAC system (more on this later) wrote the following:

A PROGRAMME is a flowchart showing the operations (in block form) corresponding to the action of the calculator during the solution of the problem.

A ROUTINE is the programme written in the detailed code of a particular machine.[3]

Wheeler clearly recognized that one represents (in some "code") what one wants the computer to do at different levels of abstraction: as a flowchart, a symbolic notation describing the general nature of the actions a machine must perform, and in the "detailed code" for a "particular machine." The words *flowchart* and *routine* had, clearly, come into usage.

So what was so unique about this species of artifacts that was coming to be called *programs*? In what sense was it Janus faced?

On the one hand, its design and construction involves not matter but symbols. One *writes* a program. Writing entails an alphabet of symbols that are strung together according to certain rules. There is a syntax involved here. Writing necessitates a physical medium certainly, but in itself, what one writes is medium independent. One can write on clay tablets, on papyri, and on electronic devices as much as on paper.

On the other hand, like physical artifacts, a computer program is a dynamic thing; it consumes physical space and physical time. Most tantalizingly, a computer program, although a symbol structure, causes physical things to happen within a computer—much as thought causes bodily motion and bodily change in human beings. In other words, a computer program manifests *agency*.

Programs (or programming) is Janus faced in another way. On the one hand, programming is the means by which humans communicate with the machine, "telling" it what it must do; and the machine, in turn, must understand this communication and interpret the person's commands. On the other hand, programs are the means by which humans conceive computations, represent them to themselves, and communicate them to other human beings. The programmer then looks inward toward the physical computer and outward to herself and others like her.

11

As during the years leading up to and including the development of the ENIAC (see Chapter 7), as in conceiving the stored-program computer idea (see Chapter 8), the emergence of the computer program as a distinct kind of artifact—and programming as an activity—entailed an entanglement of several minds. For, as we can imagine, anyone who was developing a stored-program computer in that era would be forced to grapple with the problem of preparing a problem for solving on such machines.

In 1970, American computer scientist Donald Knuth (1938–) published a paper titled "Von Neumann's First Computer Program."[4] Here, Knuth described the contents of a handwritten 1945 document that he believed was likely the earliest extant computer program for the stored-program digital computer.[5] In contrast to the usual discussions of computational problems, von Neumann's program was concerned with two classic *data processing* tasks (see Chapter 3, Sections V–VII): sorting data (numbers or alphabetic character strings such as names) into nondecreasing order and merging two sequences of sorted data into a single sorted file. IBM had its own special-purpose punched-card machines to perform these two tasks: the IBM 082 sorter and the IBM 085 collator (merger), respectively.[6] von Neumann was interested in whether the order code for the proposed EDVAC could work as well for nonnumeric computations (such as sorting and merging) as for numeric ones—and how efficiently, in terms of speed, it could do so. The availability of the IBM sorter, the most common machine for this task (on punched-card data) afforded him a standard of comparison.[7]

Judging by the fragment of the original handwritten manuscript reproduced in Knuth's article, and Knuth's own commentary on it, von Neumann was not concerned with a language in which to communicate with others. It was, rather, a private notation. The program used quasinumeric symbols to refer to memory addresses (locations) and assigned actual addresses to individual instructions making up the program. He even made his program "relocatable" by designating an unspecified symbolic address "e" and assigning addresses to instructions relative to e.[8]

The physicality of his program was evident; the amount of memory consumed by the program could be estimated. And, by making assumptions about the speed of execution of individual instructions, the execution time (in seconds) of the total program could be estimated.[9] Yet, the EDVAC (for which the program was intended) did not exist! von Neumann's program described a computational process for (in present-centered language) a virtual machine; in fact, what was still a hypothetical machine. There was no physical computer on which the program could be imposed that would "understand" or "interpret" the program and operate accordingly. The program was an abstract artifact in this sense. If von Neumann's sorting program of 1945 was indeed the earliest surviving instance of a program for a stored-program computer, the Janus-faced nature of programs-as-artifacts, their liminality, was manifest at its very inception.

III

Alluding to von Neumann's sorting program, Goldstine would remark that the problem of programming had not been scrutinized sufficiently up to that time,[10] and this was hardly surprising considering the embryonic stage of the field. There would soon be some attempt to rectify this situation, as Arthur Burks, Goldstine, and von Neumann went about preparing their lengthy report *Preliminary Discussion of the Logical Design of an Electronic Computing Instrument* in 1946 (see Chapter 8, Section XV).

Early that year, Goldstine and von Neumann developed a kind of graphical notation as an aid to help describe programs. They named this notation a *flow diagram*. Its objective was, as the name suggested, to express graphically the flow of control through the instructions as they were selected from memory and executed—a sense of *motion* through a computation. The flow diagram would also exhibit the status (contents) of variables at key points during the course of computation. Goldstine would recall that he was soon convinced of the *necessity* of such a notation in programming.[11] Thus, the challenge in both expressing and understanding a flow diagram lay in the melding of the dynamic (the flow of control) with the static (the states of the variables at key points).

The point about necessity is worth noting. Concern for the preparation of a mathematical problem as a computation reach back to Ada Lovelace, as we have seen (see Chapter 2, Section VIII). However, now we see the emergence of a concern for a systematic notation for expressing computer programs. In Goldstine's flow diagram, we see the beginnings of another part of the stored-program computing paradigm: what would later be called *programming languages*.

In their 1947 memorandum titled *Planning and Coding Problems for an Electronic Computing Instrument*, Goldstine and von Neumann articulated explicitly at the very beginning the complexity of their problem.[12] A computer's "control organ" does not just move from one instruction to the next in a linear fashion. If this was the case, there would be no problem. The complexity lay in that the control organ has to "jump" every now and then, forward or backward, and sometimes it has to repeat sequences of instructions. In other words, the control organ must execute branches and iterations. And because in the IAS computer (for which this document was written)[13] the instructions in the Selectron-based main memory (see Chapter 8, Section XV) could be modified by other instructions, there was also the possibility that, in repeating a sequence of instructions, the instructions may have been altered.[14]

The intricacies of programming were being put on the table, and the future programmer of the IAS computer was forewarned by Goldstine and von Neumann that the actual sequence of instructions executed in real time may not coincide with the ordering of the instructions in the program text. The latter is static; the former, dynamic. The point they were making, that the relation of the actual computer program to the mathematical procedure being programmed was not simply a matter of translation, was an important early insight into the complexity of the programming activity. It was not simply a question of translating a piece of mathematical text into code.[15]

In the literary realm, as every thoughtful translator of literary texts written in one language into another has recognized, translation is a creative process, for it entails not just a linguistic conversion, but a mapping from one culture to another. Literary translation has often been referred to as *transcreation* to acknowledge the creative aspect of this process.[16]

The problem of "coding" (that is, programming) is also a problem of mapping from one culture to another—in the case of a solution to a mathematical problem, for example, mapping from mathematical culture to machine culture. Ever since Lovelace, those who have attempted to prepare problems for automatic computation have realized this, but it seems fair to say that Goldstine and von Neumann were probably the first to treat this problem of intercultural translation *as a problem in its own right*, and to bestow on it a huge measure of respect.

A program, a "coded instruction sequence," itself *seems* a static entity—simply a sequence of instructions residing in specific locations of memory. This static appearance is misleading. What one must keep in mind is that a program "text" represents a *process*. And so the art of preparing a program should begin, as Goldstine and von Neumann advised, by planning the course of the *process* itself, its dynamic aspect, and *then* extract from this the actual instruction sequence as a "secondary" operation.[17] Here, Goldstine and von Neumann were grappling with an entirely new intellectual experience, and the insight it led them to was that one should first master the process (a dynamic entity), then program text (a static entity) can be extracted from the process.

Thus, the planning of a program should begin by depicting graphically the movement of the "control organ" through the instructions held in memory as the program is being executed. This graphic depiction ("schematic") is the flow diagram for *the control organ*.[18]

At the heart of why the program text does not mirror the process undertaken by the control organ is the phenomenon of repetition—the fact that the control organ may have to move several times through the same locations in memory to repeat a sequence of instructions.[19] The authors gave a litany of examples from mathematical situations of this sort. A repetitive process—or "iterative" process—would be best "visualized as a loop." Goldstine and von Neumann called it an *inductive loop*. And although a linear sequence of operations with no iteration within it would be represented by a directed line, iterative (or inductive) loops would be symbolized by directed lines that closed in on themselves.

And so the language of the flow diagram unfolds. New symbols are introduced to represent how or when the control organ enters into a process and when it exists—to signify alternative pathways within a process, to specify conditions that cause the control organ to select one or the other of the alternative pathways, to describe actual arithmetic and other numeric operations performed during the course of the process.

The actual (arithmetic) operations performed during the course of a computational process are described by expressions and the destinations of the expression values—in present-centered language, by means of assignment statements. However, Goldstine's flow diagramming language also has something very interesting: "assertion boxes."[20]

An assertion given in an assertion box inserted in a certain point in a flow diagram specifies certain relations are always satisfied whenever the control organ reaches that point.[21] This concept of assertions, describing relations between variables, such as $x + y = n$, or $x < z$, that *always* hold at certain points in the process is a way of stating that, in the midst of all the changes that occur during the course of a process, certain relations always hold—rather as the ancient Greek philosopher Parminedes insisted: behind all the appearance of change there is an unchanging constancy. As we will see later, this concept of static assertions placed within the representations of a dynamic process such as a computer program will become one of the linchpins in the development of (in present-centered language) *programming methodology*. Goldstine and von Neumann anticipated this later development, although it does not seem that they *influenced* those developments. They articulated a programming methodology of their own: programs (or coding, in their language) begins with the construction of flow diagrams.[22]

Their flow diagramming notation had a syntax. There were rules and principles that would have to be followed in drawing a flow diagram, and the reader of such a diagram would have to be conversant with the syntactic principles. In this sense, their flow diagram was more than a notational system; it was a language. Having first drawn the flow diagram showing the overall flow of control (the "dynamic" or "macroscopic" picture, in their language), the programmer then proceeds to code the instructions for the individual tasks shown in the "operation boxes" within a flow diagram. They called this the "static" or "microscopic" stage of programming. The main virtue here was that one could work on the coding of the individual operation boxes independent of one another.[23] In contemporary language, their programming methodology advocated a blend of the hierarchical (macroscopic/microscopic) and the modular (independence of the individual boxes).

Figure 9.1 gives a flavor of how a Goldstine–von Neumann flow diagram might look. The boxes marked # signify assertions; the other boxes specify operations. At two points in the flow diagram alternate pathways are shown, with the path chosen depending on whether the pertinent expression is positive or negative. Iterations, possibly nested in other iterations, are also shown in the diagram.

IV

If *Preliminary Discussion of the Logical Design of an Electronic Computing Instrument* by Burks and colleagues was a manuscript for the architecture of a stored-program computer, *Planning and Coding Problems for an Electronic Computing Instrument* was as surely a manifesto for a methodology of programming that computer. As we have seen, this methodology enfolded both the design of a language in which to describe programs as well as the process of translating a problem into a computation.

However, there was much more to programming and its methodology than this. At the time Goldstine and von Neumann wrote *Planning and Coding Problems for an*

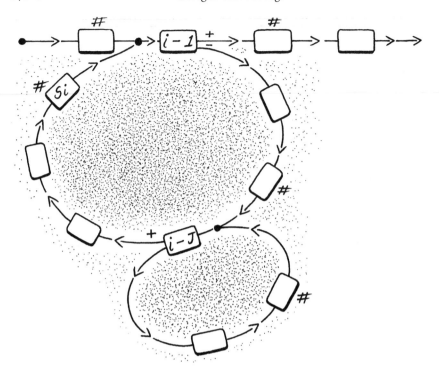

FIGURE 9.1 The Goldstine-von Neumann Flow Diagram.

Electronic Computing Instrument, work was already underway in Cambridge in England on the EDSAC. And Maurice Wilkes understood clearly that as soon as the EDSAC was working, the focus of interest must shift to the realm of programming. He understood that even the simplest task demanded of the EDSAC required a nontrivial program of some sort.[24] And so, very early during the EDSAC project, he assembled a group of people interested in the problem of program development. A committee was assembled to create a library of *subroutines* on which users could draw without having to write them from scratch every time they were needed.[25]

Thus, it was not enough to create a language for expressing a program in some human-comprehensible term; it was not enough to show how the description should be transformed into code for a real computer. "Higher level" building blocks had to be created to facilitate the ordinary user's task of programming a stored-program computer. The subroutine was such a type of building block.

The idea of the subroutine had actually occurred to John Mauchly even before this time. In January 1947, he presented a paper titled *Preparation of Problems for EDVAC-Type Machines* at the Harvard symposium on digital computing machines organized by Howard Aiken (see Chapter 8, Section XVI). In this paper, Mauchly dwelled on a basic decision problem that all computer designers would face: to distinguish between operations that must be built into the machine (hardwired, in present-centered terms) and those that should be programmed.[26] He made the point that this would depend on the frequency of operations and the ease with which the "nonbuilt" operations could be programmed on a given machine.

He then noted that some operations that are not "built-in" may still occur with sufficient frequency that, although it may not be justified to "build them into" the machine, one should not have to program them *ab initio* every time. Rather, he imagined magnetic tapes that would contain small programs that performed these operations, prepared once and for all, which could then be summoned into use whenever needed by different programmers for their respective programs. Mauchly used the term *subroutines* to signify such frequently used and usable programs. But, he warned, they must be sufficiently flexible to be genuinely general purpose.[27] In fact, half of Mauchly's paper was devoted to the topic of subroutines and how to implement them in a practical way.

That same year, a month after Mauchly's presentation, in his lecture to the London Mathematical Society (see Chapter 8, Section VIII), Alan Turing also mentioned, although far more briefly, the necessity of what he called "subsidiary tables"—essentially, subroutines.[28]

There is also anecdotal evidence, recalled many years later, that Grace Murray Hopper, who had worked with Aiken on the development of the Harvard Mark I and coauthored a three-part paper on that machine (see Chapter 5, Sections V and VI), was aware of the subroutine concept at that time (the mid 1940s). Recollecting her experiences in a keynote address given at a conference on the history of programming languages in June 1978, she spoke of writing subroutines, although they were not called as such, but rather thought of simply as "pieces of code."[29]

Thus the concept of the subroutine was much "in the air" in the mid to late 1940s. The question of who "invented" the subroutine, like the larger question of who "invented" the stored-program computer, is highly problematic, for it depends on what we mean by *invention*.

If we were to signify by "invention" the *conceptualization* of an idea, then Mauchly should probably have the credit. If Hopper's recollection was correct, then the *term* "subroutine" existed as early as 1944. Mauchly, however, clearly conceived the notion of subroutines existing as entities (on magnetic tape) independent of the physical computer but summoned to use on and by the physical computer when required. Subroutines are programs that would become building blocks in the creation of larger programs. Here was an idea of the *autonomy* of a computer program—an artifact at once apart from the physical computer but with a usefulness that depended on the physical computer—a realization of the liminality of programs (see Prologue, Section III).

On the other hand, if invention in the world of useful artifacts entails not just the conception or ideation but the *construction* of the first artifacts that carry the idea into a complete, demonstrable form, then it would seem that David Wheeler in the Cambridge University Mathematical Laboratory was the "real" inventor of the subroutine as a class of liminal computational artifacts.

V

Wheeler, as a student of Trinity College, Cambridge, read for the mathematics tripos and obtained his degree in 1948.[30] He joined the EDSAC project as a research student immediately after graduation.[31] When the time came for the EDSAC group to think about how the machine should be used, Wilkes suggested to Wheeler that he should "imagine" that the machine was completed and investigate how it should be used.[32]

This kind of "imagining" could never have happened in the days when an artifact's conceptual design existed entirely in the mind of a single creator, and the creator made the artifact based on his private mental concept, had computer designs still been at the "craft stage" (see Chapter 2, Section VIII).[33] Wheeler's "imagining" was possible because the EDSAC existed, if not materially, then in abstract form as a design that was shared by members of the EDSAC team. In present-centered language, this design was the EDSAC architecture—a liminal artifact, abstract on the one hand, yet its physical realization sufficiently well understood that Wheeler could "imagine" the workings of the physical computer as if it had been completed and in use.

Wheeler's response was twofold. The first was the development and use of subroutines and the creation of a subroutine library. At the Cambridge conference in June 1949, Wheeler presented a paper titled *Planning the Use of a Paper Library* and began by noting that "different problems have many parts in common."[34] He went on to say that these "parts" may be prepared "once and for all" but—echoing Mauchly—they must be sufficiently flexible so that they can be adapted to differing problem contexts, thus the prospect of a library of subroutines.[35]

Then, after defining "programme" and "routine," he explained that a subroutine "is the coded form of an element in a routine (e.g., square root, input and binary decimal conversion, etc.)" (see Section I, this chapter). He went on to state the advantages of a subroutine and a library of such entities: simplification of the task of preparing problems for computation, facilitating the understanding of routines by other users, and, if the subroutines are correct then the chances of errors in a routine as a whole are considerably reduced. These advantages originate in the fact that subroutines are larger functional "units" in a program than the order codes themselves.

Wheeler did not just conceive an idea, however; he actually built subroutines and demonstrated how they could be used. He identified certain problems engendered by the subroutine concept and proposed solutions to them.

One of the problems was that instructions (orders) within a subroutine refer to memory locations (addresses) of the "data" (*operands*, as they were being called by 1951[36]) relevant to that subroutine only. This meant that the subroutine would have to be placed in a fixed set of locations in the EDSAC memory. It would always have to be placed in that same set of locations. Wheeler proposed, instead, a more flexible solution that allowed for the "relocatability" of a subroutine, which involved putting the subroutine on the tape in such a way that it deferred fixing its location in memory until when it would be input into the machine. The latter task, in turn, would necessitate a "special" subroutine.[37]

Another problem was to make a subroutine for a particular kind of task sufficiently general by using parameters that could be set to specific values for each instance of the subroutine's use. These parameters could be "external"—set to values at the beginning of the subroutine's use, which would remain fixed throughout the execution of the subroutine—or "internal," meaning that their values could vary during the solution of the problem.[38]

A third problem was where and how a subroutine should be invoked for execution. Here, Wheeler distinguished between two types of subroutines. In the first, and simpler, situation, control is transferred to the beginning order of the subroutine and, when the latter ends, execution control simply flows to the order located immediately after the subroutine in memory. Wheeler termed such a subroutine "open."[39] But, this was not very flexible, for if the subroutine was required to be used at several points in the main program, as many copies of the subroutine would have to be inserted in the appropriate places. Instead, Wheeler conceived the *closed* subroutine, which would be called from some location within a program and, on its execution, control would be transferred to the point in the "calling" program immediately after the location from when the subroutine was called.[40]

So, a closed subroutine can be placed anywhere in the EDSAC memory, *outside* the main program. When it was needed to be called from a point in the calling (main) program—say, from address n—control "jumps" to the first instruction in the subroutine. At the end of the subroutine's execution, control "jumps back" to address $n + 1$. This mechanism came to be called the *Wheeler jump* (Figure 9.2).

VI

Wheeler's other major invention was as consequential as that of the subroutine. To understand the nature of this second contribution, let us follow his own words:

> It is inconvenient to write our orders in their binary form, and so we shall write them in the following form. The first five binary digits [within an order, called the *function digits*, which specify the function or operation to be performed] will be represented by the capital letter that represents these digits on the keyboard perforator. The next 11 binary digits [signifying the operand in memory] will be represented by an integer n in the normal decimal form. This integer is the address referred to in the order.... The last digit [signifying the length of the operand, "long" (binary 1) or "short" (binary 0)] will be represented by D if...[long] and if...[short] it will be represented by F.[41]

Thus, an instruction that in binary form is 11100 0 00000001110 1 would be written as *A 14 D*. Wheeler was using a *symbolic* notation to specify an instruction. A fragment of a program would look like that presented in Table 9.1.[42]

We have seen that the flow diagram invented by Goldstine and von Neumann was also a symbolic system, as was the notation von Neumann used to describe his sorting

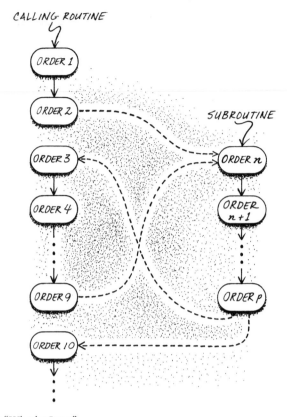

FIGURE 9.2 The "Wheeler Jump".

TABLE 9.1 A Fragment of an Assembly Language Program for the EDSAC

Location of order	Order
100	H 103 F
101	E 108 F
102	P 5 F
103	J F

program. However, Wheeler's symbolism was more consequential. It was more than a notation. We realize this when he writes about his "initial orders":

> As the reading of data from input tape is controlled directly by orders held in the store we require some process to start the machine. Orders have been wired on a set of uniselectors and when the starting button of the machine is pressed these are automatically placed in the store and the action of these orders causes the tape to be read. These orders are called initial orders.[43]

At first blush, it seems that the initial orders act simply to load a program from paper tape into EDSAC memory and begin its execution—what came to be called a program *loader*.[44] However, the initial orders do much more. To begin with, the instructions were written and punched on paper tape in the symbolic form just described, then the initial orders read the symbols on the tape and (a) *translated* them automatically, one order at a time, into binary form—representing the functions to be performed by the orders and the addresses of the numbers to be accessed on which the function would be performed (that is, the operands); (b) *assembled* the orders in proper fashion (the function digit, the operand addresses, and the length discrimination digits); and (c) placed the assembled orders into the EDSAC memory by means of a special order.[45]

In present-centered terms, this was a *programming system*—an ensemble of "application-independent" programs that makes the computer usable to the "ordinary" programmer.[46] Wheeler had invented a rudimentary but usable programming system—arguably the very first—comprising, in his case, an *assembly language* to write EDSAC programs in symbolic form, an *assembler* that translated the assembly language programs automatically into binary form, and a *loader* that would load the assembled code into memory prior to its execution.

An assembler is one of the simpler types of automatic language translators, although, as the architecture of the stored-program computer evolved in complexity, this translation process would evolve concomitantly in complexity.[47] Wheeler's "initial orders" combined the functions of assembler and loader.

VII

Wheeler's two major inventions, the closed subroutine and the assembly language/assembler–loader programming system perhaps make him the first *systems programmer*—a person who writes and implements programs that aid others who are the users of the computer. Interestingly, the Manchester Mark I group working contemporaneously eschewed the idea of symbolic programming and assembly,[48] although, as we will see, in the realm of systems programming they more than compensated for this decision in later projects.

The EDSAC project not only heralded the first fully operational stored-program computer, but also it unfolded and expanded the stored-program computer paradigm in directions that perhaps Wilkes himself had not contemplated when he began the project in 1946.

The very idea of a computing *machine* had been enlarged. The machine was now a symbiosis of two kinds of artifacts, the physical computer built of electronic and electromechanical components and the liminal, quasi-autonomous "two-faced" artifact called computer program (or, later, *software*) that would serve as the interface between the human user and the physical computer. We see here, the interplay of two kinds of computational artifacts, the material and the liminal.

Moreover, a distinction between two classes of programs had emerged, although names for these classes were yet to come. There were the programs that were written to solve the computational problems of interest to users of the machine. In present-centered terms, these were the *application programs*. And there were the programs that would facilitate the running of application programs—what would be called *system programs*.

The paradigm had not shifted. Its core was still the concept of the stored-program computer principle as the EDVAC report had prescribed. However, the physicality of the stored-program computer had been *decentered* within the paradigm. The physical computer now coexisted in equal footing with the liminal programs. It was not enough to design and build a physical machine; it was as important to design and build programs that facilitated the use of the physical machine. In present-centered language, with the EDSAC, the dichotomy of the concepts of *hardware* and *software* came into existence, if not the terms themselves.

Wilkes and his colleagues fully realized just how central programs and programming was to this paradigm's efficacy. In 1951, he and two research students, Wheeler and Stanley Gill (1926–1975) published (in America, as it happened) *Preparation of Programmes for an Electronic Digital Computer*.[49] This was the first book on computer programming.

Thomas Kuhn had emphasized that one of the characteristics of a mature paradigm is the availability of texts that defined the state of knowledge within the discipline. *Preparation of Programmes for an Electronic Digital Computer* served precisely such a role for at least one significant part of the stored-program computer paradigm. In fact, the publication of this book was a proclamation of the centrality of programming in the evolving paradigm.

NOTES

1. Anon. (1950). *Report on a conference on high speed automatic calculating-machines, June 22–25, 1949*. Cambridge, UK: University Mathematical Laboratory.

2. H. H. Goldstine & J. von Neumann. (1947). *Planning and coding problems for an electronic computing instrument*. Unpublished report. Princeton, NJ: Institute of Advanced Study. This report was later published in A. H. Taub. (Ed.). (1963). *John von Neumann, collected works* (Vol. 5, pp. 8–235). New York: Pergamon.

3. D. J. Wheeler. (1949). Planning the use of a paper library. In Anon (pp. 36–40), 1950, op cit., p. 36.

4. D. E. Knuth. (1970). Von Neumann's first computer program. *ACM Computing Surveys*, 2, 247–260. Reprinted in D. E. Knuth. (1996). *Selected papers on computer science* (pp. 205–226). Stanford, CA: Center for the Study of Language and Information. All citations to this article will refer to the 1996 reprint.

5. Knuth, 1996, op cit., p. 205.

6. F. P. Brooks, Jr. & K. E. Iverson. (1969). *Automatic data processing: System/360 edition* (pp. 75–81). New York: Wiley.

7. Knuth, op cit., p. 206.

8. Ibid., p. 220.

9. Ibid., pp. 211, 222.

10. H. H. Goldstine. (1972). *The computer from Pascal to von Neumann* (p. 266). Princeton, NJ: Princeton University Press.

11. Ibid.

12. Goldstine & von Neumann, op cit., p. 1.

13. A. W. Burks, H. H. Goldstine, & J. von Neumann. (1946). *Preliminary discussion of the logical design of an electronic computing instrument.* Princeton, NJ: Institute of Advanced Study.

14. Goldstine & von Neumann, op cit., pp. 1–2.

15. Ibid., p. 4.

16. The literature on the art and science of translation is vast. The interested reader may consult, for example, G. Steiner. (1975). *After Babel: Aspects of language and translation.* Oxford: Oxford University Press; A. Dingwaney & C. Maeir. (Eds.). (1995). *Between languages and cultures.* Pittsburgh, PA: University of Pittsburgh Press; S. Chaudhuri. (2002). *Translation and understanding.* New Delhi: Oxford University Press.

17. Goldstine & von Neumann, op cit., p. 4.

18. Ibid.

19. Ibid.

20. Ibid., p. 14.

21. Goldstine & von Neumann, op cit., p. 17.

22. Ibid., p. 20.

23. Ibid.

24. M. V. Wilkes. (1985). *Memoirs of a computer pioneer* (p. 143). Cambridge, MA: MIT Press.

25. Ibid.

26. J. W. Mauchly. (1975). Preparation of problems for EDVAC-type machines. In B. Randell (Ed.), *The origins of digital computers* (2nd ed., pp. 365–360). New York: Springer-Verlag (original work published 1947; see especially p. 367).

27. Ibid.

28. A. M. Turing. (1947). Lectures to the London Mathematical Society, February 20. Reprinted in D. C. Ince. (Ed.). (1992). *Collected works of A.M. Turing: Mechanical intelligence* (pp. 106–124). Amsterdam: North-Holland (see especially p. 118).

29. G. M. Hopper. (1978). Keynote address. In R. L. Wexelblat (Ed.), *History of programming languages* (pp. 7–20). New York: Academic Press (see especially p. 8).

30. Anon. (1985). *David Wheeler, 1985 Computer Pioneer Award* [On-line]. Citation. IEEE Computer Society. Available: http://www.computer.org

31. Wilkes, op cit., p. 148.

32. Ibid., p. 143.

33. J. C. Jones. (1980). *Design methods: Seeds of human future* (2nd ed.) New York: Wiley.

34. Wheeler, op cit., p. 36.

35. Ibid.

36. D. J. Wheeler. (1951). *Automatic computing with the EDSAC.* PhD dissertation, University of Cambridge, p. 13.

37. Wheeler, 1949, op cit., p. 37.

38. Ibid.

39. Wheeler, 1951, op cit., pp. 39–40.

40. Ibid.

41. Ibid., 1951, p. 114.

42. Ibid., 1951, p. 19.

43. Ibid., 1951, p. 23.

44. D. W. Barron. (1978). *Assemblers and loaders* (3rd ed.). New York: Elsevier North-Holland.

45. Wheeler, 1951, op cit., p. 24.

46. Brooks & Iverson, op cit., p. 364.

47. Barron, op cit.

48. Ibid., p. 2.

49. M. V. Wilkes, D. J. Wheeler, & S. Gill. (1951). *Preparation of programmes for an electronic digital computer*. Cambridge, MA: Addison-Wesley.

10

Glimpses of a Scientific Style

I

IN AUGUST 1951, David Wheeler submitted a PhD dissertation titled *Automatic Computing with the EDSAC* to the faculty of mathematics (D. F. Hartley, personal communication, September 7, 2011) at the University of Cambridge.[1] The year after, in November 1952, another of Maurice Wilkes's students, Stanley Gill, submitted a thesis titled *The Application of an Electronic Digital Computer to Problems in Mathematics and Physics.*[2]

Wheeler's was not the first doctoral degree awarded on the subject of computing. That honor must surely go to Herman Hollerith for his thesis submitted to Columbia University in 1890 on his invention of an electrical tabulating system (see Chapter 3, Section IV). Nor was Wheeler's the first doctoral degree on a subject devoted to *electronic* computing. In December 1947, Tom Kilburn (codesigner with Frederic C. Williams of the Manchester Mark I [see Chapter 8, Section XIII]) had written a report on the CRT-based memory system he and Williams had developed (but called the *Williams tube*). This report was widely distributed in both Britain and the United States (and even found its way to Russia),[3] and it became the basis for Kilburn's PhD dissertation awarded in 1948 by the University of Manchester (S. H. Lavington, personal communication, August 31, 2011).

Wheeler's doctoral dissertation, however, was almost certainly the first on the subject of *programming*. And one might say that the award of these first doctoral degrees in the realm of computer "hardware" (in Kilburn's case) and computer "software" (in Wheeler's case) made the invention and design of computers and computing systems an academically respectable university discipline.

As we have witnessed before in this story, establishing priority in the realm of computing is a murky business, especially at the birth of this new discipline. Thus, if by "computer science" we mean the study of computers and the phenomena surrounding computers (as three eminent computer scientists Allan Newell, Alan Perlis (1922–1990), and Herbert Simon suggested in 1967[4]), then—assuming we agree on what "computers" are—the boundary between hardware and software, between the physical computer and the activity of computing, dissolves. Kilburn's PhD dissertation of 1948 belongs as much to computer science as does Wheeler's of 1951. If, on the other hand, computer science is viewed as one of two—or even three—"computer cultures," along with computer technology and computer mathematics,[5] then Kilburn's dissertation belongs to computer technology and Wheeler's to computer science.

One marker of the unease over this question of "identity" is that a venerable book series comprising critical surveys of various research topics that has been published continuously since 1960 continues to bear its original title *Advances in Computers*, not *Advances in Computer Science* or any other disciplinary name. In contrast, comparable book series in other fields refer to the discipline, not the object of study such as, for example, *Advances in Psychology* or *Advances in Anthropology*, and so on. The debate has not abated to this day, and this very fact suggests that it is, to a large extent, an unresolvable, perhaps even sterile, debate. Indeed, some recent thinkers have adopted *computing* or *computing sciences* as umbrella terms encompassing every discipline to do with computation. They have suggested that computer science is a subdiscipline of the "computing sciences."[6]

Certainly, during the first decade of the stored-program computer, pioneers such as Wilkes, Kilburn, and Turing in Britain; and Burks, Goldstine, and von Neumann in America freely crossed "cultural" boundaries. In narrating this story, I have assumed the definition proposed at its very beginning: computer science is the science of automatic computation and, thus, the science of automatic symbol processing (see Prologue, Section I). This subsumes the viewpoint of Newell, Perlis, and Simon cited earlier.

II

But let us return to the two dissertations authored by Wheeler in 1951 and Gill in 1952. Wheeler tells us that his dissertation presents an account of methods developed for the EDSAC, but these methods are as applicable for other computing machines.[7] As for Gill, he, too, asserts that his work as presented in his dissertation are his own particular contributions to the methods devised for the EDSAC.[8]

Both these men, then, were concerned with the development of *methods* for using the EDSAC. Yet, like Wheeler, Gill also pointed out that although the methods described were for the EDSAC, they would interest users of other similar machines.[9]

Here we see two common characteristics of these dissertations: they were both concerned with a *single computational artifact* (in their case, the EDSAC) and with the *methodology* of its use. Both authors stated categorically that what they produced were methods; their contribution to this still-embryonic science was in methodology. And although they were concerned with a particular computer, the EDSAC, they both believed that the methodology had a "universal" potential, that it embodied ideas that were valid for other similar computational artifacts.

So what shape did this methodology take?

III

Wheeler, as we have seen, invented the closed subroutine and a symbolic language that would later be called assembly language, along with a programming system for assembling and loading the program into the EDSAC memory prior to execution (see Chapter 9, Sections V and VI). Thus, when he spoke of "methods," they were his methods. His language to describe these methods is worth noting. He speaks of programs that "are usually" constructed from subroutines, that "it is convenient" to build a library of subroutines,[10] that "it is not convenient" to use subroutines in some circumstances,[11] and why "it is very necessary" to remove errors from a program before it is used.[12]

"It is convenient," "are usually," "it is not convenient," "it is very necessary." The phrases used by Wheeler are not descriptions or analyses of the way things are, but of the way things *should be*. Wheeler is not like natural scientists or pure mathematicians, who are concerned with how things are; he is concerned with how things ought to be (see Prologue, Section II). Moreover, these phrases do not describe objective situations, objects, or events of the sort that traditional engineering research deals with. *Human beings are part of the system being described*. Indeed, "description" is the wrong word. What Wheeler stated were *prescriptions*, telling the reader (particularly, the potential EDSAC user) how to go about doing certain programming tasks. And prescription is, of course, what methodology is all about.

However, scientific research, not the least research leading to the academic respectability of a PhD, must produce knowledge of some kind. In the natural sciences, knowledge is fundamentally in the form of theories, hypotheses, laws, "facts," experimental or natural observations, measurements, and so on. These kinds of knowledge declare or state properties or relationships. Colloquially, they are "know-that" knowledge; more formally, *declarative* knowledge.[13]

The kind of knowledge produced by Wheeler and described in his dissertation was not declarative knowledge. It might *seem* that he was declaring what a closed subroutine was, what initiating orders were, what interpretive subroutines were, what the EDSAC assembly language and the assembler–loader system were, but his descriptions of these entities were a means to an end. The knowledge he actually produced was *how to use* those concepts: "know-how." Hungarian-British scientist–philosopher Michael Polanyi (1891– 1976) called such a piece of knowledge an "operational principle."[14] Accordingly, I will call rules, methods, operations, and procedures that specify how to do things *operational knowledge*. Technological knowledge, no matter how grounded it is in mathematics or the natural sciences, is ultimately in the form of operational knowledge.[15]

There are, of course, operational principles in the natural sciences. Experimental techniques, methods of chemical analysis, deployment of scientific instruments all embody operational knowledge. However, the difference is crucial. Operational knowledge in the natural sciences are means to the production of declarative knowledge. A chemist learns to use a spectrometer to obtain (declarative) knowledge of the composition of a complex chemical compound, whereas in the kind of science Wheeler practiced for his PhD dissertation, declarative knowledge is at best the *means* to the production of operational knowledge. Ultimately, operational knowledge is what matters in the sciences of the artificial.

IV

We observe a similar pursuit of operational knowledge in Gill's dissertation. As the title states, his concern was to show *how* the stored-program computer in general, and the EDSAC in particular, could solve problems in mathematics and physics. The basic schema for doing this, as his chapters explicate, was (a) describe the problem, (b) discuss the general approach to its solution, and (c) specify the process.

The end product, the desired result, were procedures—in his case, in the form of EDSAC programs (specifically, subroutines). These subroutines *were* the knowledge Gill produced, as he acknowledged.[16]

However, it is not enough to describe the automatic procedures embedded in a subroutine. One must also describe the rules *humans* have to follow when deploying the subroutines. So human actions or choices are also knowledge products. Gill stipulates that one of the subroutines he had developed "may be placed anywhere" in the EDSAC memory;[17] that another subroutine "requires" some additional subroutines to be used in conjunction with it.[18] He writes that certain variables "are [to be] stored" in a certain manner in memory, that a certain number of memory locations "are required" by a certain subroutine, that a certain parameter "should be chosen" to meet a certain condition,[19] that the first order of a particular subroutine "must be placed" in a certain location in memory.[20]

The words in quotes specify what a user has to do to enable the subroutines to work successfully. Gill's awareness of the nature of the knowledge he produced was revealed at the conclusion of one of the chapters wherein he claimed that the originality of his work lay in the particular subroutines described in that chapter, along with the programming techniques described for solving differential equations.[21]

The operational knowledge produced by Wheeler and Gill was a blend of human and machine operational principles—very specifically, computer programs, procedures, notation (language) to use, and rules. Their contributions acknowledged the significance of the human being and of the necessity of a symbiosis of human and machine in automatic computing.[22]

Moreover, they were not just concerned with the method of programming the EDSAC, although that machine was the vehicle of their thinking. Their concern was more universal: the general problem of program development (in present-centered language, programming methodology). Indeed, Gill must surely be among the very first to regard this new kind of artifact called a computer program in terms of what psychologists would call *developmental* and biologists would call *ontogenetic*. I have used the word *ontogeny* earlier in this story (see Chapter 7, Section I). Biologists use this word to mean the "life history of an individual both embryonic and postnatal,"[23] whereas, to the psychologist, development refers broadly to the expansion of mental capabilities with respect to experience and competence, from infancy to adulthood.[24] Both biologists and psychologists view development as a record of change (to the body in one case, the mind in the other) from an elemental, embryonic, or undifferentiated state into a complex, differentiated, mature, and fully functioning state. This same notion was carried into the domain of programming by Gill. Thus, he explains that when using an automatic computer to solve a problem, one must first express the problem in mathematical terms, then formulate the latter in terms of the operations the computer must carry out. There is, then, a *human* process preceding the machine process, and the former is what Gill called "the development of the programme." He further noted that this development process causes the "programme" to change "form," both structurally and logically.[25]

He identified three significant kinds of change: (a) transformation of "human-oriented" statements to "machine-oriented" statements—the former more easily comprehended by human beings, and the latter interpretable by the machine; (b) transition from a sequence of general statements to a precise, machine-executable sequence of operations; and (c) transformation from symbolic statements to assertions that relate to particular circuits within the machine.[26] Gill noted that all these changes must happen before automatic computation can even begin. And the user's aim was to effect these changes simply and economically.[27]

So these changes are to be effected as part of program development "outside the machine."[28] However, program development does not end there; further changes must occur "during the input of the programme."[29] This is when the machine has its first role in this process—for example, in converting decimal numbers to binary form[30] or in inserting actual values to parameters within instructions. These tasks are performed by the initial orders. Other tasks performed by the machine in program development were the process of assembly and loading (see Chapter 9, Section VI), and the loading of subroutines into memory.

Last, program development also occurred "during the course of the calculation"[31]—that is, while a program was actually executed. Here, the agent of development was entirely the machine. A particular example was the inclusion of "interpretive routines," which is a routine held in a computer's memory and that executes instructions in another routine also held in memory, one at a time. In other words, an interpretive routine translates an instruction into a set of actions that are executed immediately before the next instruction is interpreted.[32]

The term *interpretive routine*[33] would later enter the mainstream language of programming as *interpreter*.[34] Interestingly, Gill likened the action of an interpretive routine to the operation of Alan Turing's "universal computing machine" of 1936 (see Chapter 4, Section V), which can imitate another machine.[35] This is a *very* rare instance of the early innovators of practical stored-program computers making an explicit reference to Turing's theoretical work.

Gill clearly believed that an understanding of the stages in the development of a program—with *humans and machines as co-agents* in the process—was important, that the articulation of this understanding constituted an important body of operational knowledge. Thus, his claim to the originality of his PhD dissertation lay as much (as he stated) in his contribution to this overall understanding as to the development of particular procedures (subroutines) for solving particular problems in mathematics and physics.[36]

V

These two dissertations for which PhDs were conferred by the University of Cambridge are invaluable in what they reveal about an emerging science of computing. They offer glimpses of what we may call a scientific *style* in the realm of computing research.

Discussions of style belong predominantly in the realm of art, architecture, and literature. Indeed, for some art historians the history of art *is* the history of artistic style,[37] just as the history of architecture *is* the history of architectural style.[38] For art and architectural historians, *style* refers to features of paintings, sculptures, buildings that allow works to be "placed" in their historical setting.[39]

But style also refers to the *way* in which something is done. In this sense, it characterizes some pattern in the way one perceives, visualizes, thinks, reasons, symbolizes, represents, and draws on knowledge in the pursuit of doing something. Generally speaking, we may call this *cognitive style*; understanding a person's creativity may entail unveiling his cognitive style.[40] In the realm of science, we can detect an individual scientist developing her own particular cognitive style of doing science, her *scientific style*.[41]

We can also imagine a community of like-minded people coming to share a cognitive style. This is well understood in the realms of painting (such as impressionism, surrealism), and literary writing (such as magical realism); it may also produce, among a community of scientists, a shared scientific style.

It is in this sense that Wheeler's and Gill's dissertations document a scientific style. Its fundamental trait was operationalism—the search for rules, procedures, operations, methods—but its product is operational knowledge. If a computer *science* was slowly emerging, the production or generation of operational knowledge about humans and machines *cooperating* in support of automatic computing was certainly one of its first manifestations.

NOTES

1. D. J. Wheeler. (1951). *Automatic computing with the EDSAC.* PhD dissertation, University of Cambridge.

2. S. Gill. (1952). *The application of an electronic digital computer to problems in mathematics and physics.* PhD dissertation, University of Cambridge.

3. S. H. Lavington. (1998). *A history of Manchester computers.* London: The British Computer Society (original work published 1976); S. H. Lavington & C. Burton. (2012). *The Manchester machines*; S. H. Lavington (ed.). (2012). *Alan Turing and his contemporaries* (chapter 4). London: British Computer Society.

4. A. Newell, A. J. Perlis, & H. A. Simon. (1967). What is computer science? *Science, 157,* 1373–1374.

5. P. Wegner. (1970). Three computer cultures: Computer technology, computer mathematics, and computer science. In F. L. Alt (Ed.), *Advances in computers* (Vol. 10, pp. 7–78). New York: Academic Press.

6. P. S. Rosenbloom. (2013). *On computing.* Cambridge, MA: MIT Press; P. J. Denning. (2007). Computing is a natural science. *Communications of the ACM, 50,* 13–18; P. J. Denning & P. A. Freeman. (2009). Computing's paradigm. *Communications of the ACM, 52,* 28–30.

7. Wheeler, op cit., Preface.

8. Gill, op cit., Preface.

9. Ibid.

10. Wheeler, op cit., p. 25.

11. Ibid., p. 26.

12. Ibid., p. 49.

13. S. Dasgupta. (1996). *Technology and creativity* (pp. 33–34). New York: Oxford University Press.

14. M. Polanyi. (1962). *Personal knowledge* (p. 176). Chicago, IL: University of Chicago Press.

15. Dasgupta, op cit., pp. 157–158.

16. Gill, op cit., p. 40.

17. Ibid., p. 41.

18. Ibid., p. 203.

19. Ibid.

20. Ibid., p. 204.

21. Ibid., p. 49.

22. Ibid., pp. 62–87.

23. S. J. Gould. (1977). *Ontogeny and phylogeny* (p. 483). Cambridge, MA: Belknap Press of Harvard University Press.

24. See, for example, J. Piaget. (1976). *The child & reality.* Harmondsworth, UK: Penguin Books; M. Donaldson. (1992). *Human minds: An exploration* (p. 190). Harmondsworth, UK: Penguin Books.

25. Gill, op cit., p. 63.

26. Ibid.

27. Ibid.

28. Ibid., p. 67.

29. Ibid., p. 71.

30. Ibid., p. 72.

31. Ibid., p. 77.

32. Ibid., p. 78.

33. The term was apparently coined by another member of the EDSAC group, an Australian, John Bennett (1921–2010–), who was, in fact, the first research student to join the Mathematical Laboratory in Cambridge. See M. V. Wilkes. (1985). *Memoirs of a computer pioneer* (p. 140). Cambridge, MA: MIT Press. See also Gill, op cit., p. 78.

34. F. P. Brooks, Jr. & K. E. Iverson. (1969). *Automatic data processing: System/360 edition* (pp. 365 *ff*). New York: Wiley.

35. Gill, op cit., p. 80.

36. Ibid., p. 87.

37. H. Wolfflin. (1932). *Principles of art history*. New York: Dover Publications.

38. N. Pevsner. (1962). *An outline of European architecture*. Harmondsworth, UK: Penguin Books.

39. R. Wollheim. (1984). *Painting as an art* (p. 26 et seq.). Princeton, NJ: Princeton University Press.

40. See, for example, S. Dasgupta. (2003). Multidisciplinary creativity: The case of Herbert A. Simon. *Cognitive Science, 27*, 683–707.

41. Ibid.

II

I Compute, Therefore I Am

∽ ───

I

THE 1940S WITNESSED the appearance of a handful of scientists who, defying the specialism characteristic of most of 20th-century science, strode easily across borders erected to protect disciplinary territories. They were people who, had they been familiar with the poetry of the Nobel laureate Indian poet–philosopher Rabindranath Tagore (1861–1941), would have shared his vision of a "heaven of freedom":

> Where the world has not been broken up into
> fragments by narrow domestic walls.[1]

Norbert Wiener (1894–1964), logician, mathematician, and prodigy, who was awarded a PhD by Harvard at age 17, certainly yearned for this heaven of freedom in the realm of science as the war-weary first half of the 20th century came to an end. He would write that he and his fellow scientist and collaborator Arturo Rosenbluth (1900–1970) had long shared a belief that, although during the past two centuries scientific investigations became increasingly specialized, the most "fruitful" arenas lay in the "no-man's land" between the established fields of science.[2] There were scientific fields, Wiener remarked, that had been studied from different sides, each bestowing its own name to the field, each ignorant of what others had discovered, thus creating work that was "triplicated or quadruplicated" because of mutual ignorance or incomprehension.[3]

Wiener, no respecter of "narrow domestic walls" would inhabit such "boundary regions" between mathematics, engineering, biology, and sociology, and create *cybernetics*, a science devoted to the study of feedback systems common to living organisms, machines, and social systems. Here was a science that straddled the no-man's land between the traditionally separate domains of the natural and the artificial. Wiener's invention of cybernetics after the end of World War II was a marker of a certain spirit of the times when, in the manner in which Wiener expressed his yearning, scientists began to create serious links between nature and artifact.

It is inevitable that this no-man's land between the natural and the artificial should be part of this story. Ingenious *automata*—devices that replicated, of their own steam (so to speak) certain kinds of actions performed by living things, including humans—had been known since antiquity (see Chapter 3, Section IX). However, the computer was an entirely new genus of automata for it seemed to replicate, not action, but human *thought*.

Ada, Countess of Lovelace, had cautioned her reader not to confuse the Analytical Engine as anything but a machine. It had no power to initiate any thing; it could only do what humans had "ordered" it to do (see Chapter 2, Section VIII). However, by the early 1940s, even before the stored-program digital computer of any kind had been conceived, but stimulated by such analog machines as the differential analyzer, human imagination had already stepped into the boundary region separating man from machine, the natural from the artificial—had straddled and bridged the chasm. The year 1943 was noteworthy in this respect on both sides of the Atlantic.

II

That year, in Cambridge, England, Kenneth Craik (1914–1945), trained as a philosopher and psychologist and, like his contemporary Maurice Wilkes, a fellow of St. John's College, published a short book called *The Nature of Explanation*. In a chapter titled "Hypothesis on the Nature of Thought," he explored the neural basis of thought. He suggested that the essence of the thought process is symbol processing, of a kind similar to what we are familiar with in mechanical calculating devices.[4] He drew this analogy, let us remember, in a time when, in Cambridge, the digital computer was still a few years away, when the archetypal calculating machine that he knew was the model differential analyzer,[5] that he may have seen in use in the department of physical chemistry at the university (see Chapter 8, Section XI).

Indeed, Craik argued, it was not merely that thought uses symbol processing, but that all of thought *is* symbol processing.[6] The process of thinking, as Craik conceived it, involved "the organism" carrying symbolic representations in the head of aspects of the external world, and symbolic representations of the organism's actions. Thought, then, entails the manipulation of the symbolic models by the represented actions—that is, by *simulating* actions symbolically and their effects on external reality. Such symbolic simulation *parallels* the way analog computers (such as the differential analyzer) represent analogically a system and computes on the representation.

Craik, as Wilkes recalled in his memoir, was perhaps unusual among philosophers and psychologists because he was seriously interested in gadgets. Apparently, he made pocket-size models of objects like steam engines[7]—thus, perhaps, the analogy between thinking and mechanical calculation. Unfortunately, he had no chance to pursue his hypothesis for he was hit and killed by a car while bicycling on a Cambridge street on May 7, 1945, the eve of VE Day.[8]

Craik's insight that thinking involves symbolic representations in the nervous system of things in the world, and the processing of such symbolic representations, speculative though it was, makes him one of the earliest figures in the emergence of what much later came to be named cognitive science—the study of mental processes by which humans (and some animals) make meaning of their experiences in the world.[9] However, although his ideas were widely discussed by neurophysiologists and psychologists in Britain,[10] he had no apparent impact on the other side of the Atlantic. But then, America had its own first explorers of the relationship between cerebration and computation who advanced their own, very different, and somewhat more precise views of this relationship. By coincidence, these explorers published their first work on this relationship also in 1943.

III

That year, an article titled "A Logical Calculus of the Ideas Immanent in Nervous Activity" was published by Warren McCulloch (1898–1968), a physician-turned-neurophysiologist who, like John von Neumann, was a polymath of the kind that would have warmed (and no doubt did warm) the cockles of Wiener's heart, and Walter Pitts (1923–1969), a mathematical logician. The journal in which the article appeared, *Bulletin of Mathematical Biophysics*, suggests that the target reader was a theoretical biologist. This, despite the fact, that the paper cited only three references, all authored by world-renowned logicians.[11]

These authors were interested in constructing a formalism for describing neural activity. According to current thinking in theoretical neurophysiology, the nervous system comprised a network of nerve cells, or *neurons*. A neuron connects to others through nerve fibers called axons, which branch out through finer structures called dendrites, and these end on the surfaces of other neurons in the form of entities called *synapses*.

A neuron generally has more than one synapse impinging on it. At any instant, a neuron is activated when the sum of its "input" synapses' activities reach a certain threshold. Such synapses are called *excitatory synapses*. If the threshold is not reached, the neurons remain quiescent. However, there are also *inhibitory synapses* that inhibit the excitation of neurons on which they impinge regardless of the excitation level of excitatory synapses connecting to that same neuron.

A neuron, according to the general understanding of the time, has an "all-or-none" nature; it is either active or inactive. It is, thus, a binary digital device. The neural activity of a network of neurons can be determined by the pattern of binary activity of its constituent neurons. It was this apparent binary character of neurons that prompted McCulloch and Pitts to draw on Boolean (or propositional) logic to describe neural activity—just as, 5 years earlier, Claude Shannon had analyzed relay switching circuits using Boolean logic (see Chapter 5, Section IV). They imagined the behavior of a neuron or a neuron network in terms of the language of Boolean propositions,[12] and they represented the neuron accordingly.

1. The activity of the neuron is an "all-or-none" process.
2. A certain fixed number of synapses must be excited…in order to excite a neuron at any time.
3. The only significant delay within the nervous system is synaptic delay.
4. The activity of an inhibitory synapse absolutely prevents excitation of the neuron at that time.
5. The structure of the net does not change with time.[13]

An example of a McCulloch–Pitts neuron is shown in Figure 11.1. Here, A and B signify synaptic "inputs" to the neuron, and C denotes the "output." The number in the "neuron" shows the threshold of activation. Suppose at the start of some fixed time interval t both A and B are inactive. Then, at the start of the next time interval, $t + 1$, the neuron is inactive. If either A or B is active and the other inactive, then the neuron also remains inactive because the threshold of activation has not been reached. Only if both A and B are active at the start of time interval t, will the neuron be activated at the start of the $t + 1$ time interval. Here, the neuron functions as a Boolean AND device satisfying the proposition $C = A$ AND B.

Figure 11.2 shows a neuron with two excitatory synapses A and B, and one inhibitory synapse C as inputs. The threshold value is 1. If the inhibitory synapse is inactive, then activation of A or B will excite the neuron and it will "fire." However, if the inhibitory synapse c is active, then no matter what the states of excitation of A and B, the neuron will not excite. The Boolean proposition describing this neuron is $D = (A$ OR $B)$ AND (NOT $C)$.

McCulloch and Pitts described the behavior of both single neurons and neuron networks in terms of Boolean propositions or expressions. The correspondence with switching circuit behavior as Shannon described in 1938 (see Chapter 5, Section IV) is evident to anyone familiar with Shannon's work. Although the notation used by McCulloch and Pitts and the mathematics they present to demonstrate their "logical calculus" were complex, their core result was clear. The behavior of neural activity could be described by

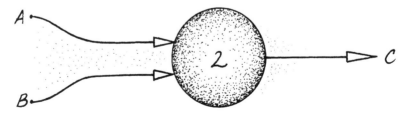

FIGURE 11.1 An Abstract Neuron with Excitatory Inputs.

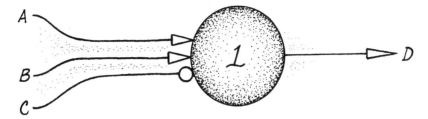

FIGURE 11.2 An Abstract Neuron with an Inhibitory Input.

Boolean (logical) expressions; conversely, any Boolean proposition could be realized by a network of McCulloch-Pitts neurons, and although the neurons themselves are simple in behavior, they can give rise to neuron systems of considerable complexity.

IV

Let us leave aside how their article was received by its primary target readers—the neurophysiological and theoretical biological community. Its place in this story lies in that it caught the attention of the irrepressible von Neumann. Tucked away in the EDVAC report, written two years after the publication of the McCulloch-Pitts article, was an observation of the "all-or-none" character of relay elements in digital computing devices.[14] But then, von Neumann continued, the neurons in the brains of "higher animals" also manifest this binary character; they possess two states: "quiescent" and "excited."[15] Referring to the McCulloch-Pitts article, von Neumann noted that the behavior of neurons could be "imitated" by such binary artifacts as telegraph relays and vacuum tubes.[16]

The parallel between binary circuit elements (relays and vacuum tubes) in a digital computer and neurons in the brain is thus established. Drawing on the McCulloch-Pitts neuron, von Neumann envisioned digital circuits as a network of idealized circuit elements, which he called *E-elements*, that "receives the excitatory and inhibitory stimuli and emits its own stimuli"[17] after an appropriate fixed "synaptic delay."[18] A significant portion of the EDVAC report is then devoted to the description of the E-elements and networks of E-elements, including the structure and behavior of arithmetic circuits modeled by such networks.[19]

von Neumann had, albeit briefly, almost casually identified a relationship between the circuits in the brain and circuits in the digital computer, but this was merely a scenting of blood. For a man of his restless intellectual capacity and curiosity, these allusions in the EDVAC report were only the beginning of a new scientific track.

In September 1948, a number of scientists from different disciplines—mathematics, neurophysiology, and psychology—assembled in Pasadena, California. They were participating in a conference titled Cerebral Mechanisms in Behavior, funded by the Hixon Foundation and, thus, named the Hixon Symposium.[20] This symposium has an important place in the histories of psychology and cognitive science. Behaviorism, the dogma that eschewed any discussion of mind, mentalism, cognition as being within the purview of scientific psychology—a dogma that became the dominant paradigm in American experimental psychology throughout much of the first half of the 20th century from the time of World War I—came under serious attack from people such as McCulloch and neuropsychologist Karl Lashley (1890–1958).

And there was von Neumann. In a lecture later published in the Hixon Symposium proceedings as a 40-page chapter, he pursued in some detail the blood he had scented 3 years before. He titled his exposition "The General and Logical Theory of Automata."[21]

If Leonardo Torres y Quevedo had redirected the old idea of automata from active to *thinking* artifacts in 1915 (see Chapter 3, Section IX), if Alan Turing had launched a branch of intellectual inquiry into how abstract automata could work with his *Entscheidungsproblem* paper of 1936 (see Chapter 4, Section III), then by way of his Hixon paper, Neumann surely gave the field a name. The subject of *automata theory* is not the automata of Hellenistic antiquity, but abstract computational machines such as the Turing machine. The epicenter of what would later be called *theoretical computer science* lay at the door of automata theory.

V

The kind of theory von Neumann advocated for the study of automata lay in the realm of mathematics and logic. In this he followed the approach adopted by McCulloch and Pitts. It was to be an *axiomatic* theory. Beginning with fundamental undefined concepts, assumptions, and propositions (axioms), and using well-understood rules of reasoning, one derives logical consequences of these fundamentals (see Chapter 4, Section I for a brief discussion of the axiomatic approach). The axiomatic world, familiar to those of a mathematical or logical disposition,[22] is a formal world, quite unlike the severely empirical world that people like Wilkes, Kilburn, and Mauchly inhabited. Abstract automata, like actual digital electronic computers, are artifacts—inventions of the human mind—but electronic computers belong to the realm of the empirical; abstract automata belong to the realm of the formal. And so, axiomatizing the behavior of abstract automata meant that their building blocks be treated as "black boxes" with internal structures that are ignored (or abstracted away), but with functional behaviors that are well defined and visible.[23] Defining the behavior of McCulloch-Pitts neurons by logical (Boolean) expressions was an instance of the axiomatization of actual neurons. Their internal structure, which obeys the laws of physics and chemistry, can be ignored.[24]

This approach is bread and butter to mathematicians and logicians, and, indeed, to certain theoretical physicists and biologists. But, von Neumann cautioned, there is a fundamental limitation of the axiomatic approach when applied to empirical objects such as neurons. The approach is only as good as the fundamental assumptions or axioms. One must be sure that the axioms are *valid* and are *consistent* with observed reality. The formal world must have resonance with the empirical world. To ensure this validity, the theorist has to rely on the empirical scientists—in the case of neurons, the neurophysiologists and biochemists.[25]

von Neumann's primary concern was not neurons in the head but "artificial automata"—more specifically, computing machines.[26] And although such automata are vastly less complicated than the nervous system, he found the idea of investigating the behavior of neural machines in terms of automata enticing—hence the comparative study of neural systems in living matter and artificial automata. More ambitiously, it could be claimed that he was aiming to establish a *universal* automata theory that applied as much to the natural as to the artificial, unifying nature and artifact in some specific sense. von Neumann was, of course, quite aware that the neuron has both binary, digital ("all-or-none"), *and* nondigital or analog characteristics.[27] In contrast, computing machines of the kind recently conceived were digital.[28] Nonetheless, as a stage of the axiomatic approach one could consider the living organism *as if* it was a purely digital automaton.[29] This suggested, to von Neumann, that there were two kinds of automata—natural and artificial, a first step in unification and universalization. Moreover, even though such artifacts as the electromechanical relay and the electronic vacuum tube were digital entities, they were really rather complicated analog mechanisms that obeyed the laws of physics. They *become* digital entities under certain restricted conditions.[30] There was, then, a small difference between such devices and biological neurons.[31] Neither was really of an all-or-nothing character, but both could be so regarded if (a) they could operate under certain conditions in an all-or-nothing manner and (b) such operating conditions were the normal conditions under which they would be used.[32]

Like relays and vacuum tubes, biological neurons are electrical switching units.[33] This, of course, was the assumption undergirding the McCulloch-Pitts model of nervous activity, which enabled them to draw on Boolean logic to describe the behavior of neuron networks.

However, McCulloch and Pitts were not interested in computers per se, whereas von Neumann was. And so, comparison between organisms and computing machines—between the natural and the artificial—followed: their relative sizes in terms of the number of basic switching elements (the central nervous system, according to estimates of the time, had 10^{10} neurons[34]; existing machines such as the ENIAC or the IBM version of the Harvard Mark I had about 20,000 switching elements—relays and vacuum tubes[35]), the relative sizes of the switching organs ("the vacuum tube … is gigantic compared to a nerve cell," the ratio of the sizes "about a billion" to one[36]), and the relative switching speeds (that is, the speed at which digital elements can switch states from active to inactive or vice versa); vacuum tubes were vastly faster than neurons, with the switching speed ratio being something like 1200:1.[37]

von Neumann did not actually present an axiomatic theory of automata but, rather, the promise of such a theory. There were already, he noted, prior results that would contribute to this theory: the McCulloch-Pitts theory according to which the functions of nervous activity can be described by a formal (or abstract or idealized) Pitts-McCulloch neural network,[38] and Turing's description and construction of an abstract computing machine (in particular, his formulation of a universal automaton that could perform computations performed by any other computing machine).[39]

But von Neumann went beyond what Turing or McCulloch and Pitts had offered. He reasoned that if automata theory was to be universal in scope, embracing the natural and the artificial, it had to tackle the problem of *self-reproduction*, for in this lay the essence of biological systems. And for this, Turing's universal computing machine did not suffice. Turing's machine could only produce as output, strings of os and 1s on a tape. von Neumann's vision was more daring; he desired automata that could produce as output *other automata.*[40]

So the "General" in the title of his article went beyond unifying natural and artificial computers. Although the universal Turing machine allowed for computational universality, what von Neumann sought was also *constructive* universality.[41] It was no longer a matter of comparing cerebration with computation, but of uniting the organic and the mechanical in a more fundamental sense—the possibility, so to speak, of "artificial life."

von Neumann then speculated in a general way on the construction of such a self-reproducing automaton. Consider first an automaton A that has associated with it a description of itself, $d(A)$. Using this description, A produces a copy of itself. However, A is not self-reproducing because it does not make a copy of its own description, $d(A)$. So next consider another automaton, B, that when supplied with $d(A)$, makes a copy of just this description.

Suppose now that machines A and B are combined by way of a control device C—call this combination A + B + C automaton D—that, when provided with $d(A)$, passes it to A for constructing a copy of A, passes $d(A)$ to B to produce a copy of $d(A)$, and inserts the copy of $d(A)$ into the new automaton A. So D can reproduce A along with the description $d(A)$ of A.

Last, consider the machine D provided with its own description $d(D)$. Call this combination automaton E. What E can do is produce another identical automaton E. E *is thus self-reproducing* because it can produce E that can produce another E and so on.

As von Neumann put it, $d(D)$ "is roughly effecting the function of a gene" whereas the copying automaton B "performs the fundamental act of reproduction, the duplicating of the genetic material, which is clearly the fundamental operation in the multiplication of living cells."[42]

von Neumann's "general theory of automata" was, first, a comparative study of biological and artificial neuron systems; second, it explored, in a highly speculative way, the idea of self-reproducing automata, thereby positing a general theory that could mimic the self-reproducing capacity of biological cells. It embraced not only the computing automaton *à la* Turing, but also something startlingly new: a self-constructing automaton. In fact, this would be the beginning of an entirely different branch of automata theory that came to be called *cellular automata theory*, which considered how *arrays* of individual automata ("cells") could work to transmit information between cells, perform computation, and construct various computational organs.[43]

VI

New scientific paradigms, new artistic and literary styles, and new technological movements are created by a select few. The birth of new creative impulses belong to the realm, primarily, of intellectual history rather than to social or cultural history. It is only when that impulse or movement is recognized as a paradigm that it spreads to the larger population. Revolutionary science, art, design *then* become normal science, art, design. Which is why we find the birthing years of computer science dominated by a small number of people, some of whom appear, disappear, and reappear during these early years. It is as if, having carved out a space of their own—indeed, *created* a space of their own—having been led to a virgin land they invent for themselves a space within that land before other newcomers have the chance to come on it. von Neumann was one such person, as we have seen. Turing was surely another (and he will appear once more very soon). Shannon was a third such person.

Shannon, as we have also seen, in 1938, connected the technological art of switching circuit design with the abstract, symbolic logic of Boolean algebra. It is, perhaps, for this reason that the design of circuits that input, process, and output the Boolean values—1 and 0 or TRUE and FALSE—is called logic design.[44] In fact, during the late 1940s, Shannon did much more. In 1948, then a mathematician at the Bell Telephone Laboratories in Murray Hill, New Jersey, Shannon published an article on a mathematical theory of communication.[45] A year later, with Warren Weaver (1894–1978), a mathematician and preeminent science administrator at the Rockefeller Foundation, Shannon published a book that developed this theory more fully.[46]

The mathematical theory of communication is otherwise and more succinctly called *information theory*, which forms the theoretical foundation of telecommunications engineering and has also influenced the study of human communication.[47] The word *information* is used in information theory in a specific sort of way; it has nothing to do with how "information" is understood in everyday language. We usually think of information as being *about* something. In common parlance, information has *meaning*, there is a semantic aspect to it. In information theory, however, information is devoid of meaning. It is simply the commodity that is transmitted across communication "channels," whether between human beings, along telegraph wires, or across telephone lines. The unit of information in information theory is called the *bit* (short for *binary digit*, a term coined by another distinguished Bell Laboratory mathematician and Shannon's colleague, John W. Tukey [1915–2000][48]). It *means* nothing but itself, just as a unit of money refers to nothing but itself.

Shannon is commonly referred to as the Father of Information Theory, but—like all such glib journalistic appellations—this, too, much be viewed quizzically if only because the history of the origins of information theory began well before Shannon.[49] What is beyond dispute is that he has a preeminent place in the creation of information theory.

Insofar as the transmission and storage of information bits are prominent aspects of the design of computer systems, Shannon's contribution to information theory has an obvious place in the history of computing. But this is *not* why he appears in this part of our story. Shannon was one of those individuals who, during the 1940s crossed interdisciplinary boundaries with total insouciance, who ignored the narrow domestic walls the poet Tagore had dreamed of demolishing. He was, after all, a contemporary of Wiener, and it is this trait that ushers him into this chapter.

For Shannon, consummate applied mathematician and engineering theorist though he was, was also intrigued with *what computers could do*. He was interested in the computer as far more than an instrument of numeric computation. He envisioned machines that would design circuits, route telephone calls, perform symbolic (not numeric) mathematical computations, translate from one language to another, make strategic military decisions, reason logically, orchestrate melodies.[50] In other words, he was interested in the computer *as an intelligent being* in the most eclectic sense of "intelligence." He believed that such computers were not only theoretically possible, but also economically viable— that is, they were feasible from an engineering point of view.[51]

Shannon ruminated on these ideas in 1950. Notice that these possibilities formed the other face of the natural–artificial wall. Craik and von Neumann had dwelled on the possibility of regarding human neural activity and thought in computational terms. Shannon was envisioning computers as capable of the kind of neural processing that produces human intelligent thought and action. If Craik and von Neumann contemplated human cognition in mechanical terms, Shannon was imagining machines in human cognitive terms. But, both perspectives converged to a common theme: *computing* (in some broad sense) *and mind–brain processing were related*.

The great French philosopher René Descartes (1596–1650) had famously uttered the dictum *cogito ergo sum*, "I think, therefore I am"—meaning, basically, that the very act of thinking is proof of one's mental existence. Craik, von Neumann, and Shannon were among the first who were claiming that *I compute, therefore I am*. The "I" here could as well be the computer as a human being.

However, Shannon was not merely speculating on the possibility of machine intelligence. He was an applied mathematician above all else and, as such, he was interested in specific problems and their solutions. Thus, in November 1949, the editor of the venerable British *Philosophical Magazine* (with a pedigree reaching back to the 18th century) received a manuscript authored by Shannon titled "Programming a Computer for Playing Chess."[52] The article was published in March 1950.[53] Less than a year earlier, the EDSAC and the Manchester Mark I had run their first programs.

VII

Chess is, of course, among the most sophisticated board games. As Shannon pointed out, the "problem" of chess playing is, on the one hand, extremely well-defined in terms of the rules that determine legal chess moves and the goal of the game (to checkmate the opponent); yet, it is neither too trivial nor too difficult to achieve the goal. To play well, demands considerable thought.

These very characteristics had prompted others long before Shannon to try and design chess-playing machines. One of these was by Leonardo Torres y Quevedo, the Spanish engineer–inventor whose *Essays in Automatics* (1914) we encountered in Chapter 3, Section IX. Evidently, among the "thinking automata" Torres y Quevedo had envisioned was a chess-playing machine he designed in 1914 for playing an end game of king and rook against king. Torres y Quevedo's machine played the side with king and rook, and could checkmate the human opponent in a few moves regardless of how the latter played.[54]

Shannon would have liked to design a special-purpose chess computer. Rather wistfully, he rejected the idea because of cost. So he began with the assumption that he would have at his disposal a stored-program digital computer along the lines available at the time. The challenge was to *simulate* a chess-playing machine on what was an "arithmetic computer." Or, in present-centered language, to design a *virtual* chess machine that could be implemented on a typical stored-program computer.

Chess, unlike many other board or card games, has no chance element in it. Moreover, it is a game of "perfect information" in that each player can see all the pieces on the board at all times. Shannon refers to the monumental and seminal book on the interdisciplinary field of game theory invented in 1944 by the ever-fertile von Neumann and German-American economist Oskar Morgenstern (1902–1977).[55] Along with cybernetics, information theory, and the computer, game theory was yet another of the extraordinary intellectual creations of the mid 1940s. Referring to the von Neumann-Morgenstern book, Shannon noted that any particular position (that is, configuration of the pieces on a chess board) at any time would lead to one of three possibilities: White winning, Black winning, or a draw. However, there is no algorithm that can determine, in a *practical* way, which of these situations prevails in any given position. Indeed, as Shannon noted, if that was the case, chess would not be at all interesting as a game.[56]

In principle, in any position, the following algorithm would work. The machine considers all possible next moves for itself. For each such next move it then considers all possible moves by its opponent. Then, for each of those, it considers all possible moves for itself—and so on until the end is reached. The outcome in each end situation will be a win, loss, or draw. By working backward from the end, the machine would determine whether the current position would force a win, loss, or draw.

In current language, this strategy is known as *exhaustive search* or *brute-force search*.[57] And, to repeat, this strategy would work in principle. However, in practice even using a high-speed electronic computer, the amount of computation required would be unimaginably large.

Shannon, referring to the pioneering experimental studies of chess play conducted by Dutch psychologist and chess master Adriaan De Groot (1914–2006) in the mid 1940s, noted that, in typical positions, there are about 30 possible legal moves.[58] Shannon estimated that, assuming a typical game to last about 40 moves to resignation of one of the players, something like 10^{120} alternatives would have to be considered from the initial position. Assuming the computer could ascertain one alternate position each microsecond, he calculated that something like 10^{90} years would be required to compute an optimal move.[59]

So exhaustive search was ruled out. More practical strategies were required. Rather than dream of a "perfect chess" machine, the aim should be to produce a machine that could perform at the level of a "good" human chess player.[60] This would involve a strategy that evaluated the "promise" of a position P using some appropriate "evaluation function" $f(P)$, with the "promise" depending on such considerations as the overall positions of the pieces on the board at any particular stage of the game, the number of Black and White pieces on the board, and so on.[61]

Shannon gave an example of an evaluation function $f(P)$ for a position P that uses different "weights" (measures of importance) to the various types of chess pieces on the board. Assuming that the machine explores only one move deep—that is, it explores its own next move—a possible strategy would suppose that $M_1, M_2, \ldots, M_n$ are the possible moves that can be made by the machine in a position P. If M_1P, M_2P, and so forth, signify the resulting positions when M_1, M_2, and so on, are made, then choose the move M_q that maximizes the evaluation function $f(M_qP)$.[62]

A "deeper" strategy would consider the opponent's response—that is, the strategy would "look ahead" to the opponent's possible moves. However, if the machine is playing White, Black's reply to a White move would endeavor to *minimize* $f(P)$. So if White plays M_i, Black would choose move M_{ij} such that $f(M_{ij}M_iP)$ is a minimum. In which case, White should choose his first move such that f is a maximum *after* Black chooses his minimizing (that is, best) reply.

Shannon described a simple version of what would later be called a *minmax strategy* in game play.[63] He did not actually write a program to play chess; rather, he explored possible strategies that would lead to the development of a practical, "virtual" chess-playing machine to play what, in chess is called, the middle game.[64]

It is worth noting that in deciding on a move to make using some kind of minmax strategy, Shannon was advocating the construction of a plan that would consider alternative moves, anticipate the opponent's move in response, up to a certain "depth" of look-ahead, and then decide on the actual move to play. This was precisely what Craik had envisioned in his discussion on the nature of thought in *The Nature of Explanation* (1943) (see Section II, this chapter).

VIII

Shannon's 1950 article was (probably) the first publication on the possibility of a chess-playing program. In addition, it is fair to say that the article marked the beginning of a distinct branch of the emerging computer science later called *artificial intelligence.*

But why should a computer capable of playing chess of the same level of skill as a good human chess player be deemed "intelligent" (in the ordinary human sense) in contrast to a computer capable of solving differential equations of the sort Stanley Gill explored for his PhD dissertation (see Chapter 10, Section IV)? After all, the rules of chess are quite simple and most people can learn to play chess, at least at a basic level, whereas one has to have considerable mathematical acumen to learn to solve differential equations. In what *significant* sense is the problem of playing chess (or other similar board games, such as checkers) superior to the problem of solving differential equations?

Shannon addressed this issue, albeit briefly. For the kinds of problems he identified at the beginning of his 1950 article—machines that could design, translate, make decisions, perform logical deductions, and so on—the procedures performed entailed making judgments, trying out something to see if it works, and trying something else if it does not. The solutions of such problems were never just right or wrong, but rather spanned a spectrum of possibilities, from the very best to the very worst and several shades in between. Thus, a solution might be one that is acceptably good rather than the very best.[65]

These are significant insights, anticipating much that will follow in this story. What strikes us most immediately is that problems such as chess entail ingredients of ordinary thought that humans negotiate on an everyday basis—with all the uncertainties, propensity for error, limited rationality, and subjectivity attendant on such thinking. These were the challenges Shannon broached on—and that Alan Turing would boldly confront.

IX

Perhaps it was no coincidence that among the possible things Shannon believed the computer could be programmed to do was create a machine that could translate between languages.[66] Automatic translation was much in the mind of Shannon's coauthor on information theory, Warren Weaver. In 1949, Weaver wrote a memorandum simply titled *Translation*, in which, referring to himself somewhat archly in the third person, he remembered how his wartime experience with computing machines had led him to think about automatic translation.[67]

Even more than Shannon's deliberations on a chess-playing machine, Weaver's memorandum reveals the optimism, bordering on brashness, that attended the thinking of early scientists concerned with the application of the digital computer. In the realm of translation, we have previously witnessed Herman Goldstine and von Neumann grapple with the problem of coding (programming) as an act of translation—mapping from a mathematical culture to machine culture—and producing a computational text from mathematical text (see Chapter 9, Section III). We have witnessed David Wheeler invent an artificial symbolic language ("assembly language") to write programs in and a means (an "assembler") to translate such programs to machine-executable form ("machine language"; see Chapter 9, Section VI).

What Weaver was contemplating was of a different qualitative order altogether—translating text from one *natural* language to another using the computer. As it turned out, Weaver's memorandum of 1949 marked the beginning of a discipline straddling linguistics and computing called *machine translation.*[68]

We have also previously noted that translating literary text is a creative process involving not only the conversion of words in one language to another, but a mapping of one linguistic culture to another (see Chapter 9, Section III), wherein the translation enacts a complicated interweaving of understanding and interpretation.[69] The prospect of *machine* translation, in the literary sense of translation, thus seems still more formidable.

But Weaver was not alone in this contemplation. Across the Atlantic, at Birbeck College, London University, Andrew D. Booth (1918–2009), a physicist working in Desmond Bernal's famed laboratory—and like many scientists of the time, drawn into computers and computing through his particular brand of research—was also dwelling on the possibility of machine translation.[70] However, Booth (who may have influenced Weaver, who visited the Englishman in 1948[71]) was, at the time, concerned with mechanizing a dictionary.[72] Weaver had more vaulting ambitions, in which such language issues as polysemy (that is, the phenomenon of multiple meanings of words) and word order would enter the frame.

Weaver was neither a linguist nor a literary translator. As a mathematician-turned-science policy shaper (employed by the Rockefeller Foundation), as Shannon's collaborator on a mathematical theory of communication, Weaver was drawn to cryptography as a source of analogical insight to the problem of machine translation. Airily and rather extraordinarily, he confessed to being "tempted" to propose that a book written in Chinese is nothing but a book written in English but using Chinese code.[73] For Weaver, the act of translation became a problem of deciphering—a position that would surely make translators, translation theorists, and literary scholars wince. Possible methods of cryptology would become, he said, when properly interpreted, "useful methods of translation."[74]

These "useful methods of translation" used in cryptography could have an interesting attribute. Deciphering a message was a process that made use of "frequencies of letters, letter combinations, interval between letters and letter combinations, letter patterns, etc."[75] So translation, from this point of view, was a process that entailed finding certain statistical regularities in texts. But these regularities, Weaver continued, were—broadly speaking—language independent.[76] This meant, according to him, that among all the languages invented by humankind, there were certain properties that were statistically invariant across the languages.[77]

Languages, in other words (as Weaver saw them), had, deep down, certain *invariant* characteristics. This suggested to Weaver a way of tackling the problem of machine translation. Rather than translate directly from one natural language to another—say, from Russian to Portuguese—perhaps the proper strategy is to translate "down" from the source language to the shared base language, to an as-yet-undiscovered "universal language," and then translate "up" from the latter to the target language.[78]

Weaver's conception of a "universal language" is striking because it seems to anticipate, in a general sort of way, the idea of "linguistic universals"—linguistic features common to (most) languages, such as the presence of the categories nouns and verbs, patterns of word order—which would be discussed by linguists during the 1960s.[79] At any rate, it is at the level of a universal language that Weaver believed that human communication takes place, and it would be at this level that the process of machine translation should begin. How this would happen he did not elaborate. He recognized that much work on the logical structure of language would have to be done before automatic translation could be tackled effectively. However, in any case, regardless of whether the approach he was advocating led to success in machine translation, it would surely produce "much useful knowledge about the general nature of communication."[80]

Machine translation has to do with natural language, the most human of human characteristics, one that separates humans from nonhumans. Yet, strangely enough, machine translation never quite penetrated into the innards of artificial intelligence in the way computer chess would; rather, it became an enterprise and a research tradition of its own. But, like the computer chess project, the machine translation enterprise as imagined by Weaver turned out to be a far more difficult problem than early machine translation researchers had anticipated. In any case, within a decade of the Weaver memorandum, the study of the structure of language itself would be turned topsy-turvy by a young linguist named Noam Chomsky.

X

Shannon was by no means the only person at the time who was thinking about thinking machines. Indeed, soon after the ENIAC seeped into public consciousness, the term *electronic brain* began to appear in the popular press. No less a personage than Lord Louis Mountbatten (1900–1979) used the term to describe the ENIAC in a talk he delivered to the (British) Institute of Radio Engineers (IRE) in 1946.[81] As Sir Maurice Wilkes recollected in 1985, this reference to computers as electronic brains excited much debate in the British press.[82] An American participant in the early development of the commercial computer, Edmund C. Berkeley (1909–1988), a founding member of the ACM in 1947 (see Chapter 8, Section XVI) and its first secretary, published in 1949 a book called *Giant Brains, or Machines That Think*.[83] So the climate was already in place for serious discussions of thinking machines in the later 1940s.

Indeed, well before Shannon's manuscript on computer chess was submitted for publication, Turing had dwelt on the topic. Like Shannon, he was much interested in the uses of the digital computer. As early as 1945, in his definitive report on the ACE being developed at the NPL in Teddington (see Chapter 8, Section IX), Turing asked whether a machine could play chess.[84] Three years later, he submitted a report to the NPL, then still his employer, titled *Intelligent Machinery*.[85]

However, Turing's thoughts on thinking machines came into public notice most famously—insofar as an article in one of England's most august philosophical journals could be said to excite "public" notice—with an article titled "Computing Machinery and Intelligence" in the October 1950 issue of *Mind*.[86]

XI

Turing began with the question: Can machines think? But, wishing to avoid the pitfalls of defining such terms as *machine* and *think*, he proposed a thought experiment that he called the "imitation game." Imagine, first, he wrote, a man (**M**), a woman (**W**), and an interrogator (**I**) who may be of either sex. **I** is placed in a room separate from the room occupied by **M** and **W**. The purpose of the game is for **I** to put questions to **M** and **W** (without knowing which one of them is the man and which is the woman) in such a fashion that **I** can determine, from the answers, which is the man and which is the woman. The answers, of course, from **M** and **W** must be given in written or typewritten form to mask the sex of the answerer.

Turing then suggested replacing either **M** or **W** by a computer C. In this situation, **I** offers questions to either a human **H** or a computer **C**, and the task for **I** is to ascertain from the answers which is a human and which is the machine.

The original question, "Can machines think?" could now be reformulated as: Are there imaginable digital computers that would do well in the imitation game?[87] The former question Turing dismissed as too meaningless. As for the latter, he predicted that, within 50 years, computers with an adequate memory capacity (implying, it would seem, that this was the crucial factor) would be able to play the imitation game successfully and pass his test criterion.[88] Indeed, he further predicted that, by the end of the 20th century, the idea of thinking machines would be deemed commonplace.[89]

We are reminded here of Austrian–British philosopher of science Sir Karl Popper (1902–1994) famously insisting that science progresses through a succession of "bold conjectures" followed by attempted refutations of the conjectures.[90] Turing defended his prediction precisely as such a bold conjecture, arguing that conjectures are so often the means for pursuing promising paths of research.[91]

Turing's imitation game, in which the machine's responses to the interrogator's questions might fool the latter into thinking that the machine is the human, has come to be called the *Turing test*. Any machine that can fool the interrogator at least 30% of the time would, in Turing's view, be deemed an intelligent or thinking machine. The essence of the game was, of course, that the interrogator could ask *any* question whatsoever, spanning the whole range of human experience.

Turing expended considerable space to countering anticipated objections to his proposal. He discussed these under a number of broad headings of which perhaps the most interesting were the following.[92]

> *Theological objection*: Thinking is a function of man's immortal soul. God has given
>   an immortal soul to humans only, and not to animals or machines—hence, no
>   animal or machine can think.
>
> *Mathematical objection*: Here, Turing referred to the implications of Kurt Gödel's
>   Incompleteness Theorem (see Chapter 4, Section I)—that there are certain lim
>   its to the power of purely mechanical (or formal) systems and procedures, even
>   computing machines. Thus, machines suffer from certain kinds of "disabilities"
>   that humans (who are not mechanical or formal systems) are not prone to.
>
> *Argument from consciousness*: That machines cannot "feel" in the sense that humans
>   feel emotions, in which case one cannot identify machines with humans.

In each of these cases, Turing advanced a response. For example, he was not "impressed" with the theological argument for various reasons, including its arbitrary separation of humans from animals, and the fact that this objection was Christianity based. Moreover, theological arguments in the past have been falsified by advances in (scientific) knowledge.

As for the mathematical objection, Turing pointed out that there may well be similar limitations to the human intellect. It has never been *proved* that the human intellect does not suffer from similar disabilities as do formal systems.

About the argument from consciousness, Turing speculates on a version of the imitation game involving just **I** and **C** in which **C** responds to **I**'s questions or comments about a sonnet in such a fashion that leads an observer to conclude that **C**'s response is convincingly humanlike.

Turing also addresses Lovelace's caution—that a programmable computing machine (in her case, the Analytical Engine) could not originate anything but, rather, it could do only what it was programmed to do (see Chapter 2, Section VIII). In response, Turing quoted David Hartree (whom we encountered in Chapter 8, Section XI) who, in his book *Calculating Instruments and Machines* (1949), considered the possibility of a computer as *learning* from its past "experiences."[93] Suppose, Turing writes, the existence of a real, contemporary computer with such learning capacity. Because the Analytical Engine of Lovelace's time was a general-purpose ("universal") computing machine, this, too, could be programmed to "mimic" the learning machine.[94]

Another version of Lovelace's warning could be that machines "never take us by surprise." But this, Turing argued, was an empirical question. Machines, he said, frequently take him by surprise, because he—like others—is himself constrained in his capacity to reason, calculate, make decisions, and so on. He pointed out that philosophers and mathematicians alike are prone to the fallacy that as soon as a fact is presented to someone all the consequences of the fact are revealed immediately.[95] If this were so, then perhaps the fact that a computer is programmed to do something means that one would know all that the computer produces by executing the program, and there would, indeed, be no surprises. But that presumption is quite false.

NOTES

1. R. Tagore. (1912). *Gitanjali (Song Offerings)* (poem 35). London: The India Society. This collection of poems, which won Tagore the Nobel Prize the year after their publication, has been republished or anthologized many times. See, for example, A. Chakravarty. (Ed.). (1961). *A Tagore reader* (pp. 294–307). Boston, MA: Beacon Press. The poem from which the lines are taken here appears on p. 300.

2. N. Wiener. (1961). *Cybernetics: Or control and communication in the animal and the machine* (2nd ed., p. 2). Cambridge, MA: MIT Press (original work published 1948).

3. Ibid.

4. K. J. W. Craik. (1967). *The nature of explanation* (p. 52). Cambridge, UK: Cambridge University Press (original work published 1943).

5. Ibid., p. 60.

6. Ibid., p. 58.

7. M. V. Wilkes. (1985). *Memoirs of a computer pioneer* (p. 23). Cambridge, MA: MIT Press.

8. Ibid.

9. J. Bruner. (1990). *Acts of meaning.* Cambridge, MA: Harvard University Press.

10. M. A. Boden. (2006). *Mind as machine: A history of cognitive science* (Vol. 1, pp. 216–217). Oxford: Clarendon Press.

11. W. S. McCulloch & W. Pitts. (1943). A logical calculus of the ideas immanent in nervous activity. *Bulletin of Mathematical Biophysics, 5,* 115–133. Reprinted in J. A. Anderson & E. Rosenfield. (Eds.). (1988). *Neurocomputing* (pp. 18–27). Cambridge, MA: MIT Press. All citations here refer to the reprinted version.

12. Ibid., p. 19.

13. Ibid.

14. J. von Neumann. (1945). *First draft of a report on the EDVAC* (p. 4). Unpublished report. Philadelphia, PA: Moore School of Electrical Engineering.

15. Ibid., p. 5.

16. Ibid.

17. Ibid., p. 9.

18. Ibid.

19. Ibid., pp. 10–17.

20. L. A. Jeffress. (Ed.). (1951). *Cerebral mechanisms in behavior: The Hixon Symposium.* New York: Wiley.

21. J. von Neumann. (1951). The general and logical theory of automata. In Jeffress, op cit., pp. 1–41. Reprinted in A. H. Taub. (Ed.). (1961–1963). *John von Neumann: Collected works* (Vol. 5, pp. 288–326). Oxford: Clarendon Press. All citations refer to the reprinted article.

22. Ibid., p. 289.

23. Ibid.

24. Ibid., pp. 289–290.

25. Ibid., p. 290.

26. Ibid.

27. Ibid., p. 297.

28. Ibid.

29. Ibid.

30. Ibid. pp. 297–298.

31. Ibid.

32. Ibid., p. 298.

33. Ibid.

34. Ibid., p. 300.

35. Ibid., p. 298.

36. Ibid., p. 300.

37. Ibid.

38. Ibid., p. 309.

39. Ibid., p. 314.

40. Ibid., p. 315.

41. I have borrowed these terms from J. R. Sampson. (1976). *Adaptive information processing* (p. 58). New York: Springer-Verlag.

42. von Neumann, op cit., p. 317.

43. J. von Neumann. (1966). *Theory of self-reproducing automata*. In A. W. Burks (Ed.), Urbana, IL: University of Illinois Press; E. F. Codd. (1968). *Cellular automata*. New York: Academic Press; A. W. Burks. (Ed.). (1970). *Essays on cellular automata*. Urbana, IL: University of Illinois Press.

44. G. G. Langdon, Jr. (1974). *Logic design: A review of theory and practice*. New York: Academic Press.

45. C. E. Shannon. (1948). A mathematical theory of communication. *Bell Systems Technical Journal, 27*, 379–423, 623–656. Also available online: http://cm.bell-labs.com/cm/ms/what/shannonday/shannon1948.pdf

46. C. E. Shannon & W. Weaver. (1949). *The mathematical theory of communication*. Urbana, IL: University of Illinois Press.

47. See, for example, C. Cherry. (1968). *On human communication*. Cambridge, MA: MIT Press.

48. Shannon, op cit., p. 379. So far as is known, this article was the first to introduce the term *bit* in the published literature.

49. Cherry, op cit., pp. 41–52.

50. C. E. Shannon. (1950a). Programming a computer for playing chess. *Philosophical Magazine, 41*, 256–275. Also available online: http://archive.computerhistory.org/projects/chess/related_materials/text/2-0%. Citations to this article refer to the online edition, which is not paginated. This quote is from p. 1.

51. Ibid.

52. Ibid.

53. In February 1950, before Shannon's article in *Philosophical Magazine* appeared, a more popular and briefer article by Shannon was published in an American science periodical: C. E. Shannon. (1950b). A chess-playing machine. *Scientific American, 182*, 48–51.

54. Shannon, 1950a, op cit., p. 2.

55. J. von Neumann & O. Morgernstern. (1944). *Theory of games and economic behavior.* Princeton, NJ: Princeton University Press.

56. Shannon, 1950a, op cit., p. 3.

57. See, for example, A. Barr & E. A. Feigenbaum. (Eds.). (1981). *The handbook of artificial intelligence* (Vol. I, pp. 26–27). Stanford, CA: HeurisTech Press.

58. A. D. De Groot. (2008). *Thought and choice in chess.* Amsterdam: Amsterdam University Press. The original 1946 edition was in Dutch.

59. Shannon, 1950a, op cit., p. 4.

60. Ibid., p. 4.

61. Ibid., p. 5.

62. Ibid., pp. 6–7.

63. Barr & Feigenbaum, op cit., pp. 84–85. See also E. Charniak & D. McDermott. (1985). *Introduction to artificial intelligence* (pp. 281–290). Reading, MA: Addison-Wesley.

64. Shannon, 1950a, op cit., p. 9.

65. Ibid., p. 1.

66. Ibid.

67. W. Weaver. (1949). *Translation.* Memorandum. New York: The Rockefeller Foundation. Also available online: http://www.mt_archive.info/weaver-1949.pdf

68. Anon. (1998). Milestones in machine translation, no.2: Warren Weaver's memorandum 1949. *Language Today, 6,* 22–23; Y. Bar-Hillel. (1960). The present status of automatic translation of languages. In F. L. Alt (Ed.), *Advances in computers* (Vol. I, pp. 91–163). New York: Academic Press.

69. G. Steiner. (1975). *After Babel: Aspects of language and translation.* Oxford: Oxford University Press; S. Chaudhuri. (1999). *Translation and understanding.* New Delhi: Oxford University Press.

70. Weaver, op cit., p. 6.

71. Ibid.

72. Ibid.

73. Ibid., p. 10.

74. Ibid.

75. Ibid., p. 2.

76. Ibid.

77. Ibid.

78. Ibid., p. 11.

79. J. H. Greenberg. (Ed.). (1963). *Universals of language.* Cambridge, MA: MIT Press.

80. Weaver, op cit., p. 12.

81. Wilkes, op cit., p. 195.

82. Ibid., pp. 195–197.

83. E. C. Berkeley. (1949). *Giant brains, or machines that think.* New York: Wiley.

84. A. M. Turing. (1945). *Proposal for the development of an electronic computer.* Unpublished report. Teddington: National Physical Laboratory. Printed in D. C. Ince. (Ed.). (1992). *Collected works of A.M. Turing.* Amsterdam: North-Holland.

85. A. M. Turing. (1948). *Intelligent machinery.* Unpublished report. Teddington: National Physical Laboratory. Printed in B. Meltzer & D. Michie. (Eds.). (1970). *Machine intelligence 5* (pp. 3–23). New York: Halsted Press.

86. A. M. Turing. (1950). Computing machinery and intelligence. *Mind, LIX*, 433–460. Reprinted in M. Boden. (Ed.). (1990). *Philosophy of artificial intelligence* (pp. 40–66). Oxford: Oxford University Press. All citations refer to the reprinted article.

87. Ibid., p. 48.

88. Ibid., p. 49.

89. Ibid.

90. K. R. Popper. (1968). *Conjectures and refutations: The growth of scientific knowledge*. New York: Harper & Row.

91. Turing, op cit., p. 49.

92. Ibid., pp. 49–55.

93. D. R. Hartree. (1949). *Calculating instruments and machines*. Urbana, IL: University of Illinois Press.

94. Turing, op cit., p. 56.

95. Ibid., p. 57.

12

"The Best Way to Design…"

∾

I

IN FEBRUARY 1951, the Ferranti Mark I was delivered to the University of Manchester. This was the commercial "edition" of the Manchester Mark I (see Chapter 8, Section XIII), the product of a collaboration between town and gown, the former being the Manchester firm of Ferranti Limited.[1] It became (by a few months) the world's first commercially available digital computer[2] (followed in June 1951 by the "Universal Automatic Computer" [UNIVAC], developed by the Eckert-Mauchly Computer Corporation[3]).

The Ferranti Mark I was unveiled formally at an inaugural conference held in Manchester, June 9 to 12, 1951. At this conference, Maurice Wilkes delivered a lecture titled "The Best Way to Design an Automatic Calculating Machine."[4] This conference is probably (perhaps unfairly) more known because of Wilkes's lecture than for its primary focus, the Ferranti Mark I. For during this lecture, Wilkes announced a new approach to the design of a computer's control unit called *microprogramming*, which would be massively consequential in the later evolution of computers.

Wilkes's lecture also marked something else: the search for order, structure, and simplicity in the design of computational artifacts; and an attendant concern for, a preoccupation with, the *design process* itself in the realm of computational artifacts.

We have already seen the first manifestations of this concern with the design process in the Goldstine-von Neumann invention of a flow diagram notation for beginning the act of computer programming (see Chapter 9, Section III), and in David Wheeler's and Stanley Gill's discussions of a method for program development (Chapter 10, Section IV). Wilkes's lecture was notable for "migrating" this concern into the realm of the physical computer itself.

11

We recall that, in May 1949, the Cambridge EDSAC became fully operational (see Chapter 8, Section XIII). The EDSAC was a serial machine in that reading from or writing into memory was done 1 bit at a time (bit serial)[5]; and, likewise, the arithmetic unit performed its operations in a bit-by-bit fashion.[6] Soon after the EDSAC's completion, while others in his laboratory were busy refining the programming techniques and exploring its use in scientific applications (see Chapter 9, Sections V–VIII; and Chapter 10), Wilkes became preoccupied with issues of *regularity* and *complexity* in computer design and their relation to *reliability*.[7]

Reliability, in Wilkes's view, depended on the amount of equipment the machine has, its complexity, and the degree of repetition of the units.[8] As for complexity, by this he meant the extent to which the physical connections between the units within a computer convoluted their *logical* relationships. A machine can be built more easily if its components were designed and implemented by different people, then they could go about their business without interfering, or having to interact, with one another. Likewise, if the components are connected in a transparent way, the machine is easier to repair.[9]

Thus, for Wilkes, complexity was related to the machine's internal organization. A regular or orderly organization lessened the obscurity of the interrelatedness of the components. In the EDSAC, the paragon of such virtue was the main memory unit, which consisted of 32 independent mercury tanks connected to common input and output "buses" (that is, communication paths).

The culprits, in contrast, were the EDSAC arithmetic unit and the control circuits. Because the arithmetic unit was a serial device (performing its operations in a bit-by-bit manner, rather as humans add two numbers in a digit-by-digit manner), it, too, was unstructured and irregular. However, during summer and early autumn 1950, Wilkes visited the United States and, during the course of this visit, he met Julian Bigelow (1913–2003)—one of the cofounders, with Norbert Wiener and Arturo Rosenblueth of cybernetics—in Princeton. Bigelow was then engaged in the development of the IAS computer at the Institute of Advanced Study under von Neumann's direction (see Chapter 8, Section XV). Through their discussions, Wilkes came to realize that a parallel arithmetic unit would have the same kind of regularity as the memory unit.[10]

Indeed, as Wilkes admitted in his Manchester lecture, regularity and simplicity is obtained, in general, when identical, repetitive units are used rather than a collection of different units—even if the number of identical units is more than the number of distinct units.[11] And just as the EDSAC memory, comprised of 32 identical memory tanks, was orderly, regular, and thus not complex (see Figure 8.2), so also would be a parallel arithmetic unit that consisted of an array of identical circuits performing semi-independent operations in parallel, on the different bit pairs corresponding to the two numbers involved (Figure 12.1).[12]

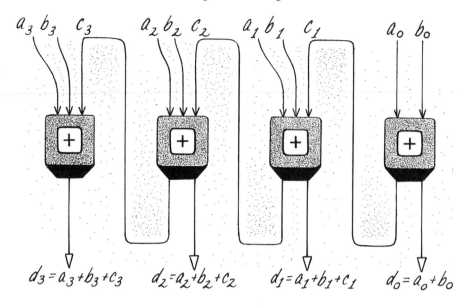

FIGURE 12.1 An Adder Unit.

So if one builds a parallel machine, one has a good example, in a parallel arithmetic unit, of a functional component consisting of multiple identical units.[13]

There remains the control unit within the computer—that is, as Wilkes put it, everything else in a machine apart from the memory unit and the registers and adding circuits comprising the arithmetic unit.[14] The control circuits in the EDSAC were responsible for issuing control signals to all other parts of the machine so that the latter could execute the EDSAC instructions in the desired sequence. The problem was that there was no systematic procedure to design the control unit. It was an ad hoc enterprise, the outcome of which was a control circuit that obscured completely the interrelationship of its elements.[15] There was no transparency. The resulting logical design of the control circuit had no structure, no orderliness. Computer designers would call such a structure *random logic*.[16] And so Wilkes arrived at the main thrust of his lecture: to propose a way in which the control unit could be made more systematic and, thus, simpler in organization and design.[17]

III

The modern reader of this article by Wilkes will be struck by the informality of its mode of presentation; the writing style is artless, more along the nature of a lecture (as indeed it was). There are no references, for example. In approximately 1300 words, aided by a single diagram, Wilkes laid out a "best way" of designing a computer's control unit—a technique he called microprogramming.

What is especially striking is what the lecture reveals of Wilkes's mentality. Although an applied mathematician by formal training, in the realm of computers he was very much the engineer. It is worth noting that Wilkes's academic position in Cambridge University at the time of his retirement in 1980 was (besides being director of the University Computer Laboratory) professor of computer *technology*.

If Alan Turing and John von Neumann represented the beginning of theoretical computer science, Wilkes was the archetypal empirical computer scientist. We cannot imagine him speculating on such abstractions as Turing machines or self-reproducing automata (see Chapter 4, Section IV; and Chapter 11, Section IV). Yet, the issue that caught Wilkes's attention was essentially a *conceptual* problem, even abstract, although it derived from the practical problem of the reliability and maintainability of computers.

An interesting attribute of conceptual problems is that their recognition by individuals is often prompted by very personal perspectives, more of a philosophical, aesthetic, or even ethical nature than a strictly empirical or technical consideration. Wilkes identified a conceptual rather than a strictly empirical problem.[18] He once remarked that, without a particular philosophical point of view, the problem he began to investigate (and the solution to which he presented at the Manchester conference) would not make too much sense.[19] Elsewhere, he would comment that his problem was essentially a private problem.[20]

IV

Creativity always originates in the past. Ideas, concepts, solutions have their traces in what came before. What makes a person creative is the *way* in which he or she draws on the past to bring about the present—and that will, perhaps, shape the future.[21] The creative being extracts ideas from the past and fuses them in unexpected and surprising ways to produce something quite different from the ingredients. Hungarian-British writer Arthur Koestler (1905–1983) called this process *bisociation*.[22]

So it was with Wilkes's invention of microprogramming. His search for an ordered, regular structure for the computer's control unit led him to other kinds of circuits that manifested the kind of order he sought. In the EDSAC itself, as we have seen, the memory unit manifested such an order, but there was another unit that seemed relevant because it had organizational order. A part of the machine was concerned with decoding the operation code within an instruction and then reencoding in a different way to provide the signals sent to the different units that would execute that instruction collectively. This reencoding was performed by a circuit called the *diode matrix* and, Wilkes believed, "something similar" could be used to implement the control circuits.[23]

A diode matrix is a regular, two-dimensional array of intersecting horizontal and vertical wires—that is, an array of intersecting orthogonal wires—in which the horizontal wires serve as inputs to the circuit and the vertical ones serve as the outputs from the

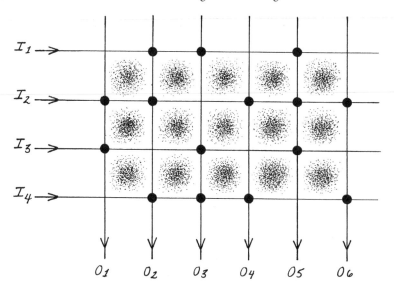

FIGURE 12.2 A Diode Matrix

circuit. The points of intersection between the horizontal and the vertical wires serve as sites of diodes. The presence of a diode causes the signal (if any) on the diode input to be passed through ("gated") to the diode output line; in the diode matrix, the diode input is a horizontal line and the output is a vertical line. Each horizontal line in the matrix connects to one or more diodes; each vertical line transmits an input signal on the connected diode to the vertical line that connects to the diode output (Figure 12.2).

The problem with the diode matrix encoder in the EDSAC was that it was completely inflexible. It was used to issue a fixed set of control signals corresponding to a particular operation code ("opcode") within an instruction. However, if an instruction allowed for *different* interpretations of the opcode, then the diode matrix encoder was of no use. More important, the task of executing a *sequence* of instructions (which was the real job of the main control unit in a computer) demanded the flexibility of being able to select different sets of control signals depending on the actual instructions—a flexibility that could not be met by the diode matrix.

It is said that travel broadens the mind. For the creative person, whether in the arts or sciences, whether in the humanities or engineering, travel certainly fosters creativity. So it was with Wilkes. As already mentioned, from June to September 1950, Wilkes was in the United States visiting various universities where work was in progress in computer development. One of the places was MIT, where, under the direction of engineer and systems scientist Jay Forrester (1918–), the Whirlwind computer was then under construction. In this machine, the duration of each arithmetic operation (except for multiplication) spanned exactly eight clock pulse intervals. The control signals corresponding to each operation were derived from a diode matrix. The regularity of this control unit made an immediate impression on Wilkes.[24]

However, he wanted far greater flexibility than what either the EDSAC diode matrix-based encoder or the Whirlwind diode matrix-based control unit could provide. In the latter case, for instance, each arithmetic instruction required a fixed sequence of control signals to be issued regardless of the context of its execution. But, as noted, in general, an instruction may demand a variable sequence of control signals depending on the operands or on some condition being generated during the course of instruction execution.

It was after his return to England in September 1950, sometime that winter, when the solution came to him.[25] He found an analogy between the functional flexibility he desired of his control unit and the functional flexibility of computer *programs*. That is, he likened the desired flexibility for control signal sequences required to execute a *single instruction* to the flexibility of instruction sequences within a *program*. From this analogy, Wilkes arrived at the concept of the control unit as a programmed computer in miniature—a computer within a larger computer, rather like a homunculus in the brain.

There still lay the problem of how this programlike flexibility could be attained using a regular, diode matrixlike circuit. The solution he arrived at was to use *two* diode matrices, one that would serve to store the control signals in the form of *microinstructions*, much as the computer's main memory stores a program's instructions. The execution of a microinstruction would cause a set of control signals to be issued in parallel.[26] The second diode matrix, organized in tandem with the first, stored the addresses of the "next" microinstruction to select for execution and to control sequencing of the microinstructions. Analogous to a program stored in a computer's main memory as a sequence of instructions, the sequence of microinstructions (along with the addresses) stored in the two diode matrices constituted a *microprogram*. The diode matrices formed the "microprogram store" (or "control store") collectively.[27] The overall control unit came to be called a *microprogrammed control unit* (Figure 12.3).

V

Wilkes delivered his Manchester lecture in July 1951. In November 1952, the first manuscript devoted entirely to microprogramming was dispatched to the editor of the *Proceedings of the Cambridge Philosophical Society* and was published the following year.[28] The article described in great detail the architecture of a microprogrammed control unit as it might be deployed in a parallel machine.

Wilkes, as remarked, was the quintessential empirical scientist–engineer. Design-as-theory, implementation-as-experiment, testing, and evaluation formed an inextricably entwined quadruple in his mind. Armed with a theory of microprogramming, he would want to see if it worked in practice. As it was, by about the time the EDSAC was operational, he was already ruminating on a machine that would succeed the EDSAC, and he had decided on a parallel machine.[29]

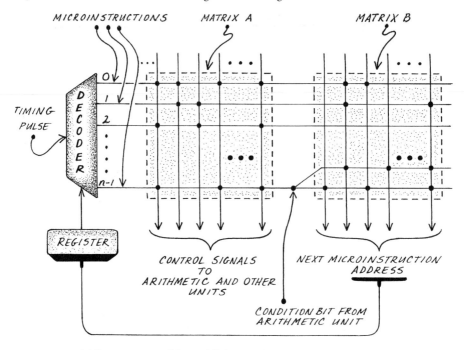

FIGURE 12.3 A Microprogrammed Control Unit.

This successor, the EDSAC 2, begun in 1953 and fully operational in 1958, was this empirical test of his microprogramming idea.[30] As such, it was a brilliant example in the history of computer design of a successful experimental corroboration of a new principle of design. Microprogramming was used to implement practically all aspects of control in this machine; every significant unit in the machine, including memory, input, and output, were driven from the microprogrammed control unit. As a test of the principles, it was a spectacular success.[31]

VI

However, the EDSAC 2 was more than an empirical confirmation of microprogramming principles. It was an experimental test bed for a number of ideas Wilkes had broached in his 1951 article in Manchester.[32] They included the attractiveness of parallel computing (as the term was then understood). A parallel arithmetic unit, certainly, but also with access to main memory, and not in the bit-by-bit mode of the ultrasonic memory used in the EDSAC (or the EDSAC 1, as it began to be called, in deference to its successor) but in bit-parallel fashion. The Williams CRT invented by Frederic C. Williams and Tom Kilburn in Manchester was a possibility (see Chapter 8, Section XIII). Indeed, this memory device had found its way into some of the commercial computers that were being manufactured and marketed rapidly during the early 1950s.[33] But, for Wilkes and his

Cambridge colleagues, it demanded too much "careful engineering" and "careful nursing" to guarantee acceptable performance.[34]

Besides, a new kind of memory had emerged in the United State. Forrester, at MIT, had developed a memory made of magnetizable ferrite "cores" shaped rather like doughnuts. The cores were arranged in a two-dimensional matrix, with each core representing a bit, and the corresponding bits of a set of n such matrices organized in parallel would constitute the n bits of a word of memory. If orthogonal wires were threaded through the central hole in a core and a current was sent through the wires, the core would be magnetized in one direction or the other, and these magnetic states would represent the binary digits 1 and 0. The cores were threaded with wires in such a fashion that the bits of word could be accessed, read out, and written into in parallel, and very rapidly. As a comparison, involving commercial computers during the early 1950s, the UNIVAC 1 (in 1951) had a delay line memory with an access time of 300 microseconds, the IBM 701 (in 1953) using the Williams tube had an access time of 30 microseconds, and the UNIVAC 1103 (in 1953) and the IBM 704 (in 1954) both used ferrite cores with access times of 10 microseconds.[35]

Wilkes, on his visit to America in summer and fall 1950 had witnessed the core memory being implemented on the Whirlwind at MIT—and as in the case of seeing the control matrix in the same machine, this made a strong impression on him.[36] By summer 1953, they were receiving, in Cambridge, England, reports from Cambridge, Massachusetts, of the success of the core memory.[37] In the EDSAC 2, not only was the read/write main memory implemented using ferrite core technology, but also the read-only microprogram store was a matrix of 1024 cores.[38]

VII

This story of the "best way to design" a computer will be incomplete unless we contemplate the consequences of Wilkes's invention. As we have noted, creativity involves as much the future as the past; one may create something never *before* known, but one may also create something that influences what comes *afterward*.

The trouble with the latter—that is, the consequences of an act of creation—is that one never knows when that might happen. An idea or concept, a discovery or an invention may lie dormant, unattended, for years—until someone perceives its significance in some particular context. Until that moment, that act of creation is inconsequential.

Microprogramming, as a computer design principle, manifested something of this nature. During the 1950s, from the time when Wilkes first outlined the idea, not too many people were enticed by it as a way of designing a computer's control unit. Apart from papers emanating from the EDSAC 2 group, only seven or eight publications on the topic are on record for the entire decade.[39]

The 1960s showed a marked increase in interest in microprogramming: articles originating in Britain and the United States, in Italy, France, Russia, Japan, Australia, and

Germany were published. During that decade, some 44 publications were reported by Wilkes in his literature survey of 1969.[40]

The tipping point that transformed microprogramming from an experimental, exploratory technique belonging to the computer design laboratory into something like a computer design subparadigm was a decision made by IBM during the early 1960s—by which time they were as surely the undisputed leaders in the electronic computer industry as they had formerly been the leaders of the electromechanical punched-card data processing industry. The then-head of IBM's Hursley Laboratory in the United Kingdom drew corporate IBM's attention to the EDSAC 2. The result was the company's decision to use microprogramming as a key design philosophy in the IBM System/360 series of computers marketed during the early to mid 1960s.[41] The enormous technical and commercial success of the IBM 360 led to the large-scale adoption of microprogramming in commercial computers thereafter. When IBM talked, others listened! Later in this story we will visit this event in more detail because of the significance of the IBM 360 in another respect. As we will also see, microprogramming played a vital role.

VIII

The EDSAC 2 held its microprogram in read-only memory. In his Manchester article of 1951, tucked away at the very end, Wilkes envisioned the possibility of a read/write microprogram store that could be written into (thus erasing previous contents) as well as read from. This led to the intriguing possibility that, if the contents of the "erasable" microprogram memory could be changed, then one could design a computer *without a fixed order code* (in present-centered terms, instruction set). Instead, the programmer could design her own order code to meet her particular requirements, and change the contents of the microprogram store accordingly.[42]

What Wilkes called "erasable store" came to be known as *writable control store* (or writable control memory), and with the later development of semiconductor memories, the writable control store became a practical reality during the early 1970s.[43] Wilkes's speculation of "a machine with no fixed order" became a practical possibility. A machine with microprogramming capability for a writable control store and no "fixed order" came to be called a *universal host machine*.[44] During the 1970s, a number of interesting universal host machines were designed and built, both in universities and by companies, to explore their applications.[45] Here was another consequence of Wilkes's invention that he *had* anticipated, albeit speculatively. In these machines, the computer *user* (not the designer) would microprogram the host to suit his or her requirements—thus, customize the host into a desired target machine. Programming could then dissolve into microprogramming.

NOTES

1. T. Kilburn. (1951). The new computing machine at the University of Manchester. *Nature*, *168*, 95–96.

2. S. H. Lavington. (1998). *A history of Manchester computers* (2nd ed., p. 25). Swindon, UK: The British Computer Society.

3. S. Rosen. (1969). Electronic computers: A historical survey. *Computing Surveys*, *1*, 7–36 (see especially p. 10).

4. M. V. Wilkes. (1951). *The best way to design an automatic calculating machine*. Report of the Manchester University Computer Inaugural Conference, Manchester, July 1951. Reprinted in E. Mallach & N. Sondak. (Eds.). (1983). *Advances in microprogramming* (pp. 58–60). Dedham, MA: Artech House. See also M. V. Wilkes. (1986). The genesis of microprogramming. *Annals of the History of Computing*, *8*, 116–126 (especially pp. 118–121). All citations refer to the Mallach-Sondak reprint.

5. Recall that the EDSAC main memory was implemented as an ultrasonic storage device consisting of a bank of tanks filled with mercury. At one end of each tank, electrical pulses arriving at fixed time intervals were converted by quartz crystals into acoustic pulses that traveled along the length of the tank, were converted at the output end into electrical pulses, were amplified, and passed back to the input end for recycling. The pulses emerging at the output end could also be "read out" to other parts of the computer for processing. Thus, the train of pulses circulating through each tank represented information "stored" in the device, with each pulse (or absence thereof) representing a bit. In the EDSAC, there were 32 such memory tanks, each capable of storing 32 17-bit numbers. Reading out a particular number from a tank would entail a delay until the first bit of that number appeared at the output of a particular tank; there would be a further delay until the remaining 16 pulses (bits) appeared one by one. Hence the bit-serial nature of the EDSAC memory. For more on ultrasonic memories, see M. V. Wilkes. (1956). *Automatic digital computers*. London: Wiley.

6. In a serial arithmetic unit, all operations are done one digit-pair at a time—that is, they follow the way humans normally perform arithmetic operations. In binary computers, the numbers are held as bit strings, so the operations are performed one bit-pair at a time. For an early discussion of serial arithmetic units, see Wilkes 1956, op cit.

7. Wilkes, 1951, op cit., p. 58.

8. Ibid.

9. Ibid.

10. M. V. Wilkes. (1985). *Memoirs of a computer pioneer* (pp. 164–165). Cambridge, MA: MIT Press.

11. Wilkes, 1951, op cit., p. 58.

12. In a parallel arithmetic unit, operations are performed in a bit-parallel manner. For example, an add operation on two 4-bit binary numbers would involve four independent and identical adding circuits (called *half-adders*), each of which would have as inputs one pair of the positionally corresponding bits of the two numbers. For an extensive description of various parallel arithmetic units of the immediate post-EDSAC era, see R. K. Richards. (1957). *Arithmetic operations in digital computers* (pp. 82–92). Princeton, NJ: van Nostrand.

13. Wilkes, 1951, op cit., p. 59.

14. Ibid.

15. Ibid.

16. For an example of random logic in the design of a computer's control unit, see, for example, S. Dasgupta. (1989). *Computer architecture: A modern synthesis. Volume I: Foundations* (pp. 170–173). New York: Wiley.

17. Wilkes, op cit., p. 59.

18. For a discussion of empirical and conceptual problems in the natural sciences, see L. Laudan. (1977). *Progress and its problems* (pp. 11–69). Los Angeles, CA: University of California Press. For a discussion of empirical versus conceptual problems in the design of artificial sciences, see S. Dasgupta. (2009). *Design theory and computer science* (pp. 13–30). Cambridge, UK: Cambridge University Press (original work published 1991).

19. M. V. Wilkes. (1984). *The origins and development of microprogramming*. Presented at a public lecture at the University of Louisiana, Lafayette, Louisiana, October 29.

20. M.. V. Wilkes in an interview with S. Dasgupta, December 19, 1991, Olivetti Research Laboratory, Cambridge, UK.

21. S. Dasgupta. (2011)."Contesting (Simonton's) blind variation, selective retention theory of creativity. *Creativity Research Journal, 23*, 2, 166–182 (see especially pp. 170–172).

22. A. Koestler. (1964). *The act of creation*. London: Hutchinson.

23. Wilkes, 1986, op cit., p. 117.

24. M. V. Wilkes. (1981). The design of a control unit: Reflections on reading Babbage's notebooks. *Annals of the History of Computing, 3*, 116–120 (see especially p. 118).

25. Wilkes, 1985, op cit., p. 178.

26. Thus, a microinstruction actually encoded multiple operations called *microoperations;* the execution of each microoperation caused a specific control signal to be issued.

27. S. Dasgupta. (1979). The organization of microprogram stores. *ACM Computing Surveys, 11*, 39–65.

28. M. V. Wilkes & J. B. Stringer. (1953). Microprogramming and the design of the control circuits in an electronic digital computer. *Proceedings of the Cambridge Philosophical Society, 49*, 230–238.

29. Wilkes, 1985, op cit., pp. 184–185.

30. M. V. Wilkes, W. Renwick, & D. J. Wheeler. (1958). The design of a control unit of an electronic digital computer. *Proceedings of the Institution of Electrical Engineers, 105*, 121–128.

31. M. V. Wilkes. (1992). EDSAC 2. *IEEE Annals of the History of Computing, 14*, 49–56 (see especially p. 52).

32. Wilkes, 1985, op cit., p. 187.

33. R. Moreau.(1984). *The computer comes of age* (pp. 56–58). Cambridge, MA: MIT Press.

34. Wilkes, 1985, op cit., p. 185.

35. Moreau, op cit., p. 68.

36. Wilkes, 1985, op cit., p. 185.

37. Ibid.

38. Ibid., p. 188.

39. M. V. Wilkes. (1969). The growth of interest in microprogramming: A literature survey. *Computing Surveys, 1*, 139–145.

40. Ibid.

41. Wilkes, 1992, op cit., p. 56.

42. Wilkes, 1951, op cit., p. 60.

43. Dasgupta, 1979, op cit.

44. Dasgupta, 1989, op cit., pp. 214–227.

45. R. F. Rosin, G. Frieder, & R. H. Eckhouse, Jr. (1972). An environment for research in microprogramming and emulation. *Communication of the ACM*, *15*, 248–260; A. B. Salisbury. (1976). *Microprogrammable computer architectures*. New York: Elsevier; E. I. Organick & J. A. Hinds. (1978). *Interpreting machines: Architecture and programming of the B1700/B1800 series*. New York: North-Holland.

13

Language Games

I

IT MUST HAVE been entirely coincidental that two remarkable linguistic movements both occurred during the mid 1950s—one in the realm of natural language, the other in the domain of the artificial; the one brought about largely by a young linguist named Noam Chomsky (1928–), the other initiated by a new breed of scientists whom we may call *language designers*; the one affecting linguistics so strongly that it would be deemed a scientific revolution, the other creating a class of abstract artifacts called *programming languages* and also enlarging quite dramatically the emerging paradigm that would later be called computer science.

As we will see, these two linguistic movements intersected in a curious sort of way. In particular, we will see how an aspect of Chomskyan linguistics influenced computer scientists far more profoundly than it influenced linguists. But first things first: concerning the nature of the class of abstract artifacts called programming languages.

II

There is no doubt that those who were embroiled in the design of the earliest programmable computers also meditated on a certain *goal*: to make the task of programming a computer as natural as possible from the human point of view. Stepping back a century, we recall that Ada, Countess of Lovelace specified the computation of Bernoulli numbers in an abstract notation far removed from the gears, levers, ratchets, and cams of the Analytical Engine (see Chapter 2, Section VIII). We have seen in the works of Herman Goldstine and John von Neumann in the United States, and David Wheeler in England that, even as the first stored-program computers were coming into being, efforts were being made to achieve the goal just mentioned. Indeed, a more precise statement of this goal was in evidence: to compose computer programs in a more abstract form than in the machine's "native" language.

The challenge here was twofold: to describe the program (or algorithm) in such a language that other humans could comprehend, without knowing much about the computer for which the program was written—in other words, a language that allowed communication between the writer of the program and other (human) readers—and also to communicate the program to the *machine* in such fashion that the latter could execute the program with minimal human intervention.

The flow diagram invented by Goldstine and von Neumann was a pictorial kind of language that realized this twofold goal only in part, because a flow diagram, although appropriate for human–human communication, could not serve as a means of human–machine communication without further human intervention. The assembly language Wheeler created for the EDSAC facilitated the goal of automatic human–machine communication. A program written in this assembly language could be transformed automatically into EDSAC machine language using another program, the "assembler" (see Chapter 9, Section VI). However, Wheeler's language was specific to the EDSAC, as were all subsequent assembly languages. To write programs in the EDSAC assembly language, one must be intimately familiar with the EDSAC.

III

Even before Goldstine and von Neumann began constructing the flow diagram notation, tucked away in a small village in the Alps, German computer designer Konrad Zuse was developing a programming language that, as would emerge much later, was well ahead of its time.

The year was 1945. The war in Europe had finally ended, if not the one in the Pacific. Zuse was in his retreat along with the Z4 computer, the only one of his wartime inventions to survive (see Chapter 5, Section XI). Germany was in ruins. It was not the time to pursue practical work in computing. In any case, the Z4 was barely working.[1] Instead, Zuse turned to the design of a language he called *Plankalkül* (or *program calculus*) that could serve to specify computational problems using some general symbolic notation.[2]

Zuse's 1945 manuscript on Plankalkül and its use in constructing programs was never published at the time. It lay ignored or unnoticed until 1972, when it appeared in a German journal. That same year, two German scientists, Friedrich Bauer and H. Wössner brought Plankalkül to the attention of the English reading world with an article in the silver jubilee issue of *Communications of the ACM*.[3]

Thus, Zuse could claim priority once more. In building the Z3, which became operational in 1941, he was the first to have built a fully operational, general-purpose, programmable computer (see Chapter 5, Section XI); in developing Plankalkül in 1945, he invented what was arguably the first programming language that was not tied to a specific computer. Indeed, as Zuse would reflect years later, there *was* no computer in 1945 that conformed to the principles laid out in Plankalkül.[4]

In present-centered language, Plankalkül was a *machine-independent* programming language or (also in present-centered language) a *high-level* programming language. His goal in designing Plankalkül, as stated by Zuse in his 1945 manuscript, was "to provide a purely formal description of any computational procedure."[5]

Of course, what Turing had offered in his 1936 *Entscheidungproblem* paper was a formal way of specifying computation. Zuse's goal was far more practical: to describe formally algorithms that did not reference any specific physical computer and yet *assumed an underlying, implicit, abstract "model" of a real computer that, in principle, could interpret and execute algorithms described in this language*. Zuse had undoubtedly grasped, almost a decade before others, an essential characteristic of a programming language.

Plankalkül was never carried to the stage at which it could be implemented—the second goal of a programming language, to enable human–machine communication. As such, it remained a "paper language," one that met the desire for human–human communication of algorithms. It illustrated the *kinds* of features a generalized, machine-independent programming language should have.

Perhaps most impressive was Zuse's recognition of the concept that would later be called *data structures* or *information structures*—abstract representations of the various kinds of data objects with which algorithms have to deal. There were features in Plankalkül that could define a range of data structures, beginning with the most primitive, the "bit" or Boolean data (having values 1 or 0), spanning integers and real numbers, and extending to "composite" data objects such bit sequences, arrays of arbitrary dimensions, and "records," comprised of two or more composite data objects that would allow, for example, paired items such as names and dates of birth to be specified as a single data object.[6] These sorts of data structures anticipated by almost a decade features that would become established aspects in later and more mature programming languages.

One of Zuse's seemingly innocuous, but in fact quite profound, inventions was the concept of the "assignment" operation; he used the symbol => to denote this.[7] An assignment, say, of the form

$$Z + 1 => Z$$

where Z is an integer variable, in Plankalkül notation signified that the "current" integer value of Z is "augmented" by one—that is, the current value of Z is incremented by one and this becomes Z's "new" value. The assignment operator => thus indicates a *process* involving both a direction and a temporal flow of data. As Donald Knuth and Luis Trabb Pardo, in their extensive survey of early programming languages pointed out, an operator such as the assignment was quite unknown in mathematics—indeed, it signified "a distinct break between computer science thinking and mathematical thinking."[8]

Zuse recognized the necessity of "conditional commands"[9]—the ability to decide to go one way or another during the course of computation on the presence or absence of a condition. Thus, Plankalkül allowed for the specification (in present-centered language) of "If *cond* Then *action*" statements; if the state of computation at that point in the program is such that *cond* is true, then perform *action*; otherwise, proceed to the next statement in the program. The language also provided for "iteration"; until such-and-such condition is met, continue to execute such-and-such sequence of statements repetitively.[10] And, quite remarkably, Zuse provided for one program to be specified and be invoked from another program—this, at least 2 years before John Mauchly conceived the idea of the subroutine in general terms, and 4 years before Wheeler invented a concrete mechanism for subroutine programming and activation for the EDSAC (see Chapter 10, Sections IV and V). Indeed, both the "calling" and the "called" programs were expressible in a uniform manner that, later, was termed *procedure*.[11]

To a later eye, the notation Zuse created for Plankalkül would seem clumsy at best, dreadfully opaque at worst. The invention of notation, we will see, will become a contentious issue among later language designers, and Zuse certainly had no antecedents to guide him. But the *features* denoted by the notation in Plankalkül were unmistakably modern; and insofar as Zuse's goal was concerned, the language was remarkably comprehensive in its power. The original (1945) manuscript included Plankalkül descriptions of a wide variety of algorithms that, in the words of Knuth and Pardo, were "far more complex than anything written before."[12] There were programs for sorting, performing integer and floating-point arithmetic in binary notation, determining whether a logical (Boolean) formula was syntactically correct, even algorithms for chess moves.[13] Bauer and Wösner presented, in their article, Plankalkül programs for the syntax checking of Boolean expressions and one of the chess-playing programs.

As the saying goes, sometimes an invention is too far ahead of its time and the world is not quite ready for it. Perhaps Plankalkül suffered from this fate.

IV

Such early investigators as Wheeler in Cambridge or Goldstine in Princeton did not use the word *language*. Zuse, hidden away in his village in the Alps, labored on what he called a *kalkül*—a calculus. Perhaps the earliest explicit use of "language" in the context of programming was in an unpublished report by Arthur Burks in 1951, then at the University of Michigan in *An Intermediate Program Language as an Aid in Program Synthesis*.[14] Burks's language incorporated features for assignment, conditional branching, and iteration.[15]

In 1950, Zuse's Z4 computer, rebuilt, finally found a home in the Swiss Federal Institute of Technology (ETH) in Zurich, Switzerland.[16] Here, Heinz Rutihauser (1918–1970), a

Swiss mathematician and numeric analyst, embarked, circa 1951, on what in German he called "*automatische rechenplan fertigung*" ("automatic machine code generation"). This coheres with the most common term used during the early 1950s: *automatic programming*—meaning, an environment that allowed the programmer to deploy symbolic notation to specify a program at a level of abstraction higher than that of the "real" machine itself.[17]

We see here the emergence of what, in present-centered language, would be called an *intermediate* or *virtual* machine more abstract than the actual physical computer. This virtual computer would be programmed in symbolic notation (representing the order code for the virtual machine), and the task of an automatic programming system would be to translate mechanically this virtual machine program into the order code for the real machine. The virtual machine was easier to program than the real machine but the two were closely coupled. Most such systems, during the early 1950s, entailed, or were elaborations of, assembly languages and assemblers, which translated the assembly language programs into the real machine's "native" language in the manner pioneered by Wheeler in Cambridge for the EDSAC (see Chapter 9, Section VI). The term automatic programming would prevail through the 1950s. In 1954, the Symposium on Automatic Programming for Digital Computers was held in Washington, DC, sponsored by the Office of Naval Research; and in 1960, an annual publication bearing the title *Annual Review of Automatic Programming* was launched. This publication, with that title, continued until 1994.

V

A certain thinking trend was, however, taking shape. This trend was toward abstraction—to move programming away, albeit cautiously, from the physical machine in a direction tending toward what humans found more natural for specifying computations. For those who were concerned with mathematical or scientific computations, this meant abstracting from the physical computer toward mathematical expressions and formulas. This was the reverse of what was previously the case. Beginning with Babbage and Lovelace, the strategy formerly had been to *reduce* mathematical thought to the level of the machine, to reduce algorithms to machine order code.

But, by around 1954, this trend was being reversed. There were those who desired to express their programs in mathematical or algebraic notation itself.[18] Automatic programming now came to mean the use of programs to *translate* efficiently algorithmic expressions and formulas stated in a mathematical language into economic machine code.[19]

In fact, by 1952, the problem had been recognized as twofold: (a) to design a mathematical language in which to express computations and (b) to develop a programming system that could translate programs cheaply in such languages into efficient machine code. This was what Corrado Böhm (1923–), an Italian and later a distinguished theoretical computer scientist, set about doing as a graduate student at ETH Zurich in 1950 to 1952. In his doctoral dissertation, Böhm described both a language and a complete translator for that language.[20] This was what Halcombe Laning (1920-2012) and N. Zierler set about doing at MIT, where they created a "program for translation of mathematical equations for Whirlwind I."[21] This was what, in England, Alick Glennie (1925–2003) of the Royal Armament Research Establishment desired to do when he designed a system he called AUTOCODE for the Ferranti/Manchester Mark I computer (see Chapter 8, section XIII, for more on the Manchester Mark I; the Ferranti Mark I was the industrial version of the Manchester University Mark I). Glennie—"the unsung hero" in the story of programming languages and automatic programming, according to Knuth and Pardo[22]—delivered a lecture on AUTOCODE at Cambridge University in February 1953 based on notes he had prepared in December 1952,[23] in which he asserted that programming notation must make it easier to make the programming task "comprehensible."[24]

By 1953/1954, the word *compiler* was being used to mean the kind of process required to translate programs written in algebraic form into machine code.[25] Indeed, Glennie's AUTOCODE system, according to Knuth and Pardo, was the first implemented compiler that was actually used.[26]

It was this trend in thinking toward abstraction that led John Backus (1924–2007) and his team at IBM in New York to conceive and develop an automatic programming system around a language he called FORTRAN.

VI

The FORTRAN (an abbreviation for FORmula TRANslator) project began in early 1954. Backus, a master's degree holder in mathematics from Columbia University, joined IBM in 1950 as a programmer for one of their state-of-the-art electromechanical calculating machines. When the IBM 701 was built in 1953 (this the company's first stored-program electronic computer), Backus led the development of an *interpretive* system for the 701 called Speedcode.[27] That is, a program written in Speedcode would be read an order (or statement) at a time, then translated automatically into the 701's machine code and executed immediately. In other words, the orders (or statements) are interpreted one at a time.

With the development of the IBM 704, IBM more or less came to monopolize the large-scale scientific computing arena.[28] Although the IBM 704 was not delivered until 1956, the FORTRAN project began in 1954 and was prompted by the planned advent of the 704. The idea was to design a language that would enable engineers and scientists to write programs themselves for the 704. The language of programming was to be "algebraic" or "formulaic" in form.

This was not the only factor. In 1954, programming accounted for a very large portion—estimated at about three quarters—of the cost of operating a computer installation.[29] Automatic programming could help reduce this cost.

The problem was that, in a culture in which programs were habitually written at virtually the level of a machine's "native language" (that is, assembly language), there was "widespread skepticism" that an automatic programming system could produce machine code as efficient as "hand-coded" programs.[30] Backus and his group were, of course, acutely aware of this skepticism. They recognized that, for such a system to be accepted and used widely, they would have to demonstrate the comparative efficiency of programs produced by automatic systems.[31]

And so even though Backus's group wanted a language to facilitate the scientist's and engineer's task of programming the 704, the design of the language itself became subservient to this imperative. The real problem, as they saw it, was to design a compiler that could produce efficient programs. The actual language design itself happened on the fly, so to speak—driven by the compiler imperative.[32]

As Backus would remember in 1981, the FORTRAN project seemed to defy the idea that all new ideas and inventions draw on prior ideas, and that something like what Arthur Koestler called *bisociation* worked to meld prior, possibly unrelated, concepts into something new (see Chapter 13, Section IV). The closest automatic programming system (in broad philosophy) was the one developed for the MIT Whirlwind I by Laning and Zierler (as mentioned earlier). Although this system was, as Backus acknowledged, "the world's first algebraic compiler"[33] and was completed before the first version of FORTRAN, it had apparently no influence on the design of FORTRAN. Nor, apparently, did any of the other related projects elsewhere, many of which Backus and his group were unaware.[34]

VII

The original goal was to design a language that, although algebraic or formulaic in form, was still tied to a particular computer, the IBM 704—that is, it would be a liminal computational artifact (see Prologue, Section IV). That FORTRAN would evolve into a genuinely machine-independent (or, as the term would emerge, *high-level*) programming language, an abstract computational artifact—and arguably the first language with this characteristic—lends it a special place in the early history of computer science.

But FORTRAN represented something more. Thus far in this story of programming languages, their design and the design of their translators belonged to the realm of what we may call *Little Science*. The work was done by one or two persons, reflecting almost entirely the creative spirit and ideas of these individuals—thus it was with Goldstine and von Neumann, with Wheeler, with Zuse and Rutihauser, with Böhm and Glennie, with Laning and Zierler.

FORTRAN changed all of this. Much as the design of computers in the final years of the 1940s became, relatively speaking, *Big Science*, even in university settings. For example, at the time the Manchester Mark I was commissioned, the group led by Frederic

C. Williams had at least eight members[35]—so also "automatic programming" entered the realm of Big Science with the FORTRAN project.[36] A paper presented at a conference in Los Angeles in 1997 titled *The FORTRAN Automatic Coding System* had 13 coauthors.[37]

The size of the FORTRAN team was, of course, a symptom of the complexity of the project, and this complexity lay in that FORTRAN was a *system* comprised of a language, a computer program for automatic translation, a computer, a text, and a social community. Each of these components influenced, and was in turn influenced by, one or more of the other components.

The FORTRAN language was designed, on the one hand, with an anxious eye toward its translatability into efficient IBM 704 machine code; and on the other, as a means of expressing algorithms in an algebraic form that would be "natural" to scientists and engineers, the intended users of the language. Thus, the acceptability of FORTRAN as a tool by the community of its potential users—the community of expected IBM 704 users and members of an IBM computers user group called SHARE, formed in 1955—depended both on the language as a vehicle for expressing algorithms *and* the efficiency of the executable machine code. The designers of the translator (compiler) bore responsibility of ensuring that FORTRAN programs could be translated automatically into IBM 704 machine code that would compare favorably in efficiency with "hand-coded" programs. If the FORTRAN language was the interface between the user community and an IBM 704 installation, the FORTRAN compiler was the interface between the language and the 704 machine itself.

Strictly speaking, the FORTRAN language was one part of the user community–704 installation interface. The user had to learn the language; a *text* was needed that would describe the language—a programmer's guide to FORTRAN. Like any endeavor that created practical artifacts for human use, the FORTRAN project entailed a melding of objective principles of design with subjective perceptions and beliefs—mathematics, logic, design principles fused with psychology.

VIII

The FORTRAN language design began in early 1954. Before the year's end, a preliminary 29-page report on the language was written[38] and distributed to prospective IBM 704 customers.[39] Armed more with faith than empirical evidence (as Backus confessed) the authors of the report, in their introduction, assured readers that FORTRAN programs would not only execute as efficiently as "laboriously" hand-coded programs would, but also that FORTRAN would facilitate the production of much more complex programs than could be hand coded.[40]

Here, "FORTRAN" meant not the language but the translator; "coding" referred not to the act of writing programs in the FORTRAN language, but to the process of producing machine code automatically by the compiler; the "human coder" was not the

FORTRAN programmer but the programmer in the 704's assembly (or machine) language. Vocabulary was being refined.

Soon after the preliminary report was written, Backus and two of his language code-signers gave talks on FORTRAN to groups of IBM customers in various cities—customers who had ordered the IBM 704 (which had been announced around May 1954). By and large, they found their audience skeptical about this new prospect.[41]

The design and implementation of the FORTRAN compiler (still called *translator*, at the time)—written in the "native" language of the IBM 701 that would execute the compiler—began in earnest in early 1955.[42] By summer 1956, "large parts of the system was working."[43] The complete compiler was available in early 1957.[44] Also in summer 1956, David Sayre (1924–2012), a PhD in crystallography from Oxford University, began writing a document describing the language. The outcome was the *Programmer's Reference Manual* (1956).[45] In early 1957, Backus and his whole group presented a paper on the FORTRAN system at the Western Joint Computer Conference in Los Angeles, California.[46] That same year, the *Programmer's Primer* for the FORTRAN system was published by IBM.[47]

IX

The FORTRAN language as it was originally conceived in 1954 to 1956 (Backus called it FORTRAN *I*[48]) would evolve in its features and capabilities over several versions: FORTRAN II, III, and IV; it spawned other "dialects." It became, among other things, a machine-independent or high-level language. To speak later of FORTRAN was to speak of a language genus, one might say. However, the fundamental and unmistakable *style* of this genus was established with the original ancestor. We get a sense of this style in the little and trivial program written in the "original" FORTRAN shown in Table 13.1.

This program reads an array of 20 integers into an array data structure A. It then initializes X, Y, Z, and W to zero, then scans in sequence the integers in A and keeps count (in X) of the number of integers that are between −50 and +50 and tallies the total of these numbers in Y. It also keeps count of the number of integers that fall outside the range in a separate counter (Z) and also adds the total of these numbers in W. When all 20 numbers in A have been accounted for, it prints out the values of the counters and the corresponding totals and stops.

The formulaic nature of most of these *statements*—by 1956, this word was used to refer to each of the basic meaningful units of action, although they were originally called formulas,[49] hence, no doubt, the name of the language—is quite apparent. Yet, algebraic or formulaic though they seemed, they were not mathematical expressions but descriptions of actions to be performed by a computer. $X = X + 1$ is not an algebraic expression in FORTRAN (indeed, mathematically or logically it would not make sense); rather, it signifies an action. The = is not the mathematical equality symbol; it denotes the

TABLE 13.1 A FORTRAN Program

```
          DIMENSION A(20)
          READ A
          X=0
          Y=0
          Z=0
          W=0
          DO 2 I=1,20
          IF ABS(A(I)) > 50 GO TO 1
          X=X+1
          Y=Y+A(I)
          GO TO 2
  1       Z=Z+1
          W=W+A(I)
  2       CONTINUE
          PRINT X,Y
          PRINT Z,W
          STOP
```

assignment operation, synonymous with Zuse's => in Plankalkül (see Section III, this chapter). The statement means: Read the value of the variable X, increment by one, and write the resulting value into X.

Other statements in Table 13.1, such as the *DO* or *IF* would seem, however, less transparent to the neophyte FORTRAN user; the former denotes an iteration, the latter a conditional branch. The purpose of the FORTRAN *Programmer's Reference Manual* was to explain *all* aspects of the language for the user's benefit. Such an explanation took the form of first specifying the legal form of each statement type and the rules governing this form, and an explanation of what the statement meant.

Form and meaning. In the realm of a natural language like English, linguists usually call form the *syntax* of the language, and the meaning its *semantics*. The FORTRAN *Programmer's Manual* of 1956 marked the emergence of a new consciousness among language designers about the linguistic (rather than merely the notational) nature of programming languages. The terms *syntax* and *semantics* (as we will see) would come to be used very soon thereafter, but we find a presence of this consciousness in the writing of the *Programmer's Manual*.

The text describing a programming language must describe all and only what the language is about. For the user of that language, the text is all. But, unlike the postmodernist's "text," which can be "read" in as many different ways as there are readers, and the writer's intention is not relevant, the text describing a programming language must provide only one "reading"—there should be only one way of making meaning, one way of interpreting the language.

The FORTRAN group took this obligation seriously. In the *Programmer's Manual* each type of statement is described in terms of its form and meaning, syntax and semantics.

> "DO n i = m_1, m_2" or "DO n i = m_1, m_2, m_3" where n is a statement number, I is a...variable, and m_1, m_2, m_3 are each either an unsigned...constant or a nonsubscripted...variable. If m_3 is not stated it is taken to be 1.[50]

Here, then, was the "general form" of the *DO* statement. Alongside were given examples: DO 30 I=1,10, DO 30 I=1, M, 3. Then followed the meaning of the *DO* statement:

> The DO statement is a command to "DO the statements which follow, to and including the statement with statement number n, repeatedly, the first time with i=m_1, and with I increased by m_3 for each succeeding time; after they have been done with i equal to the highest of this sequence of values which does not exceed m_2 let control reach the statement following the statement with statement number n....[51]

Conciseness and elegance—attributes valued by mathematicians, as many of the FORTRAN group were—is in evidence in certain sections of the language description. "Recursion," the mathematical strategy of defining a concept in terms of itself (such as defining the factorial of a number recursively, $N! = N*(N-1)!$, and $0!=1$) was used to specify the rules for forming algebraic expressions (such as $X+Y$):

> By repeated use of the following rules, all permissible expressions may be derived...
> 4. If E is an expression the (E) is an expression
> 5. If E and F are expressions...then E+F, E-F, E*F, E/F are expressions....[52]

X

Yet, by Backus's own admission, language design played a secondary role in the FORTRAN endeavor.[53] Rather, as (it was once said) Britain acquired India as part of its empire in a fit of absent-mindedness, so also, it almost seems, reading Backus, that the FORTRAN language was designed absent-mindedly. But Backus and his colleagues, collectively, were too much the engineer–scientists to be absent-minded, even in a metaphorical sense. What Backus really implied, as he would write in 1981, was that—no matter how satisfying the FORTRAN programming language was—as a programming tool, it would never have sufficed. The emphasis had to be on program efficiency. It was this criterion that ruled above all else.[54]

The burden of responsibility for producing efficient IBM 704 machine code from a FORTRAN program—later, the former came to be called *object program* or *object code* and the latter, *source program* or *source code*—fell on the compiler or, more precisely, on the compiler writer. By the time the first book-length texts and monographs on compilers began to appear during the mid to late 1960s,[55] a great deal of knowledge had accumulated on the theory, design, and implementation of compilers. And the programmers who built the first FORTRAN compiler made no small contribution to this branch of what, in the 1960s, came to be called *programming systems*.[56]

A compiler is a computer program of a rather complex and peculiar sort, for it manipulates and processes other computer programs. It takes as input a program written in a machine-independent or high-level programming language (such as FORTRAN, the source program) and produces as output a *functionally* equivalent program (the object code) that is executable on a specific computer.[57] A complier, then, is an *automatic* translator in the strict linguistic sense; it transforms automatically a text in a programming language *L* into another functionally equivalent text specified in a machine language *M*. Both texts are programs. Both texts are liminal. But, the abstract aspect of a program in the programming language (when it describes an algorithm meant *only* for human–human communication, a piece of "social text") is more pronounced than in the case of a program in a machine language.

The great difference between a compiler and the "automatic machine translators" that Warren Weaver and others had so desired (see Chapter 11, Section IX), was that automatic machine translation referred to translating texts in one *natural* language (say, Russian) into another natural language (say, English). The compiler's task is far more modest. It translates from one *artificial* language into another. And because artificial languages are invented, they can (at least in principle) be defined precisely and restricted in features, without the richness, vagueness, ambiguity, and variability of natural languages.

Thus, the challenges faced by the compiler writers (as, somewhat curiously, programmers who designed and built compilers would come to be called[58]) may not have been as overwhelming as the task faced by programmers who built automatic machine translation systems. However, the challenge of compiler writing was, in many ways, more complex than any other kind of programming experienced until then.

A compiler is, in fact, a system of many components performing many different tasks. It is an amalgam of many different algorithms of varying intricacy and complexity. It must first ensure that the program syntax adheres to the rules of the language. It must "make sense" of the overall structure, and this involves recording the flow of information and the flow of control between program components. To manage the complexity of its work, the compiler must decompose the source program into subunits (called *basic blocks*) that can be analyzed separately. The compiler must gather and record all the information about the program that is necessary for the ultimate task of the complier: generating machine code (look ahead to Figure 15.2).

Hovering like the sword of Damocles over all this is the "efficiency imperative." The proof of the pudding lies in the eating, and "eating"—in this context—means how efficient the object code is compared with "hand-coded" programs in assembly or machine language.

There is a "cultural" gap between the language of the source program and the language of the object program. The former language is abstract and symbolic. In fact, it is itself an abstract artifact; its syntax and semantics refer only implicitly to some (abstract) computer. The latter language is relatively more concrete and physical; it is liminal because, although abstract, it is very close to some real physical computer. The compiler has to straddle the two cultures and "map" texts from one to the other. The sword of Damocles mandates that the object code must be "optimized" as best as possible for both time to execute the object program and space required to store the object program in computer memory.

To repeat, by the mid 1960s, a fairly large body of knowledge about compiling would accumulate. However, the writers of the FORTRAN compiler in the mid 1950s had very little prior knowledge or experience to guide them; *they* were the producers of some of the knowledge that entered the texts and monographs of the 1960s and 1970s.

The FORTRAN compiler was, in present-centered language, a *one-pass compiler*: the source program in its original form was "fed" to the compiler just once; the latter "saw" the source program only once.[59] Thereafter, the source program would be analyzed, dissected, deconstructed—*mangled*, so to speak—all in the cause of producing "optimized" code for the IBM 704.[60]

In the case of the FORTRAN compiler, there was not a single writer. Compiler writing was a group effort and different individuals given responsibility for different "sections" of the compiler. The compiler was organized into six sections to work in sequence, each section passing its output to the one that followed, with the last section assembling the final object program in IBM 704 machine code.[61] Naturally, "code optimization" was a significant functional goal for the compiler, and various kinds of optimization strategies were distributed among the different sections. Some of the algorithms invented for object code generation and code optimization would have consequences, and they came to influence later compilers. These included an algorithm developed for compiling assignment statements involving arithmetic expressions (for example, a statement such as $X = (A[I] * B[I])/C[K])$[62] and an algorithm for allocating machine registers to variables (the *register allocation problem*, in present-centered language).[63] As a later author would write, for these reasons the FORTRAN compiler for the IBM 704 was certainly the most significant of the first generation of compilers.[64]

XI

The FORTRAN project demonstrated empirically the viability of the high-level programming language concept much as the EDSAC and the Manchester Mark I had demonstrated the viability of the stored-program computer concept. However, although the stored-program *schema* (see Chapter 8, Section V) became *the* paradigm in the realm of computer architecture, in that virtually all computers that followed adhered to this schema, this was not so in the realm of programming. Assembly languages continued to prevail, especially for writing "programming systems"—programs that created the interface between the physical machine and the "ordinary" computer user. Assemblers, loaders, subroutine linkage editors, interpreters, specialized subroutines, and the compilers themselves were written in the assembly languages of the relevant computers, because this allowed systems programmers to have direct control over machine resources in a way the high-level language programmers could not have.

Concern for program efficiency was, no doubt, the driving factor for the preference of assembly languages. However, it is also tempting to think that, much as Latin gave clerics and the learned classes in medieval Europe an esoteric tongue that separate them from the unlearned "masses"—and thus endowing the former with a certain kind of power the masses could not possess—so also each assembly language was an esoteric tongue that programmers could use to protect their guild and skills from the larger community of computer users.

XII

However, as cultural anthropologists and linguists well know, culture and language are intimately related. In the realm of computers, "culture" means the problem environment in which a community of computer users resides. FORTRAN was adopted by the community of scientists and engineers because the language matched the reality of their problem environment.

During the mid 1950s, the other major computer culture was that of business computing (or data processing). And this culture—its "universe of discourse," its "worldview"— was significantly different from the culture that embraced FORTRAN. The people who worked in data processing were not at home in the world of abstract symbols, nor were they usually mathematically savvy,[65] as Grace Hopper, Howard Aiken's collaborator on the Harvard Mark I machine of the 1940s remembered (see Chapter 5, Section VI), speaking in 1981 of her experience of the 1950s when she was employed by Remington-Rand (who had absorbed the Eckert-Mauchly Computer Corporation), the makers of the UNIVAC computers.[66] In her words, they were "word manipulators."

Hopper knew well about FORTRAN from its earliest inception.[67] She also knew about the algebraic translator Laning and Zierler had developed for the Whirlwind I.[68] At Remington-Rand in 1953/1954, under her supervision, the A-2 compiler had been built to translate programs in algebraic form into UNIVAC machine code. It was almost inevitable that, involved as she was with business computing, Hopper would want to design a language/translator that met the needs of the business computing culture.

In January 1955, Hopper and her colleagues at Remington-Rand wrote a "formal proposal for writing a data processing compiler."[69] As with Backus and his group the year before, it was not the language that dominated her thinking but the compiler. The language itself would comprise English-language words composed into sentences.[70] The outcome was a compiler for a language called FLOW-MATIC,[71] which was used by Remington-Rand customers.[72]

FLOW-MATIC's place in this story lies in that it was the first attempt to build a language/compiler system for business computing, and it had some influence on what became the most significant development in language design for this computing culture. This latter development began by way of meetings of a large group of "computer people" (including Grace Hopper) representing government, users, consultants, and computer manufacturers to decide on a "common business language for automatic digital computers."[73] The immediate outcome of these meetings was the formation of a committee, in June 1959, called Committee on Data Systems Languages (CODOSYL) and subcommittees that would examine the development of a language for business computing.[74] If the FORTRAN project manifested signs of Big Science (see Section VII, this chapter), here was Big Science in an altogether different sense: *language design-by-committee.*

The resulting language, the first complete specification of which was produced in December 1959 was named *COBOL* (COmmon Business Orientation Language).[75] Like FORTRAN, COBOL would evolve through several versions in its first dozen years of existence, as COBOL 60, COBOL 61, COBOL 61 EXTENDED, COBOL 65, COBOL 68, and COBOL 70. Like FORTRAN, COBOL formed a very distinctive language genus. Much as FORTRAN became the effective *lingua franca* of the scientific computer culture, so also COBOL emerged as the *lingua franca* of the business computing culture—at least in English-speaking parts of the world. As in the case of FORTRAN, *standards* would be established for COBOL by both national and international standardization bodies (specifically, the American National Standards Institute and the International Standards Organization).[76]

However, unlike the case for FORTRAN, COBOL did not spawn other "species" of the genus. More markedly, unlike the case for FORTRAN, in the realm of *computer science* COBOL had the uneasiest of places. As Jean Sammet (1928–), one of the original designers of the first version of COBOL (COBOL 60) remarked wistfully in 1981, "most computer scientists are simply not interested in COBOL."[77]

Perhaps this was because computer scientists were far more interested in languages that could be used to program complex, interesting *algorithms*. And with some exceptions (such as sorting and searching large files of data) this was not *really* the stuff of business computing.

XIII

It seems fair to say that the designers of programming languages, circa 1956 and 1957, were not overly conscious of the *description* of programming languages as a scientific problem in its own right, or that it was a problem of practical importance. This situation changed with the advent of what we may call the *Algol movement*, and with some computer scientists' encounters with the ideas of Noam Chomsky.

XIV

In summer 1958, a meeting was convened at ETH, the Swiss Federal Institute of Technology, Zurich, organized jointly by the ACM and the Gesellschaft für Angewandte Mathematik und Mechanic (GAMM)—the former, an American society; the latter, a German one. The objective was to discuss the design of an internationally accepted ("universal") machine-independent programming language.[78] Thus was launched a remarkable international scientific collaboration. It all began when, after the development of FORTRAN, groups of people on both sides of the Atlantic independently believed that, out of the potential Babelic profusion of tongues, a *single* tongue should emerge, a single language that would serve to *communicate programs between humans* as well as between humans and machines, an invented language that would be as abstract as mathematics and natural language are (to enable interhuman communication of computations), and as necessarily and practically close to the genre of real stored-program computers. People had been watching with unease how each new computer was spawning its own distinct programming language—or so it seemed to Alan Perlis (1922–1990), a mathematician-turned-computer scientist at the Carnegie Institute of Technology, Pittsburgh (later, Carnegie Mellon University), recalling in 1986 the situation a quarter century before.[79] The time for action to counter this trend seemed at hand.

Under the auspices of the ACM, a committee was struck in June 1957 "to study the matter of creating a universal programming language."[80] This committee spawned a subcommittee in 1958, comprising John Backus (IBM), William Turanski (Remington-Rand), Alan Perlis, and John McCarthy (MIT). Its mandate was to draft a language proposal for submission to the ACM.[81]

There were those in Europe with similar thoughts. In 1955, at an international symposium on automatic computing held in Darmstadt, (then West) Germany, several participants spoke on the need for "unification" (a term surely in the minds of many in a land split into two nations)—a single universal programming language.[82] A working group as a subcommittee of GAMM was established to design such a language. In fall 1957, this subcommittee wrote to the president of the ACM, John W. Carr, III, suggesting that the two organizations collaborate in this common enterprise[83]—thus the ACM–GAMM meeting in Zurich in summer 1958. Each organization was represented by four people, including Backus and Perlis from America, and Friedrich Bauer (1924–) and Rutihauser from Europe.[84]

The significance of this project was remarkable as an exercise in international cooperation. If the search for a *universal* is an ideal of science—of the natural sciences—then this project was whole-heartedly scientific in spirit. The members of this group were in the business of creating an artifact, no doubt, and that surely belongs to engineering; but, engineering designers are not usually interested in universals. They design and create to solve specific problems, and the solution is all, regardless of its generality. The programming "linguists" who gathered in Zurich in summer 1958 were, however, intent on the creation of a single *universal* language. Here was a gathering of "scientists of the artificial" (see Prologue, Section III) who aspired to the highest ideal of the natural sciences: universal principles, concepts, theory. The difference lay in that, in a natural science (such as physics), principles, laws, theories are deemed universal with respect to all physical time and space, whereas in the artificial science of language design its principles, syntax, and semantics would be considered universal with respect to the world of computation only. Perhaps in the emerging discipline of computer science, the only precedent to such a grand objective of universality was Turing's design of his abstract, mathematical machine during the late 1930s (see Chapter 4).

The international group identified more specific goals. They agreed that the new language should be "as close as possible to standard mathematical notation," that it should be "readable with little further explanation," that it should be used to describe numeric computations "in publications," and that it should be "readily translatable into machine code by the machine itself."[85] Both human–human communication and human–machine communication were central to their enterprise. However, the group recognized that, in using the language for publication *and* for automatic compilation, there might be discrepancies "between the notation used in publication" and the "characters available on input–output mechanisms."[86] This meant that the language for the purpose of publication and, especially, the language for the purpose of computer execution each could vary from one environment to another. They decided that, in defining their language, such variability and potential vagaries of both print fonts and input/output "hardware" would be disregarded. Rather, they would attend to an abstract representation that they called a *reference language* from which appropriate *publication* and *hardware languages* might later be spawned.[87]

So this yet-to be-designed programming language would have three "levels" of description: as a reference language, as a publication language, and as a hardware language. The group of eight, however, would concern themselves only with the reference language.

The result of this meeting of eight minds, "who met, reasoned about, argued over, insisted on, and ultimately compromised over the issues" during an eight-day period,[88] was a language they named *Algol* (an acronym for ALGOrithmic Language). Later, this version of the language was called *Algol 58*.[89]

Algol 58 had a very short life. A description of the language, edited by Perlis and Klaus Samelson (1918–1970), and coauthored by the entire group, was published in *Communications of the ACM* in 1958 and in the brand-new German journal *Numerische Mathematik* in 1959.[90]

On the one hand, Algol 58 began to be used immediately as a publication language for presenting algorithms in journals; an IBM group attempted to implement it on the IBM 709.[91] On the other hand, much as mathematicians pounce on new proofs of theorems to hunt out its flaws and possible errors, so also readers of the Algol 58 report found many definitions incomplete, contradictory, or inadequate for the description of numeric algorithms.[92] Improvements and modifications were suggested from both sides of the Atlantic. In Europe, an *ALGOL Bulletin* was launched in 1959 under the editorship of Peter Naur (1928–), a Danish astronomer-turned-computer scientist who worked for the independent computer laboratory Regnecentralen in Copenhagen.[93] This would the medium for all matters Algol.

Another international meeting on Algol was deemed necessary. In fact, there ensued more than one. Under the auspices of the United Nations Educational, Scientific and Cultural Organization (UNESCO), an international conference on "information processing" was held in Paris in June 1959. Quite apart from the Algol context, this was significant historically in that it marked the immediate prelude to the founding, in 1960, of the International Federation for Information Processing (IFIP), which became the official international umbrella organization for all individual national computing societies, the United Nations of computing, so to speak. The UNESCO Paris conference came to be later recognized as the first of the thrice yearly IFIP Congress, the official worldwide conference sponsored by IFIP.[94]

The design of the "new" Algol was on the agenda of this conference. However, proposals for change were still forthcoming, so yet another conference was held in January 1960, also in Paris, and attended by a group of 13—from America, Britain, Denmark, France, West Germany, Holland, and Switzerland.[95]

The new language proposed by this group was called *Algol 60*. A formal report on Algol 60 at the reference language level, edited by Naur and coauthored by all 13 members of the group, was quickly published, again in *Communications of the ACM* and *Numerische Mathematik*.[96]

Once more, inconsistencies were found in the report. Many discussions ensued. Another Algol meeting was found necessary, this being held at the IFIP Congress of 1962 in Rome. There were several changes in the composition of the committee. The product of their deliberations was the *Revised Report on the Algorithmic Language ALGOL 60*, edited by Naur and coauthored by the same group of 13 who had authored the first Algol 60 report. The *Revised Report* was published, this time, not only in *Communications of the ACM* and *Numerische Mathematik*, but also in the British *Computer Journal*, which had been launched in 1957.[97] It became the final, "official" definition of Algol 60.

The Algol project, spanning roughly 1958 to 1962 and culminating in the publication of the Algol 60 *Revised Report*, manifested vividly the role of *criticism* in the development of scientific knowledge. Austrian-British philosopher of science Sir Karl Popper had characterized this feature of science by way of the schema

$$P_1 \rightarrow TT \rightarrow EE \rightarrow P_2.$$

Here, P_1 is the initial problem situation (or goal), TT is a tentative theory advanced as an explanation or solution for P_1, EE is the process of error identification and elimination applied to TT relative to P1, and the outcome is a new problem situation (or revised goal) P2. The cycle renews itself until a problem situation gives rise to a tentative theory for which no error can be identified.[98]

Popper's schema was intended for the natural sciences—or rather, for any enterprise that was genuinely deemed to be called a science. We see in the succession of events in the Algol project an identical process at work in the realm of a science of the artificial.

XV

We get a sense of the nature of the Algol 60 programming style (and can compare it with that of FORTRAN) with a small example. The Algol 60 program reads in three positive integers from an input tape and computes their *greatest common divisor* (GCD). In the program, the name *buffer* refers always to the next input value on the tape. The computation of "GCD (*first, second, third*)" is done through a subroutine, called *procedure* in Algol, that computes the GCD on pairwise numbers at a time—that is, as "GCD (GCD (*first, second*), *third*)."

```
begin integer first, second, third, x, y;
      procedure gcdoftwonumbers
                 begin
                 A: if x=y then goto B;
                         if x>y then x := x-y else y := y-x;
                         goto A;
                 B: end;
            first := buffer; second := buffer; third := buffer; x := first; y := second;
            gcdoftwonumbers;
            y := third;
            gcdoftwonumbers;
            print(x);
end
```

The entire program is enclosed in an entity called *block*, which begins and ends with the "reserved" words **begin** and **end** respectively. (In Algol 60 and, indeed, all languages belonging to the Algol genus, reserved words were in bold type.) Five **integer** variables are declared inside the (outer) block, of which the first three serve to hold the three input integers and the last two are "internal" variables used for computation. Also declared within the outer block is a **procedure** named *gcdoftwonumbers*; it also comprises a block. The symbol := indicates assignment; inside the procedure, decision (or conditional) statements are specified: **if...then...** and **if...then...else...**. Also shown is the **goto** statement, which is an unconditional branch.

The flow of control through the program begins with the first assignment statement (*first := buffer*) and flows sequentially through the statements separated by semicolons. When control reaches *gcdoftwonumbers*, that procedure is called and the block inside the procedure is entered for execution. On completing the procedure, control returns to the statement (*y := third*) following the procedure call. This same procedure is called a second time. Eventually, control returns to the *print* statement after which the program terminates.

XVI

But let us return to the Paris UNESCO conference of 1959. There, John Backus presented a paper titled *The Syntax and Semantics of the Proposed International Algebraic Language of the Zurich ACM-GAMM Conference.*[99]

Syntax and *semantics*. Backus made these terms from the realm of linguistics part of the vocabulary of programming languages. But, he not only used these terms, he also proposed a notation by which the syntax of Algol 58 could be described *formally*. He introduced, in other words, a *meta-language* for the description of the syntax of a programming language. Thus did the concept of meta-language, familiar to logicians, enter the vocabulary of computer science.

Backus's meta-language came to be called *Backus Normal Form* or *BNF*.[100] Thus we find in the introductory part of the *Revised Report*, the announcement that the syntax would be specified using "metalinguistic formulae."[101]

What would these meta-linguistic formulae look like? Table 13.2 presents a description from the very beginning of the *Revised Report*. Here is how the syntax of *identifiers* (character strings that signify allowable names—of variables, labels, subroutines—in the language) was defined.

Here, the sequence of characters enclosed in < > represent meta-linguistic variables, such as <identifier> and <digit>. The symbol ::= means "defined as" or "can be"; the symbol | means "or" (and these two symbols are called *connectives*). Any symbol that is not a meta-linguistic variable or a connective stands for itself.

So in this meta-language, BNF, the first "formula" says that an identifier can be a letter or an identifier followed by a letter, or an identifier followed by a digit. The second

TABLE 13.2 A Fragment of Algol 60 Syntactic Rules

(I)	<identifier>::= <letter>| <identifier><letter>| <identifier><digit>
(II)	<digit> ::= 0|1|2|4|5|6|7|8|9
(III)	<letter>::=a|b|c|d|e|f|g|h|i|j|k|l|m|n|o|p|q|r|s|t|u|v|w|x|y|z|
	A|B|C|D|E|F|G|H|I|J|K|L|M|N|O|P|Q|R|S|T|U| V|W|X|Y|Z

TABLE 13.3 Syntactic Generation of the String 'ALGOL60' from the Rules of Table 13.2

<identifier>	
<identifier><digit>	(1)
<identifier><digit><digit>	(1)
<identifier><digit>0	(11)
<identifier>60	(11)
<identifier><letter>60	(1)
<identifier>L60	(111)
<identifier><letter>L60	(1)
<identifier>OL60	(111)
<identifier><letter>OL60	(1)
<identifier>GOL60	(111)
<identifier><letter>GOL60	(1)
<identifier>LGOL60	(111)
<letter>LGOL60	(1)
ALGOL 60	(111)

formula states that a digit can be 0 or 1 or 2 or…9. The third formula says that a letter can be a or b or…z or A or B or…Z.

These formulas establish, in fact, *syntactic rules* for how a programmer can write an identifier in Algol 60. Any identifier that obeys these rules is *syntactically correct* in the language. Any identifier that does not obey these rules is syntactically incorrect and, thus not "recognized" in Algol 60.

Consider, for example, the character string ALGOL60. Is this a syntactically correct identifier in Algol 60? We can determine this by seeing whether, beginning with the meta-lingusitic variable <identifier>, we can apply the three rules systematically and *generate* ALGOL60. One possible sequence of rules (with which rule is applied at each step shown on the right) is as noted in Table 13.3.

In fact, it can be checked easily that the character string ALGOL 60 is not syntactically correct according to rules given because a blank (here, between the L and 6) is not a recognized character.

XVII

What was the source of Backus's idea of this meta-language, BNF? Reflecting in 1981, he tells us of attending a course taught by mathematician Martin Davis (1928–) during which Davis talked about the work of Emil Post (1897–1954). It seemed to Backus that one of Post's important ideas could be used to specify the syntax of Algol 58.[102]

Post was a Polish-born American logician who taught at the City College of New York and who developed (among much else) a model of computation in 1943 in which a computation could be realized by transforming a string of symbols into another string of symbols by following certain rewriting rules called *productions*.[103] A Post production, in general, would be of the form

antecedent → *consequence*

Here, both *antecedent* and *consequence* are symbol strings, and → indicates the replacement, deletion, or addition of some part of the antecedent string to obtain the consequence string. For example, consider the single symbol 1. Then, if $ is a symbol string composed of an even number of 1s or an "empty" string, a production

$ → $11

will generate, if applied successively, the strings 11, 1111, 111111, and so on, all containing an even number of 1s.

In our example from Algol 60, we see that rule (i) can be restated as three productions:

```
<identifier>  ::=  <letter>
<identifier>  ::=  <identifier><letter>
<identifier>  ::=  <identifier><digit>
```

The meta-linguistic variables in < > are symbol strings, and what the Algol 60 *Revised Report* called "metalingustic formulae" are "productions."

XVIII

However, BNF, the meta-language used to describe the syntax of Algol 60, bears a strong similarity to another meta-language that emerged during the mid 1950s, in the work of the linguist Noam Chomsky—so much so that it is easy to believe that Backus was stimulated by Chomsky (although, according to Backus, this was not the case). In a paper presented at a conference at MIT in 1956,[104] and then in a book titled *Syntactic Structures* (1957),[105] Chomsky laid out the beginning of a new direction in linguistics that was so influential it is sometimes referred to as the *Chomskyan revolution*, in the sense that, in the opinion of a later commentator, it induced a revolution in the scientific study of natural language.[106]

The place of Chomsky in the realm of linguistic studies is, however, not our concern here, but rather how some of his basic ideas were remarkably relevant to the development of a theory of programming (and, more generally, artificial) languages, including Algol 60. His work led to a fundamental clarification of the nature of programming languages in a number of ways.

To begin with, programming language designers before Chomsky spoke of "language," but never quite clarified what they meant by this term. For example, in the case of Algol 60, an "algorithmic language," it was never stated exactly which part of the *Revised Report* constituted the language.

Chomsky helped clarify this matter when he proposed that a language is a (possibly infinite) set of sentences, each sentence being composed of a finite set of elements.[107] The "set of elements" out of which a sentence is constructed forms an "alphabet" of symbols. Thus, a sentence is a string of symbols taken from this alphabet.[108] But, the sentences or symbol strings that can be formed from an alphabet of symbols are not *all* legitimate sentences in the language. There are rules that determine which are grammatical sentences in the language and which are not. Such rules form the *grammar* of that language. In fact, according to Chomsky, the grammar of a language is a device that produces all and *only* the sentences of that language.[109]

A grammar, then, is a "device of some sort" that will *generate all* the grammatical sentences of a language and *only* those grammatical sentences. Suppose the "alphabet" of symbols includes the words found in a dictionary of that language—say, English. Then, all the grammatical sentences in English are word sequences that can be generated by the grammar for English.

What would a grammar look like and how does it generate sentences? Chomsky presented three different "models" of grammar,[110] but the one that is most illuminating for us is exemplified by the following simple grammar:[111]

(i)   Sentence → NP + VP
(ii) NP → T + Noun
(iii) VP → Verb + NP
(iv) T → the
(v)   Noun → man|ball|...
(vi) Verb → hit|took|...

In fact, these are all "rewriting" or production rules. Each is of the form X→Y, where X is a single element and Y is a string of one or more elements. The rule X→Y is interpreted as "replace X with Y" or "rewrite X as Y." The + in X+Y signifies the concatenation of X and Y; and the | signifies "or."

The rules then apply as follows: starting with the symbol "sentence," apply rule (i). This results in the string NP+VP. if any of the elements of this string can be rewritten by one of the rules (ii) to (vi), then select one such rule. Repeat this procedure until a sequence of symbols comprising only elements of the alphabet—a sentence of that language—is produced.

Thus, for example, the sentence "the man hit the ball" can be generated by this grammar by the sequence of rule applications presented in Table 13.4.

This is not the only way the rules could be applied to generate the sentence "the man hit the ball." Nor, of course, is it the only sentence that could be generated from these

TABLE 13.4 Parsing the Sentence 'the man hit the ball'

Sentence	
NP+VP	(by applying i)
NP+Verb+NP	(iii)
T+Noun+Verb+NP	(ii)
the+Noun+Verb+NP	(iv)
the+Noun+Verb+T+Noun	(ii)
the+man+Verb+T+Noun	(v)
the+man+Verb+T+ball	(v)
the+man+hit+T+ball	(vi)
the+man+hit+the+ball	(iv)

rules. Such sentences as "the man hit the man," "the man took the ball," "the ball took the man," "the ball took the ball," and so on, could also be generated from these rules. They would all be syntactically correct even though some are meaningless (that is, semantically incorrect), such as "the ball took the man."

We now have a sense of what Chomsky meant by a grammar. As he tells us, a grammar comprises of a finite set of "initial strings" and a finite set of production or rewrite rules.[112] In the previous example, there is only one initial string, "sentence," although in more elaborate grammars there would be additional initial strings such as "declaration sentence," "interrogative sentences," and so on.

XIX

We can now see how Chomskyan theory (or a miniscule part of it) relates to programming languages. His "instruction formulas" (or productions or rewrite rules) correspond to the meta-linguistic formulas of the Algol 60 *Revised Report*. They are the *syntactic rules* of Algol 60. The alphabet of symbols out of which sentences are formed in Chomsky's scheme are the basic symbols out of which Algol 60 programs are written. Chomsky's "grammatical sentences" are the set of syntactically correct *programs* that can be written using the syntactic rules defined for Algol 60. The set of basic Algol 60 symbols, together with an "initial string" (which corresponds to "sentence" in Chomsky's example grammar), which in Algol 60 is the "procedure," along with the entire corpus of meta-linguistic formulas presented in the *Revised Report* constitute the Algol 60 grammar.

There was more to the Chomskyan connection, however. Each of the rules of his simple illustrative grammar (shown previously) is of the form

$$A \rightarrow \alpha$$

where *A* is a single symbol denoting a syntactic category ("sentence," "NP," and so forth) also called a *nonterminal symbol* (because such symbols can never appear in sentences of the language) and α is a string that can contain nonterminal symbols, connectives (+), and the symbols of the language's alphabet ("man," "hit," and so on), which are called *terminal symbols*. A language with sentences that are generated by grammars having rules of just this type came to be called *context-free languages* and the corresponding grammars, *context-free grammars*. This was one of several language classes that Chomsky studied; he called it a "Type 2" language.[113]

The rules (productions) for Algol 60, as given in the *Revised Report* were all of this form. The left-hand side of each production is a meta-linguistic variable (in other words, a single nonterminal symbol); the right-hand side is a string of nonterminal and terminal symbols. To take an example, here are a few the rules for arithmetic expressions in Algol 60[114]:

<adding operator> ::= +|-
<multiplying operator> ::= x|/|...
<primary> ::= <unsigned number>|<variable>|<function designator> |(<arithmetic expression>)
...
<if clause> ::= **if** <Boolean expression>**then**
...

The irony was that Chomsky's Type 2 grammars were utterly inadequate for the description of *natural* languages; but, under the name of context-free grammars, they were preeminently suitable to describing *programming* languages. Context-free grammars and languages became extremely consequential in computer science, although of only passing interest in linguistics.

A theory of context free-languages and the automatic recognition of sentences in such languages would emerge during the 1960s.[115] One of the most fascinating topics in this realm was the problem of determining what kind of computational *power* was necessary for automata (including Turing machines) to recognize different classes of languages, including context-free languages. However, the interest in context-free languages was not just theoretical. There were enormous practical consequences. The "front end" of a compiler first had to ascertain the syntactic correctness (the "grammaticalness") of the program it was compiling—a technique called *syntactic analysis* or *parsing*—and a spate of parsing algorithms for context-free programming languages were invented during the 1960s.[116] Writing compliers became "scientific!"

xx

But what of *semantics*? What of the meaning of such things as identifiers, expressions, statements, and procedures? In the case of FORTRAN, the *Programmer's Guide* used ordinary English to present the semantics of the language. So, too, with the Algol 60 *Revised Report*. Semantics was not amenable (yet) to the kind of precise, formal descriptions that could be used for syntax. The meta-language of semantics remained English or other natural languages. Thus, although the syntax of arithmetic expressions was written in BNF, its semantics was in English:

> An arithmetic expression is a rule for computing a numerical value. In case of simple arithmetic expressions this value is obtained by executing the indicated arithmetic operations on the actual numerical values of the primaries of the expression....[117]

There will come a time (as this story will tell) when the "problem of meaning" becomes a serious subject for investigation among language designers, programmers, and computing theorists. But not yet.

XXI

One of the ironies of this story of the birth of programming languages is that although, like the crocodiles and tortoises of old, FORTRAN and COBOL would survive the vicissitudes of computing technology as the *lingua franca* of their respective target problem environments—science/engineering in the former case, business/commerce in the latter—Algol 60 as a universal language for actually *programming computers* would be virtually extinct by the 1980s. The Esperanto of the computing world it was not to be (but, then, Esperanto itself did not catch on as the universal natural language).

Algol 60, as it turned out, was the first species of the genus Algol. The language gave rise to some subspecies in the 1960s—"dialects" of Algol 60 such as Algol W, EULER, and PL/360. It also spawned other distinct species within the genus, including the influential simulation language SIMULA[118] and Algol 68, the official IFIP-sponsored "successor" to Algol 60 that, like its parent, went through first a *Report* (1969)[119] and then a *Revised Report* (1975).[120]

Algol 68 was an entirely non-American affair, its designers and implementers drawn from Europe, Britain, and Canada,[121] and it had no influence in the United States. The sheer complexity of the language—the *Revised Report* was all of 230 pages—drew sharp reactions.

In the biological world, it is widely believed, evolution generally tends toward greater complexity of organisms.[122] So also, historically, is the general trend in the made world. Cultural evolution, especially in the realm of practical artifacts, tends toward greater complexity.[123] This was evident in the evolution from Algol 60 to Algol 68, and in the development of PL/I, a programming language developed by IBM in 1964 as a language that could be used for both scientific and business computing, and as a putative successor to FORTRAN; it was to be IBM's own universal language. Like Algol 68, PL/I was a massive, complex language; unlike Algol 68, however, it has had a long life, although it could never usurp either FORTRAN's or COBOL's respective reigns.

Yet there have been exceptions to this evolutionary trend to increased complexity, even in the frantic, rambunctious world of computing. In response to what was perceived by some as the unmanageable complexity of Algol 68, Swiss computer scientist Nicklaus Wirth (1934–) created the "Algol-like" language Pascal in 1971,[124] perhaps the most influential programming language, at least in the academic computing world during the 1970s.

Algol 60 may have become extinct as a practical language for programming computers, but it had massive consequences for the development of (appropriating the great Galileo's terms) "two new sciences"—the science of programming language design and (as we will see) the science of programming. It brought to the forefront of people's consciousness the very idea of designing languages that were genuinely machine independent, genuinely abstract. It demonstrated the efficacy of a precise language for describing, communicating, publishing, and, indeed, *thinking about* computer algorithms. It heralded a concern for meta-languages for describing the syntax of programming languages. It introduced entirely new concepts in language design as well as programming style that, much as Greek culture permeated the minds and consciousness of Roman and other cultures that came after them, found their ways into the languages that came after. It demonstrated the importance of the Popperian schema of proposing a design (TT) in response to a set of goals or requirement (P1), examining the design critically, identifying and eliminating flaws or errors in the design (EE), and reformulating the goals (P2). Last (although this is not a topic we will pursue further in this story), implementation of Algol 60 compilers brought into existence an entirely new class of computer architectures that came to be called *stack machines*.[125]

The legacy of Algol 60 is far-flung.

XXII

As we have noted, the creators of the first programming languages were, almost without exception, trained formally in mathematics. Mathematical notation served as a source of inspiration and ideas for them, especially to those who aspired to create a "universal" language of computation (see Section XIV, this chapter). But, the designers of such languages such as Algol 60 were also mindful that their artifacts were not so much ends in themselves as means to other ends: the description, expression, and communication of computations between humans and from humans to machines. Toward this end, the austerity of strictly mathematical notation had to be tempered, and programming languages had to be given, on the one hand, a more "human face" and on the other, endowed with a sense of "implementability."

But there were some to whom the very austerity, economy, aesthetics of mathematical notation beckoned, and to none more so than Canadian Kenneth Iverson (1920–2004).

A graduate in mathematics and physics from Queen's University, Kingston, Ontario, Iverson did his graduate work in applied mathematics at Harvard, obtaining his PhD in 1954 with a dissertation on the automatic solutions of linear differential equations. He was a student of Howard Aiken, and years later he would acknowledge Aiken's influence on his thinking. One of the precepts he learned from Aiken was the desire for simplicity in scientific thinking.[126]

After achieving his doctorate, and as a freshly appointed assistant professor in mathematics at Harvard, Iverson was inducted into a new graduate program on "automatic data processing" initiated by Aiken.[127] As part of his new teaching duties, he embarked on the invention of a new notation for teaching and writing about computation—a notation, in other words, for strictly human consumption; a notation for pedagogic use,[128] but as much a notation as a tool of thought.[129]

We revert to the question: When does notation become a language? The dividing line is fuzzy. Swiss-American mathematician and mathematical historian Florian Cajori (1859–1930) titled his most famous book *A History of Mathematical Notation* (1928), not *A History of Mathematical Language*. On the other hand, we commonly speak of mathematics as "the language of science"—meaning, not just notation, but that the calculus of mathematics serves as a means of scientific discourse.

At any rate, in 1962, Iverson published his first book, devoted to the notation he had invented and, with breathtaking aplomb, titled his book *A Programming Language*.[130] Although the language had yet no name, this very title would, in a few years, inspire the acronym APL. Rather as John Backus's name is inextricably entwined with FORTRAN, so also Iverson's with APL.

XXIII

If brevity is the soul of wit, as Polonius claimed in *Hamlet*, then both writer and reader of APL programs must be enormously quick-witted for, in designing APL, Iverson took his mentor Aiken's ideal of simplicity to heart to mean an extreme brevity. His goal seemed to be: How little do I need to write to say something meaningful. The outcome was a notation that was uncompromisingly terse—hence the cult of the "one-liners" to express meaningful computational actions much beloved of APL devotees in later years.[131]

This brevity of expressiveness was a result of a number of factors, the most noticeable being the presence of an implicit *parallelism* in the meanings (semantics) of APL statements. We illustrate this with two small examples.

First, suppose there are two programs (or routines) named **A** and **B**. And suppose that inside **B** there is an APL statement

$\rightarrow$ **A**, n

Then, the execution of this statement results in the immediate execution of the statement numbered n in **A** and the continuation of the execution of statements in **A** following n, whereas **B** also continues on to its next statement. In other words, this statement effects both a branch to another program that is then executed *concurrently* with the continuing execution of the originating program.

A second source of implicit parallelism in APL statements lay in the fact that APL is an *array-based* language. In addition to ordinary numbers (scalars), its fundamental data *types* are vectors and matrices—two standard mathematical entities. APL's brevity of expression is exemplified by notations that express operations on entire vectors or matrices. To take an example, suppose the elements of a vector $\mathbf{x} = [\mathbf{x_1, x_2, \ldots, x_n}]$ are to be added to form a single scalar $z = \mathbf{x_1} + \mathbf{x_2} + \cdots + \mathbf{x_n}$. In an Algol-like language, this would be expressed as something like

$z := 0;$
$i := 1;$
while $i \leq n$ **do**
$z := z + x\,[i];$
$i := i + 1$

That is, after "initializing" the variables z and i, the contents of $x[i]$ is added to z iteratively with i incremented by one each time. The iteration (**while** loop) ends when the value of i exceeds n.

In APL, this task would be expressed by the statement

$z \leftarrow +/\mathbf{x}$

XXIV

As we have noted, Iverson's original intention in inventing APL (even before it came to be known by this acronym) was a notation for teaching computing. It was meant to be a pedagogic tool.[132] Indeed, when he and Frederick P. Brooks (1931–) wrote their textbook *Automatic Data Processing* (1965),[133] some of the algorithms presented therein were in APL. But well before then, in 1960, Iverson left Harvard for IBM's Thomas J. Watson Research Center, the company's headquarters for fundamental research. And much more interestingly and creatively, in 1964, Iverson's colleague and (as it turned out) long-time collaborator, Adin Falkoff (1921–2010), set out to use APL as a *machine description language*. One of IBM's major computer systems of the mid 1960s, the System/360, was described formally and precisely in APL (although the language in this exposition was still presented as a notation without a name).[134]

This work was especially seminal for it was undoubtedly the first formal description of a physical computer (more precisely, its architecture, a liminal artifact) in a quasiprogramming notation. When coupled with the description of algorithms in *Automatic Data Processing,* we find a blurring of the distinction between the computer as a material artifact, algorithms as abstract artifacts, and computer architectures as liminal artifacts. They can all be spoken about using a common language.

The description of the System/360 in APL also marks the emergence of a new language genus that came to be called *computer hardware description language* (or computer design language).[135]

By the time the description of the System/360 was published, the notation was sufficiently matured that thoughts turned to its *implementation*—the transformation of a mathematical notation for thinking about computation to a programming language.[136] In two fundamental ways, however, the language's implementation deviated markedly from the implementation of such languages as FORTRAN and Algol 60. First, the *symbols* constituting the APL notation demanded the development of a distinct character set for printers to print APL programs. Indeed, specialized APL input/output devices (called *APL terminals*) were developed.[137] Second, the execution strategy for APL programs eschewed the compile-and-execute strategy developed for FORTRAN and other contemporary programming languages (that is, first translate the whole program into a "native" machine code and *then* execute the translated program). Instead, APL statements were interpreted (by another program, the "interpreter") and executed one statement at a time. APL was implemented as an *interpretive* language.[138] A new language, implemented for the IBM System/360 and named APL\360 was thus born.[139]

NOTES

1. D. E. Knuth & L. T. Pardo. (1980). The early development of programming languages (original work published 1977). In N. Metropolis, J. S. Howlett, & G.- C. Rota (Eds.), *A history of computing in the twentieth century* (pp. 197–273). New York: Academic Press (see especially, p. 202).

2. K. Zuse. (1975). The outline of a computer development from mechanics to electronics (original work published 1962). In B. Randell (Ed.), *The origins of digital computers* (2nd ed., pp. 171–186). New York: Springer-Verlag (see especially p. 181).

3. F. L. Bauer & H. Wössner. (1972). The "Plankalkül" of Konrad Zuse: A forerunner of today's programming languages. *Communication of the ACM, 15,* 678–685.

4. Zuse, op cit., p. 101.

5. Quoted by Knuth and Pardo, op cit., p. 203.

6. Baurer and Wössner, op cit., p. 679.

7. Ibid., p. 681.

8. Knuth and Pardo, op cit., p. 206.

9. Zuse, op cit., p. 181.

10. Bauer and Wössner, op cit., p. 682.

11. Ibid., p. 683.

12. Knuth and Pardo, op cit., p. 203.

13. Ibid.

14. A. W. Burks. (1951). *An intermediate program language as an aid in program synthesis.* Report for Burroughs Adding Machine Company. Ann Arbor, MI: University of Michigan.

15. Knuth and Pardo, op cit., p. 216.

16. Zuse, op cit., p. 180.

17. J. W. Backus. (1981). The history of Fortran I, II and III. In R. L. Wexelblat (Ed.), *History of programming languages* (pp. 25–74). New York: Academic Press (see especially p. 25).

18. Ibid., p. 28.

19. J. Backus & H. Herrick. (1954). IBM 701 speedcoding and other automatic programming systems. In *Proceedings of the ONR Symposium on Automatic Programming for Digital Computers.* Washington, DC: Office of Naval Research, Department of the Navy. Cited by Backus, op cit., p. 28.

20. Knuth and Pardo, op cit., p. 222.

21. J. H. Laning, Jr. & N. Zierler. (1952). *A program for translation of mathematical equations for Whirlwind I.* Engineering memorandum E-364. Cambridge, MA: MIT Instrumentation Laboratory.

22. Knuth and Pardo, op cit., p. 227.

23. Ibid.

24. Quoted by Knuth and Pardo, op cit., p. 228.

25. See, for example, Remington-Rand, Inc. (1953). *The A-2 compiler system operations manual.* Norwalk, CT: Remington-Rand (prepared by R. K. Ridgeway and M. H. Harper).; N. B. Moser. (1954). Compiler method of automatic programming. In *Proceedings of the ONR Symposium on Automatic Programming for Digital Computers* (pp. 15–21). Washington, DC: Office of Naval Research, Department of the Navy.

26. Knuth and Pardo, op cit., p. 227.

27. Backus and Herrick, op cit.

28. S. Rosen. (1969). Electronic computers: A historical survey. *Computing Surveys, 1,* 7–36 (see especially p. 14).

29. Backus, op cit., p. 27.

30. Ibid., p. 28.

31. Ibid.

32. Ibid., p. 30.

33. Ibid., p. 28.

34. Ibid.

35. S. H. Lavington. (1998). *A history of Manchester computers* (p. 20). London: The British Computer Society (original work published 1975).

36. The terms *Big Science* and *Little Science* are due to the historian of science Derek de Solla Price. See D. K. de Solla Price. (1986). *Little science, big science—and beyond* (Exp. ed.). New York: Columbia University Press (original work published 1963). See also A. Weinberg. (1967). *Reflections on big science.* Oxford: Pergamon.

37. J. W. Backus, R. W. Beeber, S. Best, R. Goldberg, L. M. Haibit, H. C. Herrick, R. A. Nelson, D. Sayre, P. B. Sheridan, H. Stern, I. Ziller, R. A. Hughes, & R. Nutt. (1957). *The FORTRAN automatic coding system.* Proceedings of the Western Joint Computer Conference (pp. 188–197). Los Angeles, CA.

38. Backus, op cit., p. 30.

39. Ibid., p. 45.

40. Ibid., p. 30.

41. Ibid., p. 32.

42. Ibid., p. 33.

43. Ibid., p. 36.

44. Ibid.

45. IBM. (1956). *Programmer's reference manual: The FORTRAN automatic coding system for the IBM 704 EDPM.* New York: IBM Corporation.

46. Backus et al., op cit.

47. IBM. (1957). *Programmer's primer for FORTRAN automatic coding system for the IBM 704.* New York: IBM Corporation.

48. Backus, op cit.

49. Knuth and Pardo, op cit., p. 243.

50. Quoted in Backus, op cit., p. 39.

51. Ibid.

52. Ibid., p. 37.

53. Ibid., p. 30.

54. Ibid., p. 29.

55. See, for example, B. Randell & L. J. Russell. (1964). *Algol 60 implementation.* New York: Academic Press; J. A. N. Lee. (1967). *Anatomy of a compiler.* New York: Rheinhold; F. R. A. Hopgood. (1969). *Compiling techniques.* London: Macdonald.

56. S. Rosen. (Ed.). (1967). *Programming systems and languages.* New York: McGraw-Hill.

57. The source and object codes are functionally equivalent in the sense that if the source program is designed to compute a function $F(I)$ for some input data I, then if the same input is fed to the object code it will execute on its target computer and compute the same function $F(I)$.

58. For example, as illustrated by the title of the article of R. L. Glass. (1969). An elementary discussion of compiler/interpreter writing. *Computing Surveys, 1,* 55–77; and by the title of the book by J. S. Rohl. (1975). *An introduction to compiler writing.* London: Macdonald and Jane's.

59. Backus, op cit., p. 34.

60. *Optimization* was, of course, an optimistic term because *optimal*—meaning, the very *best*—is usually an unattainable, if laudable, goal. In the language of compilers, *optimization* really meant a systematic process of *improving* the object program within the practical limits of time for compilation and the cognitive limits of the compiler writer.

61. Backus, op cit., pp. 34–36.

62. P. B. Sheridan. (1959). The arithmetic translator-compiler of the IBM FORTRAN automatic coding system. *Communication of the ACM, 2,* 9–21.

63. J. Cocke & J. T. Schwartz. (1970). *Programming languages and their compilers* (pp. 510–515). New York: Courant Institute of Mathematical Sciences.

64. Hopgood, op cit., pp. 2–3.

65. G.. M. Hopper. (1981). Keynote address. In Wexelblat (pp. 7–24), op cit., p. 16.

66. S. Rosen. (1969). Electronic computers: A historical survey. *Computing Surveys 1*, 7–36 (see especially pp. 10–11).

67. Hopper, op cit., p. 15.

68. Ibid.

69. Ibid., p. 16.

70. Ibid.

71. Ibid., p. 17.

72. J.. E. Sammet. (1981a). The early history of COBOL. In Wexelblat (pp. 199–276), op cit., p. 202.

73. Ibid., pp. 200–201.

74. Ibid., p. 203.

75. Ibid., pp. 208–211.

76. J. E. Sammet. (1981b). An overview of high level languages. In M. C. Yovits (Ed.), *Advances in computers* (Vol. 20, pp. 200–260). New York: Academic Press (see especially pp. 214–215).

77. Ibid., p. 239.

78. H.. Rutihauser. (1967). *Description of Algol 60* (pp. 4–6). Berlin: Springer-Verlag; A. J. Perlis. (1981). The American side of the development of Algol. In Wexelblat (pp. 75–91), op cit., p. 78; P. Naur. (1981). The European side of the last phase of the development of Algol 60. In Wexelblat (pp. 92–139), op cit., p. 94.

79. Perlis, op cit., p. 76.

80. Ibid., p. 77.

81. Ibid.

82. Rutihauser, op cit., pp. 4–5.

83. Perlis, op cit., p. 77; Rutihauser, op cit., p. 5.

84. The full group was, from ACM, John Backus, C. Katz, Alan J. Perlis, and Joseph H. Wegstein; and from GAMM, Friedrich L. Bauer, H. Bottenbruch, Heinz Rutihauser, and Klaus Samelson.

85. Rutihauser, op cit., p. 6.

86. Ibid.

87. Ibid.

88. Perlis, op cit., p. 79.

89. Originally, in the manner of the naming of other prior languages, the name was written in upper case, ALGOL. Eventually, it became simply Algol.

90. J. W. Backus, F. L. Bauer, H. Bottenbruch, C. Katz, and A. J. Perlis (Eds.), H. Rutihauser and K. Samelson (Ed.), J. H. Wegstein (1959). Report on the algorithmic language ALGOL. *Numerische Mathematik, 1*, 41–60.

91. Perlis, op cit., p. 83.

92. Rutihauser, op cit., p. 7.

93. Perlis, op cit., p. 84.

94. Later, the IFIP Congress was renamed the IFIP World Computer Congress.

95. John W. Backus (USA), Friedrich L. Bauer (West Germany), J. Green (USA), C. Katz (USA), John McCarthy (USA), Peter Naur (Denmark), Alan J. Perlis (USA), Heinz Rutihauser

(Switzerland), Klaus Samelson (West Germany), Bernard Vauquois (France), Joseph.H. Wegstein (USA), Adriaan van Wijngaarden (Holland), and Michael Woodger (Britain).

96. P. Naur. (Ed.). (1960). Report on the algorithmic language ALGOL 60. *Communications of the ACM, 3*, 299–314.

97. P. Naur (Ed.) et al. (1962–1963). Revised report on the algorithmic language ALGOL 60. *Numerische Mathematik, 4*, 420–453; see also (1963). *Communications of the ACM, 6*, 1–17; (1962/63). *Computer Journal, 5*, 349–367. This report would be republished in many other places, including as a stand-alone publication. References to the report in our story cites, as source, its appearance as an appendix in Rutihauser, op cit.

98. K. R. Popper. (1972). *Objective knowledge*. Oxford: Clarendon Press.

99. J. W. Backus. (1959). The syntax and semantics of the proposed international algebraic language of the Zurich ACM-GAMM Conference. In *Proceedings of the 1st International Conference on Information Processing* (pp. 125–132). London: Butterworth.

100. Another expansion of BNF is *Backus Naur Form* because Naur, editor of the Algol 60 reports, made slight changes to the original notation, but, more important, made the meta-language widely known by way of the two reports.

101. Rutihauser, op cit., p. 268.

102. J. W. Backus, responding to a question about the origins of BNF, Wexelblat, op cit., p. 162.

103. E. Post. (1943). Formal reductions of the general combinatorial decision problem. *American Journal of Mathematics, 65*, 197–268.

104. N. Chomsky. (1956). Three models for the description of language. In *Proceedings of the Symposium on Information Theory* (pp. 113–124). Cambridge, MA: MIT.

105. N. Chomsky. (1957). *Syntactic structures*. The Hague: Mouton.

106. J. Lyons. (1970). *Chomsky* (p. 9). London: Fontana/Collins.

107. Chomsky, 1957, op cit., p. 13.

108. Chomsky, 1956, op cit., p. 114.

109. Ibid.

110. Ibid.

111. Chomsky, 1956, op cit., pp. 116–118; Chomsky, 1957, op cit., pp. 26–33.

112. Chomsky, 1957, op cit., p. 29.

113. N. Chomsky. (1959). On certain formal properties of grammar. *Information & Control, 2*, 136–167.

114. Rutihauser, op cit., p. 274.

115. See, for example, S. A. Greibach. (1966). The unsolvability of the recognition of linear context free languages. *Journal of the Association for Computing Machinery, 13*, 582–587; S. Ginsburgh. (1966). *The mathematical theory of context free languages*. New York: McGraw-Hill.

116. R. W. Floyd. (1963). Syntax analysis and operator precedence. *Journal of the Association for Computing Machinery, 10*; T. Kasami. (1965). *An efficient recognition and syntax analysis algorithm for context free languages*. Scientific report no. AFCRL-65–758. Bedford, MA: Air Force Cambridge Research Laboratory; P. Z. Ingermann. (1966). *A syntax-oriented translator*. New York: Academic Press; D. H. Younger. (1967). Recognition and parsing of context-free languages in time n^2. *Information & Control, 10*, 181–208; J. Earley. (1968). *An efficient context-free parsing algorithm*. PhD dissertation, Carnegie-Mellon University.

117. Rutihauser, op cit., p. 275.

118. O.- J. Dahl & K. Nygaard. (1966). SIMULA: An Algol-based simulation language. *Communications of the ACM, 9,* 671–682.

119. A. van Wijngaarden (ed.), B. J. Mailloux, J. E. L. Peck, C. H. A. Koster. (1969). Report on the algorithmic language ALGOL 68. *Numerische Mathematik, 14,* 79–218.

120. A. van Wijngaarden, B. J. Mailloux, J. E. L. Peck, C. H. A. Koster, M. Sintsoff, C. H. Lindsay, L. G. L. T. Meerttens, & R. G. Fisker. (1975). Revised report on the algorithmic language ALGOL 68. *Acta Informatica, 5,* 1–234.

121. J. E. L. Peck. (Ed.). (1971). *ALGOL 68 implementation.* Amsterdam: North-Holland.

122. J. T. Bonner. (1988). *The evolution of complexity by means of natural selection.* Princeton, NJ: Princeton University Press. See, however, D. W. McShea. (1997). Complexity in evolution: A skeptical assessment. *Philosophica, 59,* 79–112, for an alternative view of the relationship between biological evolution and the evolution of complexity.

123. S. Dasgupta. (1997). Technology and complexity. *Philosophica, 59,* 113–140.

124. N. Wirth. (1971). The programming language PASCAL. *Acta Informatica, 1,* 35–63.

125. B. Randell & L. J. Russell. (1964). *Algol 60 implementation.*New York: Academic Press; E. I. Organick. (1973). *Computer systems organization: The B5700/6700 series.* New York: Academic Press; R. W. Doran. (1979). *Computer architecture: A structured approach.* New York: Academic Press.

126. K.. E. Iverson. (1981). Transcript of presentation. In Wexelblat (pp. 674–682), op cit., p. 682.

127. A.. D. Falkoff & K. E. Iverson. (1981). The evolution of APL. In Wexelblat (pp. 661–674), op cit., p. 663.

128. In January 1972, freshly arrived as a graduate student in computer science at the University of Alberta, Edmonton, Canada, I recall attending a talk by Iverson delivered at the College of Education.

129. K. E. Iverson. (1980). Notation as a tool of thought (Turing Award lecture). *Communications of the ACM, 23,* 444–465.

130. K. E. Iverson. (1962). *A programming language.* New York: Wiley.

131. "Devotees" is the right word. APL commanded a fierce and loyal following the likes of which was rare during the first decade of programming languages.

132. Iverson, 1981, op cit., p. 675.

133. F. P. Brooks, Jr. & K. E. Iverson. (1969). *Automatic data processing: System/360 edition.* New York: Wiley.

134. A. D. Falkoff, K. E. Iverson, & E. H. Sussenguth. (1964). A formal description of System/360. *IBM Systems Journal, 3,* 191–262.

135. For a survey of this genus as it had developed from the mid 1960s through its first two decades, see S. Dasgupta. (1982). Computer design and description languages. In M. C. Yovits (Ed.), *Advances in computers* (Vol. 21, pp. 91–155). New York: Academic Press.

136. Falkoff & Iverson, op cit., p. 664.

137. Ibid., p. 665.

138. Ibid., p. 666.

139. A. D. Falkoff & K. E. Iverson. (1966). *APL\360.* White Plains, NY: IBM Corporation; A. D. Falkoff & K. E. Iverson. (1968). *APL\360 user's manual.* White Plains, NY: IBM Corporation.

14

Going Heuristic

I

LET US REWIND the historical tape to 1945, the year in which John von Neumann wrote his celebrated report on the EDVAC (see Chapter 9). That same year, George Polya (1887–1985), a professor of mathematics at Stanford University and, like von Neumann, a Hungarian-American, published a slender book bearing the title *How to Solve It*.[1]

Polya's aim in writing this book was to demonstrate how mathematical problems are *really* solved. The book focused on the kinds of reasoning that go into making discoveries in mathematics—not just "great" discoveries by "great" mathematicians, but the kind a high school mathematics student might make in solving back-of-the-chapter problems.

Polya pointed out that, although a mathematical subject such as Euclidean geometry might seem a rigorous, systematic, deductive science, it is also experimental or inductive.[2] By this he meant that solving mathematical problems involves the same kinds of mental strategies—trial and error, informed guesswork, analogizing, divide and conquer—that attend the empirical or "inductive" sciences. Mathematical problem solving, Polya insisted, involves the use of *heuristics*—an Anglicization of the Greek *heurisko*—meaning, to find. Heuristics, as an adjective, means "serving to discover."[3]

We are often forced to deploy heuristic reasoning when we have no other options. Heuristic reasoning would not be necessary if we have algorithms to solve our problems; heuristics are summoned in the absence of algorithms. And so we seek analogies between the problem at hand and other, more familiar, situations and use the analogy as a guide to solve our problem, or we split a problem into simpler subproblems in the hope this makes the overall task easier, or we summon experience to bear on the problem and apply actions we had taken before with the reasonable expectation that it may help solve the problem, or we apply rules of thumb that have worked before.

The point of heuristics, however, is that they offer promises of solution to certain kinds of problems but *there are no guarantees of success*. As Polya said, heuristic thinking is never considered as final, but rather is provisional or plausible.[4]

Problem solving, discovering, inventing—great and small, by scientists, inventors, artists, professional practitioners (such as doctors, engineers, designers, architects) or by students or, indeed, by people in the course of their everyday life—have always involved the use of heuristics, although perhaps most people are never conscious of it as a particular method of reasoning, or that it has a name. Like Monsieur Jourdain in the play *Le Bourgeois Gentilhomme* (1670) by the French playwright Molière (1622–1673) who suddenly learned that he had been speaking prose all his life without knowing it, Polya brought to the mathematical reader's attention that he had been using heuristic reasoning all his mathematical life without knowing it.

II

An undergraduate physics major at Stanford University, where Polya taught, took some of his courses. Through them he came to know the ideas in *How to Solve It*. The undergraduate's name was Allen Newell (1927–1992). By way of Polya, he was introduced to the concept of heuristics.[5]

In 1952, while working as an applied mathematician at the RAND Corporation, the California-based think tank, Newell met a social scientist by the name of Herbert Simon (1916–2001).[6] Simon was 36 at the time. By then, he had already established a formidable reputation not only as a social scientist, but also as a polymath: later, the term "Renaissance man" would be applied to him.[7]

Simon's dissertation, for which the University of Chicago awarded him a PhD in political science in 1942, became, appropriately revised, a book titled *Administrative Behavior* (1947).[8] That same year, he published his first article on the foundations of Newtonian mechanics in the august *Philosophical Magazine*.[9] He coauthored another book on *Public Administration* (1950).[10] During the 1940s, while an assistant professor of political science at the Illinois Institute of Technology in Chicago, he began publishing papers in leading economics journals such as the *Quarterly Journal of Economics* and *Econometrica*, and established a close association with the Cowles Commission for Research in Economics, a collection of some of the most eminent economists of the post-World War II era, several of whom were future Nobel laureates as, indeed, Simon himself was.[11] He published an article in 1952 on causality in the *Journal of Philosophy*.[12] By 1950—he was then a full professor in the Graduate School of Industrial Administration at the Carnegie Institute of Technology (later, Carnegie- Mellon University) in Pittsburgh—Simon was seriously contemplating using principles of servomechanisms (from cybernetics, created by Norbert Wiener and others, circa 1948 [see Chapter 12, Section I]) in organization theory, and, in 1952, he published a very formal article in *Econometrica* on servomechanism theory applied to production control.[13] That same year, he wrote an article on the interaction of social groups in the *American Sociological Review*.[14] Perhaps most relevant to our story, by the mid 1950s, he had read Edmund Berkeley's *Giant Brains* (1950) and *Faster Than Thought* (1953), edited by Vivian Bowden.[15]

The meeting of Simon and Newell heralded the beginning of an extraordinary scientific partnership that would span some 20 years (and a friendship that ended only with Newell's death in 1992). Newell became Simon's doctoral student, but theirs was never a teacher/guru–student/disciple relationship. It was always that of collaborators–colleagues. What interests us in this story is how they transformed the idea of heuristic reasoning and problem solving as done by human beings into a research tradition or a subparadigm within the computer science paradigm itself.

III

We cannot really understand how Newell and Simon embarked on their particular intellectual enterprise without knowing something of its prehistory. It began in a discipline as far removed from computer science as one can imagine. In 1947, Simon published *Administrative Behavior* (1947), wherein he presented a fundamental insight for which he would receive the Nobel Prize in economics 31 years later. The Nobel Foundation citation for 1978 tells us that the prize was awarded for Simon's "pioneering research into the decision-making process in economic organizations."[16] This "pioneering research" was first embedded in *Administrative Behavior*, which dealt not with the economic milieu at all, but with decision making in administrative organizations. The administrative "actor," Simon pointed out (drawing on the ideas of administrative theorist Chester Barnard[17]) is a purposive (or goal-oriented) being. He desires to take action, make decisions, that lead to the attainment of goals. For Simon, purposive behavior is *rational* if the choice of means leads to the attainment of goals.

However, such purposive behavior faces several oppositions. There are limits to the decision maker's innate cognitive capabilities. There are limits to one's knowledge about all the factors that must be taken into consideration to make a fully rational decision. There are limits to the decision maker's ability to cope with the complexity of the environment in which decisions have to be made, and with the rich profusion of alternative actions (choices, decisions) and their consequences.

All these constraints suggest that, except in the simplest situations, it is virtually impossible for an individual to achieve *fully* rational behavior. There are limits to his or her rationality. The decision maker's behavior is governed by what Simon first called subjective rationality.[18] A decade later, he renamed this notion *bounded rationality*, and this is the term by which this phenomenon has come to be known.[19]

By 1950, Simon had begun to apply his theory of bounded rationality to the realm of economic decision making[20]—to build a bridge between administrative theory and economic theory. And this bridge was to be paved with the stuff of *psychology*.[21] In fact, Simon was tending toward a psychological (or behavioral) theory of what might be called a "universal decision maker," regardless of the domain in which decisions are to be made—including chess. Bounded rationality lay at the core of this theory.

His interest in chess reached back to boyhood. In high school he had studied the game seriously, to the extent that he had mastered the basic decision-making issues in chess and tic-tac-toe (H. A. Simon, personal communication, November 4, 2000). This interest intensified years later when he attended a lecture by the ubiquitous John von Neumann in 1952 on computer chess, which, as we have seen, was studied by Claude Shannon circa 1949 to 1950 (see Chapter 11, Section VII). He was sufficiently stimulated by the lecture actually to engage, by mid 1953, with the design of chess-playing programs.[22] The chess player—human or automaton—is as much constrained by bounded rationality in making decisions of which moves to make as are administrative or economic decision makers.

The operative word here is *computer* chess. In summer 1954, Simon taught himself to program the IBM 701. By then, computers were much on his mind[23]—and not just in the realm of chess. As a visiting scientist at the RAND Corporation's Systems Research Laboratory, his interest in computers had been stimulated after meeting Allen Newell, and another person, Cliff Shaw (1922–1991), "an outstandingly talented and sophisticated systems programmer."[24] Their work made Simon realize that the computer was much more than a number processor—that it was, in fact, a *general symbol processor*.[25]

Newell was also much interested in computer chess. In 1955, he presented a paper on a "chess machine" at the Western Joint Computer Conference.[26] That same year, Simon published what was perhaps his first definitive article on bounded rationality, titled "A Behavioral Model of Rational Choice" in the *Quarterly Journal of Economics*.[27]

The question was, Simon wrote, how to cope with bounded rationality. "Classic" concepts of rationality assumed complete information available to the decision maker, and that she computes all possible outcomes of choices and then selects the "best" (optimal) decision from all the possibilities. In fact, there was no empirical evidence, Simon pointed out, that people actually went about the matter in this way. His task in the article, Simon wrote, was to propose a model that would endow the decision maker with a form of rationality that was consistent with the cognitive limits possessed by organisms—including, especially, humans—in the actual kinds of environments—social as well as physical—organisms occupy.[28]

So what does a decision maker *really* do? Instead of seeking an optimal outcome he will establish an "acceptable" or "satisfactory" goal, an aspiration level[29] that will be less ambitious than the optimal. This will reduce the amount of information the individual needs to make a decision. The decision maker then *searches* the reduced "space" of possibilities for a choice that meets the aspired goal. So the decision will not be optimal. Rather, in resigned recognition of the reality of bounded rationality, the decision will be "satisfactory." Or, as Simon will coin the term in 1956, it will be *satisficing*.[30] To satisfice is to choose what is "good" rather than what is "best." The bounded rational decision maker is a satisficing, rather than an optimizing, being.

However, even satisficing leaves a formidable problem for the decision maker. How does one search the "space" of possibilities? This is where *heuristics* enters the discourse. In his design of a chess machine, Newell incorporated a variety of heuristics that the computer could deploy to select its moves. He was, of course, not the first to have done so; recall Claude Shannon's minmax strategy—a heuristic—of 1950 (see Chapter 11, Section VII). However, although Newell's immediate intent was to design a program to play chess, like Simon he had larger ambitions. Chess was a means to understand how the *mind* deals with the complexities of the real-world environment, and how computers could simulate such mindlike behavior. Newell and Simon pondered at great length the possibility of modeling human thinking by computers.[31] Here was a meeting of profoundly like minds.

IV

In September 1956, at the same symposium at MIT where Noam Chomsky presented his seminal paper in linguistics (see Chapter 13, Section XVIII), Newell and Simon announced the first fruits of their joint ruminations. They described a computer program called *Logic Theorist* (LT), which was capable of discovering proofs for theorems in symbolic logic.[32]

A computer *program* had been given a name, exactly as individual computers were given such names as the ENIAC and the EDSAC in the 1940s. This, itself, gives cause for momentary pause. It suggests that a very special artifact had been created, for here was a program that exhibited behavior akin to the highest form of human intelligence. A reader of their 1956 work would have irresistibly harked back to Alan Turing's 1950 essay "Computing Machinery and Intelligence" (see Chapter 11, Section XI).

LT was able to prove several theorems stated (and proved) in one of the chapters of *Principia Mathematica* (1910–1913), the massive treatise on the logical foundations of mathematics, authored by A. N. Whitehead and Bertrand Russell. Symbolic logic was the meta-language (see Chapter 13, Section XVI) for describing mathematics in the *Principia*, and the entities in this work were expressions (axioms and theorems) in symbolic logic and the proofs of the theorems.

By the mid 1950s, computers were being used routinely to solve complex mathematical problems such as finding roots of polynomials, evaluating matrices, and solving differential equations. What was it about LT that merited it a name of its own, an individuality, special attention?

The answer lay in the nature of proofs in axiomatic (formal) systems of the kind mathematics and symbolic logic were concerned with (see Chapter 4, Section I, for more on axiomatic systems). One begins with a set of axioms—expressions that are assumed to be true—and definitions. There will also be a small number of "rules of inference," by means of which new true expressions (theorems) can be inferred (or deduced) beginning with axioms, definitions, and other previously proved theorems. A proof of a theorem is a sequence of expressions $e_1, e_2, \ldots e_N$, where e_1 is either an axiom or a previously proved theorem, each *ei* is derived from its predecessor by applying the rules of inference and using the axioms and definitions, and *eN* is the theorem to be proved.

What makes this situation different from solving numeric problems such as differential equations is that *algorithms* exist for the solution of the numeric problems. In the case of proofs of theorems and the like, a "systematic algorithm" can be developed, but this would involve a potentially exhaustive search of all chain of inferences until one leads to an expression corresponding to the theorem of interest.[33] The situation is exactly the same as the human decision maker's problem in arriving at a "fully rational" optimal decision. The decision maker is faced with bounded rationality, which for all practical purposes prevents him from optimizing his decision. So also, although *in principle* an algorithm may be constructed that searches exhaustively the space of all possible sequences of inferences until one is found leading to the theorem of interest, such in-principle possibility is impractical computationally because of the very large numbers of pathways of inferences that might have to be explored in arriving at a valid proof.[34]

Like the human decision maker, LT must resort to heuristic reasoning and search. And, like the human decision maker operating under bounded rationality, the theorem-proving computer program must use heuristic clues, rules of thumb, and strategies of various sorts to *search* for a proof.

V

Simon would later commemorate December 15, 1955, as the day of the birth of computer-based heuristic reasoning.[35] He had begun to analyze the proof of one of the theorems in the *Principia* and, by early December, some ideas were emerging about the nature of the heuristics Whitehead and Russell had used.[36] On December 15, he simulated successfully by hand the execution of a program to generate a proof of one of the theorems in the *Principia*. So the basic strategies used in LT were discovered by "actual pencil-and-paper work."[37]

Principia Mathematica began with fundamental ("atomic") concepts such as variables (denoted by **p, q,** ... and so forth), a set of connectives (denoted by ¬ [not], + [or], —> [implies], and => [entails]) that link variables to form expressions, definitions, a set of five axioms, and three rules of inference. For our purposes here, to illustrate how LT uses heuristic reasoning, it is sufficient just to state one definition, one of the axioms, and two of the rules of inference (Table 14.1).

Suppose LT is given the expression

$E: \mathbf{p} \rightarrow \neg\mathbf{p} => \neg\mathbf{p}$

and asked to obtain a proof for it.[38] As it happens, a proof for *E* would involve the following steps:

TABLE 14.1 A Tiny Axiomatic System

Definition *D*: **p → q** *def* **¬p v q**

Axiom *A*: **r v r => r**

Inference Rules:

Rule of Substitution: If **A(p)** is any true expression containing the variable **p** and **B** is any expression, then **A(B)** is also a true expression.

Rule of Replacement: Any expression may be replaced by its definition.

1. By axiom *A*: **p v p => p**
2. Substituting **¬p** for **p**: **¬p v ¬p => ¬p**
3. Replacement of left subexpression: **p → ¬p => ¬p**, which is the expression *E*.

The question is: How can LT search for a proof of expression *E* without considering *all* the valid substitutions involving the five axioms?[39] The heuristic Newell and Simon used was to "work backward" from the expression to be proved—from the characteristics of the expression, "cues" are extracted about the most promising path to pursue.[40] Newell and Simon called this heuristic the *method of substitution*—later, in the literature of heuristic programming, it would viewed as an instance of what came to be called *backward chaining*. In the case of LT, it entailed the search for an axiom or theorem similar to the expression to be proved. If a similarity is found, then the program tries to match the expression to the similar axiom or theorem by appropriate transformations of the expression; if successful, the expression is proved and the chain of transformations *is* the proof. Otherwise, if no similar axiom or theorem is found, the strategy fails.[41]

By "similarity" Newell and Simon meant a structural matching between the expression to be proved and one or more of the axioms or theorems already proved. Precise "measures" of similarity were defined. Informally, these measures would identify the expressions

p → ¬p => ¬p
p v p => p

as similar because they have the same structure—pattern of variables and connectives—whereas

p => q v p
p v p => p

would be dissimilar because their structures do not match.

To illustrate the method of substitution heuristic, we can follow how LT produced a proof of the expression

$$E: p \rightarrow \neg p => \neg p$$

Because of their structural similarity, LT finds a match between E and the axiom

$$A: r \vee r => r$$

However, on the left hand side of =>, there is a mismatch between the connectives $\rightarrow$ in E and $\vee$ in A. To make them match, the $\vee$ in A must change to $\rightarrow$. This can be done by applying the definition D. But, before that can be done, a $\neg$ must be placed before r in A—that is, by substituting a variable $\neg t$ for r in A according to the rule of substitution. This produces

$$A': \neg t \vee \neg t => \neg t$$

Now definition D can be applied to change $\neg t \vee \neg t$ to $t \rightarrow \neg t$. The new situation is

$$E: p \rightarrow \neg p => \neg p$$
$$A'': t \rightarrow \neg t => \neg t$$

The only difference now between E and A'' is that there is a variable p in the former and a variable t in the latter. Applying the rule of substitution, p can be substituted for t in A'' resulting in

$$A^*: p \rightarrow \neg p => \neg p$$

There is now a complete match between E and A^*; a proof of E has been obtained. In this process, the method of substitution relied on cues gleaned from the features of the theorem to be proved. Such cues reduced the amount of search but, of course, there was no prior guarantee of success. The cues may have led down a blind alley. Ultimately, the criterion of success for a heuristic is whether it actually works.

In fact, the method of substitution did not work all the time. Of 67 theorems in the second chapter of the *Principia*, only 20 could be proved using this heuristic. Other heuristic principles would be needed for the other theorems.[42]

VI

LT established a bridge between human and machine cognition, so much so that Simon would write in October 1956 to Bertrand Russell of this program and what it had achieved. To which Russell replied dryly that had he and Whitehead known of this possibility, they would not have wasted the years "doing it by hand."[43]

LT was a means to an end. Newell and Simon were interested in universalizing the insights they had gained in designing this program to the realm of human problem solving in general. Moreover, the paper on LT was published in a journal on information theory, a mathematical branch of communication engineering (see Chapter 11, Section VI), and was unlikely to be read by psychologists, those who might be most interested professionally in the nature of heuristic thinking.

Two years later, in 1958, Allen Newell, Cliff Shaw, and Herbert Simon published an article titled "Elements of a Theory of Human Problem Solving" in *Psychological Review*, a prominent American journal in psychology. Their theory, they stated, "explain[ed] problem-solving behavior in terms of what we shall call *information processes*."[44] It was an explicitly computational theory to explain the observed or observable behavior of organisms.[45]

For Simon and Newell, the terms *information processing* and *symbol processing* were synonymous. Over time, they seemed to prefer the latter term. If, in their earliest joint publications, they chose to use *information processing*, their last joint publication (in 1975) spoke firmly of symbol systems, which are at the core of intelligent behavior.[46]

Let us then refer to their theory as a *symbol processing model* (SPM) of cognition. SPM absorbs and generalizes Simon's previous model of the "universal decision maker" into a "symbolic problem solver." SPM was a theory of symbolic problem solving regardless of whether the problem solver was a human being, a computer, or some other kind of organism. SPM represented a certain *class* of problem-solving mechanisms of which LT was a concrete exemplar. We have seen that Simon's theory of the decision maker was entwined with a satisficing activity in which heuristics were used to overcome bounded rationality. So, also, SPM viewed problem solving as a heuristics-driven enterprise. LT did not go about its task using "simple algorithms" that applied "brute force" to search exhaustively for a solution to a given problem.[47] This was what "conventional" computers did. The algorithmic approach was not feasible in the kind of problem solving in which LT was engaged. In finding a proof for a theorem, the choices of inferences at each stage were extremely large—an embarrassment of riches—from which the program had to select an inference that seemed most promising for the purpose of arriving at a proof. Thus, the method of proof for LT used heuristics. It also used a kind of *learning* in the sense that, once LT proved a theorem, this was stored away in its memory as a potential aid in proving other theorems.[48]

SPM, in fact, provided significant insight into how the symbolic processing and mental simulation on which Kenneth Craik had speculated in his *The Nature of Explanation* (1943) could be envisioned *more precisely* (see Chapter 11, Section II)—namely, in the form of a heuristic computer program executed by a physical machine. Here was a model of how symbol structures might be represented in a material entity and how they might be manipulated, processed, and transformed into other symbol structures. Furthermore,

SPM suggested how the computer could serve as an *experimental apparatus,* a kind of microscope for the inner eye, with which one could "observe" mental phenomena. By programming the computer one could *simulate* specific higher level cognitive tasks—language understanding, chess playing, scientific concept formation, and so on—a concrete realization of Turing's thought experiment of 1950 (see Chapter 11, Section XI). If the simulation produced behavior that was consistent with what was predicted, then the computational (or symbol processing) model on which the program was based could become a theory of how humans might think and carry out cognitive tasks.

VII

Curiously, in their 1956 paper on LT, Newell and Simon did not mention the term *artificial intelligence.* This term, in fact, emerged the year before in a document describing a "summer research project on artificial intelligence" to be held in Dartmouth College in Hanover, New Hampshire, in summer 1956. The author of this proposal was John McCarthy (1927–2011).[49]

McCarthy was an assistant professor of mathematics at Dartmouth College. Later, he would move to MIT before joining Stanford University, where he founded their artificial intelligence laboratory. McCarthy is generally regarded as the coiner of the term "artificial intelligence", which, in its original sense, meant a kind of intelligence that contrasted to "natural intelligence." As the Dartmouth proposal explained, artificial intelligence was a phenomenon wherein any aspect of mental activity deemed a manifestation of intelligent action could, at least in principle, be so precisely specified that a computer could be programmed to simulate it.[50]

As we have seen, the possibility and the idea of machine intelligence had been in the minds of many ever since computing machines began to be built. Torres y Quevedo speculated on it in 1920 (see Chapter 3, Section IX); in 1943, Craik dwelled on the idea of human thinking in symbol processing terms (see Chapter 11, Section II). But, with the invention of the electronic digital computer, we find more interesting ideas—Claude Shannon's thoughts on computer chess in 1949, von Neumann comparing the brain with the computer, and Alan Turing's speculations in 1950 on what it would take for a computer to "fool" a human into thinking it was engaged with another human (see Chapter 11, Sections IV–VII).

It seems fair to say that LT was a seminal invention that transposed artificial intelligence from the realm of speculation into the realm of the real. LT was a working liminal artifact, a computer program that simulated the way human logicians went about proving theorems. It was an *actual* piece of artificial intelligence. The symbol processing model Newell, Shaw, and Simon presented in 1958 was a theory of problem solving.

It was a theory of *human* problem solving, in fact, which explained how Craik's "symbol processing in the head" could happen. As such, the Newell–Shaw–Simon paper of

1958 was seminal in the development of cognitive science, the multidisciplinary study of cognition. If, as some people believe, computational processes are at the core of cognition (in humans and animals)[51]—although not everyone does[52]—then the Newell–Shaw–Simon paper was at the very vanguard of this belief. It heralded the beginning of the "information processing paradigm" in cognitive psychology.[53] At the same time, LT was seminal to the development of the idea of artificial intelligence, both the phenomenon as envisioned by McCarthy and colleagues in 1955 and as a branch—a subdiscipline—of computer science.

VIII

If Newell and Simon were at the forefront of this new discipline, others followed very soon thereafter. Game playing and other kinds of problem solving were the main domains of inquiry. Perhaps the most influential work to follow on the tracks of Newell and Simon was the study of how machines could learn (a topic in artificial intelligence that came to be called *machine learning*) by Arthur Samuel (1901–1990) using the board game checkers ("draughts" in Britain).

While a professor of electrical engineering at the University of Illinois, Urbana, in 1947, Samuel wrote his first checkers program. It would go through many modifications. During the 1950s, as a member of the IBM Poughkeepsie laboratory, Samuel programmed the IBM 701 to play checkers. The program, described in a paper published in 1959, "self-learnt" and thereby improved its own performance.[54] In that same year, Herbert Gerlenter described (at the same first IFIP conference, where John Backus delivered his paper on the syntax and semantics of Algol [see Chapter 13, Section XVI]) a program that proved theorems in geometry at the level of "good" high school students.[55]

Such programs used heuristic reasoning and search. By the end of the 1950s, then, the *methodology* of computer science was no doubt dominated by the algorithmic approach—that is, computer scientists sought primarily to automate by inventing algorithms to solve computational problems. However, this methodology was now joined by an alternative strategy: heuristic search.

IX

Language, thought, and reality are related intimately, as distinguished linguist Benjamin Lee Whorf (1897–1941) famously proposed.[56] Whorf was alluding to natural languages, but the relationship is true in the realm of artificial languages. As we have seen, the two cultures of scientific and business computing that emerged during the 1950s gave rise to very different types of programming languages (see Chapter 13, Section XII).

The kind of computing in which Newell, Shaw, and Simon were engaged while building LT—the kind of computing with which artificial intelligence researchers became involved—as we have seen, entailed not numeric computations, but symbol processing. Expressions in logic were manipulated as symbol structures with no numeric significance; indeed, with no *semantic* content at all. Computations of the kind LT performed involved extracting subexpressions, matching two (sub)expressions, substituting (sub) expressions for other (sub)expressions, and so on. For the purpose of implementing LT on the RAND Corporation's JOHNNIAC computer, Newell and Shaw invented a programming language they called IPL (Information Processing Language).[57] The version of the language that was actually used to program LT was labeled IPL V, developed circa 1957 and implemented on the IBM 650, IBM 704, and other machines of the time.[58]

IPL, however, became a "dead language" within a relatively short time. Its significance is twofold: it was used to program LT and it was the first of a new genus of programming languages called *list processing languages*, of which the most dominant and influential species was named LISP (LISt Processing) invented by John McCarthy between 1956 and 1958.[59]

The basic concept underlying LISP (and other list processing languages) is that the fundamental symbol structures (in computational jargon, "data structures") on which computations are performed are structures called *lists*. Each element in a list is a symbol consisting of some piece of information along with information of where to find the next associated symbol. The latter information is called a *pointer*. Thus, lists are not stored in sequential location in a computer's memory. The elements of a list may be scattered all over memory, but they are linked by means of pointers.

A list processing language would contain operations that can extract parts of a list (making them lists of their own), insert elements into or delete elements from a list, find the successor elements of a list element, create new lists, and so on.

Such kinds of operations (insert, alter, delete) are not specific to list structures. But, LISP as a particular list processing language has properties and characteristics that are very distinct from such languages as FORTRAN or Algol. The latter were *procedural* languages—that is, programs are composed in the form of sequences of statement constituting procedures, which can be called from other procedures. LISP was a *functional* language, drawing its computational character from the mathematical notion of functions.

In mathematics, a function is represented symbolically by the name of the function followed by the arguments of the function, usually in parentheses. Thus, the square root of a number x, represented conventionally as $\sqrt{x}$, can be given functionally as *sqroot(x)*, and the application of this function to the value of argument x would yield the square root of that number. An arithmetic expression such as $(a * b) - (w/x)$ would be represented functionally as *minus (mpy(a,b), div(w,x))*. The syntax and semantics of LISP programs—or, rather, LISP functions—follows this general pattern.

For a flavor of what a LISP-like function looks like, let us look at a small example. Before we do, however, some preliminaries need to be established.

LISP incorporates a number of *basic* functions. They include the following. Suppose x, y are lists. Then

CAR *x* returns the first element of *x* as a list

CDR *x* returns *x* with the first element deleted

CDDR *x* returns *x* with the first two elements deleted

CONS *x, y* returns a list in which list *y* is appended to list *x*

NULL *x* returns *T* (true) if list *x* is empty

A list of elements are always depicted in parenthesis separated by a space. For example, (*A B C*) is a list of elements *A, B, C* each of which may be an "atomic" element or a list. So as examples of the use of the previously mentioned operations, we may have:

```
CAR  (A B C)  =  (A)
CDR  (A B C)  =  (B C)
CDDR (A B C)  =  (C)
CONS (A) (D E F)  =  (A D E F)
```

Now suppose we wish to define a function *ALT* that, given a list, returns the alternative elements of the list beginning with the first element. Then, in LISP, the function will be

```
(DEFUN ALT (X)
      (COND ((OR (NULL X)  (NULL (CDR X)))  X)
                 (T (CONS  (CAR X)  (ALT (CDDR X))))) 
      ))
```

What this says is that if *X* is either the empty list or if it consists of just one element (that is, CDR *X* is empty), then the function *ALT* returns as its value *X*. Otherwise, select CAR *X* and append to it the list returned by recursively calling the function *ALT* with CDDR *X* as argument.

In Algol-like notation, this same function would appear as follows:

```
ALT X:
If NULL (X) or NULL (CDR X)
then return X
else return CONS (CAR X) (ALT (CDDR X))
```

For example, if *X* is the empty list ( ), then ( ) will be returned. If *X* is the list containing a single element (A), then (A) will be returned. Suppose *X* is a list (A B C D E). Then, *ALT* will return the list (A C E).

LISP was fundamentally different from such languages as Algol and FORTRAN in that it was a language that was intended to cope with a different kind of computer culture. In its implementation, it differed from procedural languages in that programs written in the latter languages were *compiled* into a machine's "native" language before execution, whereas LISP (like APL; see Chapter 13, Sections XXII *et seq.*) was an *inter-pretive* language. The LISP interpreter examines a LISP program statement; it determines what each statement specifies and executes it on the computer before moving to the next statement.

NOTES

1. G. Polya. (1957). *How to solve it* (2nd ed.). Princeton, NJ: Princeton University Press (original work published 1945).

2. Ibid., p. vii.

3. Ibid., p. 113.

4. Ibid.

5. H. A. Simon. (1991). *Models of my life* (p. 199). New York: Basic Books.

6. Ibid.

7. S. Dasgupta. (2003). Multidisciplinary creativity: The case of Herbert A. Simon. *Cognitive Science, 27,* 683–707.

8. H. A. Simon. (1976). *Administrative behavior* (3rd ed.). New York: Free Press (original work published 1947).

9. H. A. Simon. (1947). The axioms of Newtonian mechanics. *Philosophical Magazine, 7,* 889–905.

10. H. A. Simon, D. R. Smithburg, & V. A. Thompson. (1950). *Public administration.* New York: Alfred A. Knopf.

11. Simon, 1991, op cit., p. 101.

12. H. A. Simon. (1952a). On the definition of the causal relation. *Journal of Philosophy, 49,* 517–528.

13. H. A. Simon. (1952b). Application of servomechanism theory to production control. *Econometrica, 20,* 247–268.

14. H. A. Simon. (1952c). A formal theory of interaction in social groups. *American Sociological Review, 17,* 202–211.

15. Simon, 1991, op cit. pp 197-198.

16. S. Carlson. (1979). The prize for economic science. In *Les Prix Nobel 1978.* Stockholm: The Nobel Foundation.

17. C. I. Barnard. (1938). *The function of the executive.* Cambridge, MA: Harvard University Press.

18. Simon, 1976, op cit., p. 76.

19. H. A. Simon. (1957). Rationality in administrative decision making. In H. A. Simon. *Models of man* (pp. 196–206). New York: Wiley.

20. H. A. Simon. (1950). *Administrative aspects of allocative efficiency.* Cowles Commission discourse paper, economics no. 281.

21. H.. A. Simon to T. C. Koopmans, September 29, 1952. Herbert A. Simon papers. Carnegie-Mellon University Archives, Pittsburgh, PA. Further reference to material contained in these archives will be abbreviated HASP.

22. H.. A. Simon to J. von Neumann, June 24, 1953, HASP, op cit.

23. Simon, 1991, op cit., p. 201.

24. Ibid.

25. Ibid.

26. A. Newell. (1955). The chess machine: An example of dealing with a complex task by adaptation. *Proceedings of the Western Joint Computer Conference, 7*, 101–108.

27. H. A. Simon. (1955). A behavioral model of rational choice. *Quarterly Journal of Economics, 69*, 99–118.

28. Ibid., p. 99.

29. Ibid., p. 104.

30. H. A. Simon. (1956). Rational choice and the structure of the environment. *Psychological Review, 63*, 129–138 (see especially p. 129).

31. Simon, 1991, op cit., p. 201.

32. A. Newell & H. A. Simon. (1956). *The Logic Theory machine: A complex information processing system.* Technical report P-868. Santa Monica, CA: The RAND Corporation. Also published in *IRE Transactions on Information Theory, IT-2*, 61–79. Citations of this work refers to the RAND report.

33. Newell & Simon, op cit., p. 27.

34. Ibid.

35. Simon, 1991, op cit., p. 206.

36. Ibid., p. 205.

37. Ibid.

38. Newell & Simon, op cit., p. 26.

39. Ibid., p. 30.

40. Ibid.

41. Ibid.

42. Ibid., p. 37.

43. H. A. Simon to B. Russell, October 2, 1956; B. Russell to H. A. Simon, November 2, 1956. HASP, op cit.

44. A. Newell, J. C. Shaw, & H. A. Simon. (1958). Elements of a theory of human problem solving. *Psychological Review, 65*, 151–166 (see especially p. 151).

45. Ibid.

46. A. Newell & H. A. Simon. (1976). Computer science as empirical inquiry: Symbols and search (Turing Award Lecture). *Communications of the ACM, 19*, 113–126. Reprinted in Anon. (1987). *ACM Turing Award lectures: The first twenty years 1966–1985* (pp. 287–313). New York: ACM Press (see especially p. 290).

47. Newell, Shaw, & Simon, op cit., p. 156.

48. Ibid., p. 165.

49. There were three others who were the proposal's "originators": Marvin Minsky (1927–), then a Harvard Junior Fellow and later, cofounder, with McCarthy, of the Artificial Intelligence Project at MIT; Nathaniel Rochester (1919–2001) of IBM, a designer of the IBM 701 and, at the time, manager of information research in IBM's Poughkeepsie laboratory; and Claude Shannon, whom we have already encountered, a mathematician at Bell Telephone Laboratories.

50. J. McCarthy, M. L. Minsky, N. Rochester, & C. E. Shannon. (1955). *A proposal for the Dartmouth summer research project on artificial intelligence* [On-line]. August 31. Available: http://www-formal.stanford.edu/jmc/history/dartmouth/dartmouth.html

51. B. von Eckerdt. (1993). *What is cognitive science?* Cambridge, MA: MIT Press; Z. W. Pylyshyn. (1984). *Computation and cognition.* Cambridge, MA: MIT Press.

52. J. Bruner. (1990). *Acts of meaning.* Cambridge, MA: Harvard University Press.

53. See, for example, R. Lachman, J. L. Lachman, & E. C. Butterfield. (1979). *Cognitive psychology and information processing.* Hillsdale, NJ: Lawrence Erlbaum Associates.

54. A. L. Samuel. (1959). Some studies in machine learning using the game of checkers. *IBM Journal of Research & Development, III,* 210–229.

55. H. Gerlenter. (1959). Realization of a geometry theorem proving machine. In *Proceedings of the International Conference on Information Processing* (pp. 273–282).London: Butterworth.

56. B. L. Whorf. (1956). *Language, thought and reality.* Cambridge, MA: MIT Press.

57. Simon, 1991, op cit., p. 213.

58. Ibid.

59. J. McCarthy. (1981). History of LISP. In R. L. Wexelblat (Ed.), *History of programming languages* (pp. 173–185). New York: Academic Press.

15

An Explosion of Subparadigms

⌒

I

IN 1962, PURDUE University in West Lafayette, Indiana, in the United States opened a department of computer science with the mandate to offer master's and doctoral degrees in computer science.[1] Two years later, the University of Manchester in England and the University of Toronto in Canada also established departments of computer science.[2] These were the first universities in America, Britain, and Canada, respectively, to recognize a new academic reality formally—that there was a distinct discipline with a domain that was the computer and the phenomenon of automatic computation.

Thereafter, by the late 1960s—much as universities had sprung up all over Europe during the 12th and 13th centuries after the founding of the University of Bologna (circa 1150) and the University of Paris (circa 1200)—independent departments of computer science sprouted across the academic maps on North America, Britain, and Europe. Not all the departments used *computer science* in their names; some preferred *computing*, some *computing science*, some *computation*. In Europe non-English terms such as *informatique* and *informatik* were used. But what was recognized was that the time had come to wean the phenomenon of computing away from mathematics and electrical engineering, the two most common academic "parents" of the field; and also from computer centers, which were in the business of offering computing services to university communities. A scientific identity of its very own was thus established. Practitioners of the field could call themselves *computer scientists*.

This identity was shaped around a paradigm. As we have seen, the epicenter of this paradigm was the concept of the stored-program computer as theorized originally in von Neumann's EDVAC report of 1945 and realized physically in 1949 by the EDSAC and the Manchester Mark I machines (see Chapter 8). We have also seen the directions in which this paradigm radiated out in the next decade. Most prominent among the refinements were the emergence of the historically and utterly original, Janus-faced, liminal artifacts called computer programs, and the languages—themselves abstract artifacts—invented to describe and communicate programs to both computers and other human beings. We have seen that a curious aspect of this new science was its concern for, indeed preoccupation with, procedures. The knowledge that had accrued and that characterized the field by the end of the 1950s was fundamentally *procedural knowledge*—"know-how" knowledge. Algorithms, numeric methods, heuristic search, linguistic tools, design methods were what this new breed of scientists were concerned with. *Methodology* was as much a domain of inquiry as the physical artifacts themselves.

There was strangeness to this new paradigm. There was strangeness to this new identity, for here was invented a new *intellectual tradition*. The mature natural sciences—geology, biology, physics, chemistry, astronomy—and the mature engineering sciences on which the engineering fields rested—mechanics, thermodynamics, fluid mechanics, physical metallurgy, metal physics, process chemistry, and so forth—had not seen the likes of such a science. Even electrical engineering and mathematics, both historically concerned with continuous phenomena, the two disciplines in which the first generation of professors of computer science were mostly trained, stood some distance from computer science.

II

But the computer science that was in place when the first departments of computer science emerged in the groves of academe in 1962 to 1965 was far from stable. If the appearance of a dominant paradigm is supposed to mark a *mature* science, then the computer science of the early 1960s challenged this view. As a paradigm, computer science was far from mature. It was volatile; it was dynamic. The core of the paradigm was not in any danger of being overthrown. No one suggested an alternative to the concept of the stored-program computer as a rival computational model. *That* would occur in the mid 1970s with what would be called the *data flow computing style*[3] and the *functional programming style*.[4] Yet, no one would call what transpired during the 1960s "normal science" in Thomas Kuhn's unflattering sense (see Chapter 6, Section II).

Rather, within the stored-program computing paradigm as a whole there were regions where *subparadigms* were being created—local earthquakes that shifted the regions with consequences for neighboring regions, as it were. The outcome was to alter significantly "local landscapes" within the paradigm without destabilizing the paradigm itself. In our story, the end of the birth of computer science was marked not by a whimper but a rather big bang—by an explosion of subparadigms created during the 1960s.

III

Of course, to partition this chapter of our story neatly into a split between calendrical decades is too facile. Some of the subparadigm shifts began during the 1950s and reached maturity during the 1960s. A notable instance was the development of a theory of what came to be called variously and synonymously *sequential circuits, sequential machines, finite-state machines, finite automata*.

A physical computer comprises, ultimately, of switching circuit components. Some of these take (Boolean) values as inputs and, after a certain delay, produce (Boolean) outputs. But these circuits have no "memory" of their past behavior. These circuits came to be called *combinational circuits* and were the kind Claude Shannon analyzed using Boolean algebra in 1938 (see Chapter 5, Sections III and IV). The circuits in a computer that decode instructions and then encode the decoder's output and issue control signals that cause the instruction to be executed are combinational circuits (see Chapter 12, Section IV).

Other circuits have "memory" of their immediate past states. A counter that counts from 0 to 9 (and then returns to 0) is an example. At each time step, a new pulse causes the state of the device to change, so that if the present state represents the digit n, then its next state would represent the digit $n + 1$ (for $0 \leq n \leq 8$), and it would represent 0 if $n = 9$. Such devices with response to inputs that depend on its internal state are sequential circuits or machines. Registers, accumulators, shift registers, main memory, control units—all components of a computer—are instances of sequential circuits. The most basic sequential circuit element is the "flip-flop," which can have only one of two states: 1 and 0. Depending on its present state, and the input value (1 or 0), flip-flops either stay in its present state or switch to the other state.

The structure of combinational and sequential circuits involve components that are abstractions of physical—electronic, electrical—circuit elements. Their behavior is, correspondingly, abstractions of such things as currents, voltages, and resistances. It does not matter whether these circuits are built from relays, vacuum tubes, or transistors, which were invented in 1948 by Willam Shockley (1910–1989), John Bardeen (1908–1991), and Walter Brattain (1902–1987), all of Bell Laboratories, for which they shared the Nobel prize for physics in 1956; or integrated semiconductor "chips" of the kind that appeared during the early 1960s. What was important was that *as* combinational or sequential circuits, their structure and behavior were described in terms of "logical"/binary/Boolean values and Boolean algebra.

Abstracting physical circuits up to the level of combinational and sequential circuits created a *new* kind of design activity that came to be called *logic design* and that provided a bridge between the machine, seen as a complex network of physical devices (diodes, triodes, resistors, capacitors, ferrite cores) obeying the laws of physics, and the machine, seen as a unified, functionally organized digital stored-program computer.

Shannon invented this abstraction level in the realm of combinational circuits in 1938. However, the creation of a theory of sequential circuits/machines, more complex because of the presence of memory, was initiated during the mid 1950s. This theory began with the recognition of the vital concept of an internal state of a digital device, and this concept was recognized independently by a number of people.[5]

In its most general form, a sequential machine has the following characteristics: (i) it consists of a finite set of possible states in which the machine can be; (ii) it can accept (recognize) one of a finite set of possible input values (that is, has a finite input alphabet); (iii) it can produce one of a finite set of output values (that is, has a finite output alphabet); (iv) when an input is received the circuit changes from its present state to a next state, depending on the input and the present state; and (v) the machine produces an output either depending (a) only on the present state or (b) on the present state and the input.

The overall structure of a sequential machine is shown in Figure 15.1. Notice that the (mathematical) function that produces the next state Sk (next-state function) and the function that produces the output Oj (the output function) are realized by combinational logic circuits to which the inputs are the inputs Ij and the present state Si. The "memory" device is that part of the sequential machine that holds the machine's state at any point of time.

The alternative ways in which the output function may be defined give rise to two alternative models of sequential machines that are identical with respect to (i) through (iv), but differ according to whether the output function follows (v(a)) or (v(b)). The first model came to be called the *Moore machine*, after Edward F. Moore (1925–2003), its inventor in 1956, who was then on the research staff at Bell Laboratories and, later, professor of computer sciences at the University of Wisconsin, Madison. The second model came to be called the *Mealy machine* after George H. Mealy (1927–2010), who conceived it in 1955. Mealy was also, at the time, with Bell Laboratories; later, he became a professor of computer science at Harvard University.

These two models together formed the seed of a new subparadigm, and around this seed an elaborate and mathematically sophisticated theory of sequential machines emerged during the course of the 1960s[6]—a theory that contributed, on the one hand, to automata theory[7] and, on the other, to an elegant and formal foundation for logic design.[8]

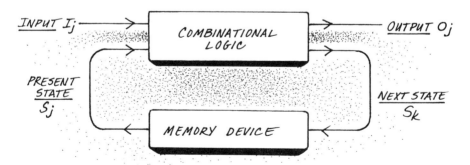

FIGURE 15.1 The Structure of a Sequential Circuit.

As an example of the latter, a computer's control unit (see Chapter 12) is an instance of a sequential machine. At any given time the device is in one of a finite set of states, $S = \{s_1, s_2, \ldots, s_m\}$. When in state s_i (that is, when the present state of the control unit is s_i), the device issues one or more control signals from a finite alphabet of control signals $C = \{c_1, c_2, \ldots, c_n\}$; the signals issued constitute collectively the unit's output o_j. The input i_q to the control unit comes from the "rest of the computer." Thus, the next state of the control unit s_k will be determined by both the present state s_i and the input i_q. Such a control unit is an instance of the Moore machine.

IV

Sequential machines were also called finite automata—finite because the number of possible states such a machine can have is finite. A sequential machine, then, has finite memory. In contrast, the Turing machine (see Chapter 4, Section IV), with its infinite tape, has infinite memory. So even though the control part of a Turing machine can only have a finite number of states, the machine as a whole is an "infinite automaton." The "machines" involved here were not physical devices; they were not material computational artifacts. The Turing machine (as previously pointed out in Chapter 4, Section IV) is a purely abstract artifact, having no physical reality. A sequential machine, in contrast, has the same liminal quality a program has. It is fundamentally abstract. Like the Turing machine, it is a mathematical entity, and can be studied, analyzed, and manipulated entirely in the abstract as mathematical objects are, as the Turing machine can be. On the other hand, a sequential machine can serve as a *design* for a physical digital circuit. The implementation of a sequential machine design would be a material artifact.

Collectively, the study of sequential machines and infinite automata came to be called *automata theory*, a field of study that came into its own during the 1950s.[9] Automata theory treats both such machines as abstract artifacts. By the end of the next decade, its status as a subparadigm within the computer science paradigm was firmly established. A marker was the publication of texts during the second half of the 1960s—texts that became seminal in characterizing the "state of the art" of the field, most notably Marvin Minsky's *Computation: Finite and Infinite Machines* (1967),[10] Michael Arbib's *Theories of Abstract Automata* (1969),[11] and *Formal Languages and Their Relation to Automata* (1969) by John Hopcroft and Jeffrey Ullman.[12]

The study of Turing machines, of course, was concerned with the fundamental problem that had led Alan Turing to create his abstract machine in the first place: what does it mean to compute? Computability, decidability, solvability were the issues with which automata theorists remained concerned. The *theory of computing* was the broad term that encompassed this subsubparadigm (as it were) of automata theory, and a number of key books explored this subsubparadigm between the late 1950s through the 1960s.[13]

V

However, there was another face to automata theory that had more practical appeal, and this went back to Noam Chomsky's celebrated monograph *Syntactic Structures* (1957) (see Chapter 13, Section XVIII). We recall that the focus of that book was the nature and form of grammar (syntactic rules) that would generate and account for sentences of a natural language such as English. Early in the book, Chomsky explored the idea of *a grammar as a machine.*

Imagine a finite-state machine with, possibly, a very large set of possible states. It has an "initial" or "starting" state and a "final" state. Beginning in its starting state, the machine goes from one state to another in sequence, each change of state being accompanied by the production of a symbol (say, an English word), until it reaches the final state and stops. We can call the sequence of symbols produced by the machine a *sentence.* Each distinct path from a starting state to a final state thus generates a distinct sentence. We can call the set of all such sentences producible by this machine a *language.*

Chomsky called any language that can be produced by this sort of a finite-state machine a *finite-state language*, and the machine itself, a *finite-state grammar.*[14]

Chomsky's finite-state grammar is, in fact, a finite-state or sequential machine wherein there is no input, and the outputs (words) are produced as a function of the state only. It is, in fact, a Moore machine. Chomsky would go on to describe several *types* of grammars and characterize the languages they would generate.[15]

In identifying grammars with automata, Chomsky summoned up a question of great interest—not to linguists, but to computer scientists interested in the theory and design of compilers for programming languages. One of the language types Chomsky identified he labeled "Type 2" came to be known to computer scientists as *context-free languages* (see Chapter 13, Section XIX). The grammars that produce context-free languages came to be called *context-free grammars.* As we have seen, the syntax of Algol 60 was defined by a context-free grammar (see Chapter 13, Section XIX). And because a programming language's compiler's first task is to ensure the syntactic correctness of a program written in that language, the segment of a compiler responsible for this task—called a *parser*—must be able to "recognize" that programs in a language like Algol 60 are, in fact, context free.

A parser is itself a computational device. And the question was raised: what kind of a computational machine is needed to recognize a context-free programming language? More generally, if there are several types of grammars, what must be the *power* of an automaton that it can recognize a particular type of language?

Thus, a subfield of the automata theory that emerged during the 1960s concerned itself with the study of automata that corresponded to these different types of languages. A finite automaton (a sequential machine) can recognize only finite-state languages (called by Chomsky "Type 3 language") that had a grammar with syntactic rules (productions) of the form

$$A \rightarrow \alpha$$
$$A \rightarrow \alpha B$$

where **A, B** are nonterminal symbols and α is a terminal symbol (see Chapter 13, Section XIX). A context-free language has a grammar with productions of the form

$$A \rightarrow \alpha$$

where **A** is a nonterminal symbol and α is a *string* of nonterminal and/or terminal symbols. A more general type of language known as *context-sensitive* language (Chomsky's Type 1) has productions of the form

$$\alpha A \beta \rightarrow \alpha \pi \beta$$

where **A** is a nonterminal symbol and α, β, π are strings of terminal and/or nonterminal symbols.

Thus, a second area of interest in automata theory that emerged during the 1960s was the determination of the kind of automata that corresponded to context-free and context-sensitive grammars. A finite automaton would recognize only finite-state languages. The other types of languages required more powerful automata—infinite machines. Turing machines of different kinds were explored as representing different types of grammars.[16]

Of course, no practical parsing algorithms would be designed along such machine principles because Turing machines consume a great deal of "time" moving back and forth along their tapes. But automata theory provided a normative standard by which to compare the different types of languages and their automatic recognition.

VI

A compiler is a programming *system*—meaning that it does not implement a single algorithm but, rather, a collection of algorithms that interact with one another in some fashion. To put this in another way, a compiler's overall goal is to translate programs written in some high-level, machine-independent programming language into object code for a particular computer. This task is complex enough to be decomposable into several subtasks or subgoals, each of which necessitates an algorithmic solution of its own (Figure 15.2). The compiling task begins with what came to be called *lexical*

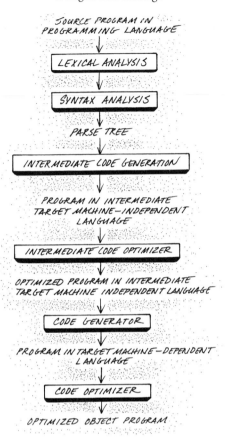

FIGURE 15.2 Structure of a Compiler.

analysis. The linguistic origin of this term is clear because a *lexeme* is the technical term for the smallest meaningful unit of sound—words. In lexical analysis, the input source program is transformed into a string of symbols in which all the (usually) multicharacter or variable-length identifiers appearing in the source program (such as reserved words in Algol such as **begin** and **end**, and variable identifiers) are replaced by single or fixed-length symbols. The output of lexical analysis (which will also include a "symbol table" that records the correspondence of fixed-length symbols with the original identifiers) is passed on to the parser, which performs syntax analysis to confirm that the program is legal syntactically, obeying the grammar of the original programming language. Assuming syntactic correctness, the parser's output in some appropriate form is passed to the "code generator," which produces object code for the target machine. As part of the code generator or as a subsequent compiler phase, there is the task of "code optimization," which makes the object code more efficient in terms of the amount of memory space required to store the object code or the amount of time required to execute the object code.

These different subtasks, in turn, may demand other subsubtasks; these engender their own problems, such as deciding which data structures should be used to represent the program and its data at various stages of the compiling process and how best to access elements from these data structures, how to represent the syntax of a programming language that leads to more efficient parsing algorithms, how best to analyze a source program for the purpose of parsing, how to represent a parser's output that facilitates efficient code generation strategies.

Thus, as a class of system programs, compilers spawned a whole range of research problems during the 1960s having to do with the invention of (especially context-free) grammars,[17] algorithms for parsing,[18] code generation strategies,[19] and code optimization techniques.[20] The first books on compilers appeared both on compiling techniques for particular programming languages[21] and, more generally, on compiling algorithms and strategies.[22] Surveys and overview papers on particular aspects of compilers were published.[23]

Inventing algorithms for various components of the compiling task was not the only issue of interest. There was the practical problem of *writing* compilers.

Compilers were usually written in assembly languages and, thus, was a long, tedious, and potentially error-prone process. Inevitably, compiler writing became an object of inquiry of intrinsic focus. The idea of compiler writing systems—more commonly called, catchily but a bit confusingly, *compiler-compilers*—emerged. Ideally, a compiler-compiler is a programming tool/language that takes as input the syntactic and semantic definition of a programming language and a description of a target machine, and produces as output a compiler for the language–machine combination. In practice, because semantics was hardly ever defined formally (although, as we shall see, inventing meta-languages for defining semantics was yet another subparadigm of this decade), compiler-compilers were largely restricted to the generation of lexical analyzers and parsers from a BNF description of the programming language of concern.

The first working compiler-compiler was developed in 1960 for the Atlas computer by a team at the University of Manchester led by Tony Brooker.[24] The topic of "compiler generation systems" became of sufficient interest that a book on the subject was published in 1970.[25]

It is fair to say that research on both compiling algorithms and compiler writing and implementing represented a distinct subparadigm within the overall paradigm, spawning a plethora of research problems in all aspect of compiling: designing/inventing context-free grammars for programming languages that enabled the task of efficient parsers, inventing algorithms for lexical analysis and parsing, and discovering procedures for code generation and code optimization. Each of these broad problem areas generated a variety of solutions. All of this was might be seen as normal science *à la* Kuhn, but it was far from "puzzle-solving" or "mopping up," as Kuhn would describe normal science.[26]

VII

We noted that the technique of microprogramming invented by Maurice Wilkes in 1951 properly came of age during the early 1960s with the design and implementation of the IBM System/360 series of computers (see Chapter 12, Sections VII and VIII). The IBM 360 also marked the beginning of the discipline and subparadigm of *computer architecture*.

Recall that John von Neumann's celebrated 1945 report on the EDVAC described what von Neumann called the logical design of the stored program computer (see Chapter 8, Section III). The idea was to frame the conceptual structure and organization of what a computer should be like based on the stored-program principle. Specifics of the physical aspects of such a machine were left largely unstated, although possibilities (and von Neumann's own preferences) were discussed.

This logical design became the essence of the new paradigm. It was assimilated by people like Wilkes, Williams, and Turing in England, and von Neumann and his collaborators in America into a common mental schema (see Chapter 8, Section V), which was interpreted, elaborated, and refined in different ways by these various researchers as implementations of actual physical computers.

The term computer architecture was not used by von Neumann or any of these other pioneers then and for years later, but we are left in no doubt that what would later be called computer architecture was anticipated by von Neumann when he laid emphasis on the logical design of computers.

It was one of several achievements of the designers of the IBM System/360 (in particular, Gene Amdahl [1922–], Frederick Brooks [1931–], and Gerrit Blaauw [1924–]) to first use the term "architecture" in the context of computers. Their original meaning was the collection of *functional* attributes of a computer, as seen by the programmer—that is, the conceptual structure and functional behavior of the computer as distinct from its internal organization and physical implementation—the outer façade of the computer, as it were.[27]

The IBM System/360 was not a specific physical computer. Rather, *System/360* referred to an architecture: a liminal artifact. Actual implementation of this architecture would entail the creation of any one of a range or *family* of physical computers, the System/360 family. Each resulting machine was a material computational artifact (called a model in IBM parlance, each identified by a model number), with its own cost–performance characteristic, depending on the physical technology and specific internal organization and design. To put this in another way, distinct physical machines each with its own physical, organizational, and technological characteristics could serve as *hosts* to implement the same System/360 architecture. As it happened, the efficacy of this approach was ensured by microprogramming the different hosts so that they each *appeared* as a System/360 "virtual" machine. This technique was called *emulation*[28]—a term first introduced in this context in 1965[29] (Figure 15.3).

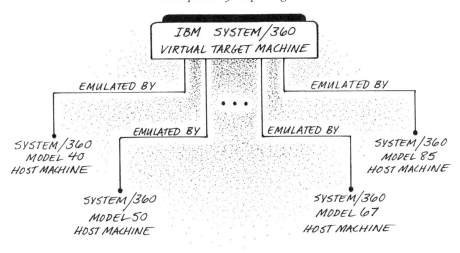

FIGURE 15.3 IBM System/360 Emulation Schema.

To the user (the programmer), these different physical computers were functionally identical. This meant that a program written for the "virtual" System/360 "computer" could be executed on any of the physical machines; or, a program executing on one of the models (say, Model 40) could be transported to another model (say Model 67). The major difference would lie in the performance of the computers; a higher numbered model had better performance (speed of processing) than a lower numbered model. Naturally, the faster machine was more costly than the slower one. This scheme allowed owners of System/360 physical machines to "upgrade" their systems to higher performing models if so desired without any substantial changes in the programs that would be transported from the old to the new.

The System/360 designers thus introduced the concept of computer architecture during the early to mid 1960s. The concept would evolve and become more complex in the decade that followed. A discipline of computer architecture as a branch of computer science would be established, also in the 1970s, and the first of a (still continuing) series of annual international conferences on computer architecture was launched in 1974. The first anthology of papers on the subject was published in 1972,[30] but the seeds of this subparadigm were planted during the 1960s.[31]

VIII

Among the ways in which a science assumes its identity is by way of publications of definitive *books* proclaiming what the subject matter is about at some moment in time. Of special status are those books that are seminal—the first textbook in a particular subject or a text that stamps its authority on the field. They become indispensable to those who study or work in that field.

In 1968 to 1969, Donald Knuth (1938–), professor of computer science at Stanford University, published the first two volumes of a planned series called, collectively, *The Art of Computer Programming*. The first volume was titled *Fundamental Algorithms* (1968)[32]; the second, *Seminumerical Algorithms* (1969).[33] These works became "immediate classics." As sometimes happens, that texts come to be referred by a generally accepted abbreviation of some sort, Knuth's first two volumes of *The Art of Computer Programming* were simply referred to as 'Knuth Volume 1' and 'Knuth Volume 2', respectively.[34]

Knuth was only 30 when *Fundamental Algorithms* was published. Both before and after these two books, he had and would have many significant contributions to different subparadigms in computer science—in the realms of programming languages, programming style and methodology, algorithms, the history of programming and programming languages, and philosophical aspects of computer science. During the 1980s, he made pioneering contributions to the development of computerized typography.[35] However, it is his *Art of Computer Programming* for which he has been most recognized.

These books were about *algorithms*. The concept of an algorithm (if not the term), of course, reaches back to antiquity. Euclid's great work *Elements* described an algorithm to find the greatest common divisor of two numbers. As Knuth tells us, the word "algorithm" itself originated in the name of a ninth-century Arabic mathematics textbook writer al-Khowârazmi as "algorism."[36] The earliest reference the *Oxford English Dictionary* has for *algorithm* was in 1695 in an article in the *Philosophical Transactions of the Royal Society*.[37]

As we have seen, ever since Charles Babbage and Ada Lovelace, people have been inventing algorithms not for humans to perform, but suitable for automatic execution on computing machines. Mathematicians and logicians had concerned themselves with algorithms under the term *effective procedure*—"a set of rules which tells us how to behave," as another significant text of the late 1960s put it.[38] In fact, Turing, in his celebrated paper of 1936, proposed that any procedure that seems intuitively effective can be carried out by the kind of machine he constructed—Turing machines (see Chapter 4, Section IV). In 1950, Soviet mathematician Andrei A. Markov (1903–1979) published a book that, in English translation, was titled *The Theory of Algorithms*; its concern was to inquire whether effective procedures did or did not exist for certain kinds of problems.[39]

Knuth's concern was far more practical. His goal was to present to his readers what was known, circa 1968 to 1969, about algorithms for "real" computers. Toward this end, cautioning that algorithms were more than procedures or methods or recipes, he laid out the fundamental characteristics of algorithms:

1. *Finiteness*: An algorithm is "finite"; it always terminates (comes to a halt) after a finite number of steps.
2. *Definiteness*: Every step of an algorithm must be defined precisely and unambiguously.

3. *Input and output*: An algorithm must have one or more inputs and one or more outputs.

4. *Effectiveness*: Each of the operations to be performed as part of an algorithm must be basic enough that, in principle, it can be performed exactly by a human being using pencil and paper.[40]

In fact, strangely enough, even though from Babbage's time people had been inventing algorithms for automatic digital computers, even in Knuth's time there was uncertainty and ambiguity about what an algorithm was and its relation to programming. Thus, in a letter to the editor of *Communications of the ACM* in 1966, Knuth made the point that the word *algorithm* refers to an abstract method of computing whereas a *program* expresses an algorithm in some particular programming language. Thus, the same algorithm can be specified as different programs[41]—hence the distinction, made in this story, between algorithms as abstract artifacts and programs as liminal artifacts.

In *The Art of Computer Programming*, Knuth used several modes of describing algorithms: as sequences of steps in which the steps themselves were in a hybrid of English and mathematical notation, as flowcharts, and as programs in a "toy" assembly language of his own invention. If Wheeler's contributions to the EDSAC project highlighted the interplay of material and liminal computational artifacts (see Chapter 8, Section VII), Knuth's *Art of Computer Programming* emphasized that the algorithm as an abstract artifact is not an island of its own; it is inevitably conjoined with a corresponding liminal artifact—the program into which the algorithm must be transformed for it to be *practically* effective.

IX

But Knuth was not only concerned with the design and programming of algorithms. He ushered in a new aspect of algorithms that he called *analysis of algorithms* (or algorithmic analysis), which was concerned with the efficiency of algorithms, how well they performed. The idea was to determine the "average behavior" or "average performance" of an algorithm and, if possible, the "optimality" of the algorithm (in some precise sense).[42] This would facilitate the comparison of two or more algorithms for the same problem and deciding which was the best. With this in mind, Knuth introduced the "big O" notation, invented in 1892 by German mathematician Paul Bachmann (1837–1920).

Suppose an algorithm has been designed to parse sentences of length n symbols in some language, and suppose it is calculated that the maximum number of steps the parsing algorithm will take is *proportional* to n^2. Thus, one can say that the worst-case behavior of the algorithm is $O(n^2)$, read as *order n^2*. If another algorithm for the same problem takes an amount of time proportional to $\frac{1}{4}n^2 + n$, this is also an $O(n^2)$ algorithm. In other words, because the time required to execute both the algorithms will be dominated by the

n^2 term, they are both of the same *complexity*—that is, O(n^2) algorithms. However, if a third algorithm is invented that requires time proportional to $n\log n$, this is an O($n\log n$) algorithm, and because as n increases, n^2 "grows" more quickly than $n\log n$, the O($n\log n$) algorithm is more efficient than the O(n^2) algorithm, because the time required to execute the former algorithm will increase at a slower rate with the increase in the length (n) of the sentence than the latter algorithm.

The term *computational complexity* was also used to signify these kinds of performance characteristics.[43] Studies of the computational complexity of abstract computing machines (such as Turing machines) or algorithms that could recognize certain types of formal languages (such context-free languages) were first published in 1965.[44] These studies were largely concerned with the performance *limits* of abstract machines on certain kinds of computations. It seems fair to say that, with the publication of Knuth's *Fundamental Algorithms,* computational complexity entered the domain of algorithms designed for "real" machines. Anyone who designed or invented an algorithm would be obligated to perform an analysis of the algorithm and estimate its complexity using the big O notation.

Knuth's achievements in writing *The Art of Computer Programming* were many. Perhaps, at the most fundamental level, was his demonstration of the relationship between mathematics and practical programming via algorithm design and analysis. Mathematical fields—abstract algebra, probability theory, statistics, and the theory of numbers—became, in Knuth's books, essential mathematical *tools* for the computer scientist interested in the design and analysis of algorithms. We are reminded of how, almost 300 years before, Sir Isaac Newton (1647–1727) published his great work in physics (or natural philosophy, as it was then called), *Philosophae Naturalis Principia Mathematica* (1687; known simply by posterity as *Principia*) in which he demonstrated how mathematical analysis becomes the tool for explaining physical phenomena. Knuth's *The Art of Computer Programming* stands in the same relation to the design of algorithms (and programs) as Newton's *Principia* did to physics.

X

According to the online *Oxford English Dictionary*, the term *software* entered the culture of computing in an article in the June 1960 issue of *Communications of the ACM*. The article referred to "such software as COBOL." A year later an article in the British Computer Society's *Computer Bulletin*, in June 1961, spoke of "The programming expertise or 'software' that is at the disposal of the computer user comprising expert advice on all matters of machine code programming…."[45]

So although the first article alluded to a language (and, implicitly, its compiler) as software, the second referred to "expertise" that was available to the user. By the mid 1960s a more precise meaning of the term was in place. The British newspaper *The Observer* of December 13, 1964, referred to software as "the 'supervisory programme', the complex instructions which enable the machine to handle many tasks simultaneously."[46] The *New Scientist* of August 25, 1966, spoke of " 'software'—the programmes for operating the computer on a wide range of problems."[47]

The *Oxford English Dictionary* gives the modern meaning of software as

1. The programs and procedures required to enable a computer to perform a specific task, as opposed to the physical component of the system.
2. *esp.* The body of system programs, including computers and library routines of a particular computer and often provided by the manufacturer, as opposed to program material provided by a user for a special task.[48]

The significance of the word itself should not be overlooked: *soft*ware as opposed to *hard*ware. The physical computer was "hard"—materialistic, subject ultimately to physical laws. A program was "soft"—comprising symbols, indifferent to physical laws, changeable, plastic, with laws all their own. Moreover, this new dichotomy of hardware/software suggested, by the mid 1960s, a *new order* in computer culture. The physical computer was no longer the epicenter of computing with all else as peripheral. Rather, there were two classes of artifacts, the physical and the symbolic—the material and the liminal—and they were *equal* partners. Computing entailed a bilateral symbiotic relationship; the totality constituted a computer *system*.

Moreover, there was the increasingly transparent issue of the largeness, the complexity of system software—the "body of system programs" mentioned in the dictionary definition. Programming languages and their compilers constituted one major type of system software. And more or less at the same time as *that* class of software came into existence during the mid 1950s, another class made its appearance. And in just more than a decade, the size and complexity of *this* class of software far exceeded those of any other kind of software.

XI

Ever since David Wheeler and the EDSAC group in Cambridge conceived and implemented subroutine libraries and the first assembler, computer systems designers and researchers had sought to protect, as far as possible, the "user" from the gritty realities of the physical computer—thus, high-level programming languages and their compilers. The user was offered not so much an IBM, a UNIVAC, or an English Electric computer, but a FORTRAN, an Algol, a COBOL, or a LISP machine.

The system programmer's ambition was to create a grand illusion. The tedium of programming, the input and output processes of a computation; the intricacies of organizing a program to fit into available physical memory; managing the movement of program segments from "secondary memories" such as tapes, disks, drums, or punched cards (these being the common hardware for storing large files of program data by the end of the 1950s) into the computer's main memory; the user's frustration at having to share access to a physical computer over time—the system programmer's goal was to free the user from all such onerous responsibilities by creating the illusion that none of this mattered or was necessary; or, rather, it would be the system that would take these responsibilities on itself.

However, the system programmer was not driven by altruism alone. A computer was a machine, an expensive resource; a computer center was an information processing factory. Ever since the Industrial Revolution during the 18th century, those who owned, managed, and ran factories were obsessed with maximizing the efficiency of their machines, achieving the greatest possible output with the least possible cost. And this meant, among other things, maximizing the *use* of machines. Machines that lay idle, machines that ran below their capacity struck a chill in the bones of the factory owner.

This factory ethic would inevitably infiltrate computer culture. Users' programs that solved systems of differential equations or calculated and produced paychecks came to be called "jobs" that a computer center had to do. And in the best factory tradition, rather than process these jobs piecemeal, one by one, as they "arrived" in the computer center, jobs were collected into batches and processed in one continuous sequence until the entire batch of jobs had been processed: "batch processing." The "overhead" in preparing the computer installation to process jobs could thus be reduced.

A computer system as a factory machine posed other problems. The two main types of activities were input/output and actual computation. The latter was done by the "central processing unit" and, by the beginning of the 1960s, the former was performed by input/output devices under command of the program. The former was done at electronic switching speeds; the latter, involving moving devices—card readers and punches, printers, magnetic tape units, disks, and drums—required far more time. And so while a program performed its input/output transfers (such as large files of data) between the computer and input/output devices, the central processing unit could do nothing but, metaphorically, twiddle its thumbs. Thus, specialized "input/output processors" (called "channels" in IBM terminology[49]) were developed that could work independently of the central processor. This led to the possibility that while one program was executing its input/output operations via the specialized input/output processors, the central processor might be set to perform actual computations of another program. This would reduce the central processor's "idle time" and increase its productivity. But, this meant that, at any one time, the main memory would have to be occupied by more than one program, and the central processor would be shared between the programs. Program P_1 has control of the central processor, then requires to perform input/output, issues input/output commands to the specialized processor, releases the central processor, which is then possessed by another program P_2 occupying main memory. When the input/output is complete, P_1 may "interrupt" the execution of P_2 and control of the central processor is given back to *P1*, or *P2* may continue to execute until *it* requires to do input/output, at which time it issues the appropriate commands to the input/output processors and then relinquishes control of the central processor to *P1*. At any given time, *several* programs, sharing main memory, may take turns to take control of the central processor. This was the concept of *multiprogramming*.

It is not clear which individual or group actually *conceived* the idea of multiprogramming. It was clearly "in the air" circa 1962 to 1964. IBM implemented a form of multiprogramming on its 7094 machine (1962),[50] Manchester University's Atlas computer system apparently supported multiprogramming by January 1964, and IBM's System/360 series supported multiprogramming, calling it *multitasking*.[51]

At about the same time, a new mode of input/output came into existence. The users were no longer actually denied direct access to a computer installation—a privilege that had been taken away from them with the advent of batch processing. Rather, they would sit at a "remote terminal"—a teletype reader/printer—possibly far removed physically from where the computer center was located, and interact with the computer on a "real-time" basis. This meant that, at any time, multiple users could have what seemed to be "simultaneous" access to the computer system. This, too, was an illusion. The user *thought* that he or she had exclusive access to the machine. This illusion was created by a combination of software and hardware that enabled the system's resources to be *time-shared* between multiple users, with each user given a time quantum to actually access the system before it was passed to another for a time quantum, and so on. However, switching between users happened at electronic speeds, hence the user's illusion. But all this must happen automatically; there must be minimal human intervention. The effectiveness of the grand illusion demanded that the illusion be created by the computing system itself.

Compilers were, of course, one class of such system programs. The other major class of system software that emerged from the mid 1950s went by various names: "monitor", "supervisor", "executive". Eventually, the term that came to be more or less generally accepted was *operating system*. An example of a basic form of an operating system was implemented for the IBM 709 circa 1958. The machine came with input/output subroutines and a monitor that managed the execution of FORTRAN jobs.[52] However, it was during the 1960s that the operating system properly came of age—an age at which it manifested itself in full, lush, huge, complex glory. And with its emergence was created a plethora of research problems and a gathering of new subparadigms.

How did this happen?

XII

The size of a computer's main memory obsessed computer designers and frustrated computer users. Even though main memory grew spectacularly in capacity from the comically small (from a present-centered perspective) size of the EDSAC memory (1024 or "1K" locations) to what commercial machines had to offer during the mid 1960s—the IBM general-purpose System/360 series of machines announced in 1964 had up to 524,288 (512K) bytes (8-bit addressable locations) of main memory[53]—it never seemed enough, thus the need for a much larger, cheaper (but considerably slower) "secondary memory" (or "backup storage") to be attached to the computer. A "memory hierarchy" was thus created involving the relatively faster, smaller main memory and the relatively slower, larger secondary memory. Thus was created the burden of managing this memory hierarchy so that when parts of a program and/or its data were necessary for execution, they would be transferred from secondary to main memory. This came to be called the *memory management problem*.

In 1962, a group at the University of Manchester led by Tom Kilburn published an article proposing a solution to this problem. They called their idea "one-level store."[54] Their idea was an instance par excellence of the grand illusion. In their case, it was to give users the illusion of (practically) unlimited memory space. This idea came to be called *virtual memory*.[55]

Kilburn and colleagues implemented this idea on the Atlas computer, designed and built at the University of Manchester in collaboration with Ferranti, their corporate partner on the Mark I (see Chapter 8, Section XIII). Manchester University had never ceased to build experimental computers since their Mark I endeavor. Atlas was the fourth of the Manchester computers[56] (later, two more would emerge). Atlas was commissioned in December 1962 and was considered to be "the most powerful computer in the world" at the time.[57] It offered the user a virtual memory of one million 48-bit words, even though the physical main memory comprised only 16,384 (16K) words.[58]

A virtual memory, then, is a grand illusion. It consists of a "virtual address space" partitioned into fixed-length subspaces called *pages*, so that a single program would occupy one or (usually) more pages, or variable-length subspaces called *segments*, each occupied by a functionally distinct program module (such as an Algol procedure or block). A program would reside physically at all times as a collection of pages or segments in secondary memory. In the case of the Atlas, this was a drum store. However, pages or segments would be transferred *automatically* from secondary memory and placed in some region of the much smaller main memory as and when required for execution. The Atlas used a paging scheme with a page size of 512 words.

Allocating main memory regions to individual program segments or program pages meant that an individual program's parts in main memory might not be stored entirely in adjacent memory words, but rather may be scattered in different regions of main memory. In a virtual memory system coupled with multiprogramming, the "virtual address space" would consist, at any time, of several user programs located either in segments or pages. Parts of an individual program ("up" for execution) would also be located in pages or segments scattered all over main memory, so that adjacent blocks of main memory would hold segments or pages of *different* programs.

The principle of organizing and storing programs in memory in the form of segments was first used in an experimental machine built at Rice University, Houston, Texas, in 1961.[59] A similar scheme was used on the Burroughs Corporation's B5500 machine circa 1961.[60] However, neither systems involved multiprogramming. The principle of segmentation and its expansion to the design of multiprogrammed virtual memory computers was explored by Jack Dennis (1931–) and his associates at MIT during the mid 1960s as part of a project called *Multics*.[61] The Multics operating system (discussed more later), in fact, used a combination of segmentation and paging.[62] That is, the virtual address space was occupied by program segments, but only pages of a program's segment would be transferred to occupy corresponding blocks ("page frames") in main memory.

The virtual memory concept as originally proposed by Kilburn and colleagues is yet another prime example of the creation of a subparadigm within the larger stored-program computing paradigm. Clearly, the "memory management problem" inhered in the overall paradigm. In this sense, the memory management problem was a "normal (computer) science" problem, in Thomas Kuhn's sense. However, the solution itself—virtual memory— was of such consequence that it created its own subparadigm; it spawned a whole range of problems that needed to be solved for virtual memory to be realizable—theoretical, experimental, design related, architectural, algorithmic—to the extent that virtual memory became a fertile research arena.[63] Among the problems to which the virtual memory concept gave rise, and were investigated by computer scientists during the 1960s, were the design of algorithms for transferring pages/segments from virtual address space into main memory, algorithms for selecting pages/segments in main memory for replacement by "incoming" pages/segments, analysis of the performance of paging and segmentation schemes, and analysis of the performance of secondary memory that implemented virtual memory. Most interestingly, the virtual memory subparadigm unveiled new phenomena that became problems in their own right. One was the peculiar nature of "program behavior" in virtual memory environments.[64]

XIII

Operating systems, as earlier noted, came of age during the 1960s. They were also, by far, the largest and most complex software artifacts built. People were not so much speaking of writing operating systems as of *building* them. And building large software systems became an engineering enterprise. In October 1968, a conference sponsored by the North Atlantic Treaty Organization (NATO) was held in Garmisch, Germany, on *software engineering*; a year later, another NATO-sponsored conference on software engineering was held in Rome, Italy.[65]

The IBM OS/360 released in 1966,[66] an operating system for the System/360, required an estimated 5000 man-years between 1963 and 1966 for its design, implementation, and documentation.[67] However, we get a more complete sense of the functional range and complexity of the most ambitious and innovative operating systems of this period by considering the Multics system.

In its mature state, Multics, built under the leadership of Fernando J. Corbató (1926–) at MIT, consisted of some 1500 program modules for a total of approximately one million lines of machine code.[68] Its structure was a direct consequence of its overall objective: to create a general computer utility analogous to electric power and telephone utilities that would run continuously and reliably, and to provide a comprehensive range of services to a population of users interacting with it through remote terminal access. The designers refined this all-encompassing objective into a collection of more specific capabilities, including time-sharing facilities, virtual memory, protection of users' programs from unauthorized access, a sophisticated programming environment in which users could work, a number of programming languages at users' disposal, an interuser communication facility (a forerunner of present-day e-mail), flexibility for enhancing the system in response to new technology and user expectations, and certain other maintenance, monitoring, and management capabilities.

Multics was thus conceived as an instance of what historian of technology Thomas Parke Hughes (1923–) would describe as a "technological system."[69] Multics had an elaborate phylogeny (see Chapter 7, Section VII). It drew upon (a) an operating system called *CTSS* (Compatible Time Sharing Computer System), also built at MIT between 1960 and 1963 that was, in fact, the first operational time-sharing system[70]; (b) the combination of the two virtual memory schemes of paging and segmentation; (c) multiprogramming; and (d) a very sophisticated scheme for protecting a user's programs and data in memory from unauthorized access by other programs.[71]

The Multics designers drew on these earlier inventions, but they combined, expanded, and generalized them, and—with this synergy—created a significantly original but enormously complex artifact. Moreover, the project constituted a significant experiment in the use of a high-level programming language (PL/I, developed by IBM) to write a large operating system.[72]

XIV

There is a price to be paid for the kind of complexity operating systems such as OS/360 and Multics manifested. How does a designer or programmer (or a programming team) *deal* with this kind of complexity? By the time of the NATO 1968 conference, there were rumblings of a "software crisis" And, as Thomas Kuhn stated, a crisis in science leads to the possibility of revolt or even revolution, a paradigm shift.[73] At the very least, it led to a serious challenge to the status quo. There were those even before the NATO conferences, even before "software crisis" became an alarmed mantra, who were willing to lead a revolution. The arch-leader was a man from Holland.

NOTES

1. J. R. Rice & S. Rosen. (1994). History of the computer science department of Purdue University. In R. DeMillo & J. R. Rice (Eds.), *Studies in computer science: In honor of Samuel D. Conte* (pp. 45–72). New York: Plenum.

2. S. H. Lavington. (1998). *A history of Manchester computers* (p. 46). Swindon, UK: British Computer Society.

3. J. B. Dennis & D. P. Misunas. (1974). *A preliminary architecture for a basic data flow processor*. CSG memo 102. Cambridge, MA: Laboratory for Computer Science, Massachusetts Institute of Technology.

4. J. W. Backus. (1987). Can programs be liberated from the von Neumann style? A functional style and its algebra of programs (ACM Turing Award lecture for 1977). In Anon. *ACM Turing Award lectures: The first twenty years 1966–1985* (pp. 63–130). Reading, MA: Addison-Wesley (original work published 1977).

5. D. A. Huffman. (1954). The synthesis of sequential switching circuits. *Journal of the Franklin Institute, 257*, 161–190; 275–303; G. H. Mealy. (1955). A method for the synthesis of sequential circuits. *Bell Systems Technical Journal, 34*, 1045–1079; S. C. Kleene. (1956). Representation of events in nervous nets and finite automata. In C. E. Shannon & E. F. Moore (Eds.), *Automata studies* (pp. 3–41). Princeton, NJ: Princeton University Press; E. F. Moore. (1956). Gedanken experiments on sequential machines. In Shannon & Moore (pp. 129–153), op cit.

6. See, for example, J. Hartmanis & R. E. Stearns. (1966). *Algebraic structure theory of sequential machines*. Englewood-Cliffs, NJ: Prentice-Hall.

7. See, for example, M. Minsky. (1967). *Computation: Finite and infinite machines*. Englewood-Cliffs, NJ: Prentice-Hall.

8. See, for example, Z. Kohavi. (1970). *Switching and finite automata theory*. New York: McGraw-Hill; G. G. Langdon, Jr. (1974). *Logic design: A review of theory and practice*. New York: Academic Press.

9. Shannon & Moore, op cit.

10. Minsky, op cit.

11. M. A. Arbib. (1969). *Theories of abstract automata*. Englewood-Cliffs, NJ: Prentice-Hall.

12. J. E. Hopcroft & J. D. Ullman. (1969). *Formal languages and their relation to automata*. Reading, MA: Addison-Wesley.

13. M. Davis. (1958). *Computability and undecidability*. New York: McGraw-Hill; M. Davis. (Ed.). (1965). *The undecidable*. Hewlett, NY: Raven Press; H. Rogers. (1967). *Theory of recursive functions and effective computability*. New York: McGraw-Hill.

14. N. Chomsky. (1957). *Syntactic structures* (pp. 18–19). The Hague: Mouton.

15. N. Chomsky. (1959). On certain formal properties of grammars. *Information and Control, 2*, 137–167.

16. Hopcroft & Ullman, op cit.

17. R. W. Floyd. (1963). Syntactic analysis and operator precedence. *Journal of the ACM, 10*, 316–333; D. E. Knuth. (1965). On the translation of languages from left to right. *Information & Control, 8*, 607–639.

18. J. Earley. (1968). *An efficient context-free parsing algorithm.* PhD dissertation, Carnegie-Mellon University; D. H. Younger. (1967). Recognition and parsing of context-free languages in time n^2. *Information & Control, 10*, 189–208.

19. H. D. Huskey & W. H. Wattenburg. (1961). A basic compiler for algebraic expressions. *Communications of the ACM, 4*, 3–9; B. Randell & L. J. Russell. (1964). *Algol 60 implementation.* New York: Academic Press.

20. F. E. Allen. (1969). Program optimization. In *Annual Review in Automatic Programming* (Vol. 5). Oxford: Pergamon Press.

21. Randell & Russell, op cit.

22. P. Z. Ingermann. (1960). *A syntax-oriented translator.* New York: Academic Press; J. A. N. Lee. (1967). *Anatomy of a compiler.* New York: Rheinhold; F. R. A. Hopgood. (1969). *Compiling techniques.* London: MacDonald.

23. R. W. Floyd. (1964). The syntax of programming languages: A survey. *IEEE Transactions on Electronic Computers, EC-13*, 346–353.

24. R. A. Brooker, I. R. MacCullum, D. Morris, & J. S. Rohl. (1963). The compiler-compiler. In *Annual Review in Automatic Programming* (Vol. 3). Oxford: Pergamon Press; R. A. Brooker, D. Morris, & J. S. Rohl. (1967). Experience with the compiler-compiler. *Computer Journal, 9*, 345–349.

25. W. M. McKeeman, J. J. Horning, & D. B. Wortman. (1970). *A compiler generator.* Englewood-Cliffs, NJ: Prentice-Hall.

26. T. S. Kuhn. (1970). *The structure of scientific revolutions* (2nd ed.). Chicago, IL: University of Chicago Press.

27. G. M. Amdahl, G. A. Blaauw, & F. P. Brooks, Jr. (1964). Architecture of the IBM System/360. *IBM Journal of Research & Development, 8*, 87–101.

28. R. F. Rosin. (1969a). Contemporary concepts of microprogramming and emulation. *Computing Surveys, 1*, 197–212.

29. S. G. Tucker. (1965). Emulation of large systems. *Communications of the ACM, 8*, 753–761.

30. C. G. Bell & A. Newell. (1971). *Computer structures: Readings and examples.* New York: McGraw-Hill.

31. S. Dasgupta. (1989). *Computer architecture: A modern synthesis* (Vol. 1). New York: Wiley.

32. D. E. Knuth. (1968). *The art of computer programming: Vol. 1. Fundamental algorithms.* Reading, MA: Addison-Wesley.

33. D. E. Knuth. (1969). *The art of computer programming: Vol. 2. Seminumerical algorithms.* Reading, MA: Addison-Wesley.

34. The third volume of the series was : D.E. Knuth (1973). *The art of computer programming: Vol. 3. Sorting and searching.* Reading, MA: Addison-Wesley—"Knuth Volume 3."

35. For collections of his papers and essays on his different interests in computer science, see, for example, D. E. Knuth. (1992). *Literate programming.* Stanford, CA: Center for the Study of Language and Information; D. E. Knuth. (1996). *Selected papers on computer science.* Stanford, CA: Center for the Study of Language and Information.

36. Knuth, 1968, op cit., pp. 1–2.

37. *Oxford English Dictionary* (2nd ed.).   Available: http://www.oed.com

38. Minsky, op cit., p. 106.

39. Knuth, 1968, op cit., pp. 8–9.

40. Knuth, 1968, op cit., pp. 4–6.

41. D. E. Knuth. (1966). Letter to the editor. *Communications of the ACM, 9*, 654.

42. Knuth, 1968, op cit., p. 7.

43. See, for example, A. V. Aho, J. E. Hopcroft & J. D. Ullman. (1974). *The design and analysis of algorithms* (pp. 2–5). Reading, MA: Addison-Wesley.

44. J. Hartmanis & R. E. Stearns. (1965). On the computational complexity of algorithms. *Transactions of the American Mathematical Society, 117,* 285–306; P. M. Lewis, II, R. E. Sterns, & J. Hartmanis. (1965). Memory bounds for recognition of context-free and context-sensitive languages. *Conference Record, IEEE 6th Annual Symposia on Switching Circuit Theory and Logic Design,* 191–202.

45. *Oxford English Dictionary* (2nd ed).   Available: http://www.oed.com

46. Ibid.

47. Ibid.

48. Ibid.

49. A. Padegs. (1964). The structure of System/360. Part IV: Channel design considerations. *IBM Systems Journal, 3,* 165–180.

50. R. F. Rosin. (1969b). Supervisory and monitor systems. *Computing Surveys, 1,* 37–54.

51. G. H. Mealy, B. I. Witt, & W. A. Clark. (1966). The functional structure of the OS/360. *IBM Systems Journal, 5,* 3–51.

52. Rosin, 1969b, op cit.

53. W. Y. Stevens. (1964). The structure of System/360. Part II: System implementation. *IBM Systems Journal, 3,* 136–143.

54. T. Kilburn, D. B. G. Edwards, M. J. Lanigan, & F. H. Sumner. (1962). One-level storage system. *IRE Transactions on Electronic Computers, EC-11,* 223–235. An earlier but much briefer paper on this same proposal was written by J. Fotheringham. (1961). Dynamic storage allocation in the Atlas computer, including the automatic use of a backing store. *Communications of the ACM, 4,* 435–436.

55. P. J. Denning. (1970). Virtual memory. *Computing Surveys, 2,* 153–190.

56. Lavington, op cit.

57. Ibid., p. 41.

58. Ibid.

59. J. K. Iliffe & J. G. Jodeit. (1962). A dynamic storage allocation scheme. *Computer Journal, 5,* 200–209; J. K. Iliffe. (1972). *Basic machine principles* (2nd ed., pp. 25–29). London: Macdonald.

60. Ibid.

61. J. B. Dennis. (1965). Segmentation and design of multiprogrammed computer systems. *Journal of the ACM, 12,* 589–602; J. B. Dennis & E. C. Van Horn. (1966). Programming semantics for multiprogrammed computations. *Communication of the ACM, 9,* 143–155; R. C. Daley & J. B. Dennis. (1968). Virtual memory, processes, and sharing in MULTICS. *Communications of the ACM, 11,* 306–312.

62. E. I. Organick. (1972). *The Multics system: An examination of its structure.* Cambridge, MA: MIT Press.

63. See, for example, Denning, op cit., for an excellent picture of this subparadigm as it was in 1970.

64. P. J. Denning. (1968). The working set model of program behavior. *Communications of the ACM, 11,* 323–333; P. J. Denning. (1968). Thrashing: Its causes and prevention. *Proceedings of the AFIPS 1968 Fall Joint Computer Conference, 33,* 915–922.

65. J. N. Buxton, P. Naur, & B. Randell. (Eds.). (1975). *Software engineering*. New York: Petrocelli (report on two NATO conferences held in Garmisch, Germany [October 1968] and Rome, Italy [October 1969]).

66. Mealy, Witt, & Clark, op cit.

67. F. P. Brooks, Jr. (1975). *The mythical man-month: Essays in software engineering* (p. 31). Reading, MA: Addison-Wesley.

68. F. J. Corbató, J. H. Saltzer, & C. T. Clingen. (1975). Multics: The first seven years. In P. Freeman (Ed.), *Software system principles* (pp. 556–577). Chicago: SRA (see especially p. 560).

69. T. P. Hughes. (1987). The evolution of large technological systems. In W. E. Bijker, T. P. Hughes, & T. J. Pinch (Eds.), *The social construction of technological systems* (pp. 51–82). Cambridge, MA: MIT Press.

70. F. J. Corbató. (1963). *The compatible time sharing system*. Cambridge, MA: MIT Press.

71. For a discussion of memory protection schemes developed in the time frame of the Multics development, see M. V. Wilkes. (1975). *Time sharing computer systems* (3rd ed., pp. 52–83). London: Macdonald & Jane's (original work published 1968).

72. F. J. Corbató. (1969). PL/I as a tool for system programming. *Datamation*, May, 68–76.

73. Kuhn, op cit.

16

Aesthetica

IN 1965, THE Dutch computer scientist Edsger Dijkstra (1930–2002), then professor of mathematics at the Technische Universiteit Eindhoven (THE) in the Netherlands, wrote a paper titled "Programming Considered as a Human Activity" and thereby announced the birth of a movement to which he gave the name *structured programming* a few years later.[1] Within the next 10 years, the movement would cause so much upheaval in the realm of programming, some came to call it a revolution—the structured programming revolution—and Dijkstra was viewed as its originator.[2]

The movement did not precipitate an overthrow of the stored-program computing paradigm as a whole, but insofar as designing and building software systems was a major component of this paradigm, structured programming altered the very essence of the subparadigm in computer science that came to be called *programming methodology*. It brought about a new *mentality* concerning programming and its methodology.

A major part of this mini-revolution actually occurred during the 1970s, but its foundations were laid during the second half of the 1960s by just a handful of publications. And Edsger Dijkstra was the revolutionary-in-chief. He laid out the gospel.

Dijkstra's undergraduate training was in mathematics and physics at the University of Leyden; he went on to obtain a PhD in computing in 1959 from the Mathematics Centrum in the University of Amsterdam and worked there until 1962 before accepting a chair in mathematics at the Technische Universiteit Eindhoven.[3]

As a computer scientist, mathematics was a source of inspiration for him, not only in terms of the method-of-proof construction, but also in the mathematician's search for *beauty* in mathematical reasoning. He quoted 19th-century English logician and mathematician George Boole, who spoke of perfectness in mathematical reasoning not just in terms of efficiency, but also in whether a method exhibited "a certain unity and harmony."[4] And he tells us that contrary to the tacit assumption on the part of many that such aesthetic considerations as harmony and elegance were unaffordable luxuries in the hurly-burly world of programming, it actually paid to cultivate elegance. This became a mantra for him.[5]

So the search for beauty in programming—a *programming aesthetic*—was a prime desideratum for Dijkstra. He did not mention English mathematician Godfrey Harold Hardy (1877–1947) and his haunting book *A Mathematician's Apology* (1940), but he would surely have approved Hardy's assertion that there is no room for ugliness in mathematics.[6] There was certainly no place for ugliness in Dijkstra's world of computing.

But Dijkstra's search for a programming aesthetic and the inspiration he took from mathematical reasoning was also prompted by a more practical consideration: mathematical reasoning also served as an exemplar of how the human mind, with its limited cognitive capacity, can deal with complexity.[7]

Programming, for Dijkstra, was a *human* activity; and as a human, he had to live with his cognitive limits.[8] Like Herbert Simon, who recognized the cognitive limits to human rationality (see Chapter 14, Section III), Dijkstra understood the limits to the human ability to cope with complexity. Simon circumvented bounded rationality by way of heuristic problem solving. Dijkstra sought for ways out from the messiness of the programming habits of his time. One way was to discipline the use of certain types of statements in programming languages—in particular, the **goto** statement in Algol-like languages. In 1968, he wrote a letter to the editor of the *Communications of the ACM* that was published under the title "Goto Statements Considered Harmful" and in which he proposed that the **goto** statement in Algol-like languages should be simply abolished from all programming languages, for it was an open invitation to make one's program unnecessarily messy, thus unnecessarily complex. The **goto** statement, he pointed out, was entirely avoidable[9] This letter proved to be astonishingly controversial because many thought it posed a threat to their very freedom as programmers, a restriction, they believed, on their "first amendment" rights as programmers.

As for large programs such as OS/360 and Multics—he was writing in the first age of massive operating systems (see Chapter 15, Section XIII)—their complexity had to be controlled, or rather mastered, in some fashion. The solution lay in the Latin adage *divide et impera*, divide and rule.[10]

But *how* should one divide to rule successfully? If a program is to be decomposed into many parts—or is to be composed *out of* many parts—then decomposition/composition of the parts must be done so that there is a harmonious fit between the parts to achieve a unity of the whole.

There was a corollary to this. Conventional wisdom on programming at the time had it that program *debugging*—weeding out errors (bugs) from a program already written—was a standard operating procedure. Dijkstra had a horror for debugging. Believing the precept "prevention is better than cure," he also believed that program development should prevent nasty bugs from entering a program *at all*, from the moment its construction begins.[11]

III

So how does one divide and rule? Dijkstra laid out the fundamentals of the gospel that became structured programming in his 1965 paper.

The programmer first identifies and completely specifies the functional requirements of the individual program components—that is, what each component is required to do. He then demonstrates, rigorously, to his own satisfaction, that if components are put together properly, then the program will solve the intended problem. He then implements the individual components independently so that their respective functional requirements are met.[12] However, an individual component of the total program may itself be of such complexity that this, in turn, may need to be decomposed into subparts using the same procedure as just mentioned.[13]

This, then, was the basic manifesto of structured programming, and Dijkstra used this term for the first time in 1969 at the NATO conference on software engineering.[14] Later, other terms would also be used to refer to this approach: *program development by stepwise refinement* and *top-down programming*.

The division into parts comes with responsibilities. One must ensure that the specifications of the components are such that, collectively, they do the job.[15] This is where aesthetics—elegance and clarity—enter the picture.[16] The insides of the components are (not yet) of concern. Indeed, they must *not* be of concern; they may not even have been constructed. The specifications describe the functional behavior of the parts, and the initial task of verification must be concerned only with these functional specifications and their "fitting together" into the desired whole so that, quite independent of the internal details of the components, when put together the components do not interfere with one another. Thus, one can guarantee the correctness of the whole program.[17]

Only when this has been achieved does the programmer proceed to the implementation of the components. This implementation, in effect its internal design and construction, must satisfy the part's exterior, functional specification. If the component is still too complex (for the "small" human brain to cope with), then it must also be divided into subcomponents, *their* functional specifications be established, verification of their working together correctly be guaranteed before constructing the interior of the subcomponents, and so on.

IV

In 1968, Dijkstra published a paper on a multiprogramming system he and a small team of colleagues were then designing and building at THE.[18] There was no reference to his "Programming Considered as a Human Activity" paper. In fact, there were no references at all, an idiosyncrasy of his style of writing scientific papers more reminiscent of a much earlier style of scientific writing than of his time. But, the paper gives us a sense of how the principle of *divide et impera* was applied in the design of a real operating system. This was not structured programming in the way described earlier; it was not "top down." Rather, it was an exercise of what, in present-centered language, would be called *bottom-up, hierarchical structured design*. However, the imperative to produce a verifiably correct system as part of the design process was still in evidence. As significantly, Dijkstra claimed that the method presented in the paper could demonstrate the logical correctness ("soundness") of the multiprogramming system in the design stage itself and thus make its empirical testing much easier after implementation.[19]

At the time the paper was written, the system had not been completed. However, Dijkstra claimed, the rigor with which the system design will be proved correct will greatly assuage any fear that the system, when implemented and put into operation, will fail.[20] We will see later how programs could be *proved* correct. What interests us, however, especially about the THE multiprogramming system, is how the credo of divide and rule was realized in the design of a complex piece of software. In fact, divide and rule applied in two different ways. First, Dijkstra conceived the whole computing system *logically* as "a society of sequential processes."[21] Each distinct user program corresponded to a sequential process; each input and output device (in operation) constituted a sequential process.[22]

A sequential process (not to be confused with sequential circuit or machine [see Chapter 15, Sections II–IV]) is a procedure or a program in a state of execution on its own "virtual" (or abstract) processor; it is a *serial* process. Sequential processes are abstract. Logically speaking each process goes about "doing its own thing," independent of other processes, except when they need to communicate with one another. A "society" of sequential processes *logically* operates concurrently each on its own virtual processor. Because the processes are abstract, there is no sense of physical time; rather, there is a sense of abstract time so that each process executes at its own abstract speed. So when two processes P_1 and P_2, working concurrently, need to communicate—for example, P_1 sends a message to P_2, which must receive it—they must be synchronized at the time communication is made. Such communication would involve P_1 writing its message into a storage area (a "buffer") and P_2 reading this message. So access to the buffer by P_1 and P_2 must not interfere with each other. This is the "mutual exclusion problem" involving shared resources that Dijkstra first studied and solved (by inventing a fundamental mechanism he called *semaphors*).[23]

The abstractness of sequential processes was important, for the "society" of such processes live and work harmoniously and cooperatively with each other quite independent of the *physical* processors (material artifacts) that actually run these processes.[24] In fact, the THE system was, in part, a realization of a *theory* of "cooperating sequential processes" Dijkstra had developed in 1965.[25]

The organization of the whole computing system into a "society" of abstract, independent but cooperating sequential processes was one aspect of the divide-and-rule strategy used in building the THE multiprogramming system. The processes were also *structured hierarchically* into multiple levels. Each level comprised one or more sequential processes that *created abstractions* out of more basic, more concrete processes or resources. Thus, the lowest level, level 0, abstracted across physical processors. Above this level, the number of processors actually shared among the processes was rendered invisible[26]; processors, so to speak, lost their individual identity.[27] At the next level, level 1, processes abstracted physical memory into segments (in the virtual memory sense [see Chapter 15, Section XII]). Above level 2, each process had its own "console" to hold "conversations" with the operator. Virtual consoles were created; the fact that there may have been only one (shared) physical console "disappeared from the picture."[28] At level 3, sequential processes concerned with buffering input streams and unbuffering output streams were realized. Virtual input/output communication units were created. Finally, at level 4, the user programs resided.[29]

Decomposing and organizing the computing system—dividing and ruling—in these two ways produced what Dijkstra would later call "hierarchical ordering of sequential processes".[30] Structuring a programming system hierarchically in this bottom-up fashion, one level at a time, has great aesthetic appeal; it is an elegant way for managing the complexity of a large system. After the sequential processes at level i have been designed, implemented, and proved correct, one need not worry about them; they become reliable components for building sequential processes at level $i + 1$.

V

But how does one *prove* that an individual program (or a sequential process) is correct? And why is it important to prove correctness as opposed to the usual method in programming of *testing* a program experimentally on a computer?

Dijkstra raised this latter issue in his 1969 paper, "Structured Programming," presented at the second NATO conference on software engineering. Proving program correctness was preferable to program testing because the latter had an inherent limitation; although empirical testing of a program can reveal the presence of errors, it could never prove their absence.[31] This assertion became a much-quoted aphorism, a mantra, in later times. The logic of the statement was impeccable. We do not know whether Dijkstra had read the writings of philosopher of science Sir Karl Popper (1902–1994),[32] but there was complete resonance between Dijkstra's aphorism and Popper's assertion that no amount of empirical evidence can ever prove the truth of a scientific theory, but just one piece of counterevidence is sufficient to falsify the theory. Thus, "falsifiability" of a scientific theory—demonstrating an error in the theory—is analogous to demonstrating the presence of a bug in a program; demonstrating the *absence* of error in a scientific theory is the analog to demonstrating the absence of a bug in a program. Neither can be shown by empirical ("inductive") means—experiment or observation.

The kind of science with which Popper was concerned were the natural sciences—physics, chemistry, biology, and the like. In the natural sciences, the object of interest being "natural," one has to perform experiments or make observations; a theory in physics or in biology *has* to be tested against reality. Popper's point was that one must test a scientific theory—that is unavoidable—but not to prove the theory (because that is logically impossible) but to *falsify* or *refute* it.

But programs—software—are artifacts; they are not discovered, but invented. Moreover, programs are *symbolic* artifacts in the same sense that mathematical theorems are symbolic artifacts. Computer science is, after all, a science of the artificial, not a science of the natural (see Chapter 1). Thus, there is a way out for programs that does not exist for a theory in a natural science. One can formally prove the correctness of a program in the same way one can formally prove the correctness of a theorem. Indeed, in this view, *a program is a theorem*. It says that "if this procedure is followed, then such and such a function will be computed." And so, as in mathematics and logic, one can apply the axiomatic approach.

We have already seen the axiomatic method "in action" in the realm of computing in Turing's work on the *Entscheidungsproblem* (see Chapter 4) and in Allen Newell's and Herbert Simon's work on the LT, or Logic Theorist (see Chapter 14, Section V). To prove a theorem in mathematics or logic, one has a set of basic definitions, axioms, and a set of rules of inference, along with a body of already proved theorems. One then applies the rules of inference on appropriate axioms, definitions, and prior theorems to construct a logically rigorous chain of inferences with an end product that is the theorem of interest; the chain of reasoning is the proof.

A similar approach can apply—indeed, for Dijkstra, *must* apply—in the case of programs. Thus, a new arena in computer science within the subparadigm of programming methodology was born: *formal program verification*.

VI

Dijkstra was by no means the first to think such thoughts. In 1949, at the Cambridge conference on automatic calculating machines where the EDSAC was first demonstrated publicly (see Chapter 8, Section XVI), the redoubtable Alan Turing presented a two-page paper in which he anticipated the germinal ideas underlying formal program verification.[33]

Turing pointed out that "checking"—his word—whether a program is correct can be greatly facilitated if the programmer states *assertions* that are expected to be true at certain points in the program. For example (using Algol-like notation), immediately after the execution of the assignment statement

    x := y + z

the assertion

    x = y + z

will always be true. Or, following the execution of the statement

    if x ≤ 0 **then** x := 0 **else** x := x + 1

the assertion

    x ≥ 0

will always be true, regardless of which of the two assignments is executed.

These assertions, Turing noted, can be such that after they are checked individually to be correct, the correctness of the whole program follows. We are reminded here of the "assertion boxes" Herman Goldstine and John von Neumann created as part of the flow diagram notation they invented for specifying algorithms (see Chapter 9, Section III).

Turing also made the distinction between what would later be called "partial" and "total" correctness. Partial correctness is the correctness of a program assuming it terminates—that is, it comes to a stop. Total correctness is concerned with proving that the program does terminate. Recall that finiteness or termination is a defining characteristic of an algorithm (see Chapter 15, Section VIII).

Turing illustrated his ideas by way of an example. The problem he used was an algorithm ("a routine," in his words) to compute the factorial of a number *n* (denoted *n!*) without using a multiply operation, with multiplication being carried out by repeated additions. The algorithm was represented by a flowchart.

Sometimes, an idea is far too ahead of its time. Turing's paper apparently made no waves at the time. It died a quiet death. It lay forgotten until well after formal program verification became an established subparadigm. The paper was "discovered" almost 20 years afterward.[34]

VII

It is quite possible to follow Dijkstra's gospel of structured programming without actually proving the correctness of the resulting program. Structured programming represented both a mentality and a method for managing the intellectual burden of developing computer programs. One can follow the divide-and-rule philosophy; proceed from the higher level specification for the programs as a whole through decomposition into parts and subparts in a top-down, hierarchical fashion without formal proofs along the way. However, the jewel in the crown of structured programming was formal verification. For this, Dijkstra's preference was the axiomatic approach of mathematics. Herein lay the aesthetics.

It is one thing to aspire to prove programs correct as one proves theorems. It is another thing to achieve this aspiration. To understand this issue we recall the fundamentals of Dijkstra's gospel. The function of an individual program must first be specified rigorously in some formal language, such as a language of logic—for example, "predicate calculus." Let us denote this specification by **S**; this describes the intended behavior of the program (yet to be written). The program itself must then be described in some appropriate programming language. Let us denote this program as **P**. The process of formal proof involves showing, by logical arguments, that **P** does indeed behave in the manner prescribed by **S**. But, this requires the availability of a precisely defined *semantics* of the language in which **P** has been written. Let us denote this semantics by σ. Verification thus requires this *ménage a trois* < **S, P,** σ >.

As we have seen, although the syntax of Algol 60 was defined formally by a context-free grammar expressed in the meta-language BNF (see Chapter 13, Section XVI), its semantics was in English. A much more formal and unambiguous meta-language than English (or any other natural language) would have to be used for the purpose of formal verification.

VIII

In fact, inventing a meta-language for a formal semantics of programming languages was very much in the air during the 1960s, quite apart from the needs of structured programming. After all, the user of a programming language would need to know the *precise* meaning of the various (precisely defined) syntactic units in the language, such as declarations of variables, assignment statements, conditional (**if then**) statements, repetition (**for**) statements, procedures (**proc**), program blocks (**begin end** statements), and so on. Furthermore, the compiler writer needed to know the precise meaning of these syntactic units to translate a program correctly in that language into object code for the target machine.

One approach, originating in the ideas of John McCarthy (the inventor of LISP [see Chapter 14, Section IX]) in 1963 and Peter Landin (1930–2009) in 1964, associated with each statement type in a programming language an *interpretation* of how that statement would be executed on a standardized ("canonical") abstract machine.[35]

This approach to defining semantics came to be called *operational semantics*, because meanings of syntactic units were defined by showing the sequence of operations that would be performed on the standardized abstract machine to execute or realize that syntactic element. The idea was a kind of formalization of the informal semantics described in English, but with respect to a formal and abstract computer.

The most developed meta-language for describing the operational semantics of a programming language was the Vienna Definition Language invented by a group at the IBM Laboratory in Vienna, inspired by McCarthy's work.[36] A formal definition of the semantics of the IBM programming language PL/I was completed in 1969.[37]

Operational semantics for proving automatically the correctness of *microprograms* (see Chapter 13) would be developed during the mid 1970s.[38] But, in the realm of structured programming and its concern with *humans* proving correctness of a program as it is developed, operational semantics did not excite much enthusiasm.[39] The seminal work on a semantics appropriate for program verification in the structured programming context was an axiomatic method by Robert Floyd (1936–2001), who at the time was with the Carnegie Institute of Technology (later, Carnegie-Mellon University) in 1967 and, influenced by Floyd, by Anthony Hoare (1934–) in 1969, who at the time was at Queen's University, Belfast.[40] This approach came to known as "Floyd-Hoare logic" or (more commonly) *Hoare logic* (rather as the Darwin–Wallace theory of evolution by natural selection in biology was reduced to, simply, "Darwinian evolution").

Although Floyd used a flowchart notation, Hoare defined the axiomatic semantics of an Algol-like language. As in mathematics and logic, Hoare defined a set of axioms describing the properties of the basic syntactic entities in his language, such as the meaning of arithmetic operators and the meaning of the basic statements in the language.

To give an example of axiomatic semantics, we consider the most fundamental execution statement in Algol: the "simple" assignment statement having the general form

$$x := E$$

where x is the identifier for a simple variable and E is an expression (such as an arithmetic expression). An English-language operational semantics for the assignments would be as follows: The expression E is evaluated; the resulting value is stored in the variable x. The axiomatic semantics of the assignment is as follows: If the assertion $\mathbf{P}(x)$, where $\mathbf{P}$ is a truth-valued function—"predicate"—with x as an argument, is to be true *after* the assignment is executed, then $\mathbf{P}(E)$ must be true immediately *before* the assignment's execution. This leads to the "axiom of assignment" expressed by the formula

$$\{\mathbf{P}_0\}\, x := E\, \{\mathbf{P}\}$$

Here, x is a variable, E is an expression, and $\mathbf{P}_0$ is obtained from $\mathbf{P}$ by substituting E for all occurrences of x in $\mathbf{P}$.

So if the assignment

$$x := x + 1$$

leads to the assertion $\mathbf{P}$: $x \geq 1$ after the assignment, then the assertion $\mathbf{P}_0$: $x + 1 \geq 1$ *must* hold before the assignment. Notationally, this situation is represented by the H*oare formula*:

$$\{x + 1 \geq 1\} \, x := x + 1 \, \{x \geq 1\}$$

The meanings of the basic statement types in a programming language (the assignment, **if then, for**, and so forth, in the case of Algol 60) were given by Hoare formulas of the general form

$\{\mathbf{P}\}\, S\, \{\mathbf{Q}\}$. Here $\mathbf{P}, \mathbf{Q}$ are true assertions and S is some legal program statement. The Hoare formula is to be read as follows: If the assertion $\mathbf{P}$ is true before the execution of S, then the assertion $\mathbf{Q}$ is true after S's execution. $\mathbf{P}$ and $\mathbf{Q}$ were named, respectively, *precondition* and *postcondition*.

In the manner of the axiomatic approach in mathematics and logic, Hoare logic, then, consists of axioms that define the meaning of the primitive concepts in the programming language, along with rules of inferences that define the semantics of "composite statements." For example, the rule of sequential composition says that if for a statement $S1$ the Hoare formula $\{\mathbf{P1}\}\, S1\, \{\mathbf{P2}\}$ is true, and if for another statement $S2$ the Hoare formula $\{\mathbf{P2}\}\, S2\, \{\mathbf{P3}\}$ is true, then we may *infer* that for the sequential composition (or sequential statement) $S1;S2$, the formula $\{\mathbf{P1}\}\, S1;S2\, \{\mathbf{P3}\}$ will be true.

The beauty of Hoare logic lay in that the assertions and inferences could be made on the program *text* without actually having actually to simulate the execution of the statements in the program. And we see how elegantly Dijkstra's structured programming principle can be married with Hoare logic.

As a very trivial example, consider the following sequence of assignment statements:

$x := x + 1;$
$y := x + z$

Suppose the variable x has some value symbolized as α and the variable z has the symbolic value β immediately before the execution of this sequence. We want to prove that after the sequence, the assertion $y = \alpha + \beta + 1$ is true. We can prove this as follows:

By axiom of assignment, the Hoare formula

$$\{x = \alpha, z = \beta\} \, x := x + 1 \, \{x = \alpha + 1, z = \beta\}$$

is true. By the same axiom, the Hoare formula

$$\{x = \alpha + 1, z = \beta\} \, y := x + z \, \{y = \alpha + \beta + 1, x = \alpha + 1, z = \beta\}$$

is also true. By applying the rule of sequential composition, the Hoare formula

$$\{x = \alpha, z = \beta\}\, x\!: = x + 1;\, y\!: = x + z \,\{y = \alpha + \beta + 1, x = \alpha + 1, z = \beta\}$$

is true, in which case our objective, to show that the postcondition of the sequential statement, $y = \alpha + \beta + 1$, has been proved formally.

As remarked earlier, structured programming became a fertile area of research during the 1970s. Important texts and papers would follow,[41] but the foundations were laid by Dijkstra, Floyd, and Hoare before the end of the 1960s.

NOTES

1. E. W. Dijkstra. (1965a). Programming considered as a human activity. In *Proceedings of the 1965 IFIP Congress* (pp. 213–217). Amsterdam: North-Holland. Reprinted in E. N. Yourdon. (Ed.). (1979). *Classics in software engineering* (pp. 3–9). New York: Yourdon Press (see especially p. 5). All citations refer to the reprint.

2. Yourdon, op cit., p. 1.

3. K. R. Apt. (2002). Edsger Wybe Dijkstra (1930–2002): A portrait of a genius (obituary). *Formal Aspects of Computing, 14,* 92–98.

4. Quoted by Dijkstra, op cit., p. 3.

5. Ibid., p. 4.

6. G. H. Hardy. (1940). *A mathematician's apology* (p. 4). Cambridge, UK: Cambridge University Press.

7. Dijkstra, 1965a, op cit., p. 5.

8. Ibid., op cit., p. 6.

9. E. W. Dijkstra. 1968a. Goto statements considered harmful. *Communications of the ACM, 11,* 147–148 (letter to the editor).

10. Dijkstra, 1965a, op cit.

11. E. W. Dijkstra. (1968b). The structure of the "THE" multiprogramming system. *Communications of the ACM, 11,* 341–346. Reprinted in E. Yourdon. (Ed.). (1982). *Writings of the revolution: Selected readings on software engineering* (pp. 89–98). New York: Yourdon Press (see especially p. 91). All citations refer to the reprint.

12. Dijkstra, 1965a, op cit., p. 5.

13. Ibid.

14. E. W. Dijkstra. (1969). Structured programming. In J. N. Buxton, P. Naur, & B. Randell (Eds.), (1976). *Software engineering: Concepts and techniques.* New York: Litton. Reprinted in Yourdon (pp. 43–48), 1979, op cit. All citations refer to the reprint.

15. Dijkstra, 1965a, op cit., p. 6.

16. Ibid.

17. Ibid.

18. Dijkstra, 1968b, op cit.

19. Dijkstra, 1968b, op cit., p. 91.

20. Ibid.

21. Ibid., 1968b, op cit., p. 92.

22. Ibid.

23. Ibid., pp. 95–98.

24. Ibid., p. 92. The assumption is, though, that there will be an underlying processor available to execute a process. Thus, sequential processes are liminal rather than purely abstract artifacts.

25. E.. W. Dijkstra. (1965b). *Cooperating sequential processes*. Technical report, Mathematics Department, Technische Universiteit Eindhoven, Eindhoven.

26. Dijkstra, 1968b, op cit., p. 92.

27. Ibid.

28. Ibid., p. 97.

29. Ibid., p. 93.

30. E.. W. Dijkstra. (1971). Hierarchical ordering of sequential processes. *Acta Informatica, 1*, 115–138.

31. Dijkstra, 1969, op cit., p. 44.

32. In particular, K. R. Popper. (1965). *Conjectures and refutations*. New York: Harper & Row; K. R. Popper. (1968). *The logic of scientific discovery*. New York: Harper & Row.

33. A. M. Turing. (1949). Checking a large routine. In Anon *Report on the conference on high-speed automatic calculating machines* (pp. 67–68). Cambridge, UK: University Mathematical Laboratory.

34. F. L. Morris & C. B. Jones. (1984). An early program proof by Alan Turing. *Annals of the History of Computing, 6*, 139–147.

35. J. McCarthy. (1963). Towards a mathematical science of computation. In *Proceedings of the IFIP Congress 63* (pp. 21–28). Amsterdam: North-Holland; P. J. Landin. (1964). The mechanical evaluation of expressions. *Computer Journal, 6*, 308–320.

36. P. Wegner. (1972). The Vienna Definition Language. *ACM Computing Surveys, 4*, 5–63.

37. O. Lucas & K. Walk. (1969). On the formal description of PL/I. In *Annual Review in Automatic Programming* (pp. 105–182). Oxford: Pergamon Press.

38. A. Birman. (1974). On proving correctness of microprograms. *IBM Journal of Research & Development, 9*, 250–266.

39. See, for example, J. de Bakker. (1980). *Mathematical theory of program correctness* (p. 4). London: Prentice-Hall International.

40. R. W. Floyd. (1967). Assigning meaning to programs. In *Mathematical aspects of computer science* (Vol. XIX, pp. 19–32). Providence, RI: American Mathematical Society; C. A. Hoare. (1969). An axiomatic basis for computer programming. *Communications of the ACM, 12*, 576–580, 583.

41. See, for example, O.-J. Dahl, E. W. Dijkstra, & C. A. R. Hoare. (1972). *Structured programming*. New York: Academic Press; D. G. Gries. (Ed.). (1978). *Programming methodology*. New York: Springer-Verlag; Yourdon, 1979, op cit.; Yourdon, 1982, op cit.

Epilogue

~

I

HISTORY NEVER ENDS, despite what American political scientist Francis Fukuyama (1952–) claimed.[1] Neither, consequently, does the writing of history. But, the writing of *a* history, like any other story, must have an ending.

The choice of where to stop a historical narrative is a matter of the narrator's judgment and, to some extent, arbitrary. English historian Edward Hallett Carr (1992–1982) famously pointed out that the historian is necessarily selective in what he or she chooses to include in the narrative.[2] That selectivity applies as much to where the narrative ends.

The story I have told here suffers from this subjectivity—both in where it begins and where it ends. This history begins in 1819, when Charles Babbage started to think about a fully automatic computing engine, and it ends in 1969—150 years later. The beginning and the ending were matters of my choice (as was everything in between). Other writers may differ in their choice of historical span as well as the contents of the history itself; but there is, I believe, a sense in where this story began and where it ended.

II

There is, I believe, a sense in beginning with Babbage. The year 1819 saw the origin of a train of thinking that led Babbage to the design of a fully automatic, programmable computing machine. English philosopher Alfred North Whitehead (1861–1947) once wrote that European philosophy was comprised of a series of footnotes to Plato. We cannot claim that the origin and evolution of computer science consisted of a series of footnotes to Babbage. As we have seen, most of the early creators were ignorant of Babbage. But, we can certainly claim that Babbage invented a machine architecture and a principle of programming that anticipated remarkably what would come a century later. There is a perceptible *modernity* to Babbage, and we recognize it because we see it in much that followed. Babbage's ghost, as it were, haunts the intellectual space of what became computer science.

III

As for ending this history in 1969, here, too, there is some rationale. It was during the 1960s that computer science assumed a distinct identity of its own. By the act of naming itself, it broke free the umbilical cords that had tied it to mathematics and electrical engineering. Universities and other academic and research institutions founded departments with names that varied slightly (computer science, computing science, computation, computing, computer and information science in the English-speaking world; informatik, informatique, and datalogy in Europe), but with references that were unmistakable. The business of these academic units was *automatic computing*—the concept itself, its nature, the mechanism to achieve it, and all phenomena surrounding the concept.

The stored-program computing paradigm emerged between 1945 and 1949. The former year marked the appearance of the seminal EDVAC report authored by John von Neumann in which he laid out the logical principles of stored-program computing; the latter year was when these principles were tested empirically and corroborated by way of the Cambridge EDSAC and the Manchester Mark I. In Thomas Kuhn's terms, all that preceded this period were "preparadigmatic."[3] However, this is neither to dismiss nor denigrate the work preceding 1945, because much of what happened before the EDVAC report *led to* the stored-program computing principles. And, although the seemingly far-removed abstractions Alan Turing created in 1936 may or may not (we do not know for sure) have shaped von Neumann's composition of the EDVAC report, the significance of the Turing machine would emerge after the founding of the stored-program computing paradigm. The Turing machine formalism offered, in significant ways, the mathematical foundations of the paradigm. In fact, some would claim that it was Turing's *Entscheidungsproblem* paper rather than the EDVAC report that *really* constituted the stored-program computing paradigm.

Now, if we were "pure" Kuhnians, we would believe that much of the excitement was over by 1949, that what followed was what Kuhn called "normal science"—essentially, puzzle solving. In fact, it was nothing like that at all. What actually happened from 1945 through 1949 was the creation of a *core* of a new paradigm. From a cognitive point of view, it marked the germination, in some minds, of a core *schema*.

It is tempting to draw a parallel with axiomatic mathematics. The basic definitions and axioms form the starting point for some branch of mathematics (such as Euclid's postulates in plane geometry or Peano's axioms in algebra), but the implications of these axioms and definitions are far from obvious—thus mathematicians' goal to explore and discover their implications and produce, progressively, a rich structure of knowledge (theorems, identities, and so forth) beginning with the axioms.

So also, the stored-program computing principle became the starting point. The implications of these principles circa 1949 were far from obvious. The 1950s and 1960s were the decades during which these implications were worked out to an impressive depth; the elemental schema lodged in people's minds about the nature of automatic computation was expanded and enriched. *The paradigm did not shift*; it was not overthrown or replaced by something else. It was not a case of a "computing revolution" as a whole; rather, new subparadigms, linked to the core, were created. If there were revolutions, they were local rather than global. The outcome, however, was that the paradigm assumed a fullness, a richness. And, as we saw, the 1960s, especially, witnessed what I have described as an "explosion of subparadigms".

IV

In the meantime, the subject that had motivated the creation of automatic computing in the first place—numeric mathematics (or numeric analysis)—grew in sophistication. But, in a certain way, it stood apart from the other subparadigms. Numeric mathematics concerned itself with "the theory and practice of the efficient calculations of approximate solutions of continuous mathematical problems"[4]—and insofar as it dealt with approximating *continuous* processes (polynomial functions, differential equations, and so on), it formed the link between the "new" computer science and the venerable world of continuous mathematics.

With the emergence of all the other new subparadigms, numeric mathematics was "decentered," so to speak. Much as, thanks to Copernicus, the earth became "just" another planet orbiting the sun, so did numeric mathematics become "just" another subparadigm. Unlike the others, it had a long pedigree; but, as a subparadigm linked to the stored-program computing core, numeric mathematics was also enormously enriched during the 1950s and 1960s. As distinguished numeric analyst Joseph Traub wrote in 1972, in virtually every area of numeric mathematics, the current best algorithms had been invented after the advent of the electronic digital computer. The sheer exuberance and promise of this artifact breathed new life into a venerable discipline.[5]

V

If we take Kuhn's idea of paradigms seriously, we must also recognize that there is more to a paradigm than its intellectual and cognitive aspects. The making of a paradigm entails social and communicative features.

Thus, another marker of the independent identity of the new science was the launching, during the 1950s and 1960s, of the first *periodicals* dedicated solely to computing—yet another severance of umbilical cords. In America, the ACM, founded in 1947, inaugurated its first journal, the *Journal of the ACM* in 1954; and then, in 1958, what became its flagship publication, the *Communications of the ACM*; and in 1969, the ACM launched the first issues of *Computing Surveys*.

Also in America, the Institute of Radio Engineers (IRE) brought forth, in 1952, the *IRE Transactions on Electronic Computers*. After the IRE merged with the American Institute of Electrical Engineers in 1963, forming the Institute of Electrical and Electronics Engineers (IEEE), a suborganization called the Computer Group was formed in 1963/1964, which was the forerunner of the IEEE Computer Society, formed in 1971. The *Computer Group News* was first published in 1966.

In Britain, the British Computer Society, founded in 1957, published the first issue of the *Computer Journal* in 1958. In Germany, *Numerische Mathematik* was started in 1959. In Sweden, a journal called *BIT*, dedicated to all branches of computer science came into being in 1961.

Commercial publishers joined the movement. In 1957, Thompson Publications in Chicago, Illinois, began publishing *Datamation*, a magazine (rather than a journal) devoted to computing. Academic Press launched a highly influential journal named *Information & Control* in 1957/1958 dedicated to theoretical topics in information theory, language theory, and computer science.

VI

The appearance of *textbooks* was yet another signifier of the consolidation of academic computer science. Among the pioneers, perhaps the person who understood the importance of texts as much as anyone else was Maurice Wilkes. As we have seen, *The Preparation of Programs for an Automatic Digital Computer* (1951), coauthored by Wilkes, David Wheeler, and Stanley Gill, was the first book on computer programming. Wilkes's *Automatic Digital Computers* (1956) was one of the earliest (perhaps the first) comprehensive textbooks on the whole topic of computers and computing, and he would also write *A Short Introduction to Numerical Analysis* (1966) and the influential *Time Sharing Computer Systems* (1968). Another comprehensive textbook (reflecting, albeit, an IBM bias) was *Automatic Data Processing* (1963), authored by Frederick P. Brooks, Jr., and Kenneth E. Iverson, both (then) with IBM. In the realm of what might be generally called *computer hardware design*, IBM engineer R. K. Richards published *Arithmetic Operations in Digital Computers* (1955), a work that would be widely referenced for its treatment of logic circuits. Daniel McCracken (who became a prolific author) wrote *Digital Computer Programming* (1957) and, most notably, a best-seller—*A Guide to FORTRAN Programming* (1961)—the first of several "guides" on programming he would write throughout the 1960s.

Among trade publishing houses, Prentice-Hall launched its Prentice-Hall Series on Automatic Computation during the 1960s. Among its most influential early texts was

Marvin Minsky's *Computation: Finite and Infinite Machines* (1967), a work on automata theory. By the time this book appeared, there were already more than 20 books in this series, on numeric analysis; the programming languages PL/I, FORTRAN, and Algol; and applications of computing. McGraw-Hill also started its Computer Science Series during the 1960s. Among its early volumes was Gerard Salton's *Automatic Information Organization and Retrieval* (1968). The author was one of the progenitors of another subparadigm in computer science during the 1960s, dedicated to the theory of, and techniques for, the automatic storage and retrieval of information stored in computer files, and this branch of computer science would link the field to library science. And, as we have seen, Addison-Wesley, as the publisher of the Wilkes/Wheeler/Gill text on programming in 1951, can lay claim to be the first trade publisher in computer science. It also published, during the 1960s, the first two volumes of Donald Knuth's *The Art of Computer Programming* (1968 and 1969, respectively). Another publisher, Academic Press, distinguished for its dedication to scholarly scientific publications, inaugurated in 1963 its *Advances in Computers* series of annual volumes, each composed of long, comprehensive, and authoritative chapter-length surveys and reviews of specialized topics in computer science by different authors.

The explosion of subparadigms during the 1960s was, thus, accompanied by a proliferation of periodicals (and, thus, articles) and books.

VII

The computer science paradigm that had emerged by the end of the 1960s, then, constituted a core practical concept and a core theory: the former, the idea of the stored-program computer; the latter, a theory of computation as expressed by the Turing machine. These core elements were surrounded by a cluster of subparadigms, each embodying a particular aspect of automatic computation, each nucleating into a "special field" within (or of) computer science, to wit: automata theory, logic design, theory of computing, computer architecture, programming languages, algorithm design and analysis, numeric analysis, operating systems, artificial intelligence, programming methodology, and information retrieval. Looking back from the vantage of the 21st century, these can be seen as the "classic" branches of computer science. They were all, in one way or another, concerned with the nature and making of computational artifacts—material, abstract, and liminal.

We have also seen that a central and vital *methodology* characterized this paradigm: the twinning of design-as-theory (or the design process-as-theory construction) and implementation-as-experimentation. Even abstract computational artifacts (algorithms and computer languages) or the abstract faces of liminal artifacts (programs, computer architectures, sequential machines) are designed. The designs *are* the theories of these artifacts. And even abstract artifacts are implemented; the implementations become the experiments that test empirically the designs-as-theories. Algorithms are implemented as programs, programs (abstract texts) become executable software, programming languages by way of their translators become liminal tools, computer architectures morph into physical computers, and sequential machines become logic or switching circuits. Turing machines are the sole, lofty exceptions; they remain abstract and, although they are designed, they are never implemented.

This methodology—design-as-theory/implementation-as-experimentation—is very much the core methodology of most sciences of the artificial, including the "classical" engineering disciplines. It is what bound the emerging computer science to the other artificial sciences on the one hand and separated it from both mathematics and the natural sciences on the other. And it was this synergy of design and implementation that made the computer science paradigm as a fundamentally *empirical*, rather than a purely mathematical or theoretical, science.

Another feature of the paradigm we have seen emerge is that, although computer scientists may have aspired for universal laws in the spirit of the natural sciences, they were rather more concerned with the *individual*. A design of a computational artifact is the design of an individual artifact; it is a theory of (or about) that particular artifact, be it an algorithm, a program, a language, an architecture, or whatever. Computer science as a science of the artificial is also, ultimately, a science of the individual.

VIII

This has been a narrative about the genesis of computer *science*—not about computers per se, nor of the "information age" or the "information society." Thus, it is not a social history of technology. However, insofar as it is concerned with computational *artifacts*, and insofar as artifacts help define *cultures*, the history I have outlined here belongs, in part, to cultural history.[6]

More fundamentally, though, this story straddles *intellectual* history on the one hand and *cognitive* history on the other.

It is intellectual history, in the older sense, celebrated by American scholar Arthur O. Lovejoy (1833–1962) in his *The Great Chain of Being* (1936) as the history of *ideas*—how ideas are consciously born, propagated, and transformed over time, and how they spawn new ideas.[7] The "newer," postmodern meaning of intellectual history is somewhat different. Rather than ideas, the focus has shifted to texts and the way language is used.[8] The history of the *idea* we have followed here is, of course, that of automatic computing. What does it mean? How does one carry it out? How do we render it practical? How do we guarantee its correctness? How do we improve its efficiency? How do we describe it? What are its limits?

But this story is also cognitive history, a term of quite recent vintage. Cognitive history attempts to understand the creative past in terms of (conscious and unconscious) *thought processes* that created that past. It involves relating goals, purpose, knowledge, even emotions, styles of doing and thinking, and how they interact in the creative moment—regardless of whether what is created is an idea, a symbolic system, or a material artifact.[9]

This particular history I have told here thus straddles the cultural, the intellectual, and the cognitive. Computer science is a science of the artificial wherein culture (artifacts and symbols), cognition (purpose, knowledge, beliefs), and ideas intersect.

IX

In this postmodern (or perhaps "postpostmodern") age, there is a social aspect to this history that is markedly visible. The protagonists in this story are all white and almost all male. The only women we have encountered are Ada, Countess of Lovelace during the mid 19th century and Grace Murray Hopper during the mid 20th century. It would be unfair to say that there were no other women who played roles in this history. This book mentions such authors as Adele K. Goldstine, Herman Goldstine's wife, collaborator, and coauthor; and Alice C. Burks, Arthur Burks's wife and coauthor. We also know of a "Miss B. H. Worsley," who was a member of Maurice Wilkes's EDSAC team and who was credited with the preparation of the "account" of the first EDSAC demonstration in June 1949.[10] The ENIAC project was, in fact, peopled by several women "computers," including Kay McNulty (later Kay Mauchly, John Mauchly's wife), who were involved in programming the ENIAC. Still, the sparseness of women in this history is glaring, to say the least. As in the case of other sciences (natural and artificial), as in art, this story is largely a story of men.[11]

It is also, as we have seen, a history of only white European-Americans (see Dramatis Personae). People of other ethnicities have not figured in this account. Whether these aspects—gender and race—of the social, intellectual, cognitive, and cultural history of computer science change during the 1970s and thereafter and, if so, in what manner, remains to be told in another tale.

X

We began this story with a brief discourse on the fundamental nature of computer science—what philosophers would call its *ontology*. Its particularity and peculiarity (we argued) stemmed from the view that computer science is the science of automatic computation, and that it entails the interplay of three kinds of computational artifacts (material, abstract and liminal), that it is a science of symbol processing, a science of the artificial, a science of the "ought," and (mainly) a science of the individual (see Prologue).

That discourse was not intended to be part of the historical narrative, but rather a 21st-century meditation that belongs more to the *philosophy* of computer science (its analysis and interpretation) than its history. And yet, as the 1960s ended (as does this story), and the computational paradigm expanded with the "explosion of subparadigms" (see Chapter 15), and the first (undergraduate and graduate) students wended their way through the first academic degree programs in computer science, there were philosophical rumblings about the discipline that *were* part of the historical narrative itself. There were skeptics who questioned the very *idea* of computer science as a science. And it lay with the members of the embryonic computer science community to defend their paradigm, their newly gotten intellectual territory, and insist on the distinct scientific identity of their new discipline.

This defense was carried into the *sanctum sanctorum* of natural science itself, into the pages of the weekly *Science*, arguably America's most prestigious and widely read periodical devoted to all branches of (especially natural) science. The defenders were three influential members of this new community: Alan Perlis, a major participant in the development of the Algol programming language (see Chapter 13, Section XIV), and Allen Newell and Herbert Simon, two of the creators of heuristic programming and artificial intelligence (see Chapter 14, Sections II–V).

Perlis, Simon, and Newell were the founding faculty, in 1965, of the computer science department at the Carnegie Institute of Technology (later, Carnegie-Mellon University) in Pittsburgh, with Perlis as its first head of department.[12] In 1967, *Science* published a very short article by these scientists titled "What Is Computer Science?," which they began by noting, a mite ruefully perhaps, that computer science professors are often asked by skeptics whether there really existed a discipline of computer science and, if so, what was its nature.[13] Their answer was categorical: a science comes into being when some domain of phenomena requires description and explanation. Computers and the phenomena surrounding them constitute such a domain; computer science is quite simply the study of computers and their associated phenomena.

But the disbelievers (not specifically named in the article) have raised many objections that Newell and colleagues were willing to confront—that the sciences deal with natural phenomena, whereas computers belong to the world of artifacts; that science is a series of quests for universal laws whereas artifacts cannot obey such laws; that computers are instruments and the behavior of instruments "belongs" to the sciences that gave rise to them (such as the electron microscope "belongs" to physics); that different parts of computer science can be parceled out to more traditional branches such as electronics, mathematics, and psychology (thus leaving nothing intrinsically that is computer science); that computers belong to the realm of engineering, not science.

Newell and colleagues refuted (rather more tersely than one might have expected) these objections. They argued, for example, that even though computers are artificial, computational phenomena are described and explained on a "daily" basis; that even if the computer is an instrument, its complexity, richness, and uniqueness are such that its behavior cannot be described or explained adequately by any other existing science. As to computers belonging to electronics or mathematics or psychology, some parts of computing do, indeed, fall within these domains, but in their entirety they belong to no one existing science. Regarding the claim that computers belong to engineering and not science, Newell, Perlis, and Simon countered that computers belong to both, just as electricity (as a phenomenon) belongs to physics and electrical engineering, and plants to both botany and agriculture.

So we see that ruminations about the ontology of computer science were integral to the history of its genesis. The very identity of computation as a distinct paradigm, of computer science as a distinct science of its own, had to be defended and justified by the first people who called themselves computer scientists.

Was this anxiety dispelled with time, during the 1970s and thereafter? In fact, this debate has continued, sporadically, into the 21st century. The Prologue of this book happens to be my own perspective on this issue, but like the aspects of gender and ethnicity in computer science, the later evolution of the ontological status of computer science remains yet another story to be told.

NOTES

1. F. Fukuyama, 1992. *The End of history and the last man*. New York: The Free Press.

2. E. H. Carr. (1964). *What is history?* (p. 12). Harmondsworth, UK: Penguin Books (original work published 1961).

3. T. S. Kuhn. (1970). *The structure of scientific revolutions* (2nd ed.). Chicago, IL: University of Chicago Press.

4. J. F. Traub. (1972). Numerical mathematics and computer science. *Communications of the ACM, 15*, 531–541 (see especially p. 538).

5. Ibid., p. 538.

6. P. Burke. (2008). *What is cultural history?* Cambridge: Polity.

7. A. O. Lovejoy. (1936). *The great chain of being*. Cambridge, MA: Harvard University Press.

8. See, for example, D. LaCapra. (1983). *Rethinking intellectual history*. Ithaca, NY: Cornell University Press; A. Brett. (2002). What is intellectual history now? In D. Cannadine (Ed.), *What is history now?* (pp. 113–131). Basingstoke, UK: Palgrove Macmillan.

9. See, for example, N. Nersessian. (1995). Opening the black box: Cognitive science and history of science. *Osiris, 10*, 196–215; D. B. Wallace & H. E. Gruber. (Eds.). (1989). *Creative people at work*. New York: Oxford University Press; S. Dasgupta. (2003). Multidisciplinary creativity: The case of Herbert A. Simon. *Cognitive Science, 27*, 683–707.

10. Anon. (1950). *Report of a conference on high speed automatic calculating machines, 22–25 June* (p. 12). Cambridge, UK: University Mathematical Laboratory.

11. For the presence of women in the history of the natural sciences and mathematics, see, for example, L. Pyenson & S. Sheets-Pyenson. (1999). *Servants of nature* (pp. 335–349). New York: W.W. Norton. For the place of women in art, see W. Chadwick. (2007). *Women, art and society* (4th ed.). London: Thames & Hudson.

12. *History*. Carnegie-Mellon University. Available: http://www.csd.cs.cmu.edu.

13. A. Newell, A. J. Perlis, & H. A. Simon. (1967). What is computer science? *Science, 157*, 1373–1374.

Dramatis Personae[1]

⌒————————————————————————————————————

Howard H. *Aiken* (1900–1973). American physicist and designer of the Harvard-IBM Mark I and Mark II electromechanical computers. Organized the first American conference on computing.

Gene *Amdahl* (1922–). American computer designer. Coarchitect of the IBM System/360 computer.

John Vincent *Atanasoff* (1903–1995). American physicist. Co-inventor and implementer of the electronic Atanasoff-Berry Computer (ABC).

Charles *Babbage* (1791–1871). British mathematician, scientist, and economist. Inventor and designer of the Difference Engine and the Analytical Engine.

John *Backus* (1924–2007). American mathematician, and programming language and meta-language designer. Invented the FORTRAN programming language. Codeveloper of the FORTRAN compiler. Inventor of the Backus Normal Form (or Backus Naur Form; BNF) notation for syntactic descriptions of programming languages.

Friedrich L. *Bauer* (1924–). German mathematician and computer scientist. Inventor of a method of mechanically evaluating arithmetic expressions. Contributor to the development of Algol 58 and Algol 60 programming languages.

Clifford *Berry* (1918–1963). American electrical engineer. Co-inventor and implementer of the Atanasoff-Berry Computer (ABC).

Julian *Bigelow* (1913–2003). American mathematician and computer designer. Contributed to the founding of cybernetics. Codeveloper of the IAS computer.

Gerrit *Blaauw* (1924–). American computer systems designer. Coarchitect of the IBM System/360 computer.

Corrado **Böhm** (1923–). Italian computer theorist. Designed and implemented an early programming language.

Léon **Bollée** (1830–1913). French inventor and manufacturer. Invented a multiplication algorithm and a mechanical multiplication machine.

George **Boole** (1819–1864). British mathematician. Inventor of Boolean algebra, a calculus for symbolic logic.

Andrew D. **Booth** (1918–2009). British physicist. Early explorer of automatic machine translation of natural languages.

John G. **Brainerd** (1904–1988). American electrical engineer. Codeveloper of the ENIAC electronic programmable computer.

Fredrick P. **Brooks** (1931–). American computer systems designer and software design manager. Coarchitect of the IBM System/360 computer and team manager of the IBM operating system OS/360 projects.

Arthur W. **Burks** (1915–2008). American mathematician, engineer, computer theorist, and philosopher of science. Codeveloper of the ENIAC electronic programmable computer, historian of the ENIAC project, and writer on cellular automata theory.

Vannevar **Bush** (1890–1974). American electrical engineer and technological visionary. Inventor of the differential analyzer, a mechanical analog computer.

Samuel H. **Caldwell** (1904–1960). American electrical engineer and codeveloper of an electromechanical version of the Bush differential analyzer.

Noam **Chomsky** (1928–). American linguist. Creator of formal models of language and the theory of transformational grammar.

Alonzo **Church** (1903–1995). American mathematician and logician. Cocreator of the concept of computability.

Joseph **Clement** (1779–1844). British engineer and machine and precise tool maker. Part collaborator in the development of the Difference Engine.

Leslie John **Comrie** (1893–1953). New Zealander astronomer. Compiler of astronomical tables using Hollerith-style tabulating machines.

Fernando J. **Corbató** (1926–). American physicist, computer scientist, and scientific manager. Contributor to the theory, design, and implementation of time-sharing computer systems, and team leader in the development of the Compatible Time Sharing System (CTSS) and the Multics operating system.

Kenneth C. **Craik** (1914–1945). British psychologist and philosopher. Speculator on the role of computationlike symbol processing in human thinking.

Jacques **Curie** (1856–1941). French physicist. Codiscoverer of piezoelectricity, used in the design of acoustic delay line memories.

Pierre **Curie** (1859–1906). French physicist and Nobel laureate. Codiscoverer of piezoelectricity, used in the design of acoustic delay line memories. Codiscoverer of the chemical elements polonium and radium.

Adriaan **De Groot** (1914–2006). Dutch psychologist and chess player. Conducted studies on the cognitive psychology of chess.

Jack B. **Dennis** (1931–). American computer scientist. Contributor to the theory and design of multiprogrammed computers and the development of the Multics operating system.

Edsger W. **Dijkstra** (1930–2002). Dutch mathematician and computer scientist. Originator of the concept of structured programming, designer of the THE multiprogramming system, and proponent of an aesthetic approach to programming.

J. Presper **Eckert** (1919–1995). American electrical engineer and entrepreneur. Co-inventor and builder of the ENIAC electronic programmable computer, conceiver of the acoustic delay line memory, and cofounder of Eckert-Mauchly Computer Corporation.

Wallace J. **Eckert** (1902–1971). American astronomer. Applied punched-card data processing machines to astronomical calculations. Codesigner of the IBM Selectric Sequence Electrical Calculator.

Adin D. **Falkoff** (1921–2010). American mathematician, computer systems designer, and scientific manager. Lead author of the first formal description of a computer system, and implementer of the APL programming language.

Robert W. **Floyd** (1936–2001). American mathematician and computer scientist. Cocreator of a theory for proving the correctness of computer programs. Inventor of an influential grammar for programming languages.

Jay W. **Forrester** (1918–). American electrical engineer and systems scientist. Inventor of the ferrite magnetic core computer memory and principal designer of the Whirlwind computer.

Stanley **Gill** (1926–1975). British mathematician and computer scientist. Contributor to programming methodology and program development techniques.

Kurt **Gödel** (1906–1978). Austrian-American mathematician. Discoverer of the Incompleteness Theorem bearing his name, describing the fundamental limits of mathematical reasoning.

Adele **Goldstine** (1920–1964). American mathematician. Computer programmer of the ENIAC electronic programmable computer and documenter of the ENIAC project.

Herman H. **Goldstine** (1913–2004). American mathematician. Administered the ENIAC project, collaborated in the design of the Princeton IAS computer, and co-invented flowchart notation for specifying computer programs.

Douglas **Hartree** (1897–1958). British mathematician, numeric analyst, and academic administrator. Builder of a version of the Bush differential analyzer.

David **Hilbert** (1862–1943). German mathematician. Postulator of key open problems in mathematics and its foundations.

C. A. R. ("Tony") **Hoare** (1934–). British computer scientist. Co-inventor of a logic for proving correctness of computer programs. Inventor of the Quicksort algorithm for sorting data.

Herman **Hollerith** (1860–1929). American inventor, statistician, and entrepreneur. Inventor of punched-card, electromechanical data processing machines.

Grace Murray **Hopper** (1906–1992). American mathematician. Codeveloper of the Harvard-IBM Mark I electromechanical computer, cocreator of the practice of computer programming, and designer of the COBOL programming language.

Kenneth E. **Iverson** (1920–2004). Canadian mathematician and programming language designer. Inventor of the APL programming language and coauthor of the first formal description of a computer system.

Joseph-Marie **Jacquard** (1752–1834). French weaver. Inventor of the Jacquard loom.

Tom **Kilburn** (1921–2001). British mathematician and circuit designer. Codesigner of the Manchester Mark I, the world's second fully operational stored program computer. Co-inventor of the Williams tube, an electrostatic computer memory.

Donald E. **Knuth** (1938–). American mathematician, computer scientist, and textbook author. Pioneer in the art of computer programming, contributor to the design and analysis of computer algorithms, author of fundamental texts on programming and algorithms, and historian of programming and programming languages.

Thomas S. **Kuhn** (1922–1996). American historian and philosopher of science. Theorist of the nature of scientific practice, change, and revolutions. Conceived the concept of the scientific paradigm and paradigm shift.

Clair D. **Lake** (1888–1958). American engineer. Codesigner and implementer of the Harvard-IBM Mark I electromechanical computer.

Peter J. **Landin** (1930–2009). British mathematician and computer theorist. Developer of the theory of operational semantics for programming languages.

Dionysius **Lardner** (1793–1859). British science writer and expositor on the Difference Engine.

Gottfried Wilhem **Liebniz** (1646–1716). German mathematician and philosopher. Co-inventor of the differential calculus and inventor of a calculating machine.

Augustus Ada, Countess of **Lovelace** (1815–1852). British mathematician. Commentator on, and composer of algorithms for, the Analytical Engine.

Percy **Ludgate** (1883–1922). Irish accountant. Designer of a mechanical computing machine.

John **Mauchly** (1903–1980). American physicist, engineer and entrepreneur. Co-inventor of the ENIAC electronic programmable computer and cofounder of the Eckert-Mauchly Computer Corporation.

John **McCarthy** (1927–2011). American mathematician and computer theorist. Inventor of the programming language LISP and co-inventor of artificial intelligence. Conceived the concept of time sharing in computer systems.

Warren **McCulloch** (1898–1968). American physician and neurophysiologist. Contributed to the early development of neurocomputing. Coconceiver of the Pitts-McCulloch neuron.

George H. **Mealy** (1927–2010). American computer theorist. Inventor of an abstract model of finite automata, later named after him.

Luigi Frederico **Menabrea** (1809–1896). Italian mathematician and politician. Expositor on the Analytical Engine.

Marvin **Minsky** (1927–). American mathematician and computational theorist. Co-inventor of artificial intelligence.

Edward F. **Moore** (1925–2003). American computational theorist. Inventor of an abstract model of finite automata, later named after him.

Oskar **Morgenstern** (1902–1977). German-American economist. Co-inventor of game theory.

Peter **Naur** (1928–). Danish astronomer and computer scientist. Codeveloper of the Algol programming language, and editor/coauthor of the Algol language definition. Co-inventor of the Backus Normal Form (or Backus Naur Form; BNF) notation for syntactic descriptions for programming languages.

Allen **Newell** (1927–1992). American mathematician and computer scientist. Cocreator of heuristic programming and codesigner/co-implementer of Logic Theorist, a program to prove theorems in logic. Cocreator of artificial intelligence and the theory of heuristic problem solving.

Max **Newman** (1897–1984). British mathematician and scientific administrator. Team leader of the Colossus project and founder of one of the first academic computing machine laboratories.

Alan J. **Perlis** (1922–1970). American mathematician and computer scientist. Contributor to the design and implementation of the Algol 60 programming language.

Walter **Pitts** (1923–1969). American mathematical logician. Contributor to the early theory of neurocomputing. Coconceiver of the Pitts-McCulloch neuron.

George **Polya** (1887–1985). Hungarian-American mathematician. Explorer of heuristic reasoning in mathematics.

Karl R. **Popper** (1902–1994). Austrian-British philosopher of science. Conceiver of the theory of falsifiability in science.

Emil **Post** (1897–1954). Polish-American logician. Inventor of Post production, a formal model of computation.

Jan A. **Rajchman** (1911–1989). American electrical engineer. Inventor of the Selectron, an electrostatic memory device.

William **Renwick** (1924–1971). British computer designer. Codeveloper of the EDSAC and other Cambridge computers.

Bertrand **Russell** (1872–1970). British mathematician, logician, philosopher, and intellectual gadfly. Coauthor of *Principia Mathematica*, a treatise on the logical foundations of mathematics.

Heinz **Rutihauser** (1918–1970). Swiss mathematician and numeric analyst. Contributor to the design, development, and exposition of the Algol programming language.

Klaus **Samelson** (1918–1980). German mathematician, physicist, and numeric analyst. Contributor to the development of Algol 58 and Algol 60 programming languages.

Arthur **Samuel** (1901–1990). American electrical engineer. Designer and implementer of a heuristic, checkers-playing computer program. Contributor to the creation of artificial intelligence.

George **Scheutz** (1785–1873). Swedish printer and journalist. Implemented (with son Edvard [1822–1881]) the Difference Engine.

Claude E. **Shannon** (1916–2001). American electrical engineer. Inventor of the theory of symbolic switching circuits, cofounder of the mathematical theory of information, and artificial intelligence visionary.

Helmut **Shreyer** (1912–1984). German engineer, designer, and implementer of an electronic version of the Z1 mechanical computer.

Herbert Alexander **Simon** (1916–2001). American polymath social, cognitive, and computer scientist and philosopher of science. Nobel laureate in economics. Inventor of the theory of bounded rationality, cofounder of heuristic programming and artificial intelligence, and codesigner/implementer of the Logic Theorist computer program for proving logic theorems.

George **Stibitz** (1904–1995). American mathematical physicist and engineer. Designer of an early series of Bell Laboratories computers.

Leonardo **Torres y Quevedo** (1852–1936). Spanish engineer. Automata visionary and theorist.

Alan Mathison **Turing** (1912–1954). British mathematician, logician, computing theorist, and computer designer. Conceived the essential abstract mechanical notion of computability, postulated a test for machine intelligence, and designed one of the first stored-program electronic digital computers.

John **von Neumann** (1903–1957). Hungarian-American mathematician and scientific polymath. Co-inventor of game theory, participant in the ENIAC project, co-inventor of the stored-program computing principle, codesigner of the IAS computer, pioneer in the development of neurocomputing, and initiator of cellular automata theory.

Thomas J. **Watson, Sr.** (1874–1956). American corporate executive and "captain of industry." Led the emergence of IBM as the leader in punched-card data processing machines and its entry into automatic electronic computing.

Warren **Weaver** (1894–1978). American mathematician and scientific administrator. Thinker on communication theory and machine translation of natural languages.

David J. **Wheeler** (1927–2004). British mathematician, computer programmer, and computer designer. Codeveloper of the EDSAC and other Cambridge computers. Inventor of assembly language programming and the closed subroutine concept.

Alfred North **Whitehead** (1861–1947). British logician and philosopher. Coauthor of *Principia Mathematica*, a treatise on the logical foundations of mathematics.

Benjamin Lee **Whorf** (1897–1941). American linguist. Postulator of the thesis that language shapes thought.

Norbert **Wiener** (1894–1964). American mathematician. Inventor of the science of cybernetics.

Maurice V. ***Wilkes*** (1913–2010). British applied mathematician. Designer of the EDSAC, the world's first fully operational stored program electronic computer and its successor, the EDSAC II. Inventor of microprogramming. Coauthor of the first textbooks on computer programming and electronic computers. Organizer of the first British conference on computing.

Frederic C. ***Williams*** (1911–1977). British electronics engineer. Codesigner of the Manchester Mark I, the world's second fully operational stored program computer. Co-inventor of the Williams tube, an electrostatic computer memory.

Nicklaus ***Wirth*** (1934–). Swiss computer scientist. Designer of several Algol-like programming languages.

Charles E. ***Wynn-Williams*** (1903–1979). British physicist and electronic scientific instrument designer. Inventor of the binary counter used in digital computers.

Konrad ***Zuse*** (1910–1995). German civil engineer. Designer of the Z series of mechanical and electromechanical computers, and designer of the Plankalkül programming language.

NOTE

1. The contributions attributed to the people listed in this cast of characters pertain only to the historical period ending in 1969. Many of them would continue to make other contributions, not mentioned here, to the evolution of computer science, post-1969.

Bibliography

Aho, A. V., Hopcroft, J. E., & Ullman, J. D. (1974). *The design and analysis of computer algorithms*. Reading, MA: Addison-Wesley.

Aiken, H. H. (1937). *Proposed automatic calculating machine*. Unpublished memorandum.

Aiken, H. H., & Hopper, G. M. (1946). The Automatic Sequence Controlled Calculator. *Electrical Engineering, 65*, 384–391, 449–454, 522–528.

Alexander, C. (1964). *Notes on the synthesis of form*. Cambridge, MA: Harvard University Press.

Allen, F. E. (1969). Program optimization. In *Annual review in automatic programming* (Vol. 5). Oxford: Pergamon Press.

Alt, F. L. (1948a). A Bell Telephone Laboratories computing machine—I. *Mathematical Tables for Automatic Computation, 3*, 1–13.

Alt, F. L. (1984b). A Bell Telephone Laboratories computing machine—II. *Mathematical Tables for Automatic Computation, 3*, 69–84.

Amdahl, G. M., Blaauw, G. A., & Brooks, F. P., Jr. (1964). Architecture of the IBM System/360. *IBM Journal of Research & Development, 8*, 87–101.

Anderson, J. A., & Rosenfield, E. (Eds.). (1988). *Neurocomputing*. Cambridge, MA: MIT Press.

Andrade, E. N. da C. (1960). *A brief history of the Royal Society*. London: The Royal Society.

Anon. (1950). *Report of a conference on high speed automatic calculating machines, June 22–25, 1949*. Cambridge, UK: University Mathematical Laboratory.

Anon. [1947] (1985). *Proceedings of a symposium on large-scale calculating machines. The Harvard Computation Laboratory*. Cambridge, MA: MIT Press.

Anon. (1985). David Wheeler, 1985 Computer Pioneer Award [On-line]. Citation. IEEE Computer Society. Available: http://www.computer.org

Anon. (1987). *ACM Turing Award lectures: The first twenty years 1966–1985*. New York: ACM Press.

Anon. (1998). Milestones in machine translation, no. 2: Warren Weaver's memorandum 1949. *Language Today, 6,* 22–23.

Apt, K. R. (2002). Edsger Wybe Dijkstra (1930–2002): A portrait of a genius. *Formal Aspects of Computing, 14,* 92–98.

Arbib, M. A. (1969). *Theories of abstract automata.* Englewood-Cliffs, NJ: Prentice-Hall.

Arbib, M. A., & Hesse, M. B. (1986). *The construction of reality.* Cambridge, UK: Cambridge University Press.

Artz, F. B. (1980). *The mind of the Middle Ages* (3rd ed., Rev.). Chicago, IL: University of Chicago Press.

Ashton, T. S. (1969). *The Industrial Revolution.* London: Oxford University Press.

Atanasoff, J. V. (1940). *Computing machine for the solution of large systems of linear algebraic equations.* Unpublished memorandum.

Atanasoff, J. V. (1984). Advent of electronic digital computing. *Annals of the History of Computing, 6,* 229–282.

Babbage, C. (1837). *On the mathematical power of the calculating engine.* Unpublished manuscript, December 26. Buxton MS7. Museum of the History of Science.

Babbage, C. [1864] (1994). *Passages from the life of a philosopher.* Piscataway, NJ: IEEE Press.

Backus, J. W. (1959). The syntax and semantics of the proposed international algebraic language of the Zurich ACM-GAMM conference. In *Proceedings of the 1st International Conference on Information Processing* (pp. 125–132). London: Butterworth.

Backus, J. W. (1981). The history of Fortran I, II and III. In R. L.Wexelblatt (Ed.), *A history of programming languages* (pp. 25–74). New York: Academic Press.

Backus, J. W. [1977] (1987). Can programs be liberated from the von Neumann style? A functional style and its algebra of programs. In Anon. *ACM Turing Award lectures: The first twenty years 1966–1985* (pp. 63–130). New York: ACM Press.

Backus, J. W., Bauer, F. L., Bottenbruch, H., Katz, C., Perlis, A. J., Rutihauser, H., Samelson, K., & Wegstein, J. H. (1959). Report on the algorithmic language ALGOL. *Numerische Mathematik, 1,* 41–60.

Backus, J. W., Beeber, R. W., Best, S., Goldberg, R., Halbit, L. M., Herrick, H. C., Nelson, R. A., Sayre, D., Sheridan, P. B., Stern, H., Ziller, I., Hughes, R. A., & Nutt, R. (1957). The FORTRAN automatic coding system. In *Proceedings of the Western Joint Computer Conference* (pp. 188–197). Los Angeles, CA.

Backus, J. W., & Herrick, H. (1954). IBM 701 Speedcoding and other automatic programming systems. In *Proceedings of the ONR Symposium on Automatic Programming for Digital Computers* (pp. 106–113). Washington, DC: Office of Naval Research, Department of the Navy.

Bar-Hillel, Y. (1960). The present status of automatic translation of languages. In F. L. Alt (Ed.), *Advances in computers* (Vol. 1, pp. 91–163). New York: Academic Press.

Barnard, C. I. (1938). *The function of the executive.* Cambridge, MA: Harvard University Press.

Barr, A., & Feigenbaum, E. A. (Eds.). (1981). *The handbook of artificial intelligence* (Vol. I). Stanford, CA: Heuristic Press.

Barron, D. W. (1978). *Assemblers and loaders* (3rd ed.). New York: Elsevier North-Holland.

Bartlett, F. C. (1932). *Remembering.* Cambridge, UK: Cambridge University Press.

Basalla, G. (1988). *The evolution of technology.* Cambridge, UK: Cambridge University Press.

Bates, M. [1950] (1990). *The nature of natural history.* Princeton, NJ: Princeton University Press.

Bauer, F. L., & Wössner, H. (1972). The "Plankalkül" of Konrad Zuse: A forerunner of today's programming languages. *Communications of the ACM, 15*, 678–685.

Bell, C. G., & Newell, A. (1971). *Computer structures: Readings and examples.* New York: McGraw-Hill.

Berkeley, E. C. (1949). *Giant brains, or machines that think.* New York: Wiley.

Birman, A. (1974). On proving correctness of microprograms. *IBM Journal of Research & Development, 9*, 250–266.

Boden, M. A. (Ed.). (1990). *Philosophy of artificial intelligence.* Oxford: Oxford University Press.

Boden, M. A. (2006). *Mind as machine: A history of cognitive science* (Vol. 1). Oxford: Clarendon Press.

Bonner, J. T. (1988). *The evolution of complexity by means of natural selection.* Princeton, NJ: Princeton University Press.

Boyer, C. B. (1991). *A history of mathematics* (2nd ed., Rev.). New York: Wiley.

Boys, C. V. (1909). A new analytical machine. *Nature, 81*, 14–15.

Brett, A. (2002). What is intellectual history now? In D. Cannadine (Ed.), *What is history now* (pp. 113–131)? Basingstoke, UK: Palgrave Macmillan.

Bromley, A. G. (1982). Charles Babbage's Analytical Engine, 1838. *Annals of the History of Computing, 4*, 196–217.

Brooker, R. A., MacCallum, I. R., Morris, D., & Rohl, J. S. (1963). The compiler-compiler. In *Annual review in automatic programming* (Vol. 3). Oxford: Pergamon Press.

Brooker, R. A., Morris, D., & Rohl, J. S. (1967). Experience with the compiler-compiler. *Computer Journal, 9*, 345–349.

Brooks, F. P., Jr. (1975). *The mythical man-month: Essays in software engineering.* Reading, MA: Addison-Wesley.

Brooks, F. P., & Iverson, K. E. (1969). *Automatic data processing: System/360 edition.* New York: Wiley.

Bruner, J. (1990). *Acts of meaning.* Cambridge, MA: Harvard University Press.

Burke, P. (2008). *What is cultural history?* Cambridge, UK: Polity.

Burks, A. W. (1947). Electronic computing circuits for the ENIAC. *Proceedings of the Institute of Radio Engineers, 35*, 756–767.

Burks, A. W. (1951). *An intermediate program language as an aid in program synthesis.* Report for Burroughs Adding Machine Company. Ann Arbor, MI: University of Michigan.

Burks, A. W. (Ed.). (1970). *Essays on cellular automata.* Urbana, IL: University of Illinois Press.

Burks, A. W. (1980). From ENIAC to the stored program computer: Two revolutions in computers. In N. Metropolis, J. S. Rowlett, & G.- C. Rota (Eds.), *A history of computing in the twentieth century* (pp. 311–344). New York: Academic Press.

Burks, A. W., & Burks, A. R. (1981). The ENIAC: First general-purpose electronic computer. *Annals of the History of Computing, 3*, 310–399.

Burks, A. W., Goldstine, H. H., & von Neumann, J. (1946). *Preliminary discussion of the logical design of an electronic computing instrument.* Unpublished report.

Bush, V. (1931). The differential analyzer, a new machine for solving differential equations. *Journal of the Franklin Institute, 212*, 447–488.

Butterfield, H. [1931] (1973). *The Whig interpretation of history.* Harmondsworth, UK: Penguin Books.

Buxton, J. N., Naur, P., & Randell, B. (Eds.). (1976). *Software engineering: Concepts and techniques*. New York: Litton.

Campbell, D. T. (1960). Blind variation and selective retention in creative thought as in other knowledge processes. *Psychological Reviews, 60*, 380–400.

Campbell-Kelly, M. (1994). Introduction. In C. Babbage. *Passages from the life of a philosopher* (pp. 7–35). Piscataway, NJ: IEEE Press.

Cannadine, D. (Ed.). (2002). *What is history now?* Basingstoke, UK: Palgrove Macmillan.

Cardwell, D. S. L. (1994). *The Fontana history of technology*. London: Fontana Press.

Carlson, S. (1979). The prize for economic science. In *Les prix Nobel 1978*. Stockholm: The Nobel Foundation.

Carr, E. H. [1961] (1964). *What is history?* Harmondsworth, UK: Penguin Books.

Casti, J. L. (2003). *The one true platonic heaven*. Washington, DC: Joseph Henry Press.

Cesareo, O. (1946). The Relay Interpolator. *Bell Laboratories Records, 23*, 457–460.

Chadwick, W. (2007). *Women, art and society* (4th ed.). London: Thames & Hudson.

Chakravarty, A. (Ed.). (1961). *A Tagore reader*. Boston, MA: Beacon Press.

Charniak, E., & McDermott, D. (1985). *Introduction to artificial intelligence*. Reading, MA: Addison-Wesley.

Chaudhuri, S. (2002). *Translation and understanding*. New Delhi: Oxford University Press.

Cherry, C. (1968). *On human communication*. Cambridge, MA: MIT Press.

Chomsky, N. (1956). Three models for the description of language. In *Proceedings of the Symposium on Information Theory* (pp. 113–124). Cambridge, MA.

Chomsky, N. (1957). *Syntactic structures*. The Hague: Mouton.

Chomsky, N. (1959). On certain formal properties of grammar. *Information & Control, 2*, 136–167.

Church, A. (1936). An unsolvable problem of elementary number theory. *American Journal of Mathematics, 58*, 345–363.

Cocke, J., & Schwartz, J. T. (1970). *Programming languages and their compilers*. New York: Courant Institute of Mathematical Sciences.

Codd, E. F. (1968). *Cellular automata*. New York: Academic Press.

Comrie, L. J. (1928). On the construction of tables by interpolation. *Monthly Notices of the Royal Astronomical Society, 88*, 506–523.

Comrie, L. J. (1932). The application of the Hollerith tabulating machine to Brown's tables of the moon. *Monthly Notices of the Royal Astronomical Society, 92*, 694–707.

Conant, J., & Haugeland, J. (Eds.). (2000). *The road since* Structure. Chicago, IL: University of Chicago Press.

Corbató, F. J. (1963). *The compatible time sharing system*. Cambridge, MA: MIT Press.

Corbató, F. J. (1969). PL/I as a tool for system programming. *Datamation*, May, 68–76.

Corbató, F. J., Saltzer, J. H., & Clingen, C. T. (1975). Multics: The first seven years. In P. Freeman (Ed.), *Software systems principles* (pp. 556–577). Chicago, IL: SRA.

Craik, K. J. W. [1943] (1967). *The nature of explanation*. Cambridge, UK: Cambridge University Press.

Crowther, J. G. (1974). *The Cavendish Laboratory, 1874–1974*. New York: Science History Publications.

Dahl, O.- J., Dijkstra, E. W., & Hoare, C. A. R. (1972). *Structured programming*. New York: Academic Press.

Dahl, O.- J., & Nygaard, K. (1966). SIMULA: An Algol-based simulation language. *Communications of the ACM, 9,* 671–682.

Daley, R. C., & Dennis, J.B. (1968). Virtual memory processes and sharing in MULTICS. *Communication of the ACM, 11,* 306–312.

D'Andrade, R. (1995). *The development of cognitive anthropology.* Cambridge, UK: Cambridge University Press.

Dasgupta, S. (1979). The organization of microprogram stores. *ACM Computing Surveys, 11,* 39–65.

Dasgupta, S. (1989). *Computer architecture: A modern synthesis. Volume 1: Foundations.* New York: Wiley.

Dasgupta, S. [1991] (2009). *Design theory and computer science.* Cambridge, UK: Cambridge University Press.

Dasgupta, S. (1992). Computer design and description languages. In M. C. Yovits (Ed.), *Advances in computers* (Vol. 21, pp. 91–155). New York: Academic Press.

Dasgupta, S. (1994). *Creativity in invention and design.* New York: Cambridge University Press.

Dasgupta, S. (1996). *Technology and creativity.* New York: Oxford University Press.

Dasgupta, S. (1997). Technology and complexity. *Philosophica, 59,* 113–139.

Dasgupta, S. (2003). Multidisciplinary creativity: The case of Herbert A. Simon. *Cognitive Science, 27,* 683–707.

Dasgupta, S. (2004). Is creativity a Darwinian process? *Creativity Research Journal, 16,* 403–416.

Dasgupta, S. (2007). *The Bengal Renaissance.* New Delhi: Permanent Black.

Dasgupta, S. (2011). Contesting (Simonton's) blind variation, selective retention theory of creativity. *Creativity Research Journal, 32,* 166–182.

Davis, M. (1958). *Computability and undecidability.* New York: McGraw-Hill.

Davis, M. (Ed.). (1965). *The undecidable.* New York: Raven Press.

Dear, P. (2006). *The intelligibility of nature.* Chicago, IL: University of Chicago Press.

De Bakker, J. W. (1980). *Mathematical theory of program correctness.* Englewood-Cliffs, NJ: Prentice-Hall.

De Groot, A. D. (2008). *Thought and choice in chess.* Amsterdam: Amsterdam University Press.

DeLillo, D. [1985] (1994). *White noise* (Viking critical ed.). New York: Penguin.

Denning, P. J. (1968a). The working set model of program behavior. *Communications of the ACM, 11,* 323–333.

Denning, P. J. (1968b). Thrashing: Its causes and prevention. *Proceedings of the AFIPS 1968 Fall Joint Computer Conference, 33,* 915–922.

Denning, P. J. (1970). Virtual memory. *Computing Surveys, 2,* 153–190.

Dennis, J. B. (1965). Segmentation and design of multiprogrammed computer systems. *Journal of the ACM, 12,* 589–602.

Dennis, J. B., & Misunas, D. P. (1974). *A preliminary architecture for a basic data flow processor.* CSG memo 102. Cambridge, MA: Laboratory for Computer Science, MIT.

Dennis, J. B., & van Horn, E. C. (1966). Programming semantics for multiprogrammed computations. *Communications of the ACM, 9,* 143–155.

De Solla Price, D. K. [1963] (1986). *Little science, big science—and beyond* (Exp. ed.). New York: Columbia University Press.

Dijkstra, E. W. (1965a). Programming considered as a human activity. In *Proceedings of the 1965 IFIP Congress* (pp. 213–217). Amsterdam: North-Holland.

Dijkstra, E. W. (1965b). *Cooperating sequential processes.* Technical report. Mathematics Department, Technische Universiteit Eindhoven, Eindhoven.

Dijkstra, E. W. (1968a). Goto statements considered harmful (letter to the editor). *Communications of the ACM, 11,* 147–148.

Dijkstra, E. W. (1968b). The structure of the "THE" multiprogramming system. *Communications of the ACM, 11,* 341–346.

Dijkstra, E. W. (1969). *Structured programming.* Technical report. Technische Universiteit Eindhoven, Eindhoven.

Dijkstra, E. W. (1971). Hierarchical ordering of sequential processes. *Acta Informatica, 1,* 115–138.

Dingwaney, A., & Maeir, C. (Eds.). (1995). *Between languages and cultures.* Pittsburgh, PA: University of Pittsburgh Press.

Donaldson, M. (1992). *Human minds: An exploration.* Harmondsworth, UK: Penguin Books.

Doran, R. W. (1979). *Computer architecture: A structured approach.* New York: Academic Press.

Earley, J. (1968). *An efficient context-free parsing algorithm.* PhD dissertation, Carnegie-Mellon University.

Eckert, J. P. (1944). *Disclosure of magnetic calculating machine.* Unpublished memorandum.

Eckert, J. P., Mauchly, J. W., Goldstine, H. H., & Brainerd, J. G. (1945). *Description of the ENIAC and comments on electronic digital computing machines.* Contract W670 ORD 4926. Philadelphia, PA: Moore School of Electrical Engineering.

Essenger, J. (2004). *Jaquard's web.* Oxford: Oxford University Press.

Falkoff, A. D., & Iverson, K. E. (1966). *APL\360.* White Plains, NY: IBM Corporation.

Falkoff, A. D., & Iverson, K. E. (1968). *APL\360 user's manual.* White Plains, NY: IBM Corporation.

Falkoff, A. D., & Iverson, K. E. (1981). The evolution of APL. In R. L.Wexelblat (Ed.), *A history of programming languages* (pp. 661–674). New York: Academic Press.

Falkoff, A. D., Iverson, K. E., & Sussenguth, E. H. (1964). A formal description of System/360. *IBM Systems Journal, 3,* 198–262.

Findlay, A. (1948). *A hundred years of chemistry.* London: Gerald Duckworth.

Floyd, R. W. (1963). Syntax analysis and operator precedence. *Journal of the Association for Computing Machinery, 10,* 316–333.

Floyd, R. W. (1964). The syntax of programming languages: A survey. *IEEE Transactions on Computers, EC-13,* 346–353.

Floyd, R. W. (1967). Assigning meaning to programs. In *Mathematical aspects of computer science* (Vol. XIX, pp. 19–32). Providence, RI: American Mathematical Society

Fotheringham, J. (1961). Dynamic storage allocation in the Atlas computer, including the automatic use of a backing store. *Communications of the ACM, 4,* 435–436.

Fukuyama, F. (1992). *The end of history and the last man.* New York: Free Press.

Fuller, S. (2000). *Thomas Kuhn: A philosophical history for our times.* Chicago, IL: University of Chicago Press.

Galison, P. (2010). Trading with the enemy. In M. Gorman (Ed.), *Trading zones and interactive expertise* (pp. 26–51). Cambridge, MA: MIT Press.

Genuys, F. (Ed.). (1968). *Programming languages.* New York: Academic Press.

Gerlenter, H. (1959). Realization of a geometry theorem proving machine. In *Proceedings of the International Conference on Information Processing* (pp. 273–282). London: Butterworth.

Gill, S. (1952). *The application of an electronic digital computer to problems in mathematics and physics.* University of Cambridge, Cambridge.

Ginsburg, S. (1966). *The mathematical theory of context free languages.* New York: McGraw-Hill.

Glass, R. L. (1969). An elementary discussion of compiler/interpreter writing. *Computing Surveys, 1,* 55–77.

Goldstine, H. H. (1972). *The computer from Pascal to von Neumann.* Princeton, NJ: Princeton University Press.

Goldstine, H. H., & Goldstine, A. (1946). The Electronic Numerical Integrator and Computer (ENIAC). *Mathematical Tables and Other Aids to Computation, 2,* 97–110.

Goldstine, H. H., & von Neumann, J. (1947). *Planning and coding problems for an electronic computing instrument.* Unpublished report.

Gombrich, E. H. (1969). *Art and illusion.* Princeton, NJ: Princeton University Press.

Good, I.J. [1976] (1980). Pioneering work on computers at Bletchley. In N. Metropolis, J. S. Rowlett, & G.- C. Rota (Eds.), *A history of computing in the twentieth century* (pp. 31–45). New York: Academic Press.

Gould, S. J. (1977). *Ontogeny and phylogeny.* Cambridge, MA: Belknap Press of Harvard University Press.

Greenberg, J. H. (Ed.). (1963). *Universals of language.* Cambridge, MA: MIT Press.

Greibach, S. A. (1966). The unsolvability of the recognition of linear context free languages. *Journal of the Association for Computing Machinery, 13,* 582–587.

Gries, D. G. (Ed.). (1978). *Programming methodology.* New York: Springer-Verlag.

Gutting, G. (1980). *Paradigms and revolutions.* Notre Dame, IN: University of Notre Dame Press.

Hardy, G. H. (1940). *A mathematician's apology.* Cambridge, UK: Cambridge University Press.

Harrison, E. (1987). Whigs, prigs and historians of science. *Nature, 329,* 233–234.

Hartmanis, J., & Stearns, R. E. (1965). On the computational complexity of algorithms. *Transactions of the American Mathematical Society, 117,* 285–306.

Hartmanis, J., & Stearns, R. E. (1966). *Algebraic structure theory of sequential machines.* Englewood-Cliffs, NJ: Prentice-Hall.

Hartree, D. R. (1949). *Calculating instruments and machines.* Urbana, IL: University of Illinois Press.

Hesse, M. B. (1966). *Models and analogies in science.* London: Sheed & Ward.

Hewett, M. (1998). Interview of Tom Kilburn. *Personal Computer World, May,* 186–188.

Hills, R. L. (1989). *Power from steam: A history of the stationary steam engine.* Cambridge, UK: Cambridge University Press.

Hills, R. L. (1990). Textiles and clothing. In I. McNeill (Ed.), *An encyclopedia of the history of technology* (pp. 803–854). London: Routledge.

Hoare, C. A. R. (1969). An axiomatic basis for computer programming. *Communications of the ACM, 12,* 576–580, 583.

Hodges, A. (1983). *Alan Turing: The Enigma.* New York: Simon and Schuster.

Hodges, H. (1971). *Technology in the ancient world.* Harmondsworth, UK: Penguin Books.

Holland, J., Holyoak, K. J., Nisbett, R. E., & Thagard, P. R. (1986). *Induction.* Cambridge, MA: MIT Press.

Hollerith, H. (n.d.) *An electric tabulating system.* Unpublished manuscript.

Hollerith, H. (1889). An electric tabulating system. *The Quarterly, Columbian University School of Mines, X,* 238–255.

Holmes, R. (2008). *The age of wonder*. New York: Vintage Books.

Hopcroft, J. E., & Ullman, J. D. (1969). *Formal languages and their relation to automata*. Reading, MA: Addison-Wesley.

Hopgood, F. R. A. (1969). *Compiling techniques*. London: MacDonald.

Hopper, G. M. (1978). Keynote address. In R. L. Wexelblat (Ed.), *A history of programming languages* (pp. 7–30). New York: Academic Press.

Huffman, D. A. (1954). The synthesis of sequential switching circuits. *Journal of the Franklin Institute, 257*, 161–190.

Hughes, T. P. (1987). The evolution of large technological systems. In W. E. Bijker, T. P. Hughes, & T. J. Pinch (Eds.), *The social construction of technological systems* (pp. 51–82). Cambridge, MA: MIT Press.

Huskey, H. D., & Wattenberg, W. H. (1961). A basic compiler for algebraic expressions. *Communication of the ACM, 4*, 3–9.

IBM. (1956). *Programmer's reference manual: The FORTRAN automatic coding system for the IBM 704 EDPM*. New York: IBM.

IBM. (1957). *Programmer's primer for FORTRAN automatic coding system for the IBM 704*. New York: Author.

Illife, J. K. (1972). *Basic machine principles* (2nd ed.), London: MacDonald.

Illife, J. K., & Jodeit, J. G. (1962). A dynamic storage allocation scheme. *Computer Journal, 5*, 200–209.

Ince, D. C. (Ed.). (1992). *Collected works of A.M. Turing: Mechanical intelligence*. Amsterdam: North-Holland.

Ingerman, P. Z. (1966). *A syntax-oriented translator*. New York: Academic Press.

Iverson, K. E. (1962). *A programming language*. New York: Wiley.

Iverson, K. E. (1980). Notation as tool of thought. *Communications of the ACM, 23*, 444–465.

Iverson, K. E. (1981). Transcript of presentation. In R. L.Wexelblat (Ed.), *A history of programming languages* (pp. 674–682). New York: Academic Press.

Jeffress, L. A. (Ed.). (1951). *Cerebral mechanisms in behavior: The Hixon Symposium*. New York: Wiley.

Jones, J. C. (1980). *Design methods: Seeds of human future* (2nd ed.). New York: Wiley.

Juley, J. (1947). The Ballistic Computer. *Bell Laboratories Records, 24*, 5–9.

Kasami, T. (1965). *An efficient recognition and syntax analysis algorithm for context free languages*. Scientific report. AFCRL-65-758. Bedford, MA: Air Force Cambridge Research Laboratory.

Kilburn, T. (1949). The Manchester University digital computing machine. In Anon. (1950). *Report of a conference on high speed automatic calculating machines, June 22–25, 1949* (pp. 119–122). Cambridge, UK: University Mathematical Laboratory.

Kilburn, T. (1951). The new computing machine at the University of Manchester. *Nature, 168*, 95–96.

Kilburn, T., Edwards, D. B. G., Lanigan, M. J., & Sumner, F. H. (1962). One level storage system. *IRE Transactions on Electronic Computers, EC-11*, 223–235.

Kleene, S. C. (1956). Representation of events in nervous nets and finite automata. In C. E. Shannon & E. F. Moore (Eds.), *Automata studies* (pp. 3–41). Princeton, NJ: Princeton University Press.

Knuth, D. E. (1965). On the translation of languages from left to right. *Information & Control, 8*, 607–639.

Knuth, D. E. (1966). Letter to the editor. *Communications of the ACM, 9*, 654.

Knuth, D. E. (1968). *The art of computer programming. Volume 1: Fundamental algorithms.* Reading, MA: Addison-Wesley.

Knuth, D. E. (1969). *The art of computer programming. Volume 2: Seminumerical algorithms.* Reading, MA: Addison-Wesley.

Knuth, D. E. (1970). Von Neumann's first computer program. *ACM Computing Surveys, 2*, 247–260.

Knuth, D. E. (1992). *Literate programming.* Stanford, CA: Center for the Study of Language and Information.

Knuth, D. E. (1996). *Selected papers on computer science.* Stanford, CA: Center for the Study of Language and Information.

Knuth, D. E., & Pardo, L. T. [1977] (1980). The early development of programming languages. In N. Metropolis, J. S. Rowlett, & G.-C. Rota. (Eds.), *A history of computing in the twentieth century* (pp. 197–273). New York: Academic Press.

Koestler, A. (1964). *The act of creation.* London: Hutchinson.

Kohavi, Z. (1970). *Switching and finite automata theory.* New York: McGraw-Hill.

Kuhn, T. S. (1970). *The structure of scientific revolutions* (2nd ed.). Chicago, IL: University of Chicago Press.

LaCapra, D. (1983). *Rethinking intellectual history.* Ithaca, NY: Cornell University Press.

Lachman, R., Lachman, J. L., & Butterfield, E. C. (1979). *Cognitive psychology and information processing.* Hillsdale, NJ: Lawrence Erlbaum Associates.

Lakatos, I., & Musgrave, A. (Eds.). (1970). *Criticism and the growth of knowledge.* Cambridge, UK: Cambridge University Press.

Landes, D. L. (1971). *Revolution in time.* Cambridge, MA: Harvard University Press.

Landin, P. J. (1964). The mechanical evaluation of expressions. *Computer Journal, 6*, 308–320.

Langdon, G. G., Jr. (1974). *Logic design: A review of theory and practice.* New York: Academic Press.

Laning, J. H., Jr., & Zierler, N. (1952). *A program for translation of mathematical equations for Whirlwind I.* Engineering memorandum E-364. Cambridge, MA: MIT Instrumentation Laboratory.

Laudan, L. (1977). *Progress and its problems.* Los Angeles: University of California Press.

Lavington, S. H. (1980). Computer development at Manchester University. In N. Metropolis, J. S. Rowlett, & G.-C. Rota (Eds.), *A history of computing in the twentieth century* (pp. 433–443). New York: Academic Press.

Lavington, S. H. (1998). *A history of Manchester computers* (2nd ed.). London: The British Computer Society.

Lavington, S. H., & Burton, C. (2012). *The Manchester machines.* S.H. Lavington (ed.), 2012. *Alan Turing and his contemporaries* (chapter 4). London: British Computer Society.

Lee, J. A. N. (1967). *Anatomy of a compiler.* New York: Rheinhold.

Lewis, P. M., II, Stearns, R. E., & Hartmanis, J. (1965). Memory bounds for recognition of context-free and context-sensitive languages. In *Conference Record, IEEE 6th Annual Symposium on Switching Circuit Theory and Logic Design* (pp. 191–202).

Lovejoy, A. E. (1936). *The great chain of being.* Cambridge, MA: Harvard University Press.

Lowes, J. L. (1930). *The road to Xanadu.* Boston, MA: Houghton-Mifflin.

Lucas, O., & Walk, K. (1969). On the formal description of PL/I. In *Annual review in automatic programming* (pp. 105–182). Oxford: Pergamon Press.

Ludgate, P. E. (1909). On a proposed analytical machine. *Proceedings of the Royal Dublin Society, 12*, 77–91.

Lyons, J. (1970). *Chomsky*. London: Fontana/Collins.

Mandler, G. (1985). *Cognitive psychology*. Hillsdale, NJ: Lawrence Erlbaum Associates.

Mauchly, J. W. (1942). *The use of high speed vacuum tube devices for calculating*. Unpublished memorandum.

Mauchly, J. W. [1947] (1975). Preparations of problems for EDVAC-type machines. In B. Randell (Ed.), *The origins of the digital computer* (2nd ed., pp. 365–369). New York: Springer-Verlag.

Mayr, E. (1982). *The growth of biological thought*. Cambridge, MA: Harvard University Press.

McCarthy, J. (1963). Towards a mathematical science of computation. In *Proceedings of the IFIP Congress 63* (pp. 21–28). Amsterdam: North-Holland.

McCarthy, J. (1981). History of LISP. In R. L. Wexelblat (Ed.), *A history of programming languages* (pp. 173–185). New York: Academic Press.

McCarthy, J., Minsky, M. L., Rochester, N., & Shannon, C. E. (1955). *A proposal for the Dartmouth Summer Research Project on Artificial Intelligence* [On-line]. August 31. Available: http://www.formal.stanford.edu/jmc/history/dartmouth/dartmouth.html

McCulloch, W. S., & Pitts, W. (1943). A logical calculus of the ideas immanent in nervous activity. *Bulletin of Mathematical Biophysics, 5*, 115–133.

McKeeman, W. M., Horning, J. J., & Wortman, D. B. (1970). *A compiler generator*. Englewood-Cliffs, NJ: Prentice-Hall.

McShea, D. W. (1997). Complexity in evolution: A skeptical assessment. *Philosophica, 59*, 79–112.

Mealy, G. H. (1955). A method for the synthesis of sequential circuits. *Bell Systems Technical Journal, 34*, 1045–1079.

Mealy, G. H., Witt, B. I., & Clark, W. A. (1966). The functional structure of the OS/360. *IBM Systems Journal, 5*, 3–51.

Medawar, P. B. (1963). Is the scientific paper a fraud? In P. B. Medawar (1990), *The threat and the glory: Reflections on science and scientists* (pp. 228–233). Oxford: Oxford University Press.

Medawar, P. B., & Medawar, J. S. (1983). *Aristotle to zoo: A philosophical dictionary of biology*. Cambridge, MA: Harvard University Press.

Menabrea, L. F. (1842). *Sketch of the Analytical Engine* [On-line]. *Bibliothéque Universelle de Genève,* 52. Available: http://www.fourmilab.ch/babbage/sketch.html

Metropolis, N., Howlett, J. S., & Rota, G.- C. (Eds.). (1980). *A history of computing in the twentieth century*. New York: Academic Press.

Minsky, M. (1967). *Computation: Finite and infinite machines*. Englewood-Cliffs, NJ: Prentice-Hall.

Mollenhoff, C. R. (1988). *Atanasoff: Forgotten father of the computer*. Ames, IA: Iowa State University Press.

Moore, E. F. (1956). Gedanken experiments on sequential machines. In C. E. Shannon & E. F. Moore (Eds.), *Automata studies* (pp. 129–153). Princeton, NJ: Princeton University Press

Moreau, R. (1984). *The computer comes of age*. Cambridge, MA: MIT Press.

Morris, F. L., & Jones, C. B. (1984). An early program proof by Alan Turing. *Annals of the History of Computing, 6*, 139–147.

Moser, N. B. (1954). Compiler method of automatic programming. In *Proceedings of the ONR Symposium on Automatic Programming for Digital Computers* (pp. 15–21). Washington, DC: Office of Naval Research, Department of the Navy.

Nagel, E., & Newman, J. R. (1959). *Godel's proof*. London: Routledge & Kegan Paul.

Naur, P. (Ed.). (1960). Report on the algorithmic language ALGOL 60. *Communications of the ACM, 3,* 299–314.

Naur, P. (Ed.), et al. (1962–1963). Revised report on the algorithmic language ALGOL 60. *Numerische Mathematik, 4,* 420–453.

Naur, P. (1981). The European side of the last phase of the development of Algol 60. In R. L. Wexelblat (Ed.), *A history of programming languages* (pp. 92–139). New York: Academic Press.

Nersessian, N. (1995). Opening the black box: Cognitive science and the history of science. *Osiris, 10,* 196–215.

Newell, A. (1955). The chess machine: An example of dealing with a complex task by adaptation. *Proceedings of the Western Joint Computer Conference, 7,* 101–108.

Newell, A., Perlis, A. J., & Simon, H. A. (1967). What is computer science? *Science, 157,* 1373–1374.

Newell, A., Shaw, C. J., & Simon, H. A. (1958). Elements of a theory of human problem solving. *Psychological Review, 65,* 151–166.

Newell, A., & Simon, H. A. (1956). The Logic Theory machine: A complex information processing system. *IRE Transactions on Information Theory, IT-2,* 61–79.

Newell, A., & Simon, H. A. (1976). Computer science as empirical inquiry: Symbols and search. *Communications of the ACM, 19,* 113–126.

Newell, A., & Simon, H. A. (1972). *Human problem solving.* Englewood-Cliffs, NJ: Prentice-Hall.

Organick, E. I. (1972). *The Multics system: An examination of its structure.* Cambridge, MA: MIT Press.

Organick, E. I. (1973). *Computer systems organization: The B5700/6700 series.* New York: Academic Press.

Organick, E. I., & Hinds, J. A. (1978). *Interpreting machines: Architecture and programming of the B1700/B1800 series.* New York: North-Holland.

Padegs, A. (1964). The structure of System/360. Part IV: Channel design considerations. *IBM Systems Journal, 3,* 165–180.

Peck, J. E. L. (Ed.). (1971). *ALGOL 68 implementation.* Amsterdam: North-Holland.

Perlis, A. J. (1981). The American side of the development of Algol. In R. L. Wexelblat (Ed.), *A history of programming languages* (pp. 75–91). New York: Academic Press.

Petroski, H. (1988). *The evolution of useful things.* New York: Alfred A. Knopf.

Pevsner, N. (1962). *An outline of European architecture.* Harmondsworth, UK: Penguin Books.

Piaget, J. (1976). *The child and reality.* Harmondsworth, UK: Penguin Books.

Polanyi, M. (1962). *Personal knowledge.* Chicago, IL: University of Chicago Press.

Polya, G. (1957). *How to solve it* (2nd ed.). Princeton, NJ: Princeton University Press.

Popper, K. R. (1965). *Conjectures and refutations: The growth of scientific knowledge.* New York: Harper & Row.

Popper, K. R. (1968). *The logic of scientific discovery.* New York: Harper & Row.

Popper, K. R. (1972). *Objective knowledge.* Oxford: Clarendon Press.

Post, E. (1943). Formal reductions of the general combinatorial decision problem. *American Journal of Mathematics, 65,* 197–268.

Pye, D. (1978). *The nature and aesthetics of design.* London: Herbert Press.

Pyenson, L., & Sheets-Pyenson, S. (1999). *Servants of nature.* New York: W.W. Norton.

Pyleshin, Z. W. (1984). *Computation and cognition.* Cambridge, MA: MIT Press.

Radnitzky, G., & Bartley, W.W., III. (Ed.). (1987). *Evolutionary epistemology.* La Salle, IL: Open Court.

Randell, B. (1971). Ludgate's analytical machine of 1909. *The Computer Journal, 14*, 317–326.

Randell, B. (1972). On Alan Turing and the origins of digital computers. In B. Meltzer & D. Michie (Eds.), *Machine intelligence 7* (pp. 3–22). New York: Wiley.

Randell, B. (Ed.) (1975a). *The origins of the digital computer* (2nd ed.). New York: Springer-Verlag.

Randell, B. (1975b). Stored program electronic computers. In B. Randell (Ed.) (1975a), *The origins of the digital computer* (2nd ed., pp. 349–354). New York: Springer-Verlag.

Randell, B. (1980). The Colossus. In N. Metropolis, J. S. Rowlett, & G.- C. Rota (Eds.), *A history of computing in the twentieth century* (pp. 47–92). New York: Academic Press.

Randell, B., & Russell, L. J. (1964). *Algol 60 implementation*. New York: Academic Press.

Remington-Rand, Inc. (1953). *The A-2 compiler system operations manual*. Norwalk, CT: Remington-Rand.

Renwick, W. (1949). The EDSAC demonstration. In Anon. (1950), *Report of a conference on high speed automatic calculating machines, June 22–25, 1949* (pp. 12–16). Cambridge, UK: University Mathematical Laboratory.

Revens, L. (1972). The first twenty five years: ACM 1947–1972. *Communications of the ACM, 15*, 485–490.

Rice, J. R., & Rosen, S. (1994). History of the computer science department of Purdue University. In R. DeMillo & J. R. Rice (Eds.), *Studies in computer science: In honor of Samuel D. Conte* (pp. 45–72). New York: Plenum.

Richards, R. K. (1955). *Arithmetic operations in digital computers*. Princeton, NJ: Princeton University Press.

Rogers, H. (1967). *Theory of recursive functions and effective computability*. New York: McGraw-Hill.

Rohl, J. S. (1975). *An introduction to compiler writing*. London: MacDonald and Jane's.

Rolt, L. T. C. (1963). *Thomas Newcomen*. London: David & Charles.

Rosen, S. (Ed.). (1967). *Programming systems and languages*. New York: McGraw-Hill.

Rosen, S. (1969). Electronic computers: A historical survey. *Computing Surveys, 1*, 7–36.

Rosenbloom, P. S. (2010). *On computing: The fourth great scientific domain*. Cambridge, MA: MIT Press.

Rosin, R. F. (1969a). Supervisory and monitor systems. *Computing Surveys, 1*, 37–54.

Rosin, R. F. (1969b). Contemporary concepts of microprogramming and emulation. *Computing Surveys, 1*, 197–212.

Rosin, R. F., Frieder, G., & Eckhouse, R. H. (1972). An environment for research in microprogramming and emulation. *Communications of the ACM, 15*, 248–260.

Rutihauser, H. (1967). *Description of Algol 60*. Berlin: Springer-Verlag.

Salisbury, A. B. (1976). *Microprogrammable computer architectures*. New York: Elsevier.

Sammet, J. E. (1981a). The early history of COBOL. In R. L. Wexelblat (Ed.), *A history of programming languages* (pp. 199–276). New York: Academic Press.

Sammet, J. E. (1981b). An overview of high level languages. M. C. Yovits (Ed.), *Advances in computers* (Vol. 20, pp. 200–260). New York: Academic Press.

Sampson, J. R. (1976). *Adaptive information processing*. New York: Springer-Verlag.

Samuel, A. L. (1959). Some studies in machine learning using the game of checkers. *IBM Journal of Research & Development, III*, 210–229.

Sen, A. K. (1992). On the Darwinian view of progress, *London Review of Books, 14*.

Shannon, C. E. (1940). *A symbolic analysis of relay and switching circuits*. Unpublished thesis, MIT.

Shannon, C. E. (1948). A mathematical theory of communication. *Bell Systems Technical Journal, 27*, 379–423, 623–656.

Shannon, C. E. (1950a). A chess-playing machine. *Scientific American, 182*, 48–51.

Shannon, C. E. (1950b). Programming a computer for playing chess. *Philosophical Magazine, 41*, 256–275.

Shannon, C. E., & Moore, E. F. (Eds.). (1956). *Automata studies*. Princeton, NJ: Princeton University Press.

Shannon, C. E., & Weaver, W. (1949). *The mathematical theory of communication*. Urbana, IL: University of Illinois Press.

Sheridan, P. B. (1959). The arithmetic translator-compiler of the IBM FORTRAN automatic coding system. *Communications of the ACM, 2*, 9–21.

Shreyer, H. (1939). *Technical computing machines*. Unpublished memorandum.

Simon, H. A. (1947). The axioms of Newtonian mechanics. *Philosophical Magazine, 38*, 889–905.

Simon, H. A. (1950). *Administrative aspects of allocative efficiency*. Cowles Commission discourse paper, economics no. 281. Yale University, New Haven, CT.

Simon, H. A. (1952a). On the definition of the causal relation. *Journal of Philosophy, 49*, 517–528.

Simon, H. A. (1952b). Application of servomechanism theory to production control. *Econometrica, 20*, 247–268.

Simon, H. A. (1952c). A formal theory of interaction in social groups. *American Sociological Review, 17*, 202–211.

Simon, H. A. (1955). A behavioral model of rational choice. *Quarterly Journal of Economics, 69*, 99–118.

Simon, H. A. (1956). Rational choice and the structure of the environment. *Psychological Review, 63*, 129–138.

Simon, H. A. (1957). Rationality in administrative decision making. In H. A. Simon. *Models of man* (pp. 196–206). New York: Wiley.

Simon, H. A. (1976). *Administrative behavior* (3rd ed.). New York: Free Press.

Simon, H. A. (1988). *Reason in human affairs*. Oxford: Basil Blackwell.

Simon, H. A. (1991). *Models of my life*. New York: Basic Books.

Simon, H. A. (1996). *The sciences of the artificial* (3rd ed.). Cambridge, MA: MIT Press.

Simon, H. A., Smithberg, D. R., & Thompson, V. A. (1950). *Public administration*. New York: Alfred A. Knopf.

Simonton, D. K. (1999). *Origins of genius: Darwinian perspectives on creativity*. New York: Oxford University Press.

Simonton, D. K. (2010). Creative thought as blind-variation and selective retention: Combinatorial models of exceptional creativity. *Physics of Life Reviews, 7*, 190–194.

Smithies, F. (1959). John von Neumann (obituary). *Journal of London Mathematical Society, 34*, 373–384.

Steadman, J. P. (1979). *The evolution of designs*. Cambridge, UK: Cambridge University Press.

Steiner, G. (1975). *After Babel: Aspects of language and translation*. Oxford: Oxford University Press.

Stern, N. (1980a). John William Mauchly: 1907–1980 (obituary). *Annals of the History of Computing, 2*, 100–103.

Stern, N. (1980b). John von Neumann's influence on electronic digital computing, 1944–1946. *Annals of the History of Computing, 2*, 349–362.

Stevens, W. Y. (1964). The structure of System/360. Part II: System implementation. *IBM Systems Journal*, *3*, 136–143.

Stibitz, G. R. (1940). Computer. In B. Randell (Ed.) (1975a), *The origins of the digital computer* (2nd ed., pp. 241–246). New York: Springer-Verlag.

Sturt, G. (1923). *The wheelwright's craft*. Cambridge, UK: Cambridge University Press.

Swade, D. (2001). *The Difference Engine: Charles Babbage and his quest to build the first computer*. New York: Viking.

Tagore, R. (1912). *Gitanjali (song offerings)*. London: The India Society.

Taub, A. H. (Ed.). (1963). *John von Neumann, collected works* (Vol. 5). New York: Pergamon.

Thomson, W. (1878). Harmonic analyzer. *Proceedings of the Royal Society*, *27*, 371–373.

Toole, B. (2011). *Ada Byron, Lady Lovelace* [On-line]. Available: http://www.agnesscott.edu/lriddle/women/love.htm

Torres y Quevedo, L. [1915] (1975). Essays on automatics (Trans. R. Basu). In B. Randell (Ed.), *The origins of the digital computer* (2nd ed., pp. 87–106). New York: Springer-Verlag.

Traub, J. F. (1972). Numerical mathematics and computer science. *Communications of the ACM*, *15*, 531–541.

Tucker, S. G. (1965). Emulation of large systems. *Communication of the ACM*, *8*, 753–761.

Turing, A. M. (1936). On computable numbers with an application to the *Entscheidungsproblem*. *Proceedings of the London Mathematical Society*, *2*, 230–236.

Turing, A. M. (1945). *Proposal for development in the mathematics division of an automatic computing engine (ACE)*. Teddington, UK: National Physical Laboratory. Unpublished report.

Turing, A. M. (1947). Lecture to the London Mathematical Society. February 20.

Turing, A. M. (1948). *Intelligent machinery*. Teddington, UK: National Physical Laboratory. Unpublished report.

Turing, A. M. (1949). Checking a large routine. In Anon. (1950), *Report of a conference on high speed automatic calculating machines, June 22–25, 1949* (pp. 67–68). Cambridge, UK: University Mathematical Laboratory.

Turing, A. M. (1950). Computing machinery and intelligence. *Mind*, *LIX*, 433–460.

Ulam, S. M. (1980). Von Neumann: The interaction of mathematics and computing. In N. Metropolis, J. S. Rowlett, & G.-C Rota (Eds.), *A history of computing in the twentieth century* (pp. 93–99). New York: Academic Press.

Usher, A. P. [1954] (1985). *A history of mechanical inventions* (Rev. ed.). New York: Dover Publications.

Van Wijngaarden, A., Mailloux, B. J., Peck, J. E. L., & Koster, C. H. A. (1969). Report on the algorithmic language ALGOL 68. *Numerische Mathematik*, *14*, 79–218.

Van Wijngaarden, A., Maiilous, B. J., Peck, J. E. L., Koster, C. H. A., Sintsoff, M., Lindsay, Meerttens, L. G. L. T., & Fisker, R. G. (1975). Revised report on the algorithmic language ALGOL 68. *Acta Informatica*, *5*, 1–234.

Von Eckerdt, B. (1993). *What is cognitive science?* Cambridge, MA: MIT Press.

von Neumann, J. (1945). First draft of a report on the EDVAC. Unpublished report.

von Neumann, J. (1951). The general and logical theory of automata. In L. A. Jeffress (Ed.), *Cerebral mechanisms in behavior: The Hixon Symposium* (pp. 1–41). New York: Wiley.

von Neumann, J. (1966). *Theory of self-reproducing automata*. Urbana, IL: University of Illinois Press.

von Neumann, J., & Morgenstern, O. (1944). *Theory of games and economic behavior.* Princeton, NJ: Princeton University Press.

Wallace, D. B., & Gruber, H. E. (Eds.). (1989). *Creative people at work.* New York: Oxford University Press.

Weaver, W. (1949). *Translation* [On-line]. Memorandum. New York: The Rockefeller Foundation. Available: http://www.mt_archive.info/weaver-1949.pdf

Wegner, P. (1970). Three computer cultures: Computer technology, computer mathematics, and computer science. In F. L. Alt (Ed.), *Advances in computers* (Vol. 10, pp. 7–78). New York: Academic Press.

Wegner, P. (1972). The Vienna Definition Language. *ACM Computing Surveys, 4,* 5–63.

Weinberg, A. (1967). *Reflections on big science.* Oxford: Pergamon.

Weiss, E. A. (1972). Publications in computing: An informal review. *Communications of the ACM, 15,* 491–497.

Wexelblat, R. L. (Ed.). (1978). *A history of programming languages.* New York: Academic Press.

Wheeler, D. J. (1949). Planning the use of a paper library. In Anon. (1950), *Report of a conference on high speed automatic calculating machines, June 22–25, 1949* (pp. 36–40). Cambridge, UK: University Mathematical Laboratory.

Wheeler, D. J. (1951). *Automatic computing with the EDSAC.* PhD dissertation, University of Cambridge.

Whorf, B. L. (1956). *Language, thought and reality.* Cambridge, MA: MIT Press.

Wiener, N. (1961). *Cybernetics: Or control and communication in the animal and the machine* (2nd ed.). Cambridge, MA: MIT Press.

Wilkes, M. V. (1951). *The best way to design an automatic calculating machine.* Presented at the Manchester University Computer Inaugural Conference, June, Manchester.

Wilkes, M. V. (1956). *Automatic digital computers.* London: Methuen.

Wilkes, M. V. (1969). The growth of interest in microprogramming: A literature survey. *Computing Surveys, 1,* 139–145.

Wilkes, M. V. (1971). Babbage as a computer pioneer. *Historia Mathematica, 4,* 415–440.

Wilkes, M. V. (1975). *Time sharing computer systems* (3rd ed.). London: Macdonald & Jane's.

Wilkes, M. V. (1981). The design of a control unit: Reflections on reading Babbage's notebooks. *Annals of the History of Computing, 3,* 116–120.

Wilkes, M. V. (1985). *Memoirs of a computer pioneer.* Cambridge, MA: MIT Press.

Wilkes, M. V. (1986). The genesis of microprogramming. *Annals of the History of Computing, 8,* 116–126.

Wilkes, M. V. (1992). EDSAC-2. *IEEE Annals of the History of Computing, 14,* 49–56.

Wilkes, M. V., & Renwick, W. (1949). The EDSAC. In Anon. (1950), *Report of a conference on high speed automatic calculating machines, June 22–25, 1949* (pp. 9–11). Cambridge, UK: University Mathematical Laboratory.

Wilkes, M. V., Renwick, W., & Wheeler, D. J. (1958). The design of a control unit of an electronic digital computer. *Proceedings of the Institution of Electrical Engineers, 105,* 121–128.

Wilkes, M. V., & Stringer, J. B. (1953). Microprogramming and the design of the control circuits in an electronic digital computer. *Proceedings of the Cambridge Philosophical Society, 49,* 230–238.

Wilkes, M. V., Wheeler, D. J., & Gill, S. (1951). *Preparation of programmes for an electronic digital computer.* Cambridge, MA: Addison-Wesley.

Wilkinson, J. H. (1980). Turing's work at the National Physical Laboratory and the construction of Pilot ACE, DEUCE and ACE. In N. Metropolis, J. S. Rowlett, & G.- C. Rota (Eds.), *A history of computing in the twentieth century* (pp. 101–114). New York: Academic Press.

Williams, F. C. (1949). Cathode ray tube storage. In Anon. (1950), *Report of a conference on high speed automatic calculating machines, June 22–25, 1949* (pp. 26–27). Cambridge, UK: University Mathematical Laboratory.

Williams, F. C., & Kilburn, T. (1948). Electronic digital computers. *Nature, 162*, 487.

Williams, F. C., & Kilburn, T. (1949). A storage system for use with binary digital computing machines. *Proceedings of the Institution of Electrical Engineers, 96*.

Wirth, N. (1971). The programming language PASCAL. *Acta Informatica, 1*, 113–140.

Wölfflin, H. (1932). *Principles of art history*. New York: Dover Publications.

Wollheim, R. (1984). *Painting as an art*. Princeton, NJ: Princeton University Press.

Wood, S. [1995] 2010. *Mary Fairfax Somerville* [On-line]. Available: http://www.agnesscott.edu/ tlriddle/women/somer.htm

Younger, D. H. (1967). Recognition and parsing of context free languages in time n^2. *Information & Control, 10*, 181–208.

Yourdon, E. N. (Ed.). (1979). *Classics in software engineering*. New York: Yourdon Press.

Yourdon, E. N. (Ed.). (1982). *Writings of the revolution: Selected readings in software engineering*. New York: Yourdon Press.

Zach, R. (2003). Hilbert's program [On-line]. *Stanford Encyclopedia of Philosophy*. Available: http://www.plato.stanford.edu/entries/hilbert-program/

Zachary, G. P. (1977). *Endless frontier: Vannevar Bush, engineer of the American century*. New York: Free Press.

Zuse, K. [1936] (1975). Method for automatic execution of calculations with the aid of computers (Trans. R. Basu, patent application). In B. Randell (Ed.), *The origins of the digital computer* (2nd ed., pp. 159–166). New York: Springer-Verlag.

Zuse, K. [1962] (1975). The outline of a computer development from mechanics to electronics (Trans. Jones & Jones). In B. Randell (Ed.), *The origins of the digital computer* (2nd ed., pp. 171–186). New York: Springer-Verlag.

Index